CHICAGO

* BY THE BOOK *

CHICAGO

⁎ BY THE BOOK ⁎

101

PUBLICATIONS

THAT SHAPED THE CITY AND ITS IMAGE

THE
CAXTON
CLUB

Introduction by Neil Harris

THE UNIVERSITY OF CHICAGO PRESS

CHICAGO AND LONDON

The University of Chicago Press, Chicago 60637
The University of Chicago Press, Ltd., London
© 2018 by The University of Chicago

Published 2018
Printed in China

27 26 25 24 23 22 21 20 19 18   1 2 3 4 5

ISBN-13: 978-0-226-46850-1 (cloth)
ISBN-13: 978-0-226-46864-8 (e-book)
DOI: https://doi.org/10.7208/chicago/9780226468648.001.0001

Chicago by the Book is part of Art Design Chicago, an initiative of
the Terra Foundation for American Art exploring Chicago's art and
design legacy, with presenting partner The Richard H. Driehaus
Foundation.

ART DESIGN CHICAGO
An initiative of the Terra Foundation for American Art exploring Chicago's art and design legacy.
TERRA FOUNDATION FOR AMERICAN ART
Presenting Partner
DRIEHAUS FOUNDATION

Chicago by the Book is supported by the Terra Foundation for
American Art.

Library of Congress Cataloging-in-Publication Data

Names: Harris, Neil, 1938– writer of introduction. | Caxton Club.
Title: Chicago by the book : 101 publications that shaped the city
    and its image / [a project of] The Caxton Club ; introduction by
    Neil Harris.
Description: Chicago ; London : The University of Chicago Press,
    2018. | Includes index.
Identifiers: LCCN 2018019128 | ISBN 9780226468501 (cloth : alk.
    paper) | ISBN 9780226468648 (e-book)
Subjects: LCSH: Chicago (Ill.)—History. | Chicago (Ill.)—In litera-
    ture. | Chicago (Ill.)—Intellectual life.
Classification: LCC F548.3 .C47 2018 | DDC 977.3/11—dc23
LC record available at https://lccn.loc.gov/2018019128

This paper meets the requirements of ANSI/NISO Z39.48-1992
(Permanence of Paper).

FACING Will Bradley (1868–1962), advertising poster for
The Chap-Book, May 1897 (no. 18).

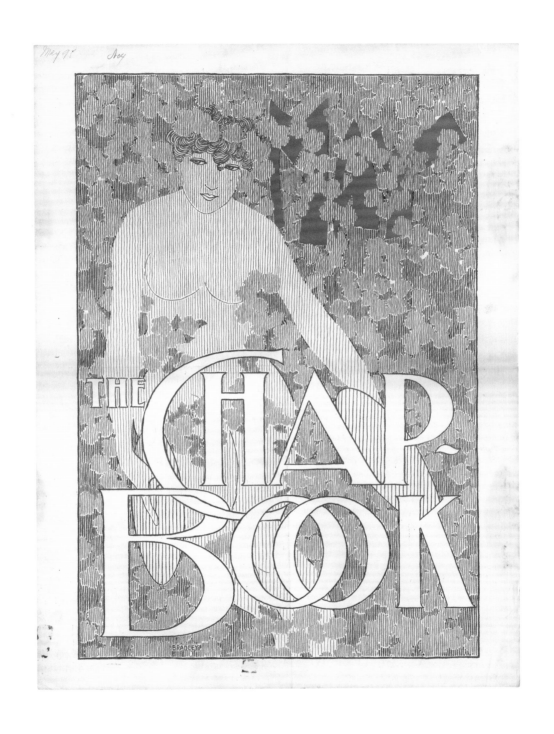

Contents

CXXVII. CHICAGO. BIRD'S-EYE VIEW AT NIGHT OF GRANT PARK, THE FACADE OF THE CI
Painted for the Comm

THE PROPOSED HARBOR, AND THE LAGOONS OF THE PROPOSED PARK ON THE SOUTH SHORE.
Club by Jules Guerin.

"Bird's-Eye View at Night of Grant Park," *The Plan of Chicago*, 1909, plate 127 (no. 29).

Preface and Acknowledgments

The Caxton Club has a sustained history of publishing. Since 1896, one year after its founding in Chicago, the Club has produced over sixty books, along with printed miscellany. The range of subjects is as broad as the interests of the members. In 2012, when it came time to embark on a new project, the Club's Publications Committee met to consider possibilities. Two years earlier, BBC Radio 4 and the British Museum had aired a series of programs and published a companion book titled *A History of the World in 100 Objects*, based on works selected from the museum's collections. Telling a story by linking items "in a way so that they can be read as a continuous narrative" because each item "stands as a kind of witness to something"[1] was an idea that appealed to the committee's cochair, Kim Coventry, who proposed that the next publication memorialize one hundred books that had shaped Chicago's identity. It would be at once a book about books and a book about books about Chicago. Eventually, in part in homage to Ben Hecht's collection of columns *A Thousand and One Afternoons in Chicago* (no. 41), as well to play on the academic introductory course designation "101," we landed on 101 as a fitting number.

In the introduction to this volume, Neil Harris describes the complex process by which the books were selected. It was a daunting undertaking, but it was also exhilarating for committee members to debate the merits and flaws of each title we considered. As Harris demonstrates, this book is a testament to the fact that the spirit of fellowship at the Club is alive and well.

We were honored to work with our fellow members of the Publications Committee—John Blew, John Chalmers, Neil Harris, Celia Hilliard, Edward C. Hirschland, and Brad Jonas—at many long meetings over several years to narrow a list of several hundred publications to just 101, to identify and contact potential authors for each title, and to gather a group of fact-checkers. We are deeply grateful to the committee members for their thoughtful, well-informed opinions, patience, humor, and goodwill.

In addition, several committee members took on additional responsibilities: Susan F. Rossen assumed the role of editor-in-chief, editing the work of eighty-seven authors and coordinating everything from contracts and photography to the book's publication. Neil Harris not only offered wise counsel from beginning to end but authored the insightful and illuminating introduction to this volume. Ed Hirschland applied his sharp editing skills and encyclopedic knowledge of Chicago history to every corner of the manuscript and generously provided access to his extensive collection of Chicagoana for images to illustrate this book. John Blew also made his collection available for photography and undertook extensive research to identify potential authors to write entries.

Ben Hecht, *A Thousand and One Afternoons in Chicago*, 1922 (no. 41).

It is a tall order to write about the impact and influence of a book in only six hundred words, but all eighty-seven authors met the challenge beautifully. We are indebted to them not only for their elegant entries but also for their enthusiasm for the project, which never flagged as we journeyed down the long, sometimes frustrating road of editing and production. Their biographies appear on pages 246–55.

Caxton Club members outside the committee also played important roles in realizing *Chicago by the Book*. We are indebted to Steve Tomashefsky for his close reading of the entire manuscript. We also thank the members who fact-checked entries: JoEllen Dickie, Teri J. Edelstein, Robert Karrow, and Alice Schreyer.

We are deeply grateful to the officers and members of the Caxton Club Council. Under the leadership of three successive presidents—Susan Hanes, Donald Chatham, and Arthur Frank—the Council steadfastly supported the project. We wish to acknowledge in particular Jackie Vossler, the Club's treasurer and program and exhibition committees chair (the latter cochaired by John Chalmers). Her leadership and fortitude led to the successful grant application made to the Terra Foundation of American Art. In addition, she managed the development of citywide programming in conjunction with the publication of *Chicago by the Book*.

The high quality and variety of illustrations that complement the entries and convey further meaning are the result of the efforts of our consulting photo editor, Bonnie Rosenberg. Without her unflagging enthusiasm, wise counsel, and attentive management of this enormous project, the book would be far less compelling. We also thank Nathan Keay for the fine photographs he took of books owned by John Blew and Ed Hirschland.

Other photographs were supplied by Chicago-based institutions that generously provided access to their rare holdings. At the Art Institute of Chicago's Ryerson and Burnham Libraries, we thank Bart Ryckbosch, archivist; Jessica Heim, archives assistant; and Joseph Tallarico, digital imaging photographer. To be acknowledged at the Chicago History Museum are Russell Lewis, executive vice president and chief historian; and Angela Hoover, rights and reproduction manager. We are grateful for the help at the Chicago Public Library of Glenn Humphreys, special collections librarian; and Michelle McCoy, archivist. We much appreciate the invaluable assistance of a large crew at the Newberry Library: Alice Schreyer, Roger and Julie Baskes Vice President for Collections and Library Services; Will Hansen, director of reader services and curator of Americana; Nora Gabor, senior program assistant for collections and library services; John Powell, digital imaging services manager; and Emerson Hunton and Tyne Lowe, digitization technicians. At the Charles

Deering McCormick Library of Special Collections at Northwestern University, we thank Martin Antonetti, director of distinctive collections; and Nicholas Munagian and Sigrid Perry, special collections library assistants.

We were helped by Michele Clark at the Frederick Law Olmsted National Historic Site and Chris Pagnozzi, audiovisual archivist, and Bob Knuth, art director, at Second City. At the Special Collections Research Center of the University of Chicago Library, we thank Daniel Meyer, director; Catherine Uecker, rare books librarian; Christine Colburn, reader services manager; Judith Dartt, digitization manager; and Barbara Gilbert, reading room coordinator. Dale Eskra of the Ephraim Historical Foundation and Valerie Wilmer also provided assistance.

We were gratified when the University of Chicago Press agreed to publish *Chicago by the Book*. Needless to say, the Press is one of the nation's leading academic publishers, with a particularly strong list devoted to Chicago subjects, and we are proud that our book is one of its titles. There are many to acknowledge: first and foremost, we thank Timothy Mennel, executive editor, for his experienced counsel and for shepherding the book through the rigorous approval stages. Jill Shimabukuro, who directs the Press's design and production department, agreed to design this book herself; its elegant and thoughtful layout reflects her passion for and understanding of books, and books about books. We are grateful to manuscript editor Ruth Goring for her artful and careful attention to this text and also to promotions manager Lauren Salas for informing Chicago and book lovers near and far that this book is not to be missed! We also thank Rachel Kelly, editorial associate, and Io-Jean Kim, international rights consultant.

We are honored to have received a grant from the Terra Foundation for American Art in conjunction with Art Design Chicago, an exploration of Chicago's art and design legacy undertaken with presenting partner the Richard H. Driehaus Foundation. At the Terra, we are grateful to Elizabeth Glassman, president and CEO; Amy Zinck, executive vice president; Jennifer Siegenthaler, program director, education grants and initiatives; and the Terra Foundation's board of trustees.

Finally, we give thanks to those Caxtonians whose generosity helped make our book possible. Robert McCamant led a targeted fundraising effort and was deeply gratified by the warm fellowship with which his appeals were answered. The names of these donors are found on page 256, along with those of additional members whose support ensured that we reached our goal.

KIM COVENTRY AND SUSAN F. ROSSEN
Cochairs, Publications Committee

Marshall Everett, *The Great Chicago
Theater Disaster*, 1904 (no. 25).

Richard Henry Dana, *Two Years before the Mast*, one of the titles in Lakeside Press's Four American Books Campaign, 1930 (no. 53).

Listing Chicago

Neil Harris

The ambitions of list books have grown dramatically in the last few years. Once largely confined to practical suggestions about reading, recipes, health, and travel destinations, or to highlighting the world of avoidable errors—*Ten Thousand Words Often Mispronounced*, *Five Thousand Words Often Misspelled*—the genre has lately exploded. Setting aside the many local business books that list utilitarian conveniences, engagement with self-improvement and pleasure seeking continues unabated. Alongside have come efforts to capture the essence of historical change, the genius of place, the joys of taste, or the assets of sponsoring institutions. On the web, the permutations are almost endless, spanning everything from the thirty celebrities who have aged the most dramatically to the hundred friendliest dogs and the ten worst college towns. Those (happily) rarely find their way into print. The magic number shifts, of course, depending on the patience of the user or the commitment of the compiler. Several recent surveys stand out for their originality and verve (Neil McGregor's 2010 *History of the World in 100 Objects* comes to mind), but quite a few are linked, perhaps inevitably, to motives of self-promotion, personal profit, or institutional enhancement.

Self-promotion provides, of course, the obvious opening for Chicagoans to join the party. This city has never shied away from letting the rest of the world know more about its many virtues. Flaunting its early motto "The City in a Garden" and boasting of its geographical destiny, Chicago faced skeptics almost from the start. Urban rivals to the east and south denounced it as the favored home of Mammon, a monument to greed, a hotbed of cupidity. Hosting a collection of philistines contemptuous of the finer things and a higher life, the city was seen as beset by graft, crime, violence, and squalor. Its various calamities across the years—fire, flood, disease, weather—were often labeled as rebukes to avarice, pride, and complacency, warnings that went unheeded. Withering assaults dating from the nineteenth century were fueled one hundred years later by the gun battles of the Al Capone years. Even Michael Jordan's feats were not enough to silence those memories.

It is not surprising that many of the texts selected for *Chicago by the Book: 101 Publications That Shaped the City and Its Image* are critical of the place they describe. A substantial portion constitutes actual exposés that have had considerable national, even worldwide, influence. Negativity, indignation, or depression is palpable in many of the most memorable presentations of this city: crushing poverty, lost opportunities, inveterate cynicism, criminal mayhem, chilling prejudice, paralyzing racism, pervasive brutality, creative corruption. Even when Chicagoans celebrate their hearth and home, they do so while acknowledging deep-seated flaws. "Where's mine?" was the motto suggested by newspaper columnist Mike Royko for the place in which he lived and worked. And the large body of unhappy émigrés, many of them artists and writers (Nelson Algren for example), has added to the litany of criticism.

And yet a metropolis that stood as one of the five largest cities in the Western world as the twentieth century began, and that counted more than three million residents in the middle of that century, has also provoked fervent tributes, declarations of loyalty, and impressive acts of philanthropy. The often-unrelenting attacks, the condescension, and the caricaturing have created defensiveness, but they have also stimulated vaulting aspirations, startling adaptations, and hidden talents.

Chicago lovers make multiple claims. The city's harsh winters strengthen endurance, its mixed athletic records encourage patience, its political problems nurture realism, its flat landscape stimulates verticality, its midwestern location discourages pretension. Narratives of affection, liberation, and devotion share space with the most brooding jeremiads. Chicago remains the "great American city" that Norman Mailer proclaimed in his searing 1968 portrait of "a strong city with faces tough as leather hide and pavement."[1] Do the encomia outweigh the critiques? Does hope rise above despair? Readers will have to decide.

The creation of *Chicago by the Book* never involved a plan to provide a balance sheet or to judge Chicago's standing in the court of historical opinion. When the arduous if stimulating task of choosing texts for inclusion began, the committee that put the plan together did not debate whether selections should be positive or negative. Instead, the group faced more open-ended questions: how were approximately one hundred publications to be chosen that reflect the nature of this city, and what criteria could be applied? At the start, the issues were multiple and bewildering. Were these to be only books written in Chicago, about Chicago, and by Chicagoans? Did they have to be set in Chicago? Did they need to be books at all? Could periodicals be included? Songs? Manuscripts? Images? The committee made decisions. Many of them. Magazines were admissible but not newspapers; songs were allowed but not manuscripts. After all, this was a project of the Caxton Club, a venerable Chicago-based organization founded in 1895 to promote appreciation of the book arts. Printing, then, had to be part of the picture. But such strictures did allow room for poetry, plays, parodies, competitions, guidebooks, proposals, novels, fantasies, investigations, reports, and a host of other forms of expression invoking the complex traditions and warring images that continue to define this city.

The eight self-appointed jurors (including me) comprised a committee of Caxtonians who worked together for over three years to formulate guidelines and make selections.[2] With claims to expertise in bibliography, history, biography, publishing, and the arts, we determined that our choices must tell

EBONY

A JOHNSON PUBLICATION

SIX WAYS TO STOP NEGRO CRIME

HARRY TRUMAN AND THE NEGRO

Was He Our Greatest
Civil Rights President?
BY CARL ROWAN

OPERA SINGERS

NOVEMBER 1959 35¢

a significant Chicago story; reflect some distinctive municipal achievement, experience, or institution; and have achieved enough recognition to leave an impact on either the city's identity or its reputation. We allowed that it would be wonderful if each selection met all our criteria, but we were realistic and agreed that two out of three might work. In some respects, the process was not totally dissimilar to what Justice Potter Stewart famously declared about pornography in the 1964 decision *Jacobellis v. Ohio*: "I know it when I see it." Personal revelation never proved to be quite sufficient, however, and we leaned heavily upon our guidelines when disagreements became prolonged.

We wanted to be comprehensive without becoming tedious or formulaic. We wanted Chicago books rather than Chicagoland books. We wanted to avoid multiple entries by the same authors and multiple commentaries by the same contributors. And we wanted the contributors themselves to reflect a range of interests, professions, backgrounds, and opinions, and to allow, at least occasionally, their own life stories to intersect with their observations.

Thus we decided early on that no single author could be allotted more than one selection and that no commentator be allowed more than two essays.[3] That was the easy part. And so was immediate acceptance of perhaps one quarter of our texts, which stood out quickly as meeting all our criteria. How, for example, could we not include *Sister Carrie* (no. 22), the Burnham Plan (no. 29), *Ebony* (no. 66), and *The Adventures of Augie March* (no. 76)? The other roughly 75 percent had to emerge after a complex process of negotiation, sustained over as many as a dozen meetings.

Our primary dilemmas concerned representation and inclusiveness. Did we want to be faithful to the city's history by ensuring that its principal interest groups, historic moments, major figures, and significant institutions were all acknowledged somehow? However sound an impulse, however appealing as a broad goal that seemed, we agreed it would not be possible.

This was not going to be a history of Chicago. We would have no acts of incorporation, legislative debates, or judicial decisions as occasions for commentary. But the pain of omitting important parts of the story was palpable. What were we to do when we determined that no truly persuasive or well-known text was available for an important subject? Should we include something, anything, for the sake of inclusion? Should we work back from the subject, identifying possible contenders, or should we concentrate on the texts themselves and reduce efforts to be absolutely comprehensive?

Those problems, like some others, were never completely resolved. But we admitted that important gaps were inevitable. One of the most significant involves religion. We wrestled with this void on a number of occasions, acknowledging that Protestant revivalism and Chicago Catholicism, for example, were poorly represented. Where are evangelist Dwight L. Moody, Archbishop George Mundelein, and Rabbi Emil Hirsch? They are missing from this book, along with many others. We simply could not agree on appropriate textual representation. Yet a book on Chicago that said little or nothing about jazz, crime, architecture, or political corruption would be even more seriously deficient. For subjects so central, we were able to identify memorable texts. Representing the major role of railroads in the history of this city turned out to be a challenge: we finally settled on a guide to a 1948 railroad fair (no. 68). Were we paying sufficient attention to the Chicago Symphony Orchestra, the Art Institute, the Field Museum? Or to one or another ethnic group? Could we identify texts that met multiple needs? We moved back and forth from subjects thought to be important to texts that merited inclusion on their own terms, and then back to the subjects, if they had been left untreated thus far.

The countless possibilities for the list were daunting. James A. Kaser's bibliographic survey *The Chicago of Fiction* (2011) records more than four thousand separate examples using the city as a setting. At its height, our list contained between two hundred and three hundred items. In good democratic fashion, we voted on all of them in several marathon sessions. While many quickly bit the dust, others attracted strenuous and ingenious defenses put forth by individual committee members. Our textual rejections include dozens of titles that could easily have been part of our book. This *salon des refusés* could constitute an interesting list on its own: *101 Omitted Chicago Books*! As Mark Twain once remarked, "There isn't a Parallel of Latitude but thinks it would have been the equator if it had had its rights." Various "Parallels of Latitude" undoubtedly will be invoked by motivated readers, eager to point out omissions and perhaps lament some of our inclusions.

Reflecting the deep knowledge of Chicago history and the bibliophilic interests of several committee members, a number of the initial proposals were of particular appeal to scholars and amateur historians: J. W. Norris's *General Directory and Business Advertiser* (1844), Rufus Blanchard's *Discovery and Conquest of the Northwest* (1880), Milo Quaife's *Chicago and the Old Northwest, 1673–1835* (1913), Thomas W. Goodspeed's *History of the University of Chicago* (1916), and Paul Gilbert's *Chicago and Its Makers* (1929) are among the nonsurvivors. Those books, reflecting major investigations, lengthy research projects, ambitious narratives, or central institutions, have earned multiple citations from those working on the history of Chicago. They could stand in, of course, for many other titles important in themselves and much relied upon by Chicago historians, however little known they might be to a broader public.

Then there were the popular books, written for different audiences, about events and personalities that seem central to the larger story but ultimately were not chosen: Charles Washburn's *Come into My Parlor: A Biography of the Aristocratic Everleigh Sisters* (1934), M. R. Werner's *Julius Rosenwald: The Life of a Practical Humanitarian* (1939), and Lloyd Wendt and Herman Kogan's *Lords of the Levee* (1943—one of several Wendt books). There were screeds like Josephine Hancock Logan's *Sanity in Art* (1937) and memoirs such as Clarence Darrow's *Story of My Life* (1932), Floyd Dell's *Homecoming* (1933), and Burton Rascoe's *Before I Forget* (1937). Those did not reflect headings that we began with, but rather categories that emerged in the course of our discussions. Once we had them, however, it was possible to argue that there were better examples available for each slot. Much of our labor, after settling tentatively on certain books, was rethinking their inclusion by proposing others. And sadly saying goodbye to earlier contenders.

To give just one example, we decided early on that the creation of the University of Chicago was an event worth recognizing. Indeed, the institution's powerful influence is reflected in a series of selections. A string of books treats its founding and early years, and several were on our list. But in the end we decided it might be interesting to include the story as told by Robert Herrick in his novel *Chimes* (no. 46). This roman à clef is not particularly sympathetic to many of the leading characters, notably the university's president William Rainey Harper, but the selection does several things simultaneously: allows representation of a somewhat neglected Chicago literary figure, challenges the self-celebrating accounts that have been the usual suspects, and introduces our readers to something new. Finally, *Chimes* might be called a bit of a surprise entry, and we sought surprises. Where there was room for the unexpected and it satisfied a thirsty category, we tried to supply it.

Another subject clamoring for attention was the 1893 World's Columbian Exposition. Its looming presence impinges on several entries, notably Rand, McNally's *Bird's-Eye Views and Guide to Chicago* (no. 14), Ida B. Wells's impassioned protest *The Reason Why the Colored American Is Not in the World's Columbian Exposition* (no. 15), and Chris Ware's *Jimmy Corrigan: The Smartest Kid on Earth* (no. 97). But details of this extraordinary event needed to be addressed head on. We decided to do so twice, in books separated by more than one hundred years. First with Rossiter Johnson's massive history of the fair (no. 19), chosen in part because its absorption with scale, details, numbers, and documentation captures part of the sensibility undergirding the great exposition. And then with Erik Larson's less authoritative but wildly popular *Devil in the White City* (no. 100), which revived fascination with the exposition in a vast new audience.

Some of our initial selections did not disappear at once but suffered a lingering demise as we buried, revived, and reinterred them. One of those intermittent entries was Edna Ferber's novel *So Big*, a 1924 Pulitzer Prize winner set in the rural outskirts of Chicago. Chief among the reasons for its demise was our determination to keep our focus on the city proper rather than on suburbs or neighboring communities. For better or worse, that is what we did, despite the interesting possibilities that might have emerged from books dealing with Evanston, Oak Park, Hinsdale, or South Holland. Other proposals sank without a trace and remain buried in our early notes. Passionate defenses were not uncommon, occasionally concluded by the phrase of concession "This is not a hill I would die on." Our decisions will, we hope, provoke discussion and greater awareness of the unexpected, forgotten, or neglected items on our list. In the end, of course, the list remains tentative and personal.

It is, we admit, the mature city that proved most appealing to us. Only six selections date from pre-Fire Chicago, a continuing source of fascination to local antiquarians and an indispensable prelude to later developments. And just twenty-two appeared in print before 1901. Some late-nineteenth-century publications on our list (nos. 10 and 11) reflect keen interest in the city's earlier history. But those histories are necessarily retrospective in character and inevitably reflect the time of their writing as much as they do their subject. By the same token, with one exception (no. 101), we avoided passing judgment on very recent texts or predicting the role they may play as sources of Chicago's reputation or identity. Thus just a handful on our list originated in the twenty-first century. And despite the thousands of novels and short stories that are included in Kaser's bibliography, fiction accounts for under 20 percent of our choices.

In the end, it is Chicago's long twentieth century—from the great exposition of 1893 to its modern formulation in Larson's 2003 best seller—that dominates our selections, with a total of seventy-five titles. In between came many of the institutions, celebrities, movements, and innovations that combine to define the metropolis to the rest of the world, as well as to its own citizens. Chicago once hoped to become North America's biggest city. The 1898 creation of Greater New York and the collapse of Chicago's massive annexation campaigns sealed the doom of this ambition, although local leaders such as the newspaper publisher Robert R. McCormick occasionally stoked the dying embers.[4] The jaunty prophecies of early promoters would be brought down to earth not only by population trends and economic developments but by shrewd if hostile observers like the *New Yorker*'s A. J. Liebling, who would permanently capture the city's also-ran destiny in his powerful portrait *Chicago: The Second City* (no. 74).

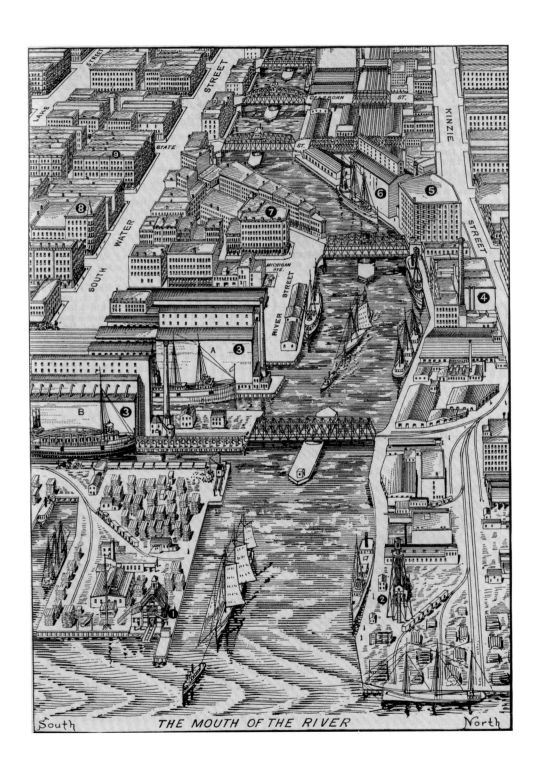

THE MOUTH OF THE RIVER

Chicago's sagging population—its rank dropping in recent decades from second to third, and perhaps soon to fourth, American city—threatens to obscure its historic role as the "shock city" of American industrialization, a place where rationalized methods of construction and manufacturing, foreign immigration, domestic migration, transport revolutions, and spasmodic population growth all came together in a combustible mixture. Anarchic, bewildering, chaotic, explosive, violent, astonishing: these were among the adjectives lavished on Chicago during its growth spurt, by streams of visitors who came to marvel at its confrontations with modernity. It was impossible, wrote the late-nineteenth-century British journalist G. W. Steevens, to "do justice to her splendid chaos," the "queen and guttersnipe of cities, cynosure and cesspool of the world!"[5]

But Chicago was not simply a victim of larger forces. It was also, as many of these texts demonstrate, an ingenious originator, with celebrated park designs, settlement houses, museums, universities, sanitary schemes, social services, architects and engineers, international expositions, musical and theatrical novelties, scientific breakthroughs, literary initiatives, public sculpture, and elaborate public landscaping. While many of Chicago's challenges have been typical if exaggerated versions of what was happening elsewhere, the responses here could be distinctive and influential. Lists of novelties and firsts associated with the city range from the mundane and trivial to the profound and unsettling. On significant civic anniversaries, newspapers and websites still trot out such items as Cracker Jacks, zippers, roller skates, and jukeboxes, improbably juxtaposed to the first self-sustaining nuclear reaction, blood bank, and juvenile court. Chicagoans seem alternately startled and pleased to learn that the first electric dishwasher, the first Twinkie, and the first remote-control devices were also produced in their town. Not unexpectedly, someone is always available to write about them and swell the long list of Chicago-related books.

Chicago's special status in the world of cities was once demonstrated by the number of places that attached its name as an indication of growth and energy. Among those basking in Chicago's stunning rise were Berlin (the "Chicago of Europe" in Mark Twain's phrase), Atlanta ("the Chicago of the South"), Novosibersk ("the Chicago of Siberia"), Budapest ("the Chicago of the Balkans"),[6] amid a string of far more improbable comparisons. Musicals, films, a John Philip Sousa march, economic theory, sociological inquiries, architecture, hot dogs, pizza—all offered their own bows to Chicago's larger-than-life reputation.

Other places, of course, can lay claim to their own enthusiastic chroniclers, rhapsodic memoirists, and bitter critics. But Chicago may possess more than its share. Today's city—embroiled in political scandal, racial tensions, angry polarization, disturbing homicide rates, heavy debt, and declining economic power—hardly offers grounds for optimism about the future. Its detractors gain fodder for their attacks each passing month. But it would be foolish to count Chicago out, or even down, for very long. Its history includes semi-miraculous recoveries from disasters of many kinds, reinventions that are as surprising as they are imaginative, and adaptations that proved to be popular and durable. Many are documented in the texts that follow. Time and time again, Chicago's population and institutions have demonstrated resilience, creativity, and optimism while responding to the huge challenges of everyday life. *Chicago by the Book* calls attention to the confessions, exaggerations, assaults, love letters, and utopian longings that have embedded themselves within the city's genetic heritage. Doing so both acknowledges Chicago's distinctive personality and hints, hopefully, at its long, bright future.

CHAPTER LXXVI   THE BATTERING-RAM

ERE quitting, for the nonce, the Sperm Whale's head, I would have you, as a sensible physiologist, simply—particularly remark its front aspect, in all its compacted collectedness. I would have you investigate it now with the sole view of forming to yourself some unexaggerated, intelligent estimate of whatever battering-ram power may be lodged there. Here is a vital point; for you must either satisfactorily settle this matter with yourself, or for ever remain an infidel as to one of the most appalling, but not the less true events, perhaps anywhere to be found in all recorded history.

You observe that in the ordinary swimming position of the Sperm Whale, the front of his head presents an almost wholly vertical plane to the water; you observe that the lower part of that front slopes considerably backwards, so as to furnish more of a retreat for the long socket which receives the boom-like lower jaw; you observe that the mouth is entirely under the head, much in the same way, indeed, as though your own mouth were entirely under your chin. Moreover you observe that the whale has no external nose; and that what nose he has—his spout hole—is on the

Herman Melville, *Moby Dick, Or the Whale*, volume 2, one of the titles in the Lakeside Press's Four American Books Campaign, 1930 (no. 53).

101

1

Narrative of the Massacre at Chicago, August 15, 1812, and of Some Preceding Events

[JULIETTE A. KINZIE] ∗ CHICAGO: ELLIS & FERGUS, 1844

Ann Durkin Keating

Juliette Augusta Magill (1806–70) was born in Middletown, Connecticut. At a young age she became enamored of the American West through the letters of an uncle, Dr. Alexander Wolcott, who served as the Indian agent in Chicago during the 1820s. In 1830 she married one of her uncle's western friends, John H. Kinzie. The couple lived first in Portage, Wisconsin, where John was an Indian agent. Juliette began to write about and draw the striking people and sights around her. After several years the couple settled permanently in Chicago, raising a large family and helping to establish St. James Episcopal Church and the Chicago Historical Society.[1]

Juliette Kinzie became an author—albeit an anonymous one—in 1844 with *Narrative of the Massacre at Chicago*, a pamphlet published in Chicago by Ellis & Fergus. In five short chapters she wrote about the experiences of the Kinzie family just before, during, and after the August 15, 1812, battle that took place as Potawatomi warriors ambushed a United States Army contingent as it withdrew from Fort Dearborn (which Kinzie labeled the Massacre at Chicago). According to an advertisement at the front of the pamphlet, "This little record taken up many years since from the lips of those who had been eye-witnesses of the events described was not designed for publication. It was made simply for the purpose of preserving for the children of the writer, a faithful picture of the perilous scenes through which those near and dear to them had been called to pass." Included in the *Narrative* is a map drawn by the author that was the first printed in Chicago.[2]

In 1856 Kinzie's *Wau-Bun: The "Early Day" in the North-West* was published by Derby & Jackson of New York and a year later was republished by D. B. Cooke of Chicago. It remains in print to this day. Kinzie's intention was to set out the early history of the region and to highlight the role of the Kinzie family in this process. At the core of *Wau-Bun* are the three chapters from the *Narrative* on the Battle of Fort Dearborn. *Wau-Bun* also includes an account of Kinzie's experiences in Wisconsin, a depiction of 1831 Chicago, and engravings of her drawings. With a strong and clear voice, she introduced people, places, and events that might otherwise have slipped from view.

Wau-Bun received attention from the press locally and nationally. On May 7, 1856, the *Chicago Daily Tribune* declared, "All classes of readers . . . will greet warmly '*Wau-bun*' and heartily thank Mrs. John H. Kinzie for giving it to the public . . . [which] will be grateful to her for the glimpse of Pioneer life she has given us with so much delicacy of feeling and of spirit." On May 25 the *New York Herald* opined about the book, "As a faithful and well-drawn picture of the life of those pioneers of the American wilderness who have paved the way for civilization, it deserves to rank with the best sketches of the sort that have as yet been published."

Twentieth-century scholars were not so laudatory. Milo Quaife, a historian of the upper Midwest, opined that "Mrs. Kinzie had but the vaguest comprehension of the historian's calling."[3] Therefore he suggested the work be used mostly as primary "source material."[4] More recently social historians have expressed appreciation of Kinzie's focus on everyday life. She is remembered as one of the first female historians in the United States, as well as an early Illinois novelist.[5]

Juliette Kinzie sketched the first map printed in Chicago, "Chicago in 1812," as the frontispiece of her *Narrative of the Massacre at Chicago*. Regularly reprinted, the map remains a touchstone for understanding the early years of the city.

2

"Zouave Cadets Quickstep Dedicated to the U.S. Zouave Cadets Governors Guard of Illinois"

A. J. VAAS, CONDUCTOR OF THE LIGHT GUARD BAND ∗ CHICAGO: ROOT & CADY, 1860

Alison Hinderliter

Some Civil War–era American soldiers, both Union and Confederate, dressed in flashy finery inspired by the French Army's Crimean War–era Zouave soldiers. The French in turn had borrowed their uniform fashion from the North African Zouaoua tribe of Berbers. The outfit included baggy breeches (sometimes decorated with braid), white leggings, open-collar jackets and vests, and occasionally brilliant red fezzes or turbans with tassels. Zouave soldiers were widely admired for their discipline and elite fighting skills.

Elmer E. Ellsworth (1837–61) moved to Chicago from New York State around 1856 to become a law clerk. In Chicago he befriended Charles A. DeVilliers, who had been a surgeon in the French Army in Algiers and who taught him sword-fighting and some Zouave drills. Ellsworth, an enthusiastic student, founded his own regiment of Zouave fighters in Chicago, creating a manual of arms for light infantry and enlisting hundreds of Chicago men. By the summer of 1859, Ellsworth's Zouave cadets were an established regiment and in constant demand to exhibit their skills. On one occasion, a competitive drill held on September 15, 1859, the cadets earned a top prize of $500 before an audience of seventy thousand. In January–February 1860, Ellsworth and some of his cadets went to train a group of Zouave soldiers in Springfield. There he met and impressed Abraham Lincoln. On January 23, 1860, Illinois governor William Henry Bissell appointed the US Zouave Cadets the Governor's Guard of Illinois.[1]

The Chicago sheet-music publishing firm Root & Cady was eager to capitalize on the popularity of Ellsworth and his Zouaves. Root & Cady was founded in Chicago in 1858 as a music store by Ebenezer Towner Root (1822–96; his brother was the composer George Frederick Root) and Chauncey Marvin Cady (1824–89), a conductor and amateur singer. Within a year of its opening, Root & Cady was Chicago's largest music store, specializing in the sale and repair of a variety of musical instruments. The store then added to its offerings printed music, first imported from New York and Boston and then, beginning in September 1859—less than one year after the company's establishment—published under the firm's own name. While there was a large and active community of sheet-music firms in Chicago in the nineteenth century, Root & Cady not only became the city's most predominant but also rose to national prominence as a major publisher of pro-Union Civil War–era music.[2]

Composer and bandleader A. J. Vaas (1820–?) had already written several polkas for Root & Cady; his work "Zouave Cadets Quickstep," the firm's fifteenth publication, was issued and entered into Library of Congress copyright on April 13, 1860. On August 20, 1860, the *Chicago Daily Tribune* reported that Root & Cady was receiving daily orders in the hundreds for this piece, which went on to be published in at least eleven editions. The beautiful cover,

This attractive lithograph by Edward Mendel graces the cover of one of the most successful tunes originated by Chicago-based music store and publisher Root & Cady. The "Zouave Cadets Quickstep" was so popular that it was reissued many times. Illustrated here is the ninth edition to appear in the year 1860.

printed by Chicago's first lithographer, Edward Mendel (1827–84), was created for at least the sixth edition onward. The figure standing second from the right in the lithograph is thought to be Ellsworth. The piece gave Root & Cady its first nationwide success. How many copies were printed and sold in total is unknown because of the destruction of Root & Cady's company records in the Great Chicago Fire of 1871.[3]

3

Chicago Illustrated 1830–1866

LITERARY DESCRIPTION BY JAMES W. SHEAHAN ESQ. ✳ ILLUSTRATIONS BY THE CHICAGO LITHOGRAPHING CO. ✳ CHICAGO: JEVNE AND ALMINI, 1866–67

David Buisseret

FACING Street life in downtown Chicago in the 1860s was a jumble of horses and well-dressed pedestrians. The view depicted here by Louis Kurz looks from State Street down Lake Street, the main commercial strip of the time. On the north side of Lake are the city's first iron-front buildings, which were destroyed by the 1871 Great Fire. At the end is the Central Railroad Depot. The telegraph poles have not yet been wired.

The publication of *Chicago Illustrated* in 1866–67 was an extraordinary act of faith in the emergent city. The work was planned for one hundred plates and eventually contained fifty-two.[1] However, this was at a time when in North America only New York and San Francisco could boast a larger number of published lithographic views, eighty or so; towns such as Baltimore, Cincinnati, Montreal, Philadelphia, Quebec, and St. Louis could muster only twenty or so such views at that time.[2] The publishers, Otto Jevne and Peter Almini, had come to Chicago from Norway and Sweden, respectively; before the publication of *Chicago Illustrated* they had been chiefly known as ornamental painters, a skill that they had learned in their homelands. After the Great Chicago Fire of 1871, they continued to follow their first profession.

For the images in their new publication, they called on a neighboring business, the Chicago Lithographing Company, which had been founded about 1865 by Louis Kurz (1833–1921) and three others. Kurz was responsible for drawing the images and played an important role in making the lithographic plates. An Austrian artist from Salzburg, he had immigrated to the United States in 1848, coming to Chicago in 1853. The Chicago Lithographing Company did not survive the Fire, but Kurz lived on for many years, undertaking numerous other lithographic projects; he became particularly famous for his (largely inaccurate) Civil War scenes.

The text for the images was provided by newspaperman J. W. Sheahan (1824–83). Born in Baltimore, he had come in 1854 to Chicago, where for six years he published the *Chicago Times* and then between 1860 and 1865 the *Chicago Post*. Sheahan was a very active journalist who, as early as January 1872, published an account of the Great Fire titled *The Great Conflagration: Chicago, Its Past, Present and Future*; the boosterism is manifest.

Sheahan's text for *Chicago Illustrated* was relatively pedestrian in comparison to the often very sprightly work of Kurz. Most of his images show buildings that would be consumed in the Fire. Constituting the best visual evidence of their appearance, the plates exude an almost palpable sense of the hustle and bustle of pre-Fire Chicago, as seen in a plate with a dramatic perspective view at State and Lake Streets of large buildings housing goods of all kinds for sale. At the end of Lake Street, which is filled with people, horse-drawn carriages, supply transports, and more, is the city's main train station, the Central Railroad Depot. The many church images in *Chicago Illustrated* remind us of the central importance to the city of the emerging parish structure (page 261). Two of the best-known plates show the giant water intake, or crib, far out in the lake, and the still-extant Water Tower[3] (on Michigan Avenue) by which lake water could be distributed in the city. In the commentary Sheahan went out of his way to emphasize the skill of the engineers in constructing a large tunnel running for a mile under the lake to the crib; clearly he felt that the work of such men could bear comparison with the great bridges and other works then being undertaken in other cities throughout the Western world.

In general *Chicago Illustrated* is a paean to the new colossus rising alongside lake. As the introductory essay breathlessly puts it, "These views . . . will contain a comprehensive picture of this marvelous city," offering "striking evidence of the city's improvement and enterprise." So they did.

4

The Great Chicago Lake Tunnel

The Causes Which Led to Its Conception; the Great Undertaking; Obstacles Encountered; How the Work Was Performed; Launch of the Crib, Etc. Together with Sketches of the Visits of Several Illustrious Parties to the Works, and a Midnight Train of Cars Beneath Lake Michigan. Also the Successful Completion of the Great Enterprise. Illustrated

[JOHN M. WING] * CHICAGO: PUBLISHED BY JACK WING, THE WESTERN NEWS COMPANY, SOLE AGENTS, 1867

Carl Smith

This sixty-four-page booklet was prepared quickly to capitalize on interest in a major undertaking critical to Chicago's health and growth. When it went into service in March 1867, the tunnel under the bottom of Lake Michigan connected a wooden intake "crib" two miles from shore to the now-iconic limestone Gothic pumping station and water tower straddling Pine Street (subsequently Michigan Avenue) at Chicago Avenue. Situating the crib this far out would fail to end the potentially catastrophic hazard to the water supply posed by the appallingly polluted Chicago River, which flowed into the lake.[1] It would take an even grander engineering achievement, the Chicago Sanitary and Ship Canal, which opened in 1900, to address the problem more effectively by reversing the direction of the river's current.

Of particular interest is the idiosyncratic career of the booklet's author-publisher, John Mansir Wing (1844–1917). He was among the legion of ambitious individuals drawn to booming Chicago. Arriving from Upstate New York in 1865, Wing became a reporter for a series of Chicago papers. He then struck out on his own, producing a booklet on another heroic piece of Chicago infrastructure, the Union Stock Yard, which opened late in 1865. Wing's was a one-man operation. He not only wrote the text but also drummed up advertising, supervised publication, and secured sales outlets.

The stockyard booklet inspired the one on the tunnel. Wing described his efforts in his diary, which provides much insight into this unconventional young man and single male life in the rising metropolis.[2] The entries are both predictably self-absorbed and surprisingly candid, including accounts of Wing's carousing and his sexual encounters with men. They also reveal the challenges facing an independent entrepreneur trying to bring a work like this to press. Wing sometimes accepted goods, including a music box and a rifle, in lieu of cash as payment from advertisers. He agonized as he awaited the delayed delivery of illustrations he had purchased from *Frank Leslie's Illustrated Newspaper*, which had recently featured the tunnel. Once the booklet appeared, he turned his considerable energies to marketing it.

The Great Chicago Lake Tunnel sold for fifty cents. Wing charged distributors—the main one was John R. Walsh's Western News Company—half that price. Disappointment with Walsh led to Wing's breaking with Western News for the two editions that soon followed, which contain more ads. In 1874 Wing (now listed as J. M. rather than Jack) issued an expanded text (titled *The Tunnels and Water System of Chicago*) that covers the extension of the water system, the building of a second intake tunnel, and the recent construction of pedestrian and carriage tunnels under the Chicago River, one at Washington Street and the other at LaSalle Street.

By that time Wing was on his way to making his fortune as publisher of two

leading trade magazines. The *Land Owner* chronicled Chicago's real estate market before and after the Great Fire, while the *Western Brewer* was devoted to the city's thriving beer industry. Wing retired a rich man in 1888, when he was still in his mid-forties. He became a serious if undistinguished book collector, immersing himself as well in the related hobby of extra illustration, which entails taking apart existing works, meticulously cutting in or inserting visual materials clipped from other sources, and then rebinding the resulting pages into new volumes. Like his diaries, these are in the collections of the Newberry Library, Chicago. But perhaps Wing's most significant contribution to the city's literary life is the generous endowment in his will of the Newberry's John M. Wing Foundation on the History of Printing, one of the most noted collections of its kind.[3]

This striking cross-sectional view is the frontispiece to John M. Wing's *Great Chicago Lake Tunnel*. It shows the tunnel under construction, with two crews working from either end toward the middle, unnoticed by people on the boats plying the surface of Lake Michigan far above. To the left is the city shoreline at Chicago Avenue; to the right, the water intake, located two miles offshore and enclosed in a "crib."

5

Chicago: Past, Present, Future

JOHN S. WRIGHT ∗ CHICAGO: SOLD BY
THE WESTERN NEWS COMPANY, AND ALL
CHICAGO BOOKSELLERS, 1868

Eric Slauter

The morning after the Great Fire of 1871, the printer of *Chicago: Past, Present, Future* hailed its author on the street. "Well, Wright, what do you think *now* of the future of Chicago?" An optimist and opportunist, John S. Wright (1815–74) had a vision: "Chicago will have more men, more money, more business within five years, than she would have had without this fire."[1]

Wright's faith in his city survived his own "pecuniary reverses": he made and lost two fortunes before writing his book.[2] Arriving in Chicago from Massachusetts in 1832, he speculated in real estate, paid for the first public school, and amassed $200,000 in property before defaulting in the panic of 1837. The inaugural issue of Chicago's first newspaper in 1839 promoted Wright's new commodities business, but that failed too.

Wright recovered. With no experience in farming or publishing, he founded the weekly newspaper *Prairie Farmer* in 1841 and encouraged growth of the grain trade. Two centuries later, the paper is still going. In 1850 he engineered a petition drive to secure a congressional land grant for the Illinois Central Railroad, furthering Chicago's development and its connections with the East and South.

Civic successes led Wright to diversify—and to more failure, first with a wool warehouse and then as a manufacturer of faulty farm equipment. Eastern creditors rated him a bad risk. He held $600,000 in property in 1856 but was ruined again in the panic of 1857. He spent the early 1860s in New York City, looking for investors while imagining a five-volume treatise that would explain the Civil War as a "confusion of theories." Few subscribers were willing to pay $13 for his insights.[3]

Trading on the dubious boast that more city property had passed through his hands than those of any others, Wright issued *Chicago: Past, Present, Future* in 1868 in a bid to reinvent himself as a real estate agent.[4] Though he envisioned a short prospectus, the book mushroomed like Chicago itself: four hundred pages are packed with financial statistics, old booster writings, a city guide, and some leftover political philosophy. Wright recounted proposals that had borne fruit, alongside others that had not—or not yet, such as his suggestion in the late 1840s that Chicago buy land for public parks to be connected by wide avenues around the city and running along the lake. Most poignantly, he balanced his account of his achievements alongside his failures. "I am poor," he told potential investors.[5]

A first printing of thirteen hundred copies met with a "cool reception."[6] Wright nevertheless persuaded the Chicago Board of Trade to subscribe to a second edition, providing a copy for each of its 1,372 members. When the board members decided they no longer wanted the books, Wright drafted a seventy-two-page appendix designed to shame them into keeping their promise. They took the copies.[7] Hopeful that this coerced patronage might secure more, Wright printed five hundred additional copies but could not convince the City Council to take them.[8]

Wright did not live long enough to see his post-Fire predictions realized. He died in a mental institution in Pennsylvania in 1874. Shortly thereafter, his widow, Catherine T. Wright, recounting a life of threats and violence, sued to recover property she claimed Wright had coerced her into selling.[9] In his obituary, former lieutenant governor William Bross said Wright's mind was "unbalanced" but that his was nevertheless "one of the most useful lives ever passed in Chicago."[10]

Whatever his failures, Wright made a lasting mark selling his city. While contemporaries saw him as a dreamer who was always "puffing" and "blowing"—a visionary in the worst sense—later generations would justifiably crown him king of the urban boosters and a prairie prophet.[11]

FACING Perhaps pre-Fire Chicago's greatest booster was John S. Wright, called by a biographer the "Prophet of the Prairies." His belief that the city would become one of the world's great commercial centers drove him to publish this book and was not diminished by the 1871 conflagration, although he did not live long enough to see the city he prophesied emerge from its ashes.

6

Report Accompanying the Plan for Laying Out the South Park

OLMSTED, VAUX & CO., LANDSCAPE
ARCHITECTS ∗ CHICAGO: SOUTH PARK
COMMISSION, 1871

Victoria Post Ranney

In the years before the Great Fire of 1871, a number of farsighted Chicagoans, aided and encouraged by Frederick Law Olmsted (1822–1903), architect in chief of New York's Central Park, began making plans to ring Chicago with parks and boulevards. These plans, established by Illinois state legislation in 1869, framed the expansion of the fast-growing city for decades to come.

The idea of a system of parks connected by boulevards was first sparked when Olmsted visited Chicago during the Civil War. Serving as executive head of the US Sanitary Commission, which advised on the health and living conditions of the Union Army, he met two public-spirited men who became key advocates for the parks: the lawyer Ezra McCagg and the sanitary reformer Dr. John Rauch.

While in California in 1865, Olmsted encountered another Chicagoan, editor William J. Bross of the *Chicago Daily Tribune*, who was visiting Yosemite Valley with a party of newspapermen. The valley had recently been set aside for public use by President Abraham Lincoln, and Olmsted headed a commission to assess its scenery and future management. Camped on the valley floor, Olmsted read to the journalists his report about this future park. Back home, Bross encouraged the landscape architect to design a park system for Chicago.[1]

With the active leadership of McCagg, Rauch, Bross, and others, three bills were drawn up to establish parks and boulevards for the North, West, and South Sides of the city. After the Illinois legislature passed the bills, in February 1869, Olmsted and his partner, Calvert Vaux (1824–95), were hired to design and implement the thousand-acre South Park (now Jackson and Washington Parks and the Midway Plaisance).

In their 1871 *Report Accompanying the Plan for Laying Out the South Park*, prepared for the Chicago South Park Commission, Olmsted and Vaux assessed Chicago's landscape and laid out in detail how it could be transformed to serve the diverse and growing population of the city. Lake Michigan, which they considered the only object of scenery near Chicago to be "of special grandeur or sublimity," could be extended inland with the construction of lagoons, ponds, and canals, all densely overhung with foliage. This scenery would be "admirably fitted to the general purposes of any park, and . . . certainly could nowhere be more grateful than in the borders of your city, not only on account of the present intensely wide-awake character of its people, but because of the special quality of the scenery about Chicago in which flat and treeless prairie and limitless expanse of lake are such prominent characteristics."[2]

Olmsted and Vaux proposed to build a pier out into the lake to accommodate steamers from the city; tired workers could then hire inexpensive small

The 1871 plan of the Chicago South Park envisioned what became Jackson Park (top) and Washington Park (bottom), with the Midway Plaisance in between. Planner Frederick Law Olmsted envisioned a water park with lagoons and canals (including the Midway) to extend inland from Chicago's greatest scenic feature, Lake Michigan. Wide, "open grounds" were to alternate with more intimate, shrubbery-filled "plaisances."

boats to explore the park, or promenade along the lakefront and the pier. A large variety of features for public enjoyment were planned: athletic fields, picnic grounds, music courts, and pavilions.

The 1871 *South Park Report* was the first comprehensive description of how coordinated open spaces could frame development of the sprawling city. Many of its ideas were implemented at the 1893 World's Columbian Exposition, which Olmsted designed in Jackson Park. It was a forerunner of Dwight Perkins and Jens Jensen's 1904 *Report of the Special Park Commission to the City Council of Chicago on the Subject of a Metropolitan Park System* (no. 26), which proposed a wider metropolitan system of parks and forest preserves, and of Daniel Burnham and Edward Bennett's 1909 *Plan of Chicago* (no. 29). Olmsted's concept of promenades, designed for people of all classes and backgrounds to enjoy together, is still being extended in projects such as the 606 and the Riverwalk today.[3]

7

Barriers Burned Away

THE REV. EDWARD P. ROE ∗ NEW YORK:
DODD & MEAD, 1872

Neil Harris

Newspaper coverage of Chicago's Great Fire of 1871 quickly went global. Individual chroniclers rushed into print with their own narratives. Surprisingly, fiction writers largely avoided the historic calamity, with the exception of *Barriers Burned Away*, a best-selling 1872 novel. Even here, in this largely forgotten book, the fire enters late, though its presence is fundamental and helped jump-start the author's profitable and prolific literary career.[1]

At the time, Edward Payson Roe (1838–88), a clergyman and Civil War veteran, was ministering in Cornwall, fifty miles north of New York City.[2] Transfixed by reports of the devastation, the thirty-three-year-old visited Chicago weeks later and conceived his first novel while walking through the stricken city. The plot may be melodramatic, the characters stereotyped, and the dialogue stiff, but Roe understood popular taste and managed to keep his many readers entertained. Ultimately more than one million copies were sold in frequent reprintings. Roe completed this lengthy sermon and portrait of a deeply divided city with the fiery climax of the blaze, hoping that "the lurid and destructive flames might reveal with greater vividness the need and value of Christian faith."[3] The text reminds us that many parsed Chicago's ordeal in Providential terms, either as a judgment on a decadent Sodom filled with Mammon worshipers or as a chance to begin its life anew on stronger, more spiritual foundations.

The hero, a young artist fresh off the farm, spends much of his time doing good works and trying to convince a refined young woman of the truths of Christianity. No easy task. The barriers in his way—and in Roe's title—are multiple: class, ethnic, and spiritual. Dennis Fleet, poor, honest, almost insufferably pious, arrives in Chicago with few assets beyond his talent and moral character. Starting at the bottom, as the cleaner in an art and antiques shop, he falls in love with the owner's daughter, Christine Ludolf, whose social ambitions and secular beliefs define the wide gulf between them. She plans to return with her father to their native Germany, their new wealth meant to burnish the status of their previously impoverished but noble family. These hopes all end with the flames, though she survives through Fleet's heroics.

Despite his somewhat generic descriptions of Chicago life and several awkward attempts at evoking high society, Roe catches some of the tensions in pre-Fire Chicago separating Yankee settlers in Chicago from German and Irish immigrants, and dramatizes the transcendent appeal of art as a means of redemption in this materialistic, money-grubbing city. Only a saving remnant recognizes this, and it will be up to those Chicagoans coming after them to realize art's promises.

The fire that resolves so many of the plot's problems also allowed Roe to confide his anxieties about crowds, class warfare, radicalism, crime, and

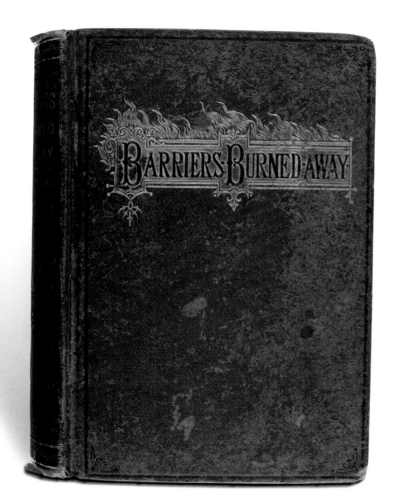

immigration. Chicago's disaster, and others of the period, intensified these ongoing fears. The conflagration's huge scale, with one third of the city burned down and more than three hundred dead, permitted apocalyptic fantasies to flourish. Roe set forth terrifying scenes of personal assault and mob violence. Surging crowds of helpless victims, driven to the shores of Lake Michigan by the flames, become targets of violent criminals. Urban legend feasted on Chicago's agony, as it would upon other debacles from flooded Johnstown, Pennsylvania, to Hurricane Katrina's New Orleans. Roe's scenes of disorder testify to increasing unease about the impact of class divisions and ethnic diversity on the nation's future, as well as continuing doubts about the role of cities in American life. All these remain with us almost 150 years later, in a city and a country larger, richer, and perhaps even more divided.

Barriers Burned Away is the only novel contemporaneous with Chicago's Great Fire of 1871 that makes the conflagration crucial to its plot. The book's success—over one million copies would eventually be sold—revealed and nurtured national fascination with such disasters. This photograph of the fire's aftermath shows what remained of the Honoré Block.

8

Montgomery Ward & Co. Catalogues

CHICAGO: 1872–1985

Sears, Roebuck and Co. Catalogues

CHICAGO: 1894–2003

Russell Lewis

A. Montgomery Ward (1844–1913) singlehandedly transformed the geography of consumption in the United States.[1] His entrepreneurial genius was creating the mail-order catalogue as his sales force and marketing tool for a rural population that encompassed 75 percent of all Americans. Realizing the enormous opportunity in rural western markets, Ward resolved to make these settlers lifelong customers by following three business principles: provide a broad array of goods, offer only high-quality items, and sell at the lowest price possible. He succeeded by cutting out the middleman and buying directly from the manufacturer. To overcome the challenge of selling unseen products to unknown consumers, Ward guaranteed a full refund if the customer was not satisfied.[2]

Chicago's manufacturing, printing, and distribution facilities and its central location made it an ideal place for Ward to launch his enterprise. While the retailer was not the first to sell products through the mail, he was the first to do so exclusively.[3] Beginning in 1872 as a single-sheet price list of 163 items, the catalogue evolved rapidly, increasing in size and sophistication as the scale of Ward's business mushroomed. It grew from 8 pages in 1874 to 152 pages in 1878 (with more than three thousand items) to 540 pages in 1890 (with over twenty-four thousand items). Woodcut illustrations, along with precise descriptions and instructions on use, became standard features. By 1904 Ward was distributing more than three million of its 1,200-page catalogue to customers free of charge.

Sears, Roebuck and Co. was formed in 1893 in Chicago and became Ward's greatest mail-order rival.[4] Its first catalogue (dated 1894 but issued in late 1893) measured 6 × 9 inches and contained 322 pages; three years later, it increased to an 8 × 11-inch format with 753 pages.[5] Sears expanded and streamlined the business that Ward had pioneered, and by 1904 it had overtaken its competitor, leading the nation in mail-order sales. The scale of Chicago's mail-order business was enormous, and the impact of the catalogues on American society pervasive; the catalogues created thousands of jobs and spurred the nation's economic growth.

Called variously the Big Book, the Farmer's Bible, and the Wish Book, the catalogues were above all extremely practical to use: they were mobile, accurate, reliable, entertaining, and regularly updated. They covered all necessities of life from cradle to grave. But the catalogues played an even larger role in shaping the way people thought about themselves and their world. They provided rural customers with a vital connection to the rest of the nation and beyond, as well as a chance to reimagine themselves. The catalogues brought city shopping to people's homes, exposing them to urban sophistication, values, and trends. They learned about the latest fashions and the newest gad-

gets, expanding their world beyond the limits of country life.[6] Catalogues even served as substitute textbooks, serving to teach reading, spelling, arithmetic, and geography in rural schools.[7]

In the 1930s, mail-order catalogue sales dipped, and Ward and Sears shifted their business focus to brick-and-mortar stores located across the country. But their catalogues remained fully integrated into consumers' lives. During World War II and the Cold War, mail-order catalogues were seen as indisputable evidence of the wealth and abundance possible in a democratic nation.

Montgomery Ward closed its mail-order catalogue operation in 1985 and went bankrupt in 2000, and Sears issued its last book in 2003.[8] For a generation of Americans who did not grow up with the catalogues, Amazon.com evokes an internet version of the experience that A. Montgomery Ward envisioned, complete with efficient home delivery.[9]

The Amazon.com sites of their day, Montgomery Ward & Co. and Sears, Roebuck and Co., used mail-order catalogues to sell to small-town and rural customers living at great distances from the retailers' bustling brick-and-mortar facilities in Chicago. The advertising broadside from around 1899 shows Ward's headquarters on Michigan Avenue, between Madison and Washington Streets.

"Warm Knitted Outfits for Children," page 170 of Sears, Roebuck and Co. catalogue, Fall and Winter 1925–26.

9

The Lakeside Annual Directory of the City of Chicago

CHICAGO: DONNELLEY, LOYD AND COMPANY, 1875–78; DONNELLEY, GASSETT & LOYD, 1879–96; THE CHICAGO DIRECTORY COMPANY, 1897–1917

Rick Fizdale

For over a century, a widespread belief emanated from Chicago claiming that local businessman Reuben H. Donnelley (1864–1929) invented the Yellow Pages.[1] His first directory, produced in 1886, was actually printed on white paper, interspersed with pink sheets to distinguish between sections, and it had a yellow cover.[2] After 1887 the cover was red, and it stayed red for a number of years. Donnelley never called his directory the Yellow Pages. He named it the Chicago Red Book, after the enduring color of its cover.[3] The first use of yellow sheets in fact predates Donnelley's initial directory by three years: in 1886, while working on a local directory, a printer in Cheyenne, Wyoming, ran out of white paper and finished the run on yellow stock.[4]

Donnelley's lasting contribution to business directories has nothing do with the hues of covers or pages. What he did was transform long, boring lists of names, addresses, and phone numbers into a major advertising medium.[5] Although he published phone books for only a few American cities,[6] telephone directories the world over looked pretty much the same because of him.

While still in college, Reuben went to work for his successful father, R.R. Donnelley, a master printer who assigned his son to a new client, the Chicago Telephone Company (CTC), which was incorporated in 1880 and was a forerunner of Illinois Bell.[7] Immediately the young man morphed into a visionary. He exploited a quirk in the arrangement between the Donnelleys and the CTC. Astonishingly, the family firm was allowed to keep all the money it charged for display ads.[8] Reuben grabbed his hat and called on the handful of businesses in the city that owned a telephone. He sold enough ads to begin a historic trend. The inside front cover of Reuben's first directory contains a full-page ad targeted at women. Headlined "Suffering Diseases Peculiar to Their Sex," it features a drawing of a woman enclosed in a semi-circular machine. The pump attached to it, operated by a bearded technician, diligently sucks illnesses out of her delicate system.[9]

Reuben began hiring salesmen to extend his reach and rapidly turned them into a crackerjack sales force, eventually considered one of the best in the nation. Not only did the salesmen sell display ads, but they increased the demand for them. In 1886, of the roughly one thousand physicians practicing medicine in Chicago, only thirty owned a phone.[10] Donnelley's drummers warned the other doctors that without phones they would lapse into irrelevance. One by one they fell in line, as did saloonkeepers, hatmakers, fortunetellers, and morticians. Indeed, everybody. More telephones led to more display ads. The world noticed and imitated Reuben Donnelley.

As if creating one advertising medium was not far-reaching enough, Donnelley used the Chicago Red Book to inspire the invention of another. From the beginning, he had organized his business directories by industry: Adver-

This full-page display advertisement (ca. 1886) for a machine from the Chicago Vacuum Medical and Surgical Institute that "vacuums" away illnesses is similar to an ad featured on the inside cover of Reuben Donnelley's first business directory (1886).

tising Agents, Agricultural Implements, Appraisers, Architects, and so on. Within each industry, the competitors were presented alphabetically. As part of their job, Donnelley's salesmen compiled company names, addresses, and phone numbers for each of their clients. But they had more information at their disposal, including the identities of key decision-makers. Reuben began selling these detailed lists and became a founding father of direct marketing.[11] He started a direct-mail division by hiring copywriters and art directors, acquiring market-research firms, and expanding his already huge publishing operation.[12] Soon he was putting out seven hundred million pieces of mail every year.[13]

As for the Yellow Pages, over the years Reuben Donnelley experimented with different colors of paper. In 1914 he permanently put yellow inside his Red Book—thirty-one years too late to be its originator.

10

Fergus' Historical Series Relating to Chicago and Illinois

CHICAGO: FERGUS PRINTING COMPANY, 1876–1903

Russell Lewis

FACING To compensate for the loss in the 1871 Fire of original manuscripts and publications that chronicled the early history of Chicago, one of the city's first publishers, Robert Fergus, produced a series of thirty-five pamphlets. Issued between 1876 and 1903, they generated enthusiasm for rebuilding the city and restoring its initial greatness.

In the aftermath of the Great Fire of 1871, while most Chicagoans struggled amid mountains of debris to imagine their city's future, a few citizens cast their gaze at its past. For Robert Fergus (1815–97), re-creating Chicago's historical records destroyed in the fire was a civic calling as important as rebuilding the city's central business district. Anointed "the historic printer of Chicago" and "practically the pioneer of publishing,"[1] Fergus eagerly seized the opportunity to remind a new generation of Chicagoans of the city's modest beginnings.

Born in Glasgow, Fergus apprenticed at the University of Glasgow printing office and soon established himself as a printer. In 1839 he immigrated to the United States, initially seeking a position in Milwaukee before settling in Chicago, which then had a population of about four thousand. He found work as a journeyman printer with Rudd & Childs, but before the end of the year he was self-employed. In 1842 he partnered with William Ellis to form Ellis & Fergus, with offices in the Saloon Building. From the early years of the business, Fergus demonstrated a sense of duty to record and disseminate the city's history. He oversaw publication of the 1844 Chicago directory, which included a historical sketch of the city from 1837 to 1844.[2] That same year, Ellis & Fergus printed Mrs. John H. Kinzie's account of the attack on Fort Dearborn as a thirty-four-page pamphlet, *Narrative of the Massacre at Chicago, August 15, 1812, and of Some Preceding Events*, one of the city's first published historical works (no. 1).[3]

Fergus' Historical Series emerged from a crucible of heightened historical consciousness in Chicago and in the nation. The destruction of the Chicago Historical Society's collection, and thus the city's historical records, in the Great Fire in 1871 (and in another fire, in 1874[4]) led to a sense of urgency to capture as much of the early history as possible from the aging community of early pioneers. The Great Fire also created another kind of urgency—a need to craft a narrative of progress to legitimize Chicago's rapid ascent and to set the stage for its rebuilding and its rise to future greatness. The national centennial and great celebratory exhibition in Philadelphia also generated broader appreciation for the past throughout the country.

Fergus inaugurated his series in 1876 with the republication of *The Annals of Chicago: A Lecture Delivered before the Chicago Lyceum, January 21, 1840*, by Joseph N. Balestier; it included a new introduction by the author and a review of the lecture by the *Chicago Daily Tribune*. In the same year he produced an astonishing eight additional publications for the series. Subsequent numbers appeared more infrequently, and by the time of Fergus's death in a train accident, a total of thirty-three had been issued (two more appeared posthumously), each selling for $1 or less. Featuring works by notable Chicagoans and Illinoisans (including Fergus), they cover the history of medicine, religion, law, Native Americans, and railroads, and feature biographical sketches as well. The series also includes a number of lectures presented at the Chicago Historical Society.[5] Alfred T. Andreas drew extensively on the series for his three-volume history of Chicago (no. 11) and personally relied on Fergus's memory to craft sections of his narrative.

Although historians today regard the series as an antiquarian effort at best, Fergus' Historical Series remains a valuable document of its time. It captures Chicago's aspirations and shapes a powerful narrative arc, from a humble past to a preeminent position among American cities to future greatness.

11

History of Chicago from the Earliest Period to the Present Time

A[LFRED]. T. ANDREAS * VOLUME 1, *ENDING WITH THE YEAR 1857* * VOLUME 2, *FROM 1857 UNTIL THE FIRE OF 1871* * VOLUME 3, *FROM THE FIRE OF 1871 UNTIL 1885* * CHICAGO: THE A. T. ANDREAS COMPANY, 1884 (VOL. 1), 1885 (VOL. 2), 1886 (VOL. 3)

Kathleen Neils Conzen

Tipping the scales at twenty pounds, the 3,304 quarto pages of Alfred T. Andreas's three-volume *History of Chicago from the Earliest Period to the Present Time* must set some kind of record as the longest, weightiest, least readable, and most consulted entry in any list of significant Chicago-related publications. The "province of the historian," Andreas argued, is not "the drawing of inferences" but rather "chronology and the presentation of facts."[1] To that end, he marshaled a twelve-member staff and scores of volunteers, including Chicago Historical Society luminaries, to collect the first-half-century documents and memories of a city that had survived the Great Chicago Fire of 1871 and the ravages of time, and to present them in three chronological volumes as "compendia of incidents ... as they transpired, rather than a general account of the event toward which the incidents tended."[2]

For a *Chicago Daily Tribune* reviewer of the first volume, the result lacked literary merit but was a valuable encyclopedic compilation enriched by maps, illustrations, and biographies of early citizens.[3] The reviewer of the second volume was less charitable: "It is voluminous, but it is not history. . . . It neglects the essentials, and gives only the nonessentials." This writer pointed out that it provides all the facts about Chicago's railroads, for example, but not the reasons for their effortless acquisition by the city; it exhaustively details Chicago's numerous boot and shoe firms but does not explain their concentration there. In contrast to recent histories of Boston and New York, he concluded, the *History of Chicago* "is big, like the Great Eastern [a leviathan steamer], and, like it, a failure."[4]

To the modern reader, the first volume's narratives of early settlement, Indian dispossession, and city founding retain the vividness, but also the bias, of the memories on which they rest. They must be read with care, a caveat that applies also to the second volume's extended Civil War and 1871 Fire accounts. The final volume eschews narrative altogether for topic-by-topic collections of formulaic laudatory biographies. Andreas disingenuously justified the *History*'s 2,236 biographies of "common-place, every-day" men and women in terms familiar to social historians today: theirs were the "actions that have made history."[5] But a business model rather than historiographical philosophy better explains their inclusion.

Alfred T. Andreas (1839–1900) was an entrepreneur who, after Civil War service, went through several fortunes in a variety of speculative initiatives, including illustrated county and state atlases and county, city, and state histories sold by subscription.[6] He augmented his income from those publications by charging residents extra for biographies, portraits, and property illustrations. Like his previous ventures, the Chicago history—Andreas's largest undertaking to date—depended upon self-commissioned biographies for

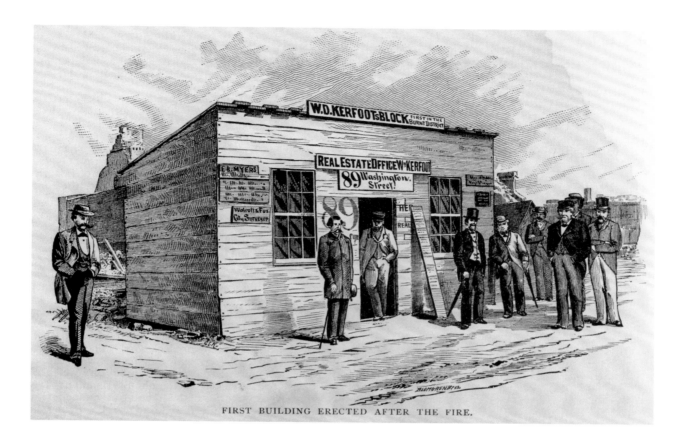

FIRST BUILDING ERECTED AFTER THE FIRE.

profit. "It is a half-million at a time, one way or the other, with Andreas," a Washington, DC, interviewer noted in 1886, "and he has always won twice out of three times in his heavy ventures."[7] Andreas claimed to have invested $32,000 in his first Chicago volume alone, and probably at best broke even with the ambitious three-volume undertaking.[8]

Yet it is precisely its much-maligned potpourri of preserved facts and its laudatory biographies that keep Andreas's *History of Chicago* on the must-consult list today. The book remains both an inescapable starting place for Chicago historiography and a significant milestone in the city's rise as a publishing center. And while those vanity biographies still await systematic historical analysis for what they can tell us about the makers of Chicago, thanks to the internet they have become a treasure trove in our age of genealogical fascination.

In his history of Chicago, A. T. Andreas followed the eighty pages in volume 2 chronicling the 1871 Fire—"Urbs Incinerata"—with fifty-one pages in volume 3 depicting the physical rebuilding of "Urbs Recondita," the city refounded. The real-estate agent W. D. Kerfoot erected his "Block," depicted here, the morning after the fire, posting a sign (not seen in this illustration) declaring: "Everything gone but wife, children and energy."

12

Reasons for Pardoning Fielden, Neebe and Schwab

JOHN P. ALTGELD * [SPRINGFIELD?, ILLINOIS], 1893

Ron Grossman

It is hard to pigeonhole Illinois governor John Peter Altgeld's *Reasons for Pardoning Fielden, Neebe and Schwab*. It does not fit into any of the standard nonfiction categories: history, biography, literary criticism, the sciences. But if its genre is elusive, its consequences are unmistakable. By writing it, Altgeld was signing a death warrant for his political career.

Born in Germany, Altgeld (1847–1902) came to the United States as an infant. In 1875 he moved to Chicago, where he practiced law, made a fortune in real estate, and became a judge. A leading member of the Progressive movement, he served as governor of Illinois from 1893 to 1897. In his first year in office, he pardoned the three survivors of a group of radicals convicted of murder during the 1886 Haymarket Riot. A notorious event in Chicago's history, it was deeply influential in the development of organized labor. It is commemorated around the world on May Day, the international workers' holiday.

About the riot's origins, Altgeld wrote, "There had been trouble, growing out of the effort to introduce an eight-hour day, resulting in some collisions with the police, in one of which several laboring people were killed, and this meeting was called as a protest against alleged police brutality."[1] Called by immigrant labor activists, the gathering was held at the city's Haymarket, near the intersection of Randolph and Des Plaines Streets. Although the speeches were fiery, the crowd was orderly. But as the rally was breaking up, a platoon of police arrived. Someone threw a bomb, killing a number of officers and workers and injuring dozens. The identity of the bomber has never been determined, but, confronted by public outrage, the authorities were determined that someone must pay for the crime.

Eight labor activists were quickly tried and convicted of murder on the theory that their writings and speeches must have influenced the culprit. By the time Altgeld became governor, four had been hanged, one had committed suicide, and three were serving prison sentences. While the Illinois Supreme Court had allowed the verdict to stand, as a Progressive, Altgeld reviewed the case and concluded that there had been a miscarriage of justice. Pardoning the three surviving "Haymarket Martyrs," Altgeld acknowledged the defendants' use of incendiary language. Romanticizing violence, they had proclaimed themselves "anarchists," a term popularly associated with bomb throwers. Yet Altgeld noted a missing link in the prosecution's theory: "It must be shown that the person committing the violence had read or heard the [defendants'] advice" (Altgeld's term for the defendants' alleged incitement).[2] Since the culprit was unknown, Altgeld asked how anyone could know what was on the bomb thrower's mind. He concluded that the case rested on a hypothetical—hardly cause to hang someone.

Freeing the surviving Haymarket Martyrs made Altgeld's final years mis-

Attention Workingmen!

---------- GREAT ----------

MASS-MEETING

TO-NIGHT, at 7.30 o'clock,

---------- AT THE ----------

HAYMARKET, Randolph St., Bet. Desplaines and Halsted.

Good Speakers will be present to denounce the latest atrocious act of the police, the shooting of our fellow-workmen yesterday afternoon.

Workingmen Arm Yourselves and Appear in Full Force!

THE EXECUTIVE COMMITTEE.

Achtung, Arbeiter!

Große

Maſſen-Verſammlung

Heute Abend, ½8 Uhr, auf dem

Heumarkt, Randolph-Straße, zwiſchen Desplaines- u. Halſted-Str.

☞ Gute Redner werden den neueſten Schurkenſtreich der Polizei, indem ſie geſtern Nachmittag unſere Brüder erſchoß, geißeln.

☛ Arbeiter, bewaffnet Euch und erſcheint maſſenhaft!

Das Executiv-Comite.

The Haymarket Riot of 1886, in which seven policemen died and for which eight demonstrators were unfairly convicted, was the violent end to what had begun as a rally to protest police brutality and demand improved working conditions and better hours for laborers. The German text on this broadside announcement indicates the involvement of activist German immigrants in organizing the demonstration.

erable. Three years after pardoning them, he was defeated for reelection. His opponents labeled him John "Pardon" Altgeld, and he was hounded as a dangerous subversive. Yet he remained a friend of the underdog. He died in Joliet, Illinois, while pleading the cause of the Boers, Dutch settlers in South Africa under attack by the British. As no clergyman was willing to conduct Altgeld's funeral, his former law partner Clarence Darrow delivered the eulogy, saying, "In the great flood of human life that is spawned upon the earth, it is not often that a man is born."[3]

13

The Cliff-Dwellers: A Novel

HENRY B. FULLER ✳ ILLUSTRATED BY
T[HURE]. DE THULSTRUP ✳ NEW YORK:
HARPER & BROTHERS PUBLISHERS, 1893

Alice Schreyer

The Cliff-Dwellers is an indelible portrait of a raw and mean Chicago, which is ironic, as it was the product of a newspaper competition for "a realistic story with a local flavor, to take advantage of the market for a Chicago story" on the occasion of the World's Columbian Exposition in 1893.[1] Written by Henry Blake Fuller (1857–1929) in a sharp departure from his previous European romances,[2] it first appeared serially in *Harper's Weekly* from June to August of that year and as a novel that September.[3] To this day the novel is renowned for its vivid delineation of a young, brash, soulless, and ruthless city where human feelings and civilized behavior are crushed by an obsession with financial and social advancement—exactly the images the fair's organizers had hoped to dispel. Still, Fuller was heralded for his realism, compared to the preeminent French writer Émile Zola, praised by the influential novelist and critic William Dean Howells, and criticized—especially by Chicagoans—for taking as his subject a city that he seemed to despise.

The book begins with a sustained metaphor invoking the recently discovered cliff-dwellings of the American Southwest, shown in an anthropological exhibit at the fair. It describes a "Bad Lands" where "great cañons—conduits, in fact, for the leaping volume of an ever-increasing prosperity" are "closed in by a long frontage of towering cliffs."[4] In one of these structures, a skyscraper called the Clifton, Fuller introduced a "tribe" of bankers, lawyers, brokers, and speculators who constitute a self-contained society. When George Ogden encounters Eugene H. McDowell, his soon-to-be brother-in-law, he "seems to see before him the spokesman of a community where prosperity had drugged patriotism into unconsciousness, and where the bare scaffoldings of materialism felt themselves quite independent of the graces and draperies of culture."[5]

The characters of *The Cliff-Dwellers* include pre-Fire "Old Settlers" (Fuller's family was among these), native Midwesterners such as the banker Erastus Brainard; and Yankee émigrés, including Ogden, the novel's putative hero. The story follows their business and personal transactions, set into motion in the halls and offices of the Clifton and extending to the lives of their wives and daughters.[6] In *Harper's* it was illustrated by Thure De Thulstrup (1848–1930), a popular Swedish-born American illustrator, but the city truly came to life through Fuller's brilliant dialogue and sharp description. Indeed, *The Cliff-Dwellers*'s main character is the city " where quality seemed to count for less than quantity, and where the 'prominent' citizen made the 'eminent' citizen a superfluity."[7] Most of the human characters remain vague and opaque; even the most dramatic plot point—the murder of Brainard by Marcus, his artistic son—is a schematic melodrama playing out the conflict between commerce and culture. Fuller's next Chicago novel, *With the Procession* (1895), presents more fully developed characters and may be a better work of fiction, but it cannot match the power of *The Cliff-Dwellers*, which evokes the voice of a prophet railing against the sins of the people he yearns to reform.

Fuller was part of an informal group of artists and writers known as the Little Room, founded in the early 1890s. Though the group counted on the Columbian Exposition to inaugurate a flourishing of the arts and culture in Chicago, such hopes soon faded. Nevertheless, the writer Hamlin Garland determined to establish "a meeting place for artists and writers, a rallying point for Midland Arts."[8] Although the Cliff Dwellers Club, established in 1907, was named after Fuller's novel, he never joined it, most likely because he doubted it would succeed.[9] He may also have been offended by the notion that he would be remembered because of it rather than for his writing.[10] More than a century later, *The Cliff-Dwellers* still is seen as a prominent milestone in American urban realism, and it is widely available in various editions.[11]

FACING Initially serialized in *Harper's Weekly*, Henry Fuller's *Cliff-Dwellers* is the first realist novel set in Chicago, characterized as home to greedy businessmen and social climbers. Here a meeting between George Ogden, a newcomer to the city and a family-business manager, is interrupted by women from families that will provide Ogden with his first and second wives, suggesting that social and marital relationships are essentially business transactions.

14

Rand, McNally & Co.'s Bird's-Eye Views and Guide to Chicago

Indispensable to Every Visitor. Containing Innumerable Details of Business and Residence Localities; the Most Charming Drives; the Various Means of Transportation, Including Routes to the Exposition, Depots, etc.; Together with Complete Directory of Churches, Clubs, Hotels, Cafés, Theaters, Amusements, Public Buildings, Parks, and Monuments—A Graphic Description, in Short, of Every Object of Any Interest in the City

CHICAGO AND NEW YORK: RAND, MCNALLY & COMPANY, 1893

Kenneth Nebenzahl

Chicago's remarkable recovery and development during the two decades after the Great Fire of 1871 made it the fastest-growing city in the world. The most dramatic representation of this was the World's Columbian Exposition of 1893, the extraordinary venture that became a defining moment in the city's history. The fair's campus, built on a marshy bog, became a beautiful urban park on the shore of Lake Michigan, supporting a tour de force of splendid architecture built to contain a vast number of unprecedented exhibits.

Promotional materials of all kinds were produced, catering to Chicagoans and the more than twenty million visitors to the fair from around the world. Maps and guidebooks were essential, and Rand, McNally & Company led the way. The Chicago-based firm's origins date to 1856, when William H. Rand (1828–1915) and Andrew McNally (1838–1904) joined forces as job printers, eventually managing the printing of the *Chicago Tribune*. Forming Rand, McNally in 1868, they began to publish railroad guides. Their first map appeared in an 1872 guide; the company quickly became a pioneer in the field of mapmaking. Rand, McNally later introduced mass-production methods that enabled it to become the largest map and atlas publisher in the United States.[1] In connection with the Columbian Exposition, the company issued several detailed maps, on various scales, of both Chicago and the fair. Its most remarkable publication of 1893 was the unique *Bird's-Eye Views and Guide to Chicago.*"[2]

The use of bird's-eye views has a long history. Many early attempts to show Jerusalem's specific buildings, bird's-eye style, are known, from the circa AD 565 Madaba mosaic map in Jordan, to Crusader-era manuscripts, woodcut versions in early printed books, and later engravings and lithographs. Late-nineteenth-century technology enabled the quality of illustrations of buildings in this guidebook to exceed that of previous printmaking. The introduction to *Bird's Eye Views* explains the visual treats to come:

A knowledge of localities and direction of streets is but partially complete unless the mind recalls with ease their separate features. While, therefore, maps and engraving might have embellished the work, a much more practical method of illustration has been chosen. This method consists of a series of accurate Bird's Eye views, executed by a unique combination of photography and topography. . . . This task has involved the use of several hundred photographs . . . in order that the views . . . may portray with perfect fidelity of detail the architectural effects rendered.[3]

The result is a graphic architectural record of what was then the second-largest city in the United States. Each building illustrated in the guide is numbered in the accompanying text, which offers much architectural detail. The fifty-nine area illustrations begin with "The Vicinity of the Board of Trade." The text identifies and describes the fourteen buildings in the area, including the Lakeside Building (1), Rookery (2), Insurance Exchange (3), Rand-McNally Building (including the Columbian Exposition headquarters: 4), Grand Pacific Hotel (9), Hotel Grace (10), Phenix [!] Building (11), Board of Trade Building (at the head of LaSalle Street: 12), Brother Jonathan Building (13), and the old Medinah Temple (14).

The views continue, radiating out from the commercial center to include railroad depots, other hotels, and major cultural buildings such as the Art Institute, and Washington Square with the Newberry Library. Also depicted are wholesale districts, the East Branch of the Chicago River and bridges, sections of the lakefront; elite residential neighborhoods; and recreational areas. Interspersed are simple plans of special areas such as the district that burned in 1871, the stockyards, Near North Side, hotels, and restaurants. Rand, McNally's *Bird's-Eye Views* preserves the picture of much of Chicago at a major moment of its history.

Of the several publications that the Chicago-based and nationally prominent map publisher Rand, McNally & Company produced to help millions of visitors to the World's Columbian Exposition navigate the fair and Chicago, this is most remarkable. Its fifty-nine main illustrations graphically represent the built environment of the nation's second-largest city. Fourteen of the buildings numbered in this image of the area around Adams and LaSalle Streets are described in the text. See also page 9.

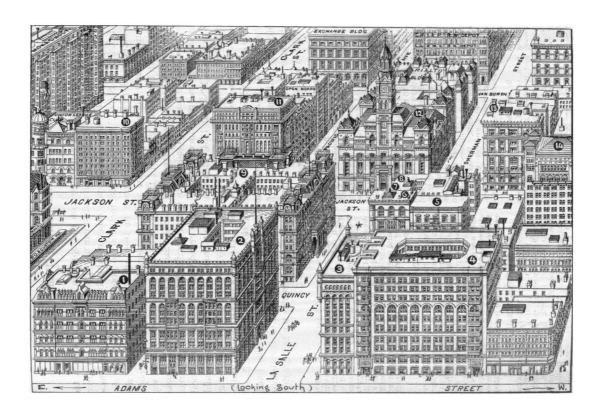

15

The Reason Why the Colored American Is Not in the World's Columbian Exposition: The Afro-American's Contribution to Columbian Literature

[IDA B. WELLS, FREDERICK DOUGLASS, I. GARLAND PENN, AND F. L. BARNETT] ✴ CHICAGO: MISS IDA B. WELLS, 1893

Toni Preckwinkle

Ida B. Wells (1862–1931) was born a slave in Holly Springs, Mississippi. She was educated at the Freedman's School and Rust College in her hometown and later at Fisk University, Nashville. Throughout her career, she combined investigative journalism with fearless personal activism. After the murder of several close friends, Wells began a crusade against lynching. In response to threats on her life, she moved to Chicago in the early 1890s.

Wells became part of Chicago's story when she edited *The Reason Why the Colored American Is Not in the World's Columbian Exposition.* She assembled essays, data, and photographs to document the African American protest against the 1893 World's Columbian Exposition. This salvo in the war against American racism was fired against the bulwarks of entrenched indifference, and it has never stopped affecting how we think and what we do.[1]

When I reread the contributions to *The Reason Why* by Wells, Frederick Douglass, I. Garland Penn, and Frederick Lee Barnett, I see the struggles of my own life in politics and public service laid open on the page. The occasion for this book was the huge public project that was the fair and that shaped the neighborhoods I represented in the Chicago City Council for two decades. The Columbian Exposition is often remembered today for its modernity, with its dazzling display of the power of electric lights and the wonders of science. But the fair took place a mere twenty-eight years after the end of slavery in the United States, and we continue to fail to recognize the consequences of slavery within our modern world.

The Reason Why is best remembered as a collection of hard-hitting essays, but it does not rely on the power of eloquence alone. The section on lynching includes graphic photographs of victims. Today video images of young black men murdered by the police serve the same function, telling the objective, terrible truth.

Wells insightfully observed that for many whites the emancipation of slaves constituted "an act of unjust punishment to them."[2] She focused on lynching, the prison system, and legalized injustice. My agenda as president of the Board of Commissioners of Cook County is often set by similar issues. Like most of the people Wells wrote about, a number of those I represent cannot vote because so many black men go to prison. The legal system created to right that wrong persists today in the unequal impact on African Americans of criminal law and restrictions on voting.

Unlike many other notable women crusaders, Wells also undertook the challenge of marriage and childrearing.[3] Her support for women's rights set her at odds with other African American leaders, just as her work on behalf of the black community isolated her from other leaders of the women's movement.

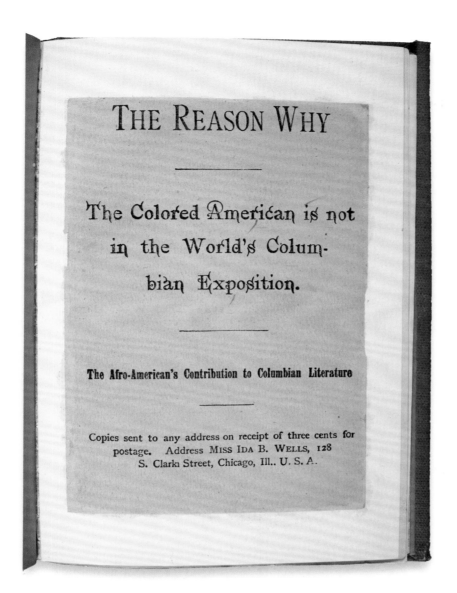

THE REASON WHY

The Colored American is not in the World's Columbian Exposition.

The Afro-American's Contribution to Columbian Literature

Copies sent to any address on receipt of three cents for postage. Address MISS IDA B. WELLS, 128 S. Clark Street, Chicago, Ill.. U. S. A.

Drawing parallels between race issues of the late nineteenth century and today, this entry considers the protest piece compiled by African American activist and journalist Ida B. Wells (seen here in a photograph of around 1892) regarding the absence of African Americans in the exhibits of the World's Columbian Exposition and their subservient role as workers in and around the fair.

Wells urged thorough investigation of what feels wrong. She advised looking for every source of data and making clear what supports one's conclusions, along with working for change openly, using the possibilities democracy bestows. There is a straight path from learning to elections, from books to voting and, if necessary, to the courthouse. The demand for the end of racial inequities raised powerfully by Wells and her coauthors continues today. When a book speaks as clearly as this one does, the authors' voices will be heard until the questions asked receive more satisfactory answers.

16

The Pullman Strike

REV. WILLIAM H. CARWARDINE, PASTOR
OF THE FIRST M. E. CHURCH, PULLMAN,
ILL. ✳ CHICAGO: CHARLES H. KERR & CO.,
1894

Leon Fink

FACING Abusive treatment and
devastating wage cuts prompted
the spring 1894 strike of Pullman's
employees and this eyewitness account by a supportive local minister.
Inspiring a national boycott of the
company's sleeping cars, the strike
was crushed by troops including the
Illinois National Guard, seen here
lined up before the Arcade Building
in the company's town, Pullman.

Composed in the last desperate weeks of one of the most cataclysmic of American labor disputes, Reverend William H. Carwardine's classic eyewitness
account of the origins and agony of the Great Pullman Railroad Strike and
Boycott of 1894 anticipates the Progressive Era muckraking genre of writing
and reportage that would continually take aim at the worst abuses of industrial capitalism. Early in the conflict, Carwardine (1855–1929), pastor of the
district's First Methodist Episcopal Church, had sermonized on the side of
workers who went on strike on May 11, 1894, against sleeping-car mogul and
Pullman Town patriarch George Pullman, following a devastating series of
wage cuts. By the time *The Pullman Strike* appeared, however, not only had
the local strikers been crushed, but so had a nationwide boycott of Pullman
sleeping cars. The latter was organized by American Railway Union president
(and future Socialist presidential standard-bearer) Eugene V. Debs, who himself would be prosecuted and jailed along with other strike leaders for breaking an injunction obtained by US Attorney General Richard Olney. In short,
even before Carwardine had finished his plaintive appeal to the public—"Go
forth, little book, like a piece of driftwood tossed out on the watery main of
life, and may God's blessing go with you"[1]—the strike's effectiveness had been
effectively curtailed by the deployment of federal troops in Chicago and other
industrial centers.

Carwardine's account has long stood as a reliable if impassioned and par-
tisan source of reporting on the simmering grievances in Pullman Town.[2]
Framed as an exposé of injustice, suffering, and squalor that played out
"behind the scenes" of what had once appeared a benevolent experiment in
industrial planning, the book is a dry accounting of worker wages, rents, and
water and gas bills with emotional testimony from the families of strikers and
the unemployed. It also offers uncommon additional details such as a description of the local war of insignia—white ribbons for strike supporters, miniature American flags for company loyalists—and an excerpt from a newspaper interview with Ohio senator John Sherman, who identified the Pullman
Company as an "outrageous monopoly" even as his own eponymous antitrust
act was deployed by the government against Debs. In the name of "applied
Christianity,"[3] Carwardine particularly assailed Pullman for his refusal to balance wage cuts with rent reductions and for rejecting numerous calls for arbi-
tration, "while thousands of dollars' worth of property was being destroyed,
. . . the trade of half the country was paralyzed, human lives were being sac-
rificed, and bloody riot hung like a pall over the city and country."[4]

Carwardine, who rose from near obscurity to take on his role during the
Pullman strike, afterward remained a prominent advocate of labor rights
from the pulpit and in print.[5] Near the end of his famous book, he offered

a clue to his inner motivation. Growing up as "an orphan boy" in New York City, Carwardine reportedly labored for six years under an abusive foreman in the composing room of the *New York Evening Post*:

In those days there was engendered in my soul a hatred against tyrannical foremen and abusive treatment of men which has never left me, and which during the past months of our long and sad winter, made my very blood boil with indignation at what I have seen and heard. Then it was that I declared if ever the opportunity presented itself to defend the true rights of laboring men, and smite those who unmercifully oppressed them, I would lift up my voice and cry aloud, in the name of the God of Israel.[6]

17

If Christ Came to Chicago! A Plea for the Union of All Who Love in the Service of All Who Suffer

WILLIAM T. STEAD ✳ CHICAGO: LAIRD & LEE, PUBLISHERS, 1894[1]

Martin E. Marty

British journalist supreme William T. Stead was lured to Chicago to report on the World's Columbian Exposition in 1893, and he stayed on to explore the city itself. One year later, writing in England, he published *If Christ Came to Chicago!*. The book's title is carefully worded: Stead invented a "Christ" and imagined his "coming" to a real "Chicago." The author had a reputation for moralism and sensationalism, and both are evident in this book.

If Christ Came to Chicago!, it was reported, sold seventy thousand copies on publication day. Readers who were attracted to it often found good reason to dwell on its concluding pages. Who then, or now, could resist exploring, or not being engrossed by, appendix A, with its "Black List" offering "names and addresses" and citing "Occupiers, Owners and Tax-Payers of Property Used for Immoral Purposes"? What follows that heading are numerous pages posting addresses on Clark, Dearborn, and other streets in the Nineteenth Precinct of the city's old First Ward. Stead dealt with many of these "house-numbers," locating "Houses of Ill Fame" or "Saloons and Assignation Houses," and scrupulously identifying those who paid taxes on them. A number of the characters also receive close-ups in chapters named, for example, "Maggie Darling" and "The Disreputables."

References to the Divine Trinity would not be out of place in a book with "Christ" in its title, but here we read of "the Chicago Trinity." They were the city's titans George Pullman, Marshall Field, and Philip Armour. Stead placed them in the company of "Boodlers," including "Dives the Tax Dodger" and "The Scarlet Woman." Finding that Chicago clergymen were failing tests of their Christian gospel, the muckraking journalist exhorted them to respond to the call of the book's subtitle: *A Plea for the Union of All Who Love in the Service of All Who Suffer*.

Stead was not only a judgmental scold. He was also an activist who later returned to Chicago to organize religious and civic leaders, supporting the Civic Federation, among other things, to advance good causes.[2] Still, progress toward Christ's ideal was too slow. Readers, the journalist thought, needed to have their imaginations stirred, so he provided a scenario for the future. "Unlike most writers who enter the field of imaginary prediction, I have endeavored scrupulously to confine myself to the practical."[3] He declared that he was only proposing advances on extant progressive beginnings such as, for example, a Council of Religious Leaders. Incidentally, he envisioned good things civically: for instance, garbage would be collected, and the Home of the Waifs and Strays would prosper.

Where Stead must have left even many devotees behind, if not stupefied, was when he invented as a "practical" future, a "Church of Chicago," which would embrace as its "effective members all the religious organizations,"

including that of Catholic archbishop John Ireland. The famed Minnesota prelate, the author noted, "had most trouble at first with his own people," but Stead believed they would come to see the need for a wider conception of Catholicism.[4]

A modern biographer has exposed Stead as an unscrupulous, sex-obsessed moralist faker, but he always found ways to make headlines as a do-gooder. Meanwhile, he was disgraced by the failures of his various start-ups and ventures and came to favor faddish spiritualism and the occult.[5] Climactically, traveling on the *Titanic* in 1912 with plans to return to Chicago, he gave up his place on a lifeboat, according to eyewitnesses. Stories of his death reinforced the image many had of his generous spirit. They would not have been surprised by this last sacrificial act if they had learned from him to pursue "the service of all who suffer."

This map from *If Christ Came to Chicago* uses bright red and black to single out the houses of ill repute and saloons that populated the Nineteenth Precinct of Chicago's First Ward, along with individuals who owned or supported them. While William T. Stead's exposé aimed to close such enterprises, it turns out he frequented them himself.

18

The Chap-Book

CHICAGO: STONE & KIMBALL (LATER
HERBERT S. STONE & CO.), 1894–98

Paul F. Gehl

Herbert Stuart Stone (1871–1915) and Hannibal Ingalls Kimball (1874–1933) were classmates at Harvard College, where they founded a publishing house, Stone & Kimball, and a little magazine, *The Chap-Book*.[1] They soon moved the firm to Chicago, where Stone supervised editorial affairs while Kimball concerned himself with business matters. *The Chap-Book* was at first a way of advertising the new firm's books, and it continued to showcase new work that would eventually find its way onto the Stone & Kimball list; but it quickly became a serious literary endeavor in its own right, claiming to speak for those who felt that literature and criticism were important social activities best expressed by young writers with a broadly transatlantic worldview. By appealing to (and achieving) an international audience, the editors proposed that Chicago was not merely an important American city but also a world cultural capital with direct ties to Britain and the Continent.

Early collaborators attributed the idea for an elegant little magazine to

Stone, a native Chicagoan. In Chicago the magazine was first printed by Frederic Goudy's Camelot Press and then by the Lakeside Press of R.R. Donnelley & Sons. Once Kimball left the partnership, a Stone & Co. imprint appeared (May 1896). In January 1897 Stone altered the format from pocket octavo (7 inches) to a more standard magazine size (12 inches), perhaps in an attempt to revive interest in the magazine, which was losing money, or to make it seem more serious. Circulation had peaked at 16,500 copies in early 1896 but dropped sharply thereafter. The July 15, 1898, issue announced that *The Chap-Book* would fold into *The Dial*, an older and less adventurous Chicago literary journal.

The Chap-Book lasted for only one hundred issues, but even in its own brief day it was considered the most influential of the early little magazines, both editorially and for its design and production standards. Harriet Monroe, in a 1915 *Poetry* magazine tribute to Stone, concluded that *The Chap-Book* had "led all [its contemporaries] in discernment and distinction."[2] Its editors embraced a variety of traditional and experimental poetry and prose and offered illustrations that drew on art nouveau, arts and crafts, and Anglo-American folk styles. Both visually and in terms of text, then, *The Chap-Book* offered a lively mix that made its college-educated audience feel up to date. It published interesting artists (among them Aubrey Beardsley, Max Beerbohm, Georges Pissarro) and important writers (Stephen Crane, Hamlin Garland, Henry James, Stéphane Mallarmé, Robert Louis Stevenson, Paul Verlaine, H. G. Wells). It presented Chicago authors to an international audience (George Ade, John Vance Cheney, Eugene Field) and offered thoughtful criticism. A substantial number of its contributors were women (Kate Chopin, Anna de Koven, Alice Morse Earle, Charlotte Perkins Stetson [later Gilman], Ella Wheeler Wilcox). Its editors took courageous stands (e.g., denouncing the British Library in 1895 for censoring Oscar Wilde's books). Into the 1940s scholars and commentators described it as innovative, even daring.

Considered critical opinion today is more uneven. *The Chap-Book* clearly reflected the playful earnestness of the American college men who created it. The editors were essentially establishmentarian and romantic but always willing to critique and even make fun of the pretensions of their own class. Their declared preference for French symbolism and edgy aestheticism was balanced by their self-conscious fashionableness, showy culture mongering, and willingness to include work by romantics and conservatives alongside more novel pieces. In the last issue the editors explained that they had merely sought out "the best writing they could procure." In fact, Stone & Kimball pioneered a theme common in later publishing and design, that Chicago looked to Europe—not just back East—for models and collaborations.

FACING Over the four years of its existence, the influential "little magazine" *Chap-Book* introduced its local subscribers to prose and poetry by both well-known and unfamiliar writers, and in turn introduced the work of Chicago's writers to its far-flung subscribers. The issues were illustrated throughout by artists working primarily in an art nouveau mode, including this striking cover image by Frank Hazenplug (1874?–1931). See also page v.

19

A History of the World's Columbian Exposition Held in Chicago in 1893 by the Authority of the Board of Directors

EDITED BY ROSSITER JOHNSON ✳ VOLUME 1, *NARRATIVE* ✳ VOLUME 2, *DEPARTMENTS* ✳ VOLUME 3, *EXHIBITS* ✳ VOLUME 4, *CONGRESSES* ✳ NEW YORK: D. APPLETON AND COMPANY, 1897 (VOLS. 1 AND 2), 1898 (VOLS. 3 AND 4)

Neil Harris

The World's Columbian Exposition of 1893 remains one of Chicago's formative experiences, helping shape the city's worldwide reputation, institutions, landscape, and civic ideals. Possibly the best publicized non-military event of nineteenth-century America, the White City, as the fair was popularly known, signaled Chicago's recovery from the Great Fire of 1871 and emphasized its status as one of the world's leading cities. Tens of millions of visitors flocked to Jackson Park on Chicago's South Side from May 1 to October 30, 1893, while thousands attended the various congresses held downtown on Michigan Avenue in the building that would become the home of the Art Institute of Chicago once the exposition closed.

Much has been written about the fair over the years, but there may be no more appropriate textual monument to its complexity, scale, seriousness of purpose, and self-celebration than the massive four-volume history commissioned by the fair's board of directors and edited by Rossiter Johnson (1840–1931). This officially sanctioned narrative, prepared as a "condensed synthesis" for general interest and to help planners of future expositions, incorporates almost every detail imaginable about the fair's planning, administration, operations, and statistical profile. Meant to preserve a "true record," its short chapters, most of them built around official reports and exhibition descriptions, are supplemented by almost one thousand photographs, many by the fair's official photographer, C. D. Arnold (1844–1927). The work as a whole documents both the fair itself and the methodical ideals of those in charge. The final volume describes the fair congresses. Four specially written, signed chapters, one in each volume, treat the fair as spectacle, as work of art, as promoter of science, and as moral agent.[1] The organizers' obsessive anticipation, study, and solving of problems, as well as endless sets of comparisons and juxtapositions, offer today's readers some insight into the taxonomic logic of the exposition, its priorities, hierarchies, values, and objectives.

Rossiter Johnson himself possessed an industrial appetite for publication and even more for compilation. Holder of a PhD (and several other degrees) from the University of Rochester, he produced, during his more than ninety years of life, an impressive series of books on many subjects: the Civil War, classic literature, Admiral George Dewey, education, rhetoric, grammar. He was a resourceful plot summarizer, creating abbreviated versions of major novels and offering selections of famous poems for general audiences. More than that, Johnson demonstrated a capacity to edit encyclopedias, anthologies, dictionaries, and collections of sources on various themes. It was presumably this editorial talent, made clear by his work on *Appletons' Cyclopaedia of American Biography*, among other texts, that led the fair's directors to assign him the task of compiling information about the fair in 1895.

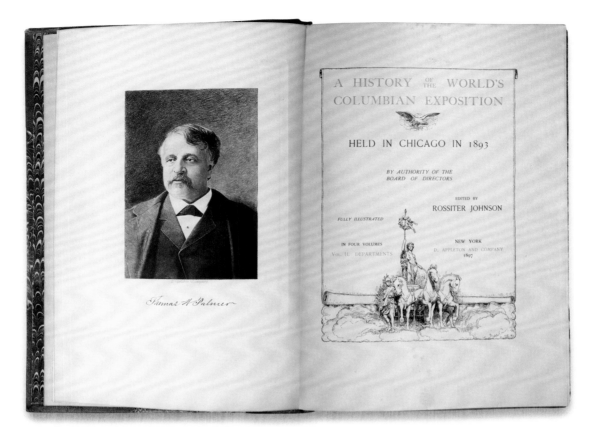

Great expositions were ultimately triumphs of organization and arrangement, as they sought comprehensive inclusion of the world's art, industry, science, agriculture, national achievements, natural resources, and human development. Doing justice to this controlled variety would have taxed the skills of an inexperienced editor, but Johnson persevered. The tone of the work is respectful and even rhapsodic, though critical observations about process and impact did find their way into the text.

Johnson's accomplishment was something of a funerary urn for the exposition, encasing cherished memories of the fair into an enormous 2,100-page container, difficult to browse, even harder to lift. As such it may have served, in the decades that followed, more as a barrier than a guide to the fair's significance. But if its size and detail discourage easy browsing, surprises await the hardy explorer. And its documentary value has been acknowledged in recent years by historians who have begun to unpack the fair's many levels of meaning, deep prejudices, and impressive accomplishments as they bring new insights and wider contexts to this fabled event.

The White City shimmering on Chicago's South Side in 1893 secured Chicago's place as one of the world's great cities. Rossiter Johnson's four-volume monument covers almost every aspect of the fair's planning, creation, management, and promotion. It includes photographs by C. D. Arnold of buildings under construction (see page 252).

20

Mr. Dooley in Peace and in War

[FINLEY PETER DUNNE] * BOSTON: SMALL, MAYNARD & COMPANY, 1898

Charles Fanning

FACING The son of Irish-born parents, journalist Finley Peter Dunne captured the world of Chicago's extensive Irish population through the voice, character, and philosophizing of saloonkeeper Martin J. Dooley, the fictional author of a nationally syndicated newspaper column that Dunne wrote weekly. Brought together in this popular book, Dunne's Dooley stories are set in and around the Irish neighborhoods' bars and liquor stores, such as George A. Regan's establishment on South Halsted, seen here in a photograph from the early 1880s.

In June 1884, sixteen-year-old Peter Dunne (1867–1936) took a job as a cub reporter for a Chicago newspaper.[1] Eight years later he was editorial chairman at the *Chicago Evening Post*, where in October 1893, at the ripe old age of twenty-six, he began a weekly column in the voice and character of Martin J. Dooley, a saloonkeeper/philosopher from the South Side Irish neighborhood of Bridgeport. Almost immediately his 750-word monologues (delivered to genial politician John McKenna or long-suffering millworker Malachi Hennessy) became a Saturday evening Chicago tradition.

Over the next seven years, some three hundred Dooley pieces appeared. Taken together, they form a coherent body of work in which a whole world comes into existence: a self-contained Irish ethnic culture with its own customs, ceremonies, sacred sites, heroes, villains, and victims. The Chicago Dooley columns are cameo etchings of archetypal immigrant themes, including memories of the turbulent crossing to North America, the shattered dream of gold in the streets, the hard life of manual labor, the pains of assimilation, the gulf between immigrants and their American-born children, and the slow rise to respectability.

Moreover, Mr. Dooley's was a vernacular dialect voice, the first such voice to transcend the stereotype of the "stage Irishman," a demeaning comic caricature of ignorance, belligerence, and garrulity that was much abroad in nineteenth-century American writing and drama. Dunne created the illusion of a speaking voice grounded in place by joining oral tradition and the written word. These are, after all, transcribed renderings of imagined conversations, many of them inspired by stories that had been told to the young Dunne by his parents and others of their generation of immigrants, in whom the Irish oral tradition was still very much alive. In fact, the Chicago Dooley pieces constitute a rare and marvelous hybrid form. Composed under deadline with imperative spontaneity, they are actually closer to talking than to writing. They bridge the gap between storytelling and short fiction. In his way, Dunne was as much a trailblazer into the American city and its ordinary people as setting for serious literature as Theodore Dreiser or Stephen Crane.

Dunne's career changed dramatically in 1898, when Mr. Dooley's satirical coverage of the Spanish-American War brought him to the attention of readers beyond Chicago. Beginning with his scoop of "Cousin George" Dewey's victory at Manila, Mr. Dooley's reports of military and political bungling during the "splendid little war" were widely reprinted, and national syndication followed. Soon Mr. Dooley was established as a premier satirist of our national life. From this point until World War I, Dunne exposed hypocrisy and folly in a wide range of national and international events and characters, among them Teddy Roosevelt's health fads and Andrew Carnegie's passion for libraries; the Boer and Boxer Rebellions and the Negro, Indian, and immigration "problems"; the Dreyfus case; and the workings of the US Supreme Court.

Dunne's first book, *Mr. Dooley in Peace and in War*, is a compilation of writings about both Mr. Dooleys: the realistic chronicler of nineteenth-century Chicago immigrant life and the creator of cutting, hilarious satire of society and politics in North America and across the globe. The book sold ten thousand copies a month for a year.[2]

21

The School and Society: Being Three Lectures by John Dewey, Professor of Pedagogy in the University of Chicago, Supplemented by a Statement of the University Elementary School

CHICAGO: THE UNIVERSITY OF CHICAGO PRESS, 1899

Michael P. Wakeford

With *The School and Society*, published in 1899, the American philosopher John Dewey (1859–1952) offered his first book-length argument for school reform based on principles of experimentalism, student centeredness, and democratic social transformation.[1] It debuted at the midpoint of Dewey's decade-long stint at the University of Chicago and three years after he founded the university's Laboratory School, the subject of the first edition's fourth chapter. Originating as three lectures delivered at the university, *The School and Society* helped put the institution and Chicago at the center of the educational-reform universe. It also punctuated Dewey's shift from the metaphysical preoccupations of his early career to the socially engaged outlook that made him a giant in the spheres of pragmatist philosophy, education, and politics over the next half century.

    The School and Society was an immediate success. As one observer commented in the months after its publication, "More eyes are now fixed upon [Dewey's school] than any other elementary school in the country and probably the world."[2] For the university's press, the book was good business; after its initial print run of one thousand copies, eleven reprints and multiple foreign translations followed in the next fifteen years.

The University of Chicago had recruited Dewey from the University of Michigan with promises that he could lead the educational research and training efforts of the brand-new institution. That facilitated Dewey's reorientation toward educational matters and the Lab School's opening, developments to which *The School and Society* owes its being. The book was inspired by various aspects of turn-of-the-century Chicago. Dewey was fascinated with the fluxing midwestern metropolis, the social intricacies of the working-class neighborhoods that lay "back of the factory system," and the class and ethnic tensions he sought to soothe. Animating the book's ideal of turning a school into a "miniature community," moreover, was Dewey's view of a school as an "embryonic society," a staging ground for a remade city.[3] *The School and Society* also identified Dewey with a broader front of Chicago reformism, drawing upon and amplifying the pioneering activity-centered pedagogy of Francis Parker's Cook County Normal School and Jane Addams's celebrated educational work with newly arrived immigrants at Hull-House (see no. 30).

The importance assigned to *The School and Society* diminished as Dewey's later books on learning—most notably, *Democracy and Education* (1916)—entered the discussion in more immediate proximity to the expanding interwar influence of progressive educators. Of course, as part of Dewey's educational corpus, *The School and Society* has been subjected to alternately laudatory and derisive reappraisals during the intervening century. Indeed, in the interwar and postwar eras the Dewey name often functioned as an epithet encapsulating criticisms that ranged from characterizing progressive education as corroding curricular structure and promoting leftist ideology to intending to substitute "social adjustment" for intellectual rigor. Nonetheless, the book's status as the classic, and perhaps the purest, statement of Deweyan ideals insulated it from the harsher critiques.[4]

Surprisingly, contemporary readers of editions of *The School and Society* other than the original one might not sense the book's Chicago ties. In 1915 a revised second edition removed the section about the Laboratory School. The original lectures that remained—though replete with descriptions of an industrializing and ethnically diverse urban world—were conspicuously devoid of direct references to the city. Purged of its most Chicago-specific content, and with Dewey eventually perched at New York City's Columbia University, *The School and Society*'s Chicago roots were partially obscured.

But they are hardly forgotten. *The School and Society* forever remains Dewey's signature "Chicago book," one that cemented the historical bond between the Windy City and a man whom some have called America's greatest philosopher.

FACING The philosopher John Dewey's first book on education, in which he promulgated a student-centered approach to schooling that embraced doing and interactivity rather than passive learning, reflects the experimental methods used at the University of Chicago's Laboratory School, which he founded in 1896. Establishing Chicago as a world-renowned center of progressive education, *The School and Society* was quickly translated into twelve languages.

22

Sister Carrie

THEODORE DREISER * NEW YORK:
DOUBLEDAY, PAGE & CO., 1900

Elliott J. Gorn

FACING The naturalistic, nonjudgmental rendering in *Sister Carrie* of the stresses of survival in Chicago and New York was seen by some as scandalous. Nonetheless, Theodore Dreiser's first novel eventually became an American classic and has been published in countless editions. The Heritage edition (1937) includes illustrations by Reginald Marsh (1898–1954), including one in which the main character, a country girl on a train bound for Chicago, is approached by a salesman whose mistress she will eventually become.

Sister Carrie begins with a pretty young woman on a train to Chicago and ends with a middle-aged man killing himself. They were lovers.

Theodore Dreiser (1871–1945) wrote in a new idiom for a new century. Published in 1900, *Sister Carrie* led the way for American naturalist fiction that left Victorian fussiness and morality behind. The first edition sold just over five hundred copies, which constituted only half of its print run. Many attributed the book's commercial failure to its relatively frank view of sex. Carrie Meeber, the main character, becomes the mistress of not one but two men and in the main does not suffer the consequences. This is Dreiser's point, that modern urban life increasingly freed the burgeoning middle class from old restraints.

Dreiser was not a man of letters, a child of privilege or learning, or an inheritor of the nineteenth century's "genteel tradition." He arrived in Chicago from Indiana at age fifteen, took a series of jobs, and ended up as a journalist. Like Carrie, Dreiser followed in the footsteps of tens of thousands of Americans, migrants from heartland states seeking work, prosperity, and excitement in the booming midwestern metropolis.

The novel opens in August 1889 with Carrie—carrying only a small satchel, ticket, bag lunch, and big dreams—on a train bound from Columbia City, Wisconsin, for Chicago. Onboard she meets Charles Drouet, a traveling salesman, the very symbol of mobility, of freedom from conventional constraints of family and community. He speaks glowingly of the city that Carrie will call home.

While Chicago enchants Carrie, she struggles there. On the brink of returning to Wisconsin, she reencounters Drouet, who helps her buy new clothes and takes her to fine restaurants. "The waiter returned with an immense tray, bearing . . . hot savory dishes. . . . Drouet fairly shone in the matter of serving. He appeared to great advantage behind the white napery and silver platters of the table. . . . His new suit creaked as he stretched to reach the plates, break the bread, and pour the coffee."[1]

Dreiser wanted readers to feel the material weight of Chicago's explosive growth and newfound wealth. Goods, luxury items, and status symbols all motivate his characters, who are pulled together and apart by where they live, whom they consort with, what they buy. Carrie becomes "the victim of the city's hypnotic influence,"[2] of the culture of consumption, of thousands of people on the streets, in stores, in theaters, in the act of seeing and being seen.

The more Drouet helps Carrie acquire the accoutrements of beauty, the more desirable she becomes. Not long after she moves in with him, she meets his friend George Hurstwood, who manages an elegant downtown saloon. Carrie is deeply impressed by Hurstwood's refined manners and expensive cloth-

CHAPTER I THE MAGNET ATTRACTING: A
WAIF AMID FORCES

When Caroline Meeber boarded the afternoon train for Chicago, her total outfit consisted of a small trunk, a cheap imitation alligator-skin satchel, a small lunch in a paper box, and a yellow leather snap purse, containing her ticket, a scrap of paper with her sister's address in Van Buren Street, and four dollars in money. It was in August, 1889. She was eighteen years of age, bright, timid, and full of the illusions of ignorance and youth. Whatever touch of regret at parting characterised her thoughts, it was certainly not for advantages now being given up. A gush of tears at her mother's farewell kiss, a touch in her throat when the cars clacked by the flour mill where her father worked by the day, a pathetic sigh as the familiar green environs of the village passed in review, and the threads which bound her so lightly to girlhood and home were irretrievably broken.

To be sure there was always the next station, where one might descend and return. There was the great city, bound more closely by these very trains which came up daily. Columbia City was not so very far away, even once she was in Chicago. What, pray, is a few hours— a few hundred miles? She looked at the little slip bearing her sister's address and wondered. She gazed at the green landscape, now passing in swift review, until her swifter thoughts replaced its impression with vague conjectures of what Chicago might be.

When a girl leaves her home at eighteen, she does one of two things.

1

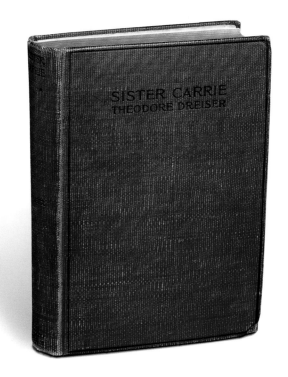

ing, and he becomes infatuated with her. His eventual downfall—in order to be with Carrie, he steals from his employers, deserts his family, runs away with her to New York, and ends up alone and penniless—is shattering.

Dreiser looked with a jaundiced eye on turn-of-the-century Chicago, but in this amoral world it is Carrie who survives. She discovers that she possesses great stage presence and goes on to a notable theater career. Nonetheless, she is never satisfied: "She longed, and longed, and longed."[3] And desire, finally, is at the heart of Dreiser's vision: for better and worse, the culture of the modern city freed individuals to crave things of the material world, and these yearnings overshadowed the life of the mind and spirit.

23

The Epic of the Wheat: The Pit, A Story of Chicago

FRANK NORRIS ✳ NEW YORK:
DOUBLEDAY, PAGE & CO., 1903

Timothy Spears

Here, midmost in the land, beat the Heart of the Nation, whence inevitably must come its immeasurable power, infinite, infinite, inexhaustible vitality. Here, of all her cities, throbbed the true life—the true power and spirit of America; gigantic, crude with the crudity of youth, disdaining rivalry; sane and healthy and vigorous; brutal in its ambition, arrogant in the new-found knowledge of its giant strength, prodigal of its wealth, infinite in its desires.[1]

The Pit, a novel by Frank Norris (1870–1902), begins at Chicago's Auditorium Theatre, where Laura Dearborn meets her future husband, Curtis Jadwin, a powerful businessman whose obsessive efforts to master the commodities exchange and corner the wheat market dominate the narrative. In the opening chapter Norris juxtaposed and intertwined the dramatic powers of business and art with the result that the young heroine, while thrilled to experience her first night of grand opera, realizes that an equally compelling drama is taking place blocks away in the Board of Trade Building, which sits "crouching on its foundations, like a monstrous sphinx, with blind eyes, silent, grave."[2]

 The mystery of the sphinx—or the market—lies at the heart of *The Pit*, the second novel in Norris's "epic" trilogy of wheat, which he began in 1899. The first, *The Octopus* (1900), set in California, describes the production of wheat; the third, *The Wolf*—never written because of Norris's premature death at age thirty-two—was to focus on the consumption of wheat, or bread, in Europe. *The Pit* is supposed to be about the distribution of wheat, but this designation

is somewhat misleading, since the novel highlights the buying and selling of future shares in wheat, not the grain itself.

Born in Chicago (he left with his family as a young teenager), Norris became a journalist as well as a novelist. In 1899 he joined Doubleday, Page & Company, which published *The Pit* after it was serialized in the *Saturday Evening Post*. *The Pit* was a major commercial success, selling almost ninety-five thousand copies during its first year in print.[3] It has remained in circulation since, attracting steady attention as an astute portrayal of Chicago's bombastic market culture. Although literary critics have complained about the florid writing and the ill-defined relation between the novel's love story and business plot, they have admired Norris's fine-grained descriptions of the trading pits at the Board of Trade—where "bulls" battle "bears" for control of the market—and how his canny representation of "fictional" values resembles the volatile manipulations of our own time.[4] Norris likewise gets credit for understanding that Chicago's proximity to the heartland and its status as the processing center for much of the nation's agricultural produce formed the basis of a commodities market that shaped the flow of capital across the world. So *A Story of Chicago* (the novel's subtitle)[5] assumes an imperial sweep reaching well beyond the city, driven by a power and vitality that Norris identified with North America as a whole.

A realist with a strong naturalist bent, Norris favored deterministic narratives, and in *The Pit* he imagined that Curtis Jadwin's final attempt to corner the market fails because the forces of nature—the wheat—overcome him. In fact, Jadwin buys more and more shares of wheat, driving up the price and prompting farmers across the Midwest to plant more crops, thus saturating the market and undermining his efforts to dictate the value of his holdings. At the end of the novel, with their fortune gone, Curtis and Laura set off to begin a new life, leaving Chicago and its mysteries behind.

The story of the rise and fall of a Chicago wheat speculator, *The Pit*—referring to the floor of the Chicago Board of Trade (seen here in a photograph of around 1900)—is a searing depiction of the greed that could corrode modern urban life at the turn of the twentieth century. The novel was initially serialized in the *Saturday Evening Post*; the first installment features an image of the speculator's beautiful, and unhappy, wife.

24

The Lakeside Classics

CHICAGO: THE LAKESIDE PRESS (R.R. DONNELLEY & SONS COMPANY), 1903–PRESENT

Kim Coventry

As head of Chicago's largest commercial printing company at the dawn of the twentieth century, Thomas Elliott Donnelley (1867–1955)[1] conceived of a printing project intended to fulfill a dual mission: first, to prove that fine books could be produced on commercial presses otherwise employed around the clock in the manufacture of mail-order catalogues, magazines, encyclopedias, trade books, and city directories; and second, to signal that his company would not participate in what had become a tradition of corporate gift-giving that had risen to the level of extravagant.[2] That marriage of pride and principle gave birth, in 1903, to the Lakeside Classics series, published annually without interruption to this day.[3]

As the nation's greatest railroad hub, Chicago was ideally situated to become a major printing center. Railroads not only supplied the necessary raw materials but were essential for the distribution of printed matter. It is not surprising that by the time that Richard Robert Donnelley, Thomas Elliott's father, joined a printing business in Chicago in 1864, Chicago boasted some thirty active printing companies.[4] The Donnelley family firm was incorporated in 1890 as R.R. Donnelley & Sons Company after several bankruptcies and attendant name changes.[5]

In the introduction to the first Lakeside Classic, *The Autobiography of Benjamin Franklin*, Donnelley wrote:

With the exception of the paper, it is entirely a product of the Press, an accomplishment possible in no other printing establishment in America. . . . If, in a modest way, this volume conveys the idea that machine-made books are not a crime against art, and that books may be plain but good, and good though not costly, its mission has been accomplished.[6]

Bibliographically, the Lakeside Classics can be classified as Americana. While the series lacked focus in its first few years, by 1911 it was centered on mid-nineteenth-century, previously published, out-of-copyright, hard-to-obtain, first-person narratives of the western frontier experience and expansion. That both filled a need and underscored the company's own pioneering roots. A few exceptions notwithstanding, the theme defined the subject matter until 1995, with the introduction of narratives that crisscross the globe, echoing the expansion of the company's business.[7] From the beginning, the Lakeside Classics have been identified and recommended by an executive editor. An independent subject expert for each book is commissioned to write a historical introduction.

Physically, however, the books have changed little since 1903: each is a small hardbound volume of quality that fits in the hand and pocket and is easy to recognize on the shelf. By 1923 J. Christian Bay could observe that the Classics were "becoming an institution near and dear to every collector of books of intrinsic value and beauty."[8] Indeed, the Classics may be longest-lived series on American history to have been published without interruption.[9] That alone places them in a class of their own, but the Lakeside Classics are also understood to be a uniquely Chicago product. They are prized by casual and serious collectors alike. In his preface to the 1928 volume, Donnelley, reflecting on the commitment to continue the series for another twenty-five years, wrote, "If the traditions of any press in America will continue for this length of time, we believe those of the Lakeside Press will."[10] The history of this venerable company and its annual Lakeside Classics is inextricably linked to, and closely interwoven with, the history of Chicago and its reputation as a place where commercial printing and the allied arts were pioneered and flourished.

Initiated by Thomas Elliott Donnelley, head of Chicago's biggest printing company (as well as one of the nation's largest), the Lakeside Classics were intended in part to prove that high-quality printing could be done on commercial presses. One volume is published each year, and the color of the binding cloth changes every twenty-five years.

25

The Great Chicago Theater Disaster

The Complete Story Told by the Survivors—Presenting a Vivid Picture, Both by Pen and Camera, of One of the Greatest Fire Horrors of Modern Times; Embracing a Flash-Light Sketch of the Holocaust, Detailed Narratives by Participants in the Horror, Heroic Work of Rescuers, Reports of the Building Experts as to the Responsibility for the Wholesale Slaughter of Women and Children, Memorable Fires of the Past, etc., etc. Profusely Illustrated with Views of the Scene of Death before, during, and after the Fire

MARSHALL EVERETT ✳ CHICAGO AND PHILADELPHIA: PUBLISHERS UNION OF AMERICA, 1904

Neil Harris

Even today it remains America's deadliest theater fire. On Wednesday, December 30, 1903, Chicago's newly opened Iroquois Theatre on Randolph Street, designed by Benjamin Marshall and praised for its elegance by the *New York Times*, was hosting a holiday-week matinee performance of *Mr. Blue Beard*. With schools closed for vacation, this lavish musical farce was perfect family entertainment. An audience of about 1,800 (including standees), supplemented by 500 cast members, musicians, and theater staff, swelled attendance to 2,300. Sparks from a klieg light ignited a stage curtain; the fire spread to scenery and shot out into the audience, and panic ensued. More than six hundred people, mainly women and children, perished in the blaze and stampede that followed. While almost every performer survived, most sitting in the balcony and gallery never made it downstairs; their bodies were found tangled together in a grotesque pile. A series of mishaps—faulty fire extinguishers, an asbestos fire curtain that did not drop properly, awkwardly placed aisles and staircases, locked doors, sudden back drafts—and a trail of neglect, incompetence, and criminality conspired to create the deadly inferno. Occurring thirty-two years after the Great Chicago Fire, the Iroquois tragedy renewed the city's international reputation as a place of conflagration and mayhem.

Local ordinances and multiple inspections had clearly proved inadequate. Municipal governments throughout the nation considered reforms ranging from proscenium curtains and panic bars to sprinkler systems and redesigned aisles and staircases.[1] Chicago mayor Carter Harrison Jr. closed every theater in the city for weeks. The legal consequences, however, were modest. Despite widespread outrage, hundreds of lawsuits, a coroner's jury, two grand juries, and five indictments for manslaughter or malfeasance, no one went to jail.

Instantly, the Iroquois horror show provoked some disaster books—the kind of publication that appears immediately after fires, earthquakes, floods, and tornados. *The Great Chicago Theater Disaster* typifies this largely by-subscription genre. Sentimental, bathetic, indignant, overwrought, moralizing, admonitory, such books revel in gory descriptions and horrific photographs, achieving something like a pornography of pain in their focus on suffering and death. Their breathless repetitions, maudlin interviews, and inconsistent observations anticipated contemporary disaster coverage, with reporters struggling to assemble a coherent narrative while information continues to unfold.

The Great Chicago Theater Disaster appeared in print under various titles and publishers, with modest textual variations.[2] Marshall Everett, the purported author (although Bishop Samuel Fallows, who introduced one version of the book, apparently collected some of its royalties), rarely shrank from any calamity. President William McKinley's assassination (1901), the Mar-

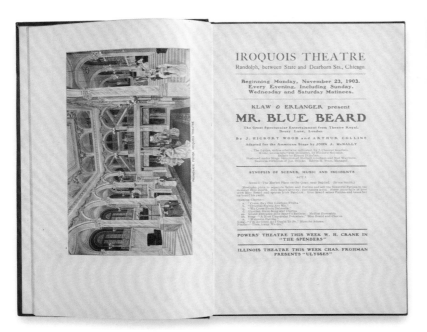

PROGRAMME PAPER, IROQUOIS THEATRE

IROQUOIS THEATRE
Randolph, between State and Dearborn Sts., Chicago.

Beginning Monday, November 23, 1903.
Every Evening, Including Sunday.
Wednesday and Saturday Matinees.

KLAW & ERLANGER present
MR. BLUE BEARD

tinique volcano (1902), the San Francisco earthquake (1906), the sinking of the *Titanic* (1912), and the Dayton flood (1913)—all were grist for his publishing mill.

Marshall Everett was a pseudonym for "Judge" Henry Neil (1863–1939), a self-promoting reformer, educator, lecturer, social activist, novelist, and journalist. His books were often copyrighted under the Neil name, although in this instance the copyright is listed under D. B. McCurdy, who appears as a Chicago publisher in later books. In the words of Chicago bookman Vincent Starrett, Marshall Everett was actually "a syndicate, with Neil at its head," assisted by various ghostwriters.[3]

In later years, while residing in Oak Park and Hinsdale, Illinois, Neil titled himself the "father of Mother's Pensions," pushing state legislation to assist mothers of fatherless children in keeping their families together.[4] His announced target was child poverty. An Illinois justice of the peace, Neil maintained something of a dual life, sparring with relief organizations over goals and methods while absorbed by a prolific publishing agenda and correspondence with celebrities ranging from George Bernard Shaw to Mahatma Gandhi. Neil's obituary in *Chicago Daily Tribune* acknowledges his record of social action but fails to mention any of the Everett books, most of them by this point, like the Iroquois fire, having been consigned to distant memory.[5]

Nearly one-quarter of the 2,300 people inside Chicago's newest theater, the Iroquois, perished in a fire on December 30, 1903. The flames began onstage and moved quickly into the audience. The eyewitness accounts that appear in Marshall Everett's chronicle and photographs such as this one—taken from the balcony days later—shook Chicago and many other American cities into revising their fire codes. See also page xviii.

26

Report of the Special Park Commission to the City Council of Chicago on the Subject of a Metropolitan Park System

COMPILED BY DWIGHT HEALD PERKINS *
[CHICAGO: CITY OF CHICAGO], 1904

Julia Bachrach

Report of the Special Park Commission to the City Council of Chicago on the Subject of a Metropolitan Park System, though somewhat obscure today, is an extremely influential book that has had a lasting impact on Chicago. Produced by architect Dwight Heald Perkins (1867–1941) and landscape architect Jens Jensen (1860–1951), this report prompted the creation of the Cook County Forest Preserve System.

In the late 1890s, Perkins and Jensen were progressive Chicagoans who were deeply concerned about the problems generated by the city's rapid industrial growth. Hundreds of thousands of immigrants lived in overcrowded tenement districts. Such neighborhoods prompted a national playground movement that called for clean and healthy breathing spaces where children could play safely. Perkins and Jensen also believed that Chicago's youth and adults needed a stronger connection with nature. Both men loved the vast stretches of unspoiled woods and wetlands at the city's outskirts and believed that these areas should be set aside for the enjoyment of urban residents.

Although Chicago had several park commissions, their jurisdictions did not span the entire city. The City Council formed the Special Park Commission (SPC) in 1899 to comprehensively study open-space needs and to create new playgrounds and parks throughout Chicago. Thanks to Perkins's influence, the SPC also advocated to save the scenic lands at Chicago's perimeter. Perkins, a founding member of the SPC, began working with Jensen on this project several years prior to the landscape architect's official appointment to the commission in 1903. That year the City Council approved a $1,500 contract with Perkins to prepare the Metropolitan Park System report.

While not an elegant volume, the report is beautifully written, cleanly designed and printed, and richly illustrated with sixty halftone photographic images and six foldout maps. Urban planning was then in its infancy, and few comparable studies or documents had been completed, which makes the report all the more remarkable. It provides a thorough history of Chicago's existing parks, analysis of the city's population and open space per capita (also in comparison with other cities), projections about population growth and future open-space needs, information about parks and preserves in other cities (most notably Boston, which had established the nation's first Metropolitan Park and Preserve System), and detailed documentation of the recommended "outer belt" lands to be conserved. Jensen's "Report of the Landscape Architect" explains the geological, topographical, prehistoric, and aesthetic significance of the region. Furthermore, he warned about continuing inappropriate land-management practices in the area, such as clear-cutting. Perkins wrote all of the other chapters and produced the large maps incorporating population and other data with geographic and site information.

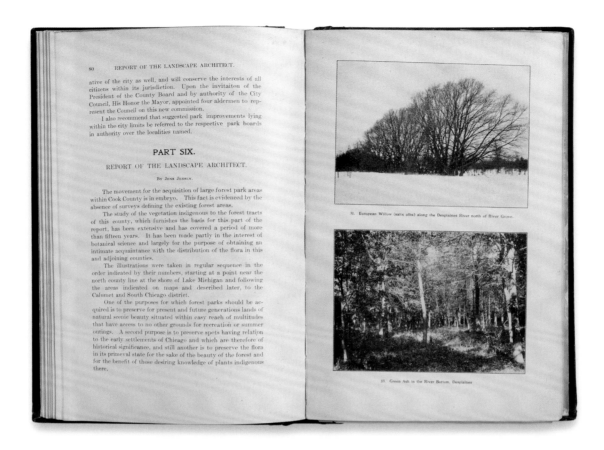

ative of the city as well, and will conserve the interests of all citizens within its jurisdiction. Upon the invitaiton of the President of the County Board and by authority of the City Council, His Honor the Mayor, appointed four aldermen to represent the Council on this new commission.

I also recommend that suggested park improvements lying within the city limits be referred to the respective park boards in authority over the localities named.

PART SIX.

REPORT OF THE LANDSCAPE ARCHITECT.

By Jens Jensen.

The movement for the acquisition of large forest park areas within Cook County is in embryo. This fact is evidenced by the absence of surveys defining the existing forest areas.

The study of the vegetation indigenous to the forest tracts of this county, which furnishes the basis for this part of the report, has been extensive and has covered a period of more than fifteen years. It has been made partly in the interest of botanical science and largely for the purpose of obtaining an intimate acquaintance with the distribution of the flora in this and adjoining counties.

The illustrations were taken in regular sequence in the order indicated by their numbers, starting at a point near the north county line at the shore of Lake Michigan and following the areas indicated on maps and described later, to the Calumet and South Chicago district.

One of the purposes for which forest parks should be acquired is to preserve for present and future generations lands of natural scenic beauty situated within easy reach of multitudes that have access to no other grounds for recreation or summer outings. A second purpose is to preserve spots having relation to the early settlements of Chicago and which are therefore of historical significance, and still another is to preserve the flora in its primeval state for the sake of the beauty of the forest and for the benefit of those desiring knowledge of plants indigenous there.

81. European Willow (salix alba) along the Desplaines River north of River Grove.

35. Green Ash in the River Bottom, Desplaines

Immediately following the report's publication, legislation was drafted to establish the Cook County Forest Preserves. After it proved to be unworkable, Perkins, Jensen, and others led hikes in the woods to further the forest-preserves movement. A second bill followed but did not withstand an Illinois State Supreme Court challenge in 1911. Among other objections, the court found the proposed statute to be so broad as to potentially include any area, including forest preserves. When, a few years later, revised forest-preserve legislation was approved by popular vote, Perkins feared that this third Forest Preserve Act would not withstand a court challenge. He was so committed to the cause that he personally challenged the bill and was joyous when he lost the case in 1916. The legislation allowed the newly founded Cook Country Forest Preserve District to purchase five hundred acres for what became the Deer Grove Preserve. Over the years, the Forest Preserve District has expanded to nearly seventy thousand acres of ecologically and scenically valuable lands, far exceeding the dreams that Perkins and Jensen had for the system.

This report laid the groundwork for what eventually became the Cook County Forest Preserves, which have since expanded to nearly seventy thousand acres. In his chapter—the beginning of which is seen here—the influential landscape architect Jens Jensen set forth the region's geographic, prehistoric, and aesthetic significance and argued for sensible land management.

27

The Jungle

UPTON SINCLAIR ∗ NEW YORK:
DOUBLEDAY, PAGE & COMPANY, 1906

Dominic A. Pacyga

FACING Upton Sinclair's portrayal in *The Jungle* of the extreme hardships and exploitation of immigrants working in Chicago's stockyards resulted from the seven weeks he lived near the stockyards. While the novel did not achieve his goal—to ameliorate the workers' plight—its raw descriptions of unsanitary practices (an inspection of pig carcasses, ca. 1890, is seen here) prompted Congress to pass the Meat Inspection and Pure Food and Drug Acts.

In 1906 a young socialist, Upton Beall Sinclair Jr. (1878–1968), published *The Jungle.* It became an instant best seller, shocked the nation, and prompted a federal investigation into Chicago's giant meat industry. *The Jungle* has been in print ever since its first publication and is one of the most important novels in American history, significant more for its historical impact than for its literary or artistic merit. Sinclair intended to expose the terrible working conditions for laborers in American industries in general, but instead he triggered a crusade for better sanitary conditions within the meatpacking industry. The author famously said, "I aimed at the public's heart, and by accident hit it in the stomach."[1]

Originally published in the socialist magazine *Appeal to Reason,*[2] *The Jungle* portrays the struggles of a Lithuanian immigrant, Jurgis Rudkus, and his family to make a life in Chicago's Back of the Yards neighborhood. While the novel paints a portrait of incredible hardships for the Rudkuses, its descriptions of the squalid working environment in Chicago's packinghouses are what immediately caught the public's attention.

For some time, the federal government had been investigating Chicago's meatpackers for monopolistic practices, and rumors had also long circulated about diseased meat being prepared under the worst possible conditions. Although the public was already prepared to accept Sinclair's portrayal of this industry, several publishers turned down the manuscript before he approached Frank Doubleday. Doubleday and his partner, Walter H. Page, assigned promotion of the book to Isaac Marcosson, who devised a campaign based on his experiences in the newspaper business. Marcosson told Page, "If the revelations in this book are true we should have guardians appointed for us if we do not publish it. It will be either a sensational success or a magnificent failure. In either case it is well worth trying." He then traveled to Chicago to verify Sinclair's accusations and returned stating that the situation was even worse than what Sinclair had described.[3] The public-relations genius sent President Theodore Roosevelt a copy of the book, which resulted in Sinclair's being invited to the White House for lunch. Overnight, the young socialist became famous.[4]

Roosevelt soon launched a federal investigation of meatpacking that resulted in one of the most important reforms of the Progressive Era. The president had long wanted to increase federal regulation of the industry, which had been rumored to have sold bad meat to the armed forces during the Spanish-Cuban-American War in 1898. Roosevelt and Indiana senator Albert J. Beveridge supported the passage of the Federal Meat Inspection Act of 1906. It and the Pure Food and Drug Act, signed into law on the same day, proved to be landmarks for the administration. Roosevelt later told his

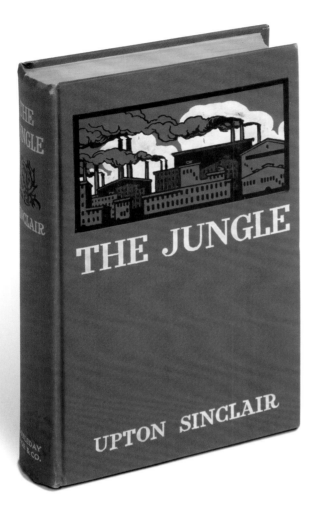

friend William Allen White, a newspaperman and politician, that Sinclair had been of service to him, but that he was basically untruthful and three-fourths of the things he said concerning Chicago's packinghouses were lies.[5]

The publication of *The Jungle* caused a national uproar. The celebrated novelist Jack London praised the book, calling it the "Uncle Tom's Cabin of wage slavery," but in the end the federal government and the large meatpackers used it to tighten regulations at the expense of smaller, independent packers who could not meet the stricter standards that had resulted from the public's agitation. While Sinclair failed in his attempt to champion the cause of labor in the United States, he did forever change the way the government regulated the meat industry.[6]

28

Musical Memories: My Recollection of Celebrities of the Half Century 1850–1900

GEORGE P. UPTON ∗ CHICAGO: A. C.
MCCLURG & CO., 1908

Celia Hilliard

George P. Upton (1834–1919) arrived in Chicago in 1855 and, within a few years, emerged as a major influence in Chicago's struggle to establish a viable cultural community. As longtime music critic at the *Chicago Daily Tribune*, he covered every facet of musical activity in the young city, doing much to lift standards, build audiences, and attract the regular appearance of concert and opera stars of international stature. His support of his friend and hero Theodore Thomas was crucial to the formation of the Chicago Symphony Orchestra, which under Thomas's leadership would become one of city's crown jewels.[1] *Musical Memories* puts in book form the substance of Upton's widely read newspaper columns, filling out the picture with candid impressions of ambitious performers, promoters, and schemers, and the fickle Chicago audiences that applauded, adored, and sometimes thwarted the cause of great music in their hometown.

After graduation from Brown University,[2] Upton moved to Chicago, then a restless, pushing metropolis surrounded by boundless prairie. He quickly found work as a reporter. He was handsome and urbane, and his fluent writing and incisive wit attracted the admiration of Joseph Medill, the *Tribune*'s publisher, who hired him in 1861. Over the next fifty years, he was assigned to many and varied editorial duties, but his national reputation rested on his standing as dean of music critics in the West. In a city increasingly preoccupied with commerce and the accumulation of wealth, he brought liberal sensibilities and a broad intelligence to his role as cultural arbiter.

In his memoir, Upton presented a vivid firsthand account of the nineteenth-century music scene in Chicago. He reported on opera troupes, festivals, band concerts, recitals, impresarios, prima donnas, composers, church choirs, and singing societies—even bell ringers and street fiddlers. He told stories of such early landmarks as Rice's Theatre, Root & Cady's music store (see no. 2), the splendid Crosby Opera House, and the renowned Auditorium Theatre, which was inaugurated with a series of dazzling entertainments in 1889. His description of the devastating effects on the city's arts scene of the 1871 Great Chicago Fire is superb.[3] Upton had a scholar's interest in research and documentation.[4] His book records many Chicago firsts and is extensively illustrated with photographs of musicians in their prime.

Of additional value are Upton's keen assessments of celebrated performers who made their careers before the days of sound recordings. He was not only judge but also confidant of many leading artists and conductors, and his tales are suffused with sympathy for the trials and hurdles of life on the stage. Even the most talented were subject to vagaries of taste, poor management, professional jealousies, ignorant reviewers, bad weather, and empty seats. Fees were insanely disparate, and a surprising number of the best-paid performers were duped by swindlers and ended their days broke and penniless. Insecurity was constant, stage fright the norm: Adelina Patti, the soprano who drew Chicago's loudest and longest ovations, earning $5,000 a night at the height of her career, confessed to Upton that whenever she saw her name in print on a playbill, she felt fear.

Upton was a prolific author and translator, and his standard opera and concert guides sold well for more than forty years after his death. It is not surprising that in 1948 a New York publicist inquired whether he might be available for a radio interview. Upton dedicated *Musical Memories* "to the Ghosts," in whose revered company he now belongs.

Among the many stories found in *Musical Memories* about the performers, impresarios, patrons, and organizations that helped establish a musical community in Chicago in the last half of the nineteenth century is one about the acute stage fright of the popular soprano Adelina Patti, seen here in the title role of Giuseppe Verdi's *Aida.*

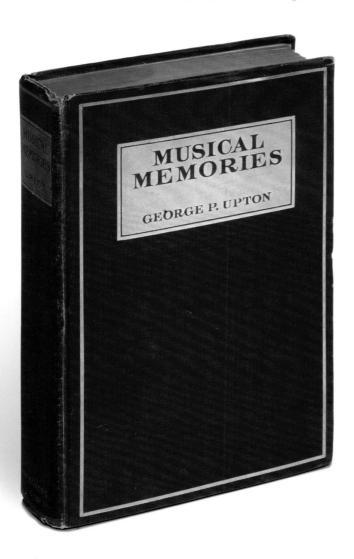

29

Plan of Chicago, Prepared under the Direction of the Commercial Club during the Years MCMVI, MCMVII, and MCMVIII

DANIEL H. BURNHAM AND EDWARD H.
BENNETT, ARCHITECTS ∗ EDITED BY
CHARLES MOORE, CORRESPONDING
MEMBER AMERICAN INSTITUTE
OF ARCHITECTS ∗ CHICAGO: THE
COMMERCIAL CLUB, 1909

Carl Smith

The *Plan of Chicago* is one of the most significant works in the history of modern city planning. Its influence is evident in many of Chicago's signature features, including the lakefront, Lake Shore Drive, Michigan Avenue, Wacker Drive, Union Station, Navy Pier, the Chicago Park District, and the Forest Preserves of Cook County. It advanced the then-innovative idea that it was both necessary and possible for cities to take an active role in the shaping of their built environment rather than allow market forces to determine growth. Prompted by such precedents as the recent remaking of Paris and the stunning array of beaux-arts buildings at the World's Columbian Exposition, held in Chicago in 1893, the *Plan* in turn inspired many other city plans and the creation of countless planning commissions and departments.

The *Plan*'s goal was to apply the fair's lessons of scale, balance, order, and unity to an unapologetically commercial and industrial metropolis of two million people that was still rapidly expanding. Congested, polluted, and unsightly, Chicago was choking on its own unregulated growth to such an extent that its future was at risk. Among those who believed that substantial intervention was needed were the Merchants and Commercial Clubs of Chicago, which early in 1907 merged under the latter's name. Their members were the city's most successful and civically engaged business leaders. They asked architect Daniel H. Burnham (1846–1912), one of their own, to take charge. He had not only directed the construction of the 1893 exposition but also worked on planning projects in other cities.[1]

While Burnham was unquestionably the key figure (the *Plan of Chicago* is often referred to as the Burnham Plan), several others played major roles. Edward H. Bennett (1874–1954), an exceptionally capable associate in Burnham's architecture firm, coordinated production from a studio constructed on top of the Railway Exchange (now Motorola) Building on Michigan Avenue, where D. H. Burnham and Company had its offices a few stories below. Burnham prepared the first draft, which was extensively edited by author, businessman, and urban-beautification advocate Charles Moore (1855–1942).

Convinced that the *Plan* required strong public support (notably voter approval of bond issues), Burnham assiduously cultivated politicians, other civic leaders, and the press, frequently hosting them in the rooftop studio to show them the plan-in-progress. Believing also that proposals had to be visually arresting in order to capture the popular mind, he hired a talented cluster of artists and draftsmen to prepare paintings and drawings that visualized how Chicago would be transformed. Especially eye-catching are the pastel-hued bird's-eye views of a reimagined Chicago by Jules Guerin (1886–1946).[2]

The planners entrusted the printing of the book, including color reproductions of the illustrations, to Commercial Club member Thomas E. Don-

COPYRIGHT, 1908, BY COMMERCIAL CLUB OF CHICAGO

I. CHICAGO. BIRD'S-EYE VIEW, SHOWING THE LOCATION OF THE CITY ON THE SHORES OF LAKE MICHIGAN, TOGETHER
WITH THE SMALLER SURROUNDING TOWNS CONNECTED WITH CHICAGO BY RADIATING ARTERIES.
Painted for the Commercial Club by Jules Guerin.

The frontispiece of the *Plan of Chicago* is artist Jules Guerin's sweeping *Chicago. Bird's-Eye View, Showing the Location of the City on the Shores of Lake Michigan, Together with the Surrounding Towns Connected with Chicago by Radiating Arteries*. The *Plan*'s frontispiece underscores the volume's overarching vision of a reimagined Chicago that extends beyond the city's limits. See also pages xii–xiii.

nelley, head of the leading printing company R.R. Donnelley. They decided to issue it as "a deluxe limited special edition" of 1,650 copies. The Commercial Club carefully staged the publication of the *Plan of Chicago* with great fanfare. It was released on July 4, 1909, accompanied by a special exhibition of many of the illustrations, curated by Burnham and Bennett, at the Art Institute of Chicago.[3] Generously sized (approximately 10 × 12 inches) and printed by the Donnelley Lakeside Press on heavyweight cream-colored paper with gilt top and deckle edges, the book is a work of art itself as well as a landmark in urban history. Coveted by collectors, the *Plan of Chicago* has been handsomely reproduced in several facsimile editions, including one in 2009, its centennial year.[4]

30

Twenty Years at Hull-House with Autobiographical Notes

JANE ADDAMS, HULL-HOUSE, CHICAGO ✳ AUTHOR OF "DEMOCRACY AND SOCIAL ETHICS," "NEWER IDEALS OF PEACE, "THE SPIRIT OF YOUTH AND THE CITY STREETS" ✳ ILLUSTRATED BY NORAH HAMILTON, HULL-HOUSE, CHICAGO ✳ NEW YORK: THE MACMILLAN COMPANY, 1910

Rima Lunin Schultz

Jane Addams (1860–1935) is a monumental figure in the history of Chicago and a towering leader in the struggle for social justice and international peace. Her work brought her both acclaim and vilification, as two artifacts in the Jane Addams Hull-House Museum attest: her Nobel Peace Medal, awarded in 1931, and a hefty FBI dossier covering decades during which she was surveilled. This daughter of the Illinois prairie made her settlement house—located in a Chicago neighborhood of sweatshops, factories, peddlers, saloons, and workers' homes—a destination for dissidents and heads of state alike. Between 1889 and 1910 she spearheaded a wide range of reform initiatives.[1]

Featuring eighteen chapters and illustrated by drawings and photographs, the book argues that democracy can work.[2] Against the voices of bigotry, it seeks to confirm the readers' faith in immigrants and their children. Contributing to Chicago's reputation as a city of immigrant neighborhoods, these narratives are intended to awaken one's moral indignation. Addams deftly used neighbors' stories to illustrate that poverty does not define a person. She framed them as moments of self-discovery, as when, during the first Hull-House Christmas, young girls refused holiday treats, too exhausted from overwork in a local candy factory. Claiming to have known nothing of child labor until that moment, Addams juxtaposed the cozy glow of fellowship to the realization that the party for the children had not connected to their lives. That was her way of emphasizing how lived experience is necessary for true social knowledge.

In *Twenty Years*, Addams traced her evolution by associating herself closely with her father, Illinois state senator John Huy Addams, and his political ally Abraham Lincoln. She defined the fulfillment of the promise of American equality and justice as her generation's mission. "Is it not Abraham Lincoln who has cleared the title to our democracy?" she asked rhetorically.[3]

Addams knew she was writing at a crucial moment. The year before, she, along with W. E. B. Du Bois and others, had established the NAACP. That same year, the centennial of Lincoln's birth, had witnessed a lynching and riot in Springfield, Illinois (not, however, recorded in *Twenty Years*).

Addams internationalized her narrative by confessing admiration for Leo Tolstoy. She had traveled to the writer's estate "with the hope of finding a clew to the tangled affairs of city poverty."[4] Tolstoy and Lincoln, Addams explained, were "cosmopolitan heroes who have become great through identification with the common lot, in preference to the heroes of mere achievement."[5]

If *Twenty Years* had been written by a man with the reputation and following of Jane Addams, we might well call it a campaign biography. An actual "campaign" came two years later, when Addams, to the roar of adulatory crowds, seconded the nomination of Theodore Roosevelt as the Progressive Party candidate for president. An anti-imperialist and antimilitarist sup-

POLK STREET, OPPOSITE HULL-HOUSE.

porting Rough Rider Teddy, Addams risked all her political capital for the chance to gain suffrage for women and a robust social reform platform she helped craft.

Twenty Years continues to be the most popular of Addams's ten books and two coauthored volumes. At age fifty, she shrewdly cut a deal with the publisher Macmillan, which agreed to six monthly installments in *American Magazine* prior to the November 1910 release of her book. *Twenty Years* immediately became a best seller, going through six printings and nearly seventeen thousand copies in the first year. It is estimated that sixty thousand copies were sold before Addams's death in 1935, and it has never gone out of print.[6] The book remains one of the most relevant texts on American democracy; readers cannot help but be awed that this one woman, Jane Addams, was able to overcome the biases of wealth, education, and gender to become a symbol for a democratic way of living.[7]

The expressionistic illustrations by Hull-House resident and artist Norah Hamilton in *Twenty Years at Hull-House* reveal not only many activities of Jane Addams's world-famous settlement house but also its setting. This drawing, titled *Polk Street, Opposite Hull-House*, shows the establishment's location in a blighted neighborhood, an intentional choice by Addams, who wished to be close to the communities being served.

31

Ausgeführte Bauten und Entwürfe von Frank Lloyd Wright [Completed Buildings and Designs by Frank Lloyd Wright]

BERLIN: ERNST WASMUTH A.G., 1910–11

David Van Zanten

In the winter of 1910–11 Ernst Wasmuth, the leading architecture and art publisher in Berlin, brought out a monograph of the early work of Frank Lloyd Wright (1867–1959) in two folios of one hundred loose plates with a lengthy introduction by the architect. Wright paid the production costs and had one thousand copies sent to him in the United States, leaving one hundred copies for Wasmuth to sell in Europe, though the publisher could buy more from Wright if needed.[1] (Fires in 1914 and 1924 at Wright's Wisconsin home, Taliesin, destroyed many of his folios.) A smaller, cheaper volume of photographs of Wright's work followed from Wasmuth in 1911, with an introductory text by the architect's friend the British arts and crafts designer C. R. Ashbee.

These folios chronologically record much of Wright's work from his first seventeen years of practice, primarily in Chicago. Their design and production are exceptional. Many of the loose 16 × 25 inch plates have tracing-paper cover sheets usually showing plans glued along their top edge over tinted boards, most of which depict large-perspective views of the same building—a system lost in the multiple subsequent republications. Why did Wasmuth make it necessary to gently raise these diagrams in order to glimpse the images? It takes a while to realize how the abstract tracing-paper plans, repeatedly transforming into the perspective realizations underneath, draw in the reader. A few plates have the plan and perspective on the same opaque board, and the profound distinctness of those images seems jarring in context.

The folio sheets won Wright admiration and imitation in Europe, where "modern" architectural design was just being discovered. Preliminary drawings or printed reproductions were shown to the Vereinigung Berliner Architekten (Association of Berlin Architects) as early as February 1910. Bruno Mohring (who had visited Wright in 1904) remarked of them in the *Deutsche Bauzeitung*, "Es liege Poesie in seinen Entwürfen" (There is poetry in his drawings). We hear that Otto Wagner presented them to his students with the words "Er kennt mehr als ich" (He knows more than I).

The plates had been prepared in Fiesole during Wright's stay there in 1909–10 with his lover, Mamah Cheney. As a type, these images were more European than American, resembling those of Wasmuth's four volumes of colored plates of the work of the Austrian Joseph Maria Olbrich (1901–13) and differing from American publications such as those reproducing the beaux arts–inflected designs of McKim, Mead & White (1914–15).[2] They were drawn by Wright's son Lloyd (1890–1978) and his assistant Taylor Woolley (1884–1965), who used line to simplify and regularize existing perspectives, suggesting the style of Wright's early renderer, Marion Mahony. Mahony and Wright had carefully worked out the signature style of Wright's self-presentation for the 1905 pamphlet of his design for Unity Temple in Oak Park.[3] It resembles that of Olbrich and of the Viennese journal *Der Architekt* but is inflected with the sense of color and linearity of Japanese prints that Wright admired and collected. He inscribed the original sheet of Mahony's 1906 rendering of the DeRhodes House "drawn by Mahony after FLW and Hiroshige."[4] Those plates, and this edition, helped establish Wright in the eyes of architects and commissioning patrons worldwide.

The first major publication anywhere of the architecture of Frank Lloyd Wright, the Wasmuth Portfolio, issued in Berlin, features plans and perspectives of buildings he designed between 1893 and 1909, including the Cheney House in Oak Park, a Chicago suburb, illustrated here. The impact of Wright's Prairie Style work and his philosophy on Europe's architecture was significant.

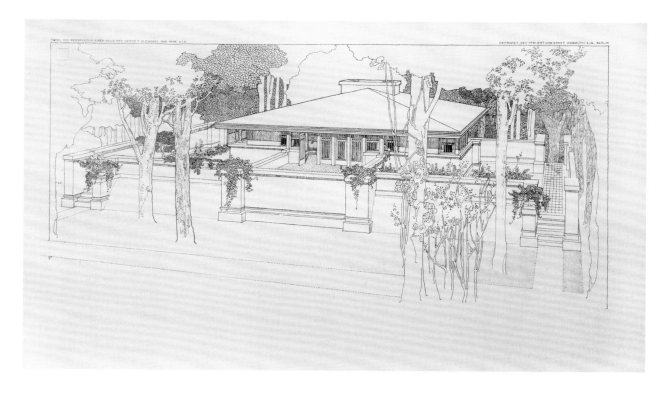

32

The Everleigh Club Illustrated, 2131–2133 Dearborn Street, Chicago

CHICAGO: [ADA AND MINNA EVERLEIGH], 1911

Edward C. Hirschland

How often does a publication bring about real change? A couple of examples come to mind: Harriet Beecher Stowe's *Uncle Tom's Cabin* (1852) and public attitudes against slavery; Upton Sinclair's *The Jungle* (1906; no. 27) and federal consumer-protection laws. A far more parochial example is *The Everleigh Club Illustrated*, a thirty-two-page, 4½ × 6 inch booklet published in Chicago in 1911 by two sisters (née Simms; they were married briefly to brothers surnamed Lester) who went by the names Ada Everleigh (1864–1960) and Minna Everleigh (1866–1948). The most successful madams in the United States and arguably the world, they opened their splendid bordello, the Everleigh Club, in 1900 in the vice district of Chicago called the Levee.[1] Here is the entire text:

The Everleigh Club[, w]hile not an extremely imposing edifice without, is a most sumptuous place within. 2131 Dearborn Street, Chicago, has long been famed for its luxurious furnishings, famous paintings and statuary, and its elaborate and artistic decorations. "The New Annex," 2133 Dearborn Street, formally opened November 1, 1902, has added prestige to the club, and won admiration and praise from all visitors. With double front entrances, the twin buildings within are so constructed as to seem as one. Steam heat throughout, with electric fans in summer; one never feels the winter's chill or summer's heat in this luxurious resort. Fortunate indeed, with all the comforts of life surrounding them, are the members of the Everleigh Club. This little booklet will convey but a faint idea of the magnificence of the club and its appointments.[2]

The booklet, of which fewer than five hundred copies were printed, consists of innocuous photographs of the club, depicting no people whatsoever. Rather, the images are of rooms with elaborate, high-quality furnishings and ornamentation.[3] Pianos abound. Just one bed is shown fully; corners of two others jut primly into view. The booklet illustrates a classy Victorian residence, hardly hinting at its real business.

Alas, one copy fell into the hands of the reform-minded mayor Carter Harrison Jr. Having the club open and thriving was one thing, but advertising it was another. Horrified by the brazenness of the publicity, Harrison ordered the club closed in October 1911. Minna destroyed the remainder of the book-

EAST VIEW OF MOORISH MUSIC ROOM.
14

ORIENTAL MUSIC ROOM.
15

lets, and only a handful are known to have survived.[4] The sisters retired with a considerable fortune to New York. They never worked again.

One might wonder why a pamphlet advertising a brothel belongs in a survey of publications about Chicago. In the first decade of the twentieth century, Chicago was known for being good at many things: transportation, manufacturing, meatpacking, music, advertising, publishing, printing, social work, amusements—and vice. If the Everleigh Club was a house of ill repute, its reputation was stellar and worldwide. Among its many well-heeled customers was Prince Henry of Prussia, brother of the kaiser, who spent a rip-roaring evening there in 1902.

The club's mystique has inspired several book-length treatments, including Charles Washburn's *Come into My Parlor: A Biography of the Aristocratic Everleigh Sisters of Chicago* (1934); Ray Hibbeler's *Upstairs at the Everleigh Club: The Inside Story of Chicago's Famed Mansion of Sex Where Millionaires, Princes and Playboys Filled the Beds* (1960?); and Karen Abbott's *Sin in the Second City: Madams, Ministers, Playboys, and the Battle for America's Soul* (2007).[5] Many articles have been written on the subject as well. All sources stress the fine treatment given to the women who worked at the club.

The Everleigh Club Illustrated is the publication that ended a legendary Chicago institution. As critic Norman Mark tartly observed, "It was one of the earliest instances of a media campaign gone awry."[6]

The most luxurious of Chicago's six-hundred-some brothels in 1910, the Everleigh Club was also the most successful, attracting wealthy clientele from around the world. Its owners, the Everleigh sisters (facing, Ada, left, and Minna), made sure its "girls" were classy and its interiors, such as the Moorish Music Room and the Oriental Music Room (above), lavish. When the club was forced by the city to close in 1911, the sisters walked away with a fortune.

33

Wacker's Manual of the Plan of Chicago: Municipal Economy, Especially Prepared for Study in the Schools of Chicago, Auspices of the Chicago Plan Commission

WALTER D. MOODY, MANAGING
DIRECTOR, CHICAGO PLAN COMMISSION
⁕ CHICAGO: [HENNEBERRY COMPANY?],
1911

Edward C. Hirschland

A plan does not do any good if it sits on the shelf.

That was certainly true of the *Plan of Chicago*, the signal achievement of Daniel H. Burnham and Edward H. Bennett in 1909 (no. 29). The antidote to the danger of not being followed was *Wacker's Manual of the Plan of Chicago: Municipal Economy, Especially Prepared for Study in the Schools of Chicago*, which was published seven times between 1911 and 1924.

Wacker's Manual was an improbable name, because the Charles H. Wacker (1856–1929) in the title had little to do with this book. Wacker was vice chairman of the Commercial Club of Chicago, which had sponsored and published the Plan. For seventeen years he was also chairman of the Chicago Plan Commission, in which capacity he tirelessly championed the Burnham Plan. But *Wacker's Manual* was not his work. The manual was in fact the creation of Walter D. Moody (1874–1920), chief publicist for the Chicago Plan Commission. Moody was an advertising and marketing wizard; that he distanced himself from his handiwork by hailing the much better known Wacker in the title was undoubtedly calculated to make the volume more popular.

What better way to make sure the Burnham Plan took root than to teach it to schoolchildren? Moody, in his own words, "was inspired with the thought to introduce into the Eighth Grade of our public schools the study of Chicago and its relation to its most important issue—an Official Plan."[1] Chicago's children would share their newfound understanding of the plan with their parents. They would grow up supporting the efforts to beautify the city, ensure public access to natural settings, streamline transportation, and accomplish all the other ideas put forth in the plan.

The company that issued the scarce first printing of the first edition, in 1911, was probably happy that its name appears nowhere in the volume, because the book was afflicted with embarrassing mistakes.[2] When they were discovered, an attempt was made to recall and destroy all copies. That would explain why this printing, the only one to have 1911 on the title page, is one of the great bibliographic rarities in Chicago history.

In short order, the second printing of the first edition appeared with the same 1911 copyright but with 1912 printed on the title page, with all problems fixed. The printer was the Henneberry Company of Chicago. Today most historians, librarians, and booksellers call this the first printing, with no reference to an earlier one—probably because they are unaware of it. A third printing appeared in 1913 and fourth in 1915, both printed again by Henneberry. A second, revised, edition was published in 1916 by the Calumet Publishing Company, Chicago.[3] A third edition, revised, with no stated printer or publisher, came out in 1920.[4] And finally, a fourth edition, revised, was published in 1924, again not attributed to any publisher.[5]

CHAPTER VII

—

WHY CHICAGO NEEDS
A PLAN

Thus far attention has been given to many things in city building of interest to us as living in one of the world's greatest cities. We understand, now, the chief elements that enter into the growth of a city, the reason great cities exist, and the means by which they are sustained. We know that mankind, in the building and conduct of cities, is constantly working to improve conditions of life in cities, and we understand something of the growth of modern cities, and the springing up of a world-wide work by mankind for the improvement of cities according to properly prepared plans.

As we think of these things, and of how other people in other cities are carrying out these tremendous plans for improvement of cities, we naturally ask ourselves about Chicago. Perhaps we wonder why Chicago was not built according to a certain plan, and we are sure to ask what the necessity is for Chicago to have a plan, and what changes should be made, if any, so that our city can be made orderly, attractive and famous. We are not satisfied to know that people in other cities in our country are at work improving their cities, and doing better work of that kind than we are.

CHICAGO. View looking North on the South Branch of the Chicago River, Showing the Suggested Arrangement of Streets and Ways for Teaming and Reception of Freight by Boat at Different Levels. Examples of the arrangement exist at Dusseldorf, Algiers, Budapest, Geneva and Paris.
[Copyrighted by the Commercial Club.]

Moody also prepared a *Teachers' Hand Book*, published in 1911, with answers to all the questions at the end of each chapter in the *Manual*. A second printing (this time spelled *Handbook*) was published in 1912 to match the second printing of the *Manual*.

With its 138 illustrations and maps (including some color reproductions of the magnificent illustrations by Jules Guerin for the *Plan*), the *Manual* was well equipped to engage its young readers. *Wacker's Manual* was an unqualified success. Through it, hundreds of thousands of Chicago schoolchildren and their parents, starting in 1911, became intimately familiar with the great Plan of 1909.

Two years after Daniel Burnham's *Plan of Chicago* appeared, Walter Moody produced this related manual as a textbook for eighth graders. He hoped not only to encourage adoption of the plan by using children to win over their parents but also to instill in the city's youths the idea that "they are the coming responsible heads of their various communities." The book remained part of the Chicago school curriculum for twenty years.

34

Poetry, A Magazine of Verse
1912–47

Poetry
1948–present

CHICAGO: THE POETRY FOUNDATION

Don Share

Founded in Chicago by Harriet Monroe (1860–1936) in 1912, *Poetry* is the oldest monthly devoted to verse in the English-speaking world. Monroe set forth her now-famous "Open Door" policy in the first volume of the magazine:

May the great poet we are looking for never find it shut, or half-shut, against his ample genius! To this end the editors hope to keep free of entangling alliances with any single class or school. They desire to print the best English verse which is being written today, regardless of where, by whom, or under what theory of art it is written.[1]

In her autobiography, *A Poet's Life*, Monroe explained that she was motivated to create *Poetry* because poets are "the most unappreciated and ill-paid artists in the world." She condemned the "common desecration of the art by prosy teachers in schools and colleges" and above all observed that "poetry had no one to speak for it, no group of powerful citizens to take a special interest in it." *Poetry* was therefore envisioned as a protest against what she saw as the desperate condition of modern poets and poetry. In retrospect it appears that the success of this venture was linked to its taking place in Chicago.

While Monroe could characterize the city at the time as "surging with . . . aspirations," she also described it as a place where a Milton might be living and "unable to find an outlet for his verse."[2] And yet it was not lost on her that the rest of the nation seemed immune to what she called stirrings of freshness in contemporary poetry. A monthly poetry magazine begun at this time in a place such as New York City might not have survived for long, certainly not for over a century: it would almost inevitably have become a coterie magazine, with lethal squabbles, and would also have faced much competition. Because Chicago was both literally and figuratively a wide-open space, *Poetry* could thrive and take bold directions without being weighed down by the burden of the past or drowned in the churnings of contemporary currents.

In its first year, *Poetry* published verse by William Carlos Williams and W. B. Yeats, Joyce Kilmer's "Trees," and Ezra Pound's "In a Station of the Metro." It also introduced Rabindranath Tagore to the English-speaking world before he became the first non-European to win the Nobel Prize in Literature. The magazine established its enduring reputation by publishing the first important poems of virtually every major modern poet. It is perhaps most famous for having published T. S. Eliot's "Love Song of J. Alfred Prufrock" (not without controversy: the literary critic Louis Untermeyer described the effect of the poem as "that of the Muse in a psychopathic ward");[3] and later John Ashbery's "Self-Portrait in a Convex Mirror." *Poetry* also championed the early works of H. D. (Hilda Doolittle), Robert Frost, Langston Hughes, Marianne Moore, Edna St. Vincent Millay, Wallace Stevens, and Tennessee Williams.[4]

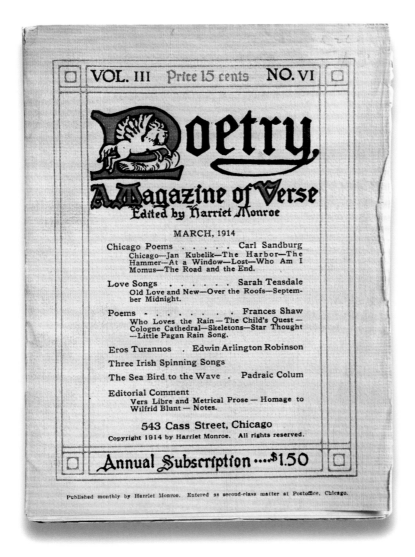

VOL. III   Price 15 cents   NO. VI

Poetry,
A Magazine of Verse
Edited by Harriet Monroe

MARCH, 1914

Chicago Poems . . . . . Carl Sandburg
Chicago—Jan Kubelik—The Harbor—The Hammer—At a Window—Lost—Who Am I Momus—The Road and the End.

Love Songs . . . . . . Sarah Teasdale
Old Love and New—Over the Roofs—September Midnight.

Poems . . . . Frances Shaw
Who Loves the Rain—The Child's Quest—Cologne Cathedral—Skeletons—Star Thought—Little Pagan Rain Song.

Eros Turannos . Edwin Arlington Robinson

Three Irish Spinning Songs

The Sea Bird to the Wave . Padraic Colum

Editorial Comment
Vers Libre and Metrical Prose — Homage to Wilfrid Blunt — Notes.

543 Cass Street, Chicago
Copyright 1914 by Harriet Monroe. All rights reserved.

Annual Subscription ····$1.50

Published monthly by Harriet Monroe. Entered as second-class matter at Postoffice, Chicago.

In the first issue of *Poetry*—the oldest continuing monthly poetry magazine in the English language—founder and editor Harriet Monroe declared that the Chicago-based magazine's mission was to "print the best English verse which is written today, regardless of where, by whom, or under what theory of art." Volume 3, number 6, includes poems by Carl Sandburg, Sara Teasdale, and others.

Poetry regularly presents new work by the most recognized poets, but its primary commitment remains to discover new voices and challenging work that expand the horizon of literature. A success from the beginning, *Poetry* magazine continues to prove that poetry is alive and well in our culture. It receives over 125,000 submitted poems annually and reaches millions of readers online; in recent years it has been awarded three prestigious National Magazine Awards for Editorial Excellence and for Podcasting. As critic Adam Kirsch wrote, "*Poetry* has done what long seemed impossible . . . it has become indispensable reading for anyone who cares about American literature."[5]

35

Catalogue of the
International
Exhibition of
Modern Art,
Association of
American Painters
and Sculptors: The
Art Institute of
Chicago, March 24
to April 16, 1913

[CHICAGO?], 1913

Paul Kruty

Between March 24 and April 16, 1913, the Art Institute of Chicago hosted the International Exposition of Modern Art, displaying over four hundred works that traced the development of European art from Goya to the cubists, along with examples by contemporary American artists. The exhibition arrived in Chicago fresh from its first, month-long showing at New York City's Sixty-Ninth Regiment Armory (hence its better-known name, the Armory Show). The Art Institute issued its own catalogue, since it was exhibiting roughly half of what the New York show had included.[1]

The idea of radical modern art as displayed at the Armory Show had been introduced in Chicago in 1912 at the W. Scott Thurber gallery, recently remodeled by Frank Lloyd Wright, in a series of exhibitions of works by Arthur Dove, Jerome Blum, and B. J. O. Nordfeldt. By October 1912, Chicago art patron Arthur T. Aldis had persuaded the New York exhibition's organizers, the artists Walt Kuhn and Arthur B. Davies, to include Chicago in their plans. Prior to the show's arrival, the *Chicago Daily Tribune* sent critic Harriet Monroe (whose *Poetry* magazine [no. 34] had begun publication the previous year) to New York to cover the exhibition, while Chicago Maecenas and lawyer Arthur Jerome Eddy purchased postimpressionist works from the New York venue.

Nevertheless, the Armory Show came as a shock to most Chicagoans, provoking a raucous response ranging from moral posturing and parody in the press to public outrage and demonstrations. The controversy spilled into so many walks of life that by June 1913 Edward Hale noted in Chicago's *Dial*

magazine that the air was "full at present of utterances concerning Futurists, Cubists, Neo-Impressionists, and Post-Impressionism."[2]

The Chicago catalogue, unlike the New York publication, contains no advertisements. It repeats the fir-tree logo of the New York catalogue's cover, while adding a frontispiece showing Michigan Avenue and the Art Institute. In addition to listing 453 entries, it reproduces sixteen works on glossy stock, beginning with Marcel Duchamp's infamous and iconic *Nude Descending a Staircase* and including paintings by Matisse, Picabia, Picasso, Redon, Henri Rousseau, and Van Gogh, and sculpture by Brancusi and Lehmbruck.[3]

Copies survive in several public collections. The Newberry Library's example, in the Arts Club of Chicago papers, includes an inscription by modern-art champion Alice Roullier, vividly recording a critical moment in Chicago's cultural history. "Went with Alice and Will Henderson and Roland Young of Welch Players. Afters [*sic*] all had dinner at Tip Top Inn then back to WPH's studio." Thus did this quartet—Roullier; Alice Corbin Henderson, cofounder of *Poetry* magazine; her husband, William Penhallow Henderson, muralist the following year for Frank Lloyd Wright's Midway Gardens and subsequent leader of the Santa Fe artists' colony; and British actor Roland Young, a sensation in the hit play of Chicago's 1913 season who in the 1930s and 1940s would become a famous Hollywood screen actor (think *Topper* and *Philadelphia Story*)—immerse themselves in the overwhelming experience provided by the exhibition.

The Armory Show changed the progress of art in Chicago. The following year Eddy published *Cubists and Post-Impressionism*, the first book in the United States to explain and support the contemporary European art movements that had so baffled and antagonized American visitors to the Armory Show. Some of Eddy's collection is in the Art Institute. In addition to establishing the importance of avant-garde art in the popular imagination, the exhibition prepared the ground for such influential designs as Midway Gardens, which combined painting, sculpture, and architecture in a single creation; the founding of the Arts Club of Chicago in 1916; and the growth of Chicago's many radical exhibition societies of the 1920s.[4]

DIRECTOR FRENCH FLEES DELUGE OF CUBIST ART

Boards Train for California Just in Time to Dodge New Pictures and Escapes Late Crop of Literature.

The cubists are coming, ho, ho, ho, ho;
The cubists are coming, ho, ho, ho, ho;
The cubists are coming from stately Manhattan;
The cubists are coming, ho, ho.

The art director has gone before,
He's said good-bye for a month or more;
The cubists are coming, and that's enough;
He cannot stand the futurist stuff.

The exhibition of European and American avant-garde art that traveled in 1913 to the Art Institute of Chicago from New York City's Armory excited viewers who hungered for new ideas and upset others who had never before seen such work. A poem published in a newspaper (above) derides the museum's director, William M. R. French, for taking a trip while the controversial show was on display in galleries such as the one seen at left.

36

You Know Me Al: A Busher's Letters

RING W. LARDNER ✳ NEW YORK: GEORGE H. DORAN CO., 1916

Lester Munson

FACING *You Know Me Al*, the first successful book by Chicago-based sportswriter and humorist Ring Lardner, is a satirical novel consisting of barely literate letters sent home by baseball player Jack Keefe. Moving from the bush leagues to the Chicago White Sox and back, Keefe is headstrong, boastful, and naive. But his letters vividly paint the knotty world of Chicago baseball: although Keefe is a fictional character, those with whom he interacts are real-life baseball personalities.

Ring Lardner (1885–1933) began writing about baseball as a teenager and perfected his craft reporting on hundreds of games during six years of work on seven newspapers in four cities, including three publications in Chicago. When he joined the *Chicago Daily Tribune* in 1913, he transformed the paper's "In the Wake of the News" column into a major voice in the media of the time. Lardner's prose was crisp and funny, describing events in idiomatic and slangy terms that left the readers laughing and hoping for more.

While building a national following with a column that was syndicated in one hundred papers, Lardner began to pen short fiction for magazines, a lucrative sideline for writers of the era. Among those efforts was a series of six pieces published in the *Saturday Evening Post* in 1914. Based on the countless hours he spent on trains and in locker rooms with the Chicago White Sox and other teams, they tell the story of Jack Keefe, a hard-throwing right-handed pitcher for the Chicago White Sox who is almost as good as he thinks he is. The narrative is epistolary: Keefe writes letters to his best friend, Al Blanchard, in rural Indianan, a country dialect that is both frustrating and delightful. The stories were published in book form in 1916 as *You Know Me Al: A Busher's Letters*; it is Lardner's most important work. Virginia Woolf and F. Scott Fitzgerald praised the book when it was published, and, in later years, appreciative critics of the work added Lardner to a roster of outstanding American humorists that included Mark Twain and Will Rogers. In a list of the one hundred best sports books of all time, *You Know Me Al* was ranked fifth overall and first as a work of fiction.[1]

Lardner presented Keefe as a country rube who is at once loathsome, lovable, oblivious, boastful, and impossible. Describing his best pitch, Keefe tells Al, "My fast one . . . was so fast that Evans the umpire couldn't see it half the time and he called a lot of balls that was right over the heart."[2] Facing the Detroit Tigers in an important game, Keefe brags that the great Ty Cobb will not be playing: "They told me he was sick, but I guess the truth is that he knowed I was going to pitch."[3]

When Charles Comiskey, the then-owner of the White Sox, plans a highly profitable barnstorming trip for his team through Japan and Europe, Keefe refuses to go because he will be not be paid anything extra and wants to spend the offseason with his infant son. Comiskey tells Keefe that Woodrow Wilson has written to him that the "king of Japan" has insisted that they bring all their star players, because the president, as Keefe puts it, is "a scared if they did not take there stars a long Japan would get mad at the united states and start a war."[4] When Keefe remains hesitant, John McGraw, an actual baseball legend and manager of the barnstorming team in Lardner's tale, informs Keefe that he will recruit Keefe's brother-in-law, a lefty, for the team. Keefe dislikes all lefties and has particular contempt for his brother-in-law. Replying to Keefe's assertion that his southpaw rival cannot travel to the West Coast in time for the trip, McGraw explains that Keefe's potential replacement will make it because he is on a train that will "come around threw canada, and it was down hill all the way."[5] This is enough for Keefe, and he joins the trip, which begins as the story comes to a close.

With a total mastery of baseball jargon and a fine ear for midwestern colloquialisms, Lardner rendered all the emotions of friendship, love, joy, disappointment, betrayal, and envy in a style that is always humorous and frequently side-splitting. Many writers (including Frank Deford, Philip Roth, and John Updike) have tried to surpass what Lardner accomplished in *You Know Me Al*, but it remains the best of sports literature. It is no surprise that in a review of the book, Virginia Woolf concluded that Lardner was the best prose writer in the United States.[6]

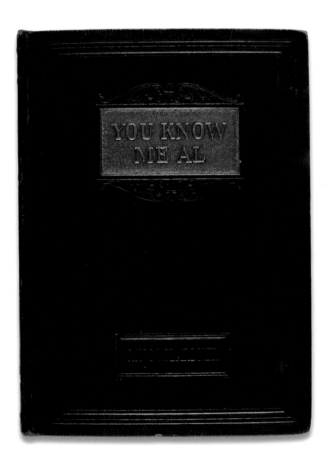

37

Chicago Poems

CARL SANDBURG ∗ NEW YORK: HENRY
HOLT AND COMPANY, 1916

Rosanna Warren

When Carl Sandburg died in 1967, he was honored at a ceremony at the Lincoln Memorial in Washington, DC. Chief Justice Earl Warren chaired the occasion, President Lyndon Johnson spoke, and poet Archibald MacLeish and scholar Mark Van Doren delivered eulogies. Whom were they praising?

"I am the people—the mob—the crowd—the mass," Sandburg boasted in his first book, *Chicago Poems*.[1] He persuaded generations of readers that this was true—some might not have read much else in the way of poetry, but they recognized in Sandburg's chanting a mythology of America to which they could assent. The poems rollick, rush, and swagger, often in lines so long they swell out beyond the margins into indented paragraphs. Sandburg refused to be contained. His poems are not hard to understand. They celebrate labor; revel in the gritty particulars of butchering, building skyscrapers and railroads, husking corn, taking dictation, streetwalking; and sneer at the wealthy and privileged. At the heart of the vision looms Chicago, greeted as a kind of god in Sandburg's most famous poem, "Chicago":

> Hog Butcher for the World,
> Tool Maker, Stacker of Wheat,
> Player with Railroads and the Nation's Freight Handler;
> Stormy, husky, brawling,
> City of the Big Shoulders.[2]

Sandburg earned his vision. Born in 1878 to a poor immigrant Swedish family in Galesburg, Illinois, he left school at thirteen and worked as a milkman, porter, bricklayer, farmhand, hotel servant, and coal-heaver before he broke into journalism, writing for the *Chicago Daily News*. A journalistic impulse drives many of his poems, a desire to record in detail the life swirling and lurching about him. He was recognized early. His second book of poems, *Cornhuskers*, received a Pulitzer Prize in 1919. In 1940 he won another Pulitzer, and in 1951 a third.[3] He did, indeed, speak for "the people," or at least for many of them.

It takes an effort now to extract some essential poetry from the massive heap of Sandburg's writing. Readers trained to weigh each syllable, judge each clause, and hunt for irony can feel clobbered by the pile-up of clichés, stock pairings, and smears of sentiment. But it is worth the effort. Poems capture the startling appearance of Lake Michigan beyond the city's buildings: "I came, sudden, at the city's edge, / On a blue burst of lake" ("The Harbor") and make one hear "the hoarse crunch of waves" ("Picnic Boat"). His language can be electrifying when "the people" speak through him: "The park policemen tell each other it is dark as a stack of black cats on Lake Michigan" ("Picnic

Boat"). It delights in Jack, "a swarthy, swaggering son-of-a-gun" ("Jack"). Every once in a while, a line has the force of a sword stroke: "I am glad God saw Death" ("The Junk Man").

MacLeish suggested that Sandburg's work needs to be honored as a whole, not poem by poem.[4] Indeed, Sandburg was a continental force. Yet he also deserves to be read in detail, for that is how one finds the veins of ore. One way to honor him would be to take seriously one of his favorite words, *yes*, from the title of his 1936 collection of poems, *The People, Yes*. He was a bard of affirmation. Robert Frost, his contemporary and rival, countered, "The People, Yes and No!"[5] American democracy, an ongoing experiment, is still working itself out between Sandburg's faith and Frost's skepticism.

Some of the phrases that have become touchstones of Chicago's image—for example, "city of the big shoulders" and "hog butcher for the world"—appear in *Chicago Poems*, the first book of verse by Chicago-based Carl Sandburg to appear under the imprimatur of a major publishing house. The collection established his national reputation.

38

City Residential Land Development: Studies in Planning; Competitive Plans for Subdividing a Typical Quarter Section of Land in the Outskirts of Chicago

EDITED BY ALFRED B. YEOMANS, LANDSCAPE ARCHITECT ✳ PUBLICATION OF THE CITY CLUB OF CHICAGO ✳ CHICAGO: THE UNIVERSITY OF CHICAGO PRESS, 1916

Daniel Bluestone

In 1916 *City Residential Land Development* contributed to the growing literature of the nascent city-planning movement. The volume presents twenty-six designs for a model 160-acre residential subdivision, submitted to a City Club of Chicago competition and exhibited at its 1913 Housing Exhibition. The book's 31-centimeter folio size, green cover, gold title lettering, and club logo make it strikingly similar to the Commercial Club's 1909 *Plan of Chicago* (no. 29). R.R. Donnelley's Lakeside Press printed both titles with text, black-and-white photographs, and handsome color renderings.[1] Alfred B. Yeomans (1870–1954), a Chicago landscape architect, edited the volume.

These publications embody different urban-planning ideals. Indeed, the City Club criticized the Commercial Club plan.[2] City Club civic secretary George E. Hooker insisted that the earlier plan focused upon "the broad structural features of the city," requiring years to implement. In the meantime, Chicago's edges were developing rapidly without "intelligent direction."[3] A resident of Hull-House, Hooker aimed to ameliorate the "housing conditions of the common people."[4] Architect William Drummond believed model subdivision designs "would count immediately," providing favorable publicity for the City Club.[5] City Club planners sought an "Organic Plan"[6] promoting "light, air, and cleanliness"[7] and "the real needs of all the people all the time."[8] This contrasted with the *Plan of Chicago*'s "Parisian standards," and monumental boulevards, parks, and symmetrical civic centers.[9]

Hooker bemoaned the Commercial Club plan's uniform cornice lines, set at twelve stories downtown, ignoring the "picturesque possibilities" of Chicago's skyscraper heritage.[10] However, the City Club plans were also detached from common Chicago urban forms. The subdivision competition limited the number of housing units to 1,280, a density comparable to that of a contemporary Chicago bungalow neighborhood. Individual homes filled most competition plans, despite the fact that by the 1910s multiple-family buildings dominated Chicago residential construction. Chicagoans had made great strides in humanely, conveniently, and economically accommodating residents in high-rise apartments and low-rise courtyard and walk-up buildings. Nevertheless, many competitors considered apartments to be a "menacing factor," violating "the appropriate and the harmonious" in residential development.[11]

Aside from the subdivision plans, the 1913 Housing Exhibition included a historical analysis of Chicago housing, an overview of contemporary housing form, a review of the "darker" side of tenements and slums, and innovative housing plans from Europe and America.[12] Competitors were explicitly directed toward English and German Garden Cities models. Garden City designers Raymond Unwin and Henry Vivian were enthusiastically received at the City Club.[13] Vivian criticized City Club members for "setting a bad

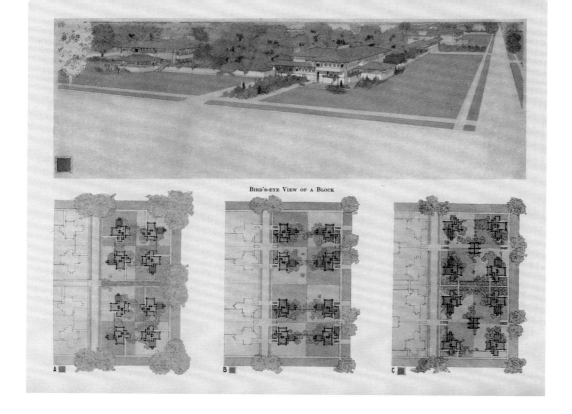

BIRD'S-EYE VIEW OF A BLOCK

example" by promoting model tenements instead of the "individual home" as the "standard home for the great mass of the people."[14]

City Club competitors generally bypassed the house-and-block forms of the existing city, promoting more suburban solutions. The publication highlighted Frank Lloyd Wright's non-juried competition entry, which expanded his 1901 Quadruple Block Plan to subdivision scale.[15] Here four houses occupied each block, with one house facing each side of the block. Foliage, walls, and room orientation sought privacy for nominally urban residents. Nevertheless, Wright accommodated two-thirds of his families in multiunit houses.[16] Most competition entries showed greater ambivalence about density and urban possibilities. Competition winner Wilhelm Bernhard (1885–1947) and other competitors did away with the prototypical interior alleys on blocks and substituted a shared realm of interior parks, gardens, and promenades for the individual yards of typical subdivisions. Retail-trade and civic buildings were carefully clustered in neighborhood centers, viewed as more appropriate than the Commercial Club's focus on a monumental civic center.[17] Plans laid out streets to discourage through traffic. Such elements became hallmarks of subsequent "neighborhood unit" designs in national urban planning, which constitute an enduring legacy of the publication.[18]

A response in part to Daniel Burnham's *Plan of Chicago* (no. 29), with its focus on the central city, the competition that occasioned this book focused on residential design, prompted by Progressive Era approaches to healthy living environments. Frank Lloyd Wright's "non-competitive" subdivision design featured his quadruple block plan, underscoring the City Club of Chicago's Garden City vision.

39

The Negro in Chicago: A Study of Race Relations and a Race Riot

THE CHICAGO COMMISSION ON RACE
RELATIONS ✳ CHICAGO: THE UNIVERSITY
OF CHICAGO PRESS, 1922

Adam Green

The Negro in Chicago: A Study of Race Relations and a Race Riot was the formal report of the Chicago Commission on Race Relations, charged by Illinois governor Frank O. Lowdon to determine the causes of the 1919 race riot in Chicago. The one-week outbreak of violence (July 27–August 3), which resulted in 38 deaths, 537 injuries, and over 1,000 homeless, brought simmering racial tensions to the surface and revealed for the first time racial segregation's consequence as a factor shaping the city. The twelve-person commission tasked a team of researchers, including Charles Spurgeon Johnson (1893–1956), research director for the local chapter of the Urban League, to draw together materials related to six factors informing local race relations before 1919: prior conflicts, everyday contacts, housing, labor, crime, and public opinion. The resulting 651-page report constituted the most comprehensive overview of racial conflict in an American city for much of the twentieth century. It provided a template for the 1968 analysis of urban racial unrest from the National Advisory Commission on Civil Disorders, a group chaired by yet another Illinois governor, Otto Kerner.

Written during the Great Migration (Chicago's African American population more than doubled between 1916 and 1919), *The Negro in Chicago* remains one of the most instructive examinations of racial inequality ever written about a northern American city. Though the 1919 riot was an exemplary case study of social panic, Johnson and his coresearchers rejected the simple explanation of mass irrationality in favor of a complex analysis of incivility fostered through multiple institutions. Drawing on 5,584 pages of recorded testimony before the city's coroner's jury, they revealed starkly disparate patterns of policing during the riot, with black communities held under curfew, while white assailants were not arrested even when standing in the vicinity of victims. Media bias and stereotype were cited as key causes, reinforcing association of black Chicagoans with a criminal nature that argued—against a preponderance of evidence—they were the primary perpetrators of the violence. While antagonisms in the workplace were found to be relatively mild compared to other spheres of relations, failure to establish an enduring biracial form of unionization in industries such as meatpacking suggested an opportunity lost to mitigate the general climate of suspicion.

Without question, the form of conflict cited by the commission as most crucial in precipitating the riot was struggles over housing. The report acknowledges prevailing assumptions that black entry into white residential neighborhoods, as both renters and owners, caused property values to drop dramatically, even though wide fluctuations in value across the South Side predated the arrival of blacks.

Both before the riot and after, white homeowner associations in several

areas, notably Greater Hyde Park, sought to stem the influx of black residents through suasion of real estate brokers, preemptive intimidation, and overt violence. Both blacks and whites grew more convinced that they comprised besieged communities, encouraging rumor and retribution to run amok after the tragic stoning and drowning of African American teenager Eugene Williams, which catalyzed the riot.

Despite the cautionary analysis of *The Negro in Chicago*, segregation in the city deepened, rather than lessened, following the report's publication. Work sorted into dual labor markets, even when blacks and whites worked within the same industrial firms. Nominally enfranchised, local African Americans found themselves tightly controlled by party overlords, both white and black. Restrictive covenants soon covered 75 percent of properties in Chicago. Thus *The Negro in Chicago* is noteworthy for its incisive analysis of the structural conditions of racial inequality and for how emphatically its recommendation of reform was rejected by the wider city, leaving a legacy of racial separation hampering municipal governance and civility into the present.

The Negro in Chicago was published three years after a violent attack by whites on Chicago's burgeoning African American population. A photograph taken during the 1919 riot shows the Ogden Café ringed by members of the National Guard who appear to be protecting it from the black Chicagoans standing near the curb.

40

"Chicago: That Todd'ling Town"

FRED FISHER ∗ FEATURED BY BLOSSOM
SEELEY ∗ NEW YORK: FRED FISHER AND
PUBLISHERS, 1922

D. W. Krummel

Chicago, Chicago, that toddl'ing Town, that toddl'ing Town[1]
Chicago, Chicago, I'll show you around, I love it,
Betch your bottom dollar you lose the blues in Chicago, Chicago,
The town that Billy Sunday could not shut down[.]

On State Street, That Great Street, I just want to say,
Just want to say,
They do things they don't do on Broadway,
Say, They have the time, the Time of their life
I saw a man he danced with his wife,
In Chicago, Chicago, my home town.

It is ironic that the best-known Chicago song came from New York. Its composer, Fred Fisher (1875–1942), emigrated from Germany in 1892,[2] settling in Tin Pan Alley, where in 1907 he established a publishing firm to promote his songs, including "Come Josephine in My Flying Machine" (1910), "Peg o' My Heart" (1913), and "Dardanella" (1919). "Chicago (That Todd'ling Town)" (1922) quickly became a favorite on records, thanks to such widely different artists as Count Basie, Tony Bennett, Tommy and Jimmy Dorsey, Duke Ellington, Leadbelly, Guy Lombardo, Anita O'Day, and Louis Prima. Frank Sinatra recorded the song several times, most famously on his 1958 album *Come Fly with Me.*[3] "Chicago" was featured in a number of movies, including *The Story of Vernon and Irene Castle* (1939) with Ginger Rogers and Fred Astaire, *Roxie Hart* (1942) with Rogers and Adolphe Menjou, and Sinatra's film *The Joker Is Wild* (1957).

The "toddle" of the title refers to a kind of bouncy foxtrot, and the tune's energetic rhythm is right for Chicago. Singers love the long "Shee" and "Cah," but, frankly, the lyrics could just as easily have celebrated Cleveland, Denver, or Seattle. This was a period of songs about major American cities, the most famous being those about St. Louis and San Francisco, as well as New York, of course. (Think Jerome Kern and Leonard Bernstein.) The line "The Bronx is up and the Battery's down" may be handy for tourists to keep in mind, but Fisher's "On State Street, That Great Street" has more gravitas.

While Fisher's song says "you lose the blues in Chicago," we do not know whether he ever heard them played in a South Side or West Side bar. Nonetheless, he was right in promising that "you, all your kids, and your wife" would have the time of your life in Chicago. Fisher could boast that the baseball-player-turned-evangelist Billy Sunday could not shut Chicago down, but his lyrics do not specify which of the city's sins Sunday would have had in mind.

This early edition of "Chicago, Chicago: That Todd'ling Town" features a portrait of Blossom Seeley (1891–1974), whose fame as a leading vaudevillian and recording star the publisher used to promote the song.

In sum, the song is great fun, even if it is a mixture of utter nonsense and jolly enthusiasm.

For what is memorable about Chicago and its music, better to recall a few of the many musicians, from ragtime to gospel to jazz, blues, and beyond, whose careers were cradled there and whose achievements have a ring of Chicago authenticity.[4] Fred Fisher did not know (or likely care) what he was talking about. "Chicago" remains the city's theme song, and it is great fun if you enjoy toddling.

41

A Thousand and One Afternoons in Chicago[1]

BEN HECHT ✳ DESIGNED AND
ILLUSTRATED BY HERMAN ROSSE ✳
CHICAGO: COVICI-MCGEE, 1922

Celia Hilliard

In 1920 H. L. Mencken famously declared Chicago "the literary capital of the United States."[2] Writers who would one day win national recognition were part of the city's boisterous community of letters, much of it nurtured in its robust newspaper culture. Among them Ben Hecht (1894–1964) was perhaps the most vigorous presence—cocky, resourceful, ambitious, a man of volcanic energies beside whom even the most talented colleagues seemed pale and toothless.

A native of Racine, Wisconsin, Hecht arrived in Chicago at age sixteen seeking work as a reporter. For the next several years, he led a knockabout existence covering major and minor news in all corners of the city, first for the *Chicago Journal* and then for the *Chicago Daily News.* He wrote essays for little magazines, began a novel, and tried playwriting. After a postwar stint in Berlin, he left the *Daily News*, determined to become a serious literary author.

His former editor, Henry Justin Smith, lured Hecht back to the *Daily News* with an unprecedented plum assignment: a daily column telling stories of urban life just under the news as it is commonly understood.[3] With a puckish nod to "Scheherazade," Hecht titled his column "1001 Afternoons in Chicago." For his vignettes, he drew upon his encounters with people from every stratum of life: judges, railway conductors, strippers, scrubwomen, financiers, hotel dandies, fishermen sitting on a pier. Though prominent personalities such as the lawyer Clarence Darrow and opera singer Mary Garden appeared on occasion, his subjects were mostly unknown. Their hapless tales are part fact, part imagined. Dutch, a once-fashionable tattoo artist, plies his needles behind a photo booth at State and Van Buren; and Peewee, manicurist at a barbershop, fends off gentleman predators: "Sometimes I give them the baby stare and pretend I don't know what's on their so-called minds."[4] Nathan, the Wabash Avenue auctioneer, possesses an ability to pass off dimestore bric-a-brac as ancient treasure with a glibness that finally backfires on him. Prospects fade, wives run away, sick children die, and prostitutes are always at a loss to tell the court why they keep at it. People, Gustave says, are like the watches he repairs: "Zo nice outside und zo busted inside."[5] Yet when Hecht gazed out over the night skyline he loved, he sensed that in spite of their struggles and disappointments, men and women were ever embarked on secret voyages, in pursuit of silent and illogical dreams.

Hecht's column first appeared in June 1921. Running on the back page of the *News*, it quickly became the paper's most popular feature. In November 1922, a collection of these pieces was published by Covici-McGee, a new firm established by the owners of an eccentric bookstore on Washington Street. The book features a striking dust jacket and pen drawings by Herman Rosse (1887–1965).[6] Hecht said that in spite of some 105 typographical errors and

the printing of whole paragraphs upside down, it was the most beautiful book he had ever seen.[7]

Sexual frankness was a strong element of all Hecht's work. After a novel he published prompted federal obscenity charges, the *News* fired him.[8] Enraged, he decamped for New York, where he and the writer Charles MacArthur scored a Broadway hit with their wisecracking newspaper comedy *The Front Page*. Hecht went on to conquer Hollywood. He won the first Oscar ever awarded for Best Original Screenplay and over time composed or doctored the scripts for a staggering number of now-classic films.[9]

Later in life, Hecht remembered his time in Chicago as Arcady, the years that had mattered. Hastily written but deeply observed, his stories in *A Thousand and One Afternoons* can be considered the wellspring of his art and surely the stuff of literature.[10]

The striking illustrations and unusual design that Herman Rosse provided for *A Thousand and One Afternoons in Chicago* punctuate this collection of boisterous stories from journalist Ben Hecht with a jazzlike graphic staccato and signal the willingness of the Chicago publisher Covici-McGee to issue titles with original content and unique presentation. This spread shows the book's title page. See also page xv.

42

The International Competition for a New Administration Building for the Chicago Tribune, MCMXXII Containing All the Designs Submitted in Response to the Chicago Tribune's $100,000 Offer Commemorating Its Seventy Fifth Anniversary, June 10, 1922

CHICAGO: TRIBUNE COMPANY, [1923]

Katherine Solomonson

Picture this volume on your drafting table, circa 1923. It is a book with real heft, bulky and broad-shouldered as an early Chicago skyscraper. But its dust jacket features a skyscraper of a different kind: the future Tribune Tower, tall and slender, crowned with a fountain of flying buttresses. Inside the book, more skyscrapers with slim proportions and fanciful crowns parade through the pages. Eye-opening and whimsical, practical and impossible, they are the entries to the Chicago Tribune Tower Competition—one of the largest, most talked about, and (to some) most outlandish design competitions of the twentieth century.

On June 10, 1922, the *Chicago Tribune* announced an international competition for the design of world's most beautiful office building for the "World's Greatest Newspaper." To achieve this, the company promoted the competition internationally, provided latitude for experimentation, and offered $100,000 in prizes as enticements. It worked. Two hundred sixty-three architects from twenty-three nations produced a broad array of designs that ranged from beaux-arts classicism to Bauhaus modernism. In the end, the jury awarded first prize to John Mead Howells (1868–1959) and Raymond Hood (1881–1934) for a Gothic-style tower with a crown distinctive enough to lend itself well to corporate advertising. Second prize went to Eliel Saarinen (1873–1950) for a structure with soaring lines culminating in a graceful—and less histrionic—stepped-back top.

After the competition, architecture journals argued the merits of various entries, especially the top two, and Chicago—internationally known for its post-Fire tall buildings—received renewed attention in debates about the skyscraper's future. But no one saw the full spectrum of entries until 1923, when the Tribune Company collected almost all of them into a book meant to memorialize the competition and provide models for future skyscraper design.[1] Many European entries, including those that became famous later—Walter Gropius and Adolf Meyer's, and Adolf Loos's, for example—arrived after the competition's deadline and remained invisible in the United States until this book came out.[2] When it landed on drafting tables, the volume offered many their first glimpse of the current creative ferment in international design.

Today *The International Competition* is a rare book, protected and seldom seen. But it has developed an afterlife in other forms. In 1980 it was republished in paperback along with a new set of "late entries."[3] Selected designs have appeared in countless publications, and many are available via the internet. Even so, it is worth returning to the original tome in its tangible form. Pick it up and you can feel its rough burlap and gold-lettered leather. Open it, and its heavy stock reveals the touch and smell of a medium that circulated new ideas about design. Peruse the entries in their original published size and order, and you learn something about the *Tribune*'s intentions and the architects' responses.[4] Compare different copies, and you find signs of use over the years, including fingerprint smudges on favorite pages. Finally, consider how the competition's influence traveled from plates in publications to countless drafting boards, and it is easy to imagine architects keeping the book open to Saarinen's proposal. For, in the end, Saarinen was the competition's real winner. Though his entry was never constructed, it was hailed as the exemplar of a new era in skyscraper design. Start looking, and you will find Saarinen's design springing up on skylines from New York to Shanghai.[5]

Howells and Hood's winning design of a Gothic-style skyscraper to house the Tribune Company graces the dust jacket of the luxury volume the newspaper giant published illustrating the submissions to its architectural competition. Twenty-three nations were represented by 263 entrants. While Finnish architect Eliel Saarinen (1873–1950) came in second, his entry, seen here, would prove more influential in the evolution of the modern skyscraper than the winner. For Walter Gropius's entry, see page 257.

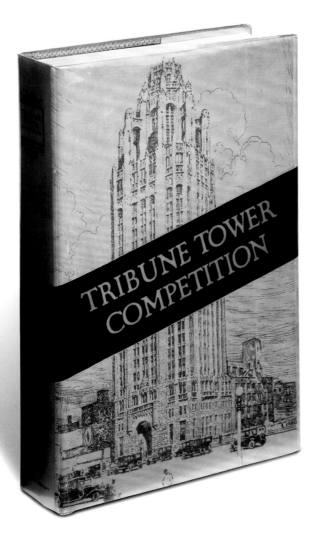

43

Weird Tales

CHICAGO: RURAL PUBLICATIONS, 1923–
24; POPULAR FICTION PUBLISHING,
1924–38; NEW YORK: WEIRD TALES,
INC., 1938–54

Carlo Rotella

In 2009, at the age of ninety-two, the great fantasy and science fiction writer Jack Vance recalled the life-altering effect on him of reading the pulp magazine *Weird Tales* as an adolescent during the Great Depression. Vance said, "I waited at the mailbox every month with my tongue hanging out for the latest issue." The stories he read there by Robert E. Howard, H. P. Lovecraft, C. L. Moore, Clark Ashton Smith, and other virtuosos of fantasy and horror played a crucial role in his becoming a writer, just as Vance's own work would in turn influence Michael Chabon, Neil Gaiman, and George R. R. Martin.[1]

The magazine that fired the young Vance's imagination came from Chicago, which was a capital of weird publishing in the early decades of the twentieth century. In the realms of self-help and spiritual guidance, the Egyptian Publishing Company, Sun-Worshiper Publishing Company, Mazdaznan Publishing Company, and especially de Laurence, Scott and Company produced a rich assortment of occult and esoteric volumes.[2] *Weird Tales*, first appearing in 1923, enjoyed a decade and a half of unmatched glory as the home of fantastic fiction under the editorship of Farnsworth Wright (1888–1940).[3] Until it moved to New York City in 1938 and went into decline, it was the finest of the fantasy pulps, and it remains perhaps the most influential fantasy periodical of all time. What *Black Mask*—the New York–based pulp magazine in which Raymond Chandler, Dashiell Hammett, and others perfected the hard-boiled detective and noir sensibility—was to crime fiction, *Weird Tales* was to fantasy, especially at the noir end of the genre's spectrum.

It was not just the writing inside the magazine that caused tongues to hang out. Its covers typically featured alluring women wearing little or no clothing and accessorized with whips, daggers, fetishistic restraints, and slavering demons. The most lurid of these cover images were painted by Margaret Brundage (1900–1976), a native Chicagoan who had attended McKinley High School and the Chicago Academy of Fine Arts (Walt Disney was a classmate at both). Unlike Frank Frazetta's pneumatic odalisques and apoplectically muscular he-men, types that have long reigned as the canonical norm in pulp fantasy art, Brundage's wan, louche characters look more like flappers and lounge lizards trapped in a bondage-themed opium nightmare.

But above all else *Weird Tales* was a treasure house of stylish writing for a popular audience, in which distinctive voices offered up heaping portions of adventure, horror, and the uncanny.

Here's Lovecraft: "Into Thalarion, the City of a Thousand Wonders, many have passed but none returned. Therein walk only daemons and mad things that are no longer men, and the streets are white with the unburied bones of those who have looked upon the eidolon Lathi, that reigns over the city."[4]

And Howard: "Then with a fierce cry Valerius' sword was sheathed in her

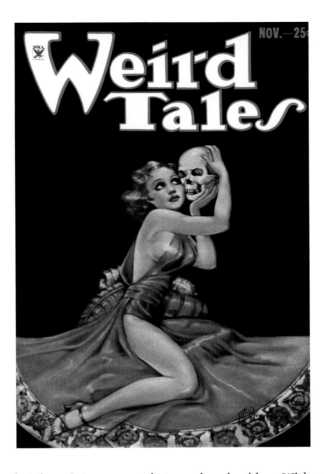

The Chicago artist Margaret Brundage designed thirty-nine covers for *Weird Tales*, the Chicago-based fantasy and horror pulp-fiction magazine with an enthusiastic national following. They proved that she could equal and even outdo male illustrators in depicting what one writer called "pin-up horror art."[7] This is her cover design for the November 1933 issue.

breast with such fury that the point sprang out between her shoulders. With an awful shriek the witch sank down, writhing in convulsions, grasping at the naked blade as it was withdrawn, smoking and dripping."[5]

And Moore: "And he could not stir in that slimy, ecstatic embrace—and a weakness was flooding that grew deeper after each succeeding wave of intense delight, and the traitor in his soul strengthened and drowned out the revulsion—and something within him ceased to struggle as he sank wholly into a blazing darkness that was oblivion to all else but that devouring rapture."[6]

Such writing was not the moralizing fantasy of J. R. R. Tolkien or C. S. Lewis, Oxford dons who courted literary respectability by dressing up their stories in the trappings of epic. *Weird Tales* offered unapologetic genre fiction, stripped to its formulaic essence and seething with pulpy vitality and a yen for strangeness.

44

The Plea of
Clarence Darrow,
August 22nd,
23rd & 25th,
MCMXXIII, in
Defense of Richard
Loeb and Nathan
Leopold Jr. on
Trial for Murder.
Authorized and
Revised Edition,
Together with a
Brief Summary of
the Facts

CHICAGO: RALPH FLETCHER SEYMOUR,
1924[1]

Gary T. Johnson

It is highly unusual for a closing statement in a murder trial to be expressed in the second-person singular. There was no jury, so the "you" in this most famous of Clarence Darrow's courtroom statements was Judge John R. Caverly. "We did plead guilty before Your Honor because we were afraid to submit our cause to a jury."[2]

Darrow (1857–1938), who established his law practice in Chicago in 1880, had long opposed the death penalty as antihumanitarian. Against all odds, his objective was to save Nathan Leopold Jr. and Richard Loeb from execution. They had kidnapped a child, killed him with a chisel, and hidden his body in a remote culvert. One fact shaped Darrow's arguments: Caverly had helped to create the Cook County Juvenile Court. This had been the first court of its kind in the nation, one where the child should "be made to feel that he is the object of its care and solicitude."[3] Because of this, Darrow believed the judge would be "kindly and discerning in his views of life."[4]

The defendants came from prominent families living in Hyde Park, where the University of Chicago is located. At ages nineteen and eighteen, respectively, Leopold and Loeb were outside the juvenile court's jurisdiction, but Darrow consistently referred to them as "children" or "boys." He asserted that executing them would be "in violation of the policy of the law to take care of the young, in violation of all the progress that has been made and of the humanity that has been shown in the care of the young."[5] Darrow knew, however, that he had to walk a fine line. To avoid the death penalty, early release must not be an option: "They should be permanently isolated from society."[6] Nor could he minimize the horror of their acts. "They killed him as they might kill a spider or a fly, for the experience. They killed him because they were made that way. Because somewhere in the infinite processes that go to the making up of the boy or the man something slipped."[7]

Both sides offered expert testimony on the youths' state of mind, but Darrow argued that the nature of the crime spoke for itself: "There is not a sane thing in all of this from the beginning to the end. There was not a normal act in any of it, from its inception in a diseased brain, until today, when they sit here awaiting their doom."[8] Why had Loeb become obsessed with crime novels? Why had Leopold come to believe in Friedrich Nietzsche's superman, someone who stood above the law? Darrow offered no definitive answers.

Darrow argued that an execution would add fuel to the fire of cruelty and hate. "And yet there are men who seriously say that for what Nature has done, for what life has done, for what training has done, you should hang these boys."[9] He nonetheless proved to be right about Judge Caverly, who imposed sentences of life imprisonment plus ninety-nine years. Darrow's unconven-

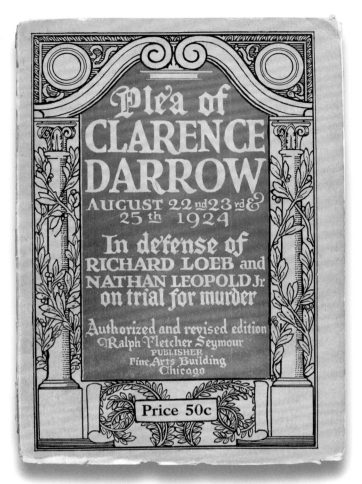

Plea of CLARENCE DARROW
AUGUST 22nd 23rd & 25th 1924

In defense of RICHARD LOEB and NATHAN LEOPOLD Jr on trial for murder

Authorized and revised edition
Ralph Fletcher Seymour
PUBLISHER
Fine Arts Building
Chicago

Price 50c

Hyde Park teenagers Richard Loeb and Nathan Leopold Jr. are seen here in a courtroom (Loeb in a light suit, Leopold in a dark one) during their murder trial. Arguing that the death penalty is antihumanitarian and only spawns more death, their lawyer, Clarence Darrow, third from the left, succeeded in persuading the judge to sentence the young men to life plus ninety-nine years in prison, but the issues he raised remain unresolved today.

tional strategy and the improbable outcome of this case helped build his national reputation as the quintessential defense lawyer.

The crime was a factor in Chicago's growing reputation for being a city of murders, but Darrow's plea, with its reliance on expert testimony, helped to reinforce the city as a locus for cutting-edge social-science research. Read the plea, and you will find that the questions of life and death are all addressed to you. What are *your* ideas of justice and mercy for juveniles? Whom do *you* blame when an individual's "machine is imperfect"? Do *you* think that punishment can cure "the hatreds and the maladjustments of the world"?[10] These are timeless questions. My guess is that Darrow's plea will have the same force in another one hundred years as it did in 1923 and as it does today.

45

A System of Architectural Ornament According with a Philosophy of Man's Powers

LOUIS H. SULLIVAN, ARCHITECT ✳
NEW YORK: PRESS OF THE AMERICAN
INSTITUTE OF ARCHITECTS, 1924

David Van Zanten

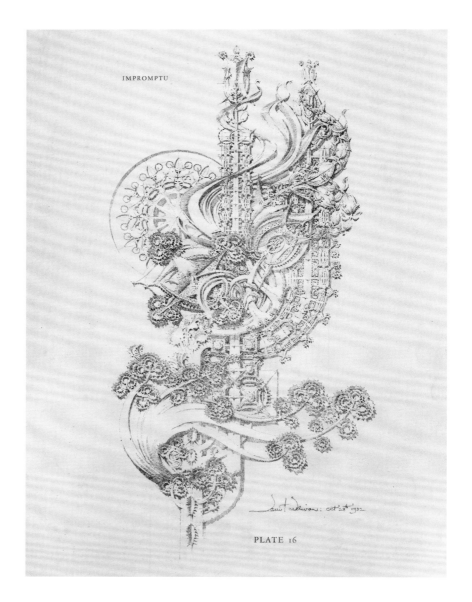

IMPROMPTU

PLATE 16

The career of Chicago architect Louis Sullivan (1856–1924) blossomed with the Auditorium Theatre of 1886–89 and culminated with the Carson Pirie Scott Department Store of 1898–1904. But, as has often been recounted, by then he had separated from his engineer partner, Dankmar Adler, and, knowing too well his own worth as a designer to compromise with practical reality, he declined into poverty, living off the charity of friends. But he was never uncreative: the twenty plates of this folio book were part of a remarkable last flash of imaginative productivity. In January 1922 he was simultaneously commissioned to write twelve essays of reminiscences for the *AIA Journal* (in the end producing sixteen) and to draw twenty plates of instruction in ornamental design for the Burnham Library at the Art Institute of Chicago. He produced them between then and mid-1923, writing in addition three of his best critical essays for *Architectural Record*: one on the design competition for the Chicago Tribune building (no. 42) and two about Frank Lloyd Wright's Imperial Hotel in Tokyo. By the time he finished, both the plates and the reminiscences they sparked had morphed into books, *A System of Architectural Ornament* and *The Autobiography of an Idea*.[1] Wright, who had worked for Sullivan early on, found both, newly printed, in his hands the day before the older architect died, on April 14, 1924.[2]

A System of Architectural Ornament starts as an essay on geometric ornamental elaboration in words and diagrams. But beginning with plate 8, it transforms into single spreading images freed from further pedagogical inscriptions and speaking only the language of pattern. The sole exceptions are found on plates 16 and 20 (page 266), which bear the signal words "Impromptu" and "FINIS," respectively, inscribed at the top. The sheets are dated, starting January 1922 and ending June 11, 1923.

The last images (plates 18–20) do not constitute an instruction manual like those of Arthur Wesley Dow and Denman Ross or the Chicago-trained Ernest Batchelder.[3] They are closer in scale, power, and geometry to Victor-Marie Ruprich-Robert's folio *Flore ornementale* (1865–75), pencil copies of which survive among Sullivan's papers. Those were Ruprich-Robert's teaching exercises at the École des Arts Décoratifs in Paris, across the street from which Sullivan had lived in 1874–75. But such comparisons only make the abstract thickness and labyrinthine fascination of Sullivan's plates more evident. They encapsulate his frustrated creativity, sometimes suggesting spatial plans, as in plate 13, which seems a reworking of Burnham's 1909 plan (no. 29) for the Chicago Loop. Sullivan's rearrangement of the last of his plates leaves a strange, frightening moonscape at the end, below that roughly inscribed word "FINIS," making it clear these diagrams might be read on more than one plane, "according with a philosophy of man's powers."

As a glimpse into this powerful, brilliant mind contemplating failure and death, the plates have few parallels, although Sullivan's admirer the architect Claude Bragdon developed such graphic elaboration into an art form that spilled over into public performances of music and theater, which in turn inspired Buckminster Fuller's geometric explorations.[4] But in Sullivan's case, if his autobiography documents the beginning of his career, his plates document the end, and both do this with passionate indirectness.

At the end of Louis Sullivan's life, the Burnham Library of the Art Institute of Chicago commissioned the impoverished and ill "father of modernist architecture" to write about his approach to architectural ornament. This and other drawings in the resulting publication showcase his understanding of ornament as a way to link the organic and inorganic, as well as nature and science.

46

Chimes

ROBERT HERRICK, AUTHOR OF
"TOGETHER," "ONE WOMAN'S LIFE," ETC.
∗ NEW YORK: THE MACMILLAN COMPANY,
1926

Hanna Holborn Gray

Chimes is a novel set in the University of Chicago's earliest years. It was written by Robert Herrick (1868–1938), who taught in the university's Department of English from 1893 to 1923. Author of some twenty-one novels, he set most of his fiction in the Chicago of the late nineteenth and early twentieth centuries, describing it as a grimy, smoke-ridden, crowded, and frenetic city of unfettered growth, materialism, commercialism, and corruption. Nostalgic for the coherence and ethical certainties he found in an idealized New England (he was born in Cambridge, Massachusetts, and attended Harvard), Herrick made Chicago into a proxy for the disintegration of values and cynical disregard of higher purposes that he considered outgrowths of urban industrial society. The leading characters of his novels are businessmen who create huge industries and fortunes and professional men (doctors, lawyers, architects) whose inherent humaneness gives way to compliance with their world's overriding pressure to achieve worldly power and success.

Chimes, written after Herrick had left Chicago, is a not even thinly disguised novel about the university. The book's title refers to the bells of Mitchell Tower. Herrick's account of the institution and its history differs significantly from the triumphalist narrative of the success of a great founder—William Rainey Harper—in propelling the university within a decade into one of America's leading academic institutions. Herrick's "President Harris" is instead a provincial midwesterner, a pudgy, ill-dressed man lacking in sophistication and mannerly restraint. He is pictured as an entrepreneurial huckster and shrewd manipulator obsessed with growth and prestige, preoccupied with ceaseless building and money raising, indebted to the barons of big business, ready to subordinate the central studies and values of the humanities to the sciences and vocational education, and indifferent to the idea of a university where meaningful learning and scholarship and scientific research should be pursued for their own sake while addressing the important questions of human existence. Herrick mocked the pretentious triviality and pedantry that mars the work of his colleagues, their engagement in academic politics and self-interested ambition, and the shallowness of students who care only for sports and social life. And Herrick was not sympathetic to what he considered the populist side of Harper's quest for the widest possible transmission of knowledge and education. Herrick's Chicago was uneasy with elite institutions, and Herrick was basically elitist in outlook.

Chimes is, in short, an academic novel that relates closely to the city of Chicago. It is a much better novel than its reputation—or lack of one—would suggest, and it offers a more complex assessment of the university's relationship with its larger community. Herrick was not a happy camper at the university or in the city, but he saw dimensions and accomplishments to admire in both. He wrote about a significant institution in Chicago, one that relied for its support on, and became part of, the social universe of the class of wealthy businessmen whom he regarded as the princes of the city and who served as influential university trustees.

Most interesting is that Herrick made the University of Chicago a kind of mirror image of the city. The founding president behaves like Chicago's builders and rulers; the professors, with a few exemplary exceptions, behave as do the professional men of the city, giving way to the same temptations. They too strive for social advancement and material goals at variance with the integrity of their calling; they too succumb to the petty and unlovely enticements of the commercial world around them. In the end, the university that Herrick wished were an ivory tower is instead a microcosm, and indeed a creature, of Chicago itself.

The University of Chicago has been rightly celebrated perhaps as "the Harvard of the Midwest," but this 1926 novel has very little good to say about it. The author, who taught English and rhetoric there from its inception until he quit in 1923, found the university's leaders—such as its founding president, William Rainey Harper (1856–1906), seen below—to be unsophisticated, its trustees greedy capitalists, and its faculty grasping social climbers.

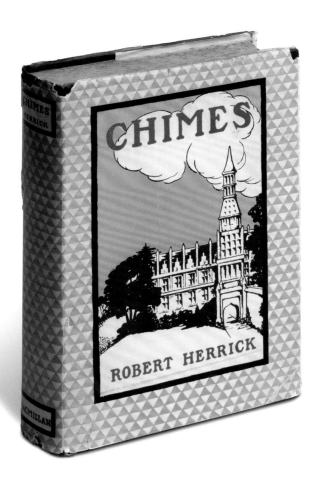

47

Touchdown!

AS TOLD BY COACH AMOS ALONZO
STAGG TO WESLEY WINANS STOUT ✳
NEW YORK, LONDON, TORONTO, BOMBAY,
CALCUTTA, MADRAS: LONGMANS, GREEN
AND CO., 1927

Robin Lester

Amos Alonzo Stagg (1862–1965) was America's first tenured college football coach; his name probably appeared in Chicago newspapers more often from 1892 to 1932 than the name of any other person then alive. He became the University of Chicago's best-known personality and the twentieth century's first celebrity coach.[1] The university founding president, William Rainey Harper, used Stagg and football as an early promotional tool. As a result, the coach created the nation's model for industrial-strength college football, prompting the rise of the roles of coaches, players, and spectators. Stagg got all other athletic conference teams to play in Chicago for bigger paychecks, he promoted himself as the unblemished evangelist of the gridiron gospel, and he transmogrified student-players into player-students. Although sports pages are unreliable historical documents, clearly Stagg was the most creative coach of the early twentieth century, inventing plays and training procedures. He also led basketball, track, and baseball teams to great success.

After the Chicago Maroons won two national and seven Big Ten conference titles—eight if one includes the last one, in 1924, shared with Red Grange's University of Illinois team—Stagg never again had a winning season in Chicago. He sensed that his sun was setting as the university began to close doors he had long forced open. Chicago administrators had become increasingly uneasy with the academic price paid for football glory and began to impose restrictions on his program, signaled by their refusal to build a giant stadium to match the national boom started by the University of Pennsylvania, Harvard, Princeton, and Yale.

At age sixty-five, the "Grand Old Man" related his memoirs to Wesley Winans Stout (1890–1971), a newspaper reporter in his thirties who had just been hired at the *Saturday Evening Post*. He proved a fortunate choice and drafted a remarkable volume about American college football. The press praised the book, and it merited a second printing within a month. *Touchdown!* is both a football history and a hagiographic memoir. It provides a running narrative of the game's English origins, its transit across the Atlantic, and its cultural transformation. And it details an exemplary American life that assures us of Stagg's extraordinary rectitude. Stagg took every opportunity to criticize the very excesses that he himself had pioneered in college football: the use of teams as advertising and fundraising arms of the institutions, runaway salaries for winning coaches, rampant recruiting of players who were academically unqualified and who were set apart from the student bodies as both physical commodities and campus elite, and cover-ups of resultant scandals.[2]

In 1932, when Stagg was seventy, the university's then-president, Robert Maynard Hutchins, refused to renew his contract, thus ending his forty-year

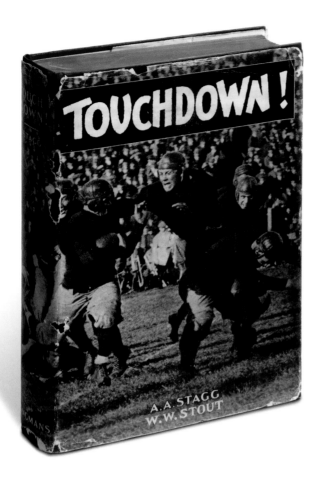

Touchdown! chronicles the career of the University of Chicago's longtime celebrity football coach Amos Alonzo Stagg, whose teams led their conference year after year under his creative but at times unscrupulous direction. Stagg is seen here with his players in 1932.

career in Chicago. In time Hutchins constructed his own myth about sports at the university and about Stagg as a purist, picturing both as being above the unseemly intercollegiate fray and opposing its excesses. A 2011 *New York Times* story on Chicago football in large part repeats the fable of unique rectitude, despite the pervasive university archival evidence historians have found of the rapacious athletic enterprise at Stagg's university.[3]

Between 2011 and 2014, the Big Ten enlarged its borders and media reach from Nebraska to New Jersey and could find only one legendary coach of unsoiled reputation after which to name its annual football championship trophy: Amos Alonzo Stagg. Never mind that Stagg and the University of Chicago had not participated in the conference for about fifty years: it was the best that they could devise after scandals had tarnished the demigods of the University of Michigan, Ohio State, and, more recently, Penn State.

48

The Gang: A Study of 1,313 Gangs in Chicago

FREDERIC THRASHER, PH.D., PROFESSOR OF SOCIOLOGY, ILLINOIS WESLEYAN UNIVERSITY, SOMETIME FELLOW IN THE DEPARTMENT OF SOCIOLOGY AND ANTHROPOLOGY, THE UNIVERSITY OF CHICAGO * CHICAGO: THE UNIVERSITY OF CHICAGO PRESS, 1927

Andrew V. Papachristos

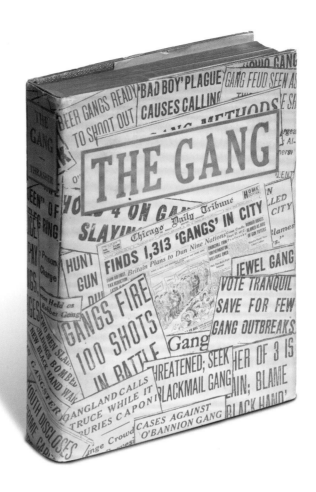

To this day, Chicago has not been able to shake its reputation as a capital of gang activity. But as this entry points out, the city has also been a center for the serious study and understanding of gangs, beginning with Frederic Thrasher's sociological analysis of the phenomenon.

Chicago is a city (in)famous for its gangs and gangsters. From the tommy-gun-driven battles over brewers during Prohibition to modern-day wars over honor and street corners, Chicago's violent reputation is linked to the imagery and behavior of its street gangs.

Chicago is also birthplace of social-scientific research on street gangs. In 1927 Frederic Thrasher (1892–1962), a PhD student in the newly formed Department of Sociology at the University of Chicago, published the results of a massive study of Chicago gangs, straightforwardly titled *The Gang: A Study of 1,313 Gangs in Chicago*. Thrasher produced a sprawling, five-hundred-page analysis of the structure, culture, geographic location, and characteristics of more than one thousand gangs in the city. *The Gang* was not a census of gangs but rather a deep sociological analysis of the gang as a unique social form. Thrasher's opus explores dozens of topics that continue to puzzle scholars and policymakers, including gang formation and evolution, the composition and structure of gangs, the role of race and ethnicity, the dynamics of gang warfare, and the role of gangs in politics and organized crime.

The centerpiece of Thrasher's work—the extent to which he had a "theory" of gangs—pivots on the ways in which gangs are linked to the larger ecology of the city. Like his mentors and peers at the University of Chicago, Thrasher believed that many of the distinctive aspects of early-twentieth-century urban life derived from the city's social ordering—the way different social groups interrelated and competed over the use of resources and certain geographic spaces.[1] Interactions among social groups—in particular, successive waves of immigrant and racial/ethnic groups—created a particular "social ecology" of the city, a distinct patterning of unique neighborhoods, each with its own unique flavor and culture. It was the coming together of these unique neighborhoods that gave the city its "mosaic-like" quality of "little worlds which touch but do not interpenetrate."[2]

The gang, according to Thrasher, occupied an *interstitial* position in the city, both spatially and socially. Thrasher held that "cracks" in the social fabric of society were created as competing groups moved throughout the city. This shifting of populations and groups—along with poverty and other social ills—diminished the social-control capacities of neighborhoods. Gangs arose to fill these interstices. For him, this interstitial quality defined the gang and gangland:

The most important conclusion suggested by a study of the location and distribution of the 1,313 gangs investigated in Chicago is that gangland represents a geographically and socially *interstitial* area in the city . . . that is, pertaining to spaces that intervene between one thing and the other . . . the gang may be regarded as an interstitial element in the framework of society, and gangland as an interstitial region in the layout of the city.[3]

Such *interstitiality* extended to include the timing of gang formation during the period of adolescence, itself an in-between period in the life course.

Much has changed in the nearly ninety years since Thrasher studied gangs in Chicago. The industrial economy that drove Thrasher's ecological thinking has given way to a global, postindustrial economy that has seen the rise and fall of cities around the world. Yet the symbiotic nature of the gang and the city still captures the curiosity of scholars. Gangs continue to arise in interstitial neighborhoods and are largely the domain of young people living in disadvantaged circumstances. No single piece of gang scholarship has come even close to the breadth of exploration found in *The Gang*, and scholars continually revisit Thrasher's theory of evolution and ecology, despite the tremendous shifts in the world around us.

49

A Portfolio of Fine Apartment Homes

COMPILED BY THE MICHIGAN ERIE OFFICE
OF BAIRD & WARNER INCORPORATED *
CHICAGO: 1928

Teri J. Edelstein

Chicago's visual identity is determined by nature, economics, and art, but geography is paramount. Lake Michigan, along with the parkland on its shores, is a constantly seen and integral aspect of the city. Lake Shore Drive made the land just to its west the most desirable real estate in the city. Developers and architects quickly exploited the Drive's extension north and built a series of luxury apartment buildings whose occupants could enjoy unencumbered views of the lakefront. In 1928 a group of real estate brokers at the 640 North Michigan branch of Baird & Warner determined to promote these buildings to an expanding wealthy class by publishing *Fine Apartment Homes.* This firm, which traces its history to 1855, before the Great Chicago Fire,[1] was confident enough of its prestige to include buildings managed by other firms as well.

The folio-sized hardcover book, embossed with gold-foliated ornament, immediately asserts its importance. And the luxuriousness and elegance of its design and production, including spectacularly printed endpapers, confirm this impression. The book functioned not only as a sales tool but also as an advertisement for the city itself: its unique geographic situation, its economic success, and its sophistication. The enthusiastic preamble declares: "No other city has ever chosen its location so fortunately as Chicago."[2]

The apartment houses listed stand north of the Chicago River and stretch beyond the city's limits to include Evanston. Nothing to the south, no matter how ambitious, is included.[3] Most of the book's eighty-three buildings were opened in a six-year period that antedated publication.[4] Neil Harris called this "an era of astounding legal, financial, architectural, and technological energy in Chicago."[5]

Each apartment receives an elegant layout; most occupy one page (a few obtain a double spread). Facade photographs (or sketches), opposite the address, sit atop a description that lauds the distinctive virtues of each structure, noting amenities, the surrounding neighborhood, and special features. These myriad conveniences include water-filtration systems, steel silver vaults, a golf course, extra maids' rooms, a chauffeur's room, and playrooms. The name of the architect (or architects) follows, and almost half a page is dedicated to the floor plans.

The descriptions provide a window into social structures and practice before the Crash. The text devoted to 6–12 East Scott Street notes: "The service quarters comprise two maids' rooms with their bath and open off a hall separating them from the kitchen. The servants' street entrance is from Scott Street and not from any court or alley. The ash, coal, and removal of waste is from an entrance on that alley." And not very coded language alludes to contemporary religious and ethnic restrictions. 227–237 East Delaware "fills a very definite demand for a residence of high type and with such restrictions as to attract the best families as tenants."[6]

The floor plans say much about the habits of privileged Chicagoans, or at least their dreams. That of Benjamin Marshall's 1550 North State Parkway is labeled in French: four "Chambre[s] de Domestique," a servants' "Salle a manger," and a separate "Office Maitre D'Hotel."[7] 900 Michigan Avenue North (now demolished) forecasts mixed-use developments of the late twentieth century, combining retail, two floors of small rentals, and a six-floor co-op.

Fine Apartment Homes represents much more than an extravagant sales brochure. It is a capsule of the values, concerns, aspirations, and increasing social segregation of a group of wealthy Chicagoans. Almost all of the buildings still stand, many of them now condominiums rather than cooperatives or rentals, housing Chicagoans who still prize gracious living, enjoying ample space, amenities, and views.

Each of the eighty-three apartment buildings featured in this appropriately lavish publication is allotted a page with a photograph of the building, a blurb, and a typical floor plan. The frontispiece illustrates a view of a stretch along Lake Shore Drive, a virtual wall of exclusive abodes that has come to symbolize Chicago's wealthiest population.

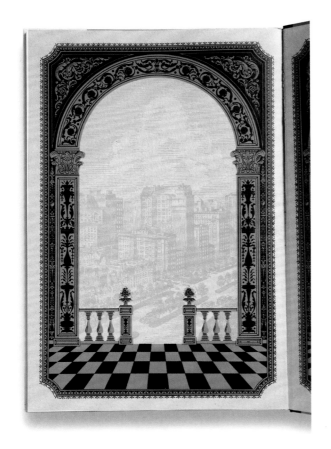

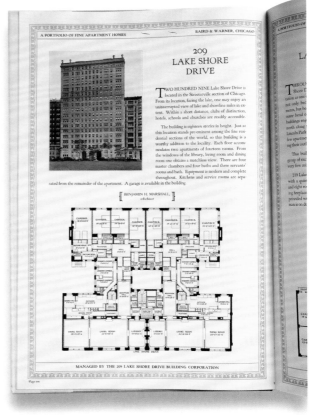

50

The Gold Coast and the Slum: A Sociological Study of Chicago's Near North Side[1]

HARVEY WARREN ZORBAUGH * CHICAGO
AND LONDON: THE UNIVERSITY OF
CHICAGO PRESS, 1929

Andrew Abbott

The Gold Coast and the Slum, by Harvey Warren Zorbaugh (1896–1965), is the most enduring monograph in the University of Chicago Press's thirty-five-volume Sociological Series, begun in 1925 by Robert E. Park and other members of the university's Sociology Department. The book sold 1,018 copies in its first three months (April to June 1929) and has remained in print continuously since.

Zorbaugh's biography explains little of how he came to write a best seller and sociological classic. Born in Cleveland, he earned an undergraduate degree at Vanderbilt in 1922 and spent the years 1922–25 doing graduate work under Park, Ellsworth Faris, and others in Chicago, living on the Near North Side for two years of that time. He became an assistant professor of education at New York University, where he spent a lifetime working on the problems of gifted children. Despite his book, he never got a PhD.

The Gold Coast and the Slum focuses on the adjacency of wealth and poverty on Chicago's Near North Side, the two separated by a "rooming house district."[2] In Zorbaugh's view, the city's social and geographical patterns reflect inevitable tension between the sharp group boundaries created by internal cohesion (be it ethnic, occupational, racial, or even age-based) and the boundary-breaking interconnections arising from the city's larger economic and social processes. Stability is merely apparent; change is reality. The book is based on extensive personal documents from Near North Side residents but also on historical documents, organizational archives, published material, governmental agency data, and interviews with residents, retailers, charities specialists, and many others. It also draws heavily on materials by Zorbaugh's fellow sociology students. Fifteen maps—important additional features—show the spatial distribution of everything from membership in the Fourth Presbyterian Church to origins of potter's-field burials. While the book is written in a fluid and even somewhat dramatic style, its extensive but well-presented data maintain the balance between popular and academic literature. The whole is enticing, readable, and also compelling.

Zorbaugh's audience certainly thought so. The university's press marketed the book heavily. But the wire services must have been responsible for the three packaged reviews that appeared very widely (the press's clipping service lists a total of seventy-two instances of these reviews): a short notice on the precariousness of "the 400" (high society);[3] a medium-sized version headlined "Murder Dwells at the Door of City Elite"; and a long piece on "How to Gate-Crash Society," based on the extensive list of "dos and don't's" included by some of Zorbaugh's elite respondents. The book sold 3,793 copies by 1935 and 6,412 by 1953.[4] In the 1950s it appeared in the first University of Chi-

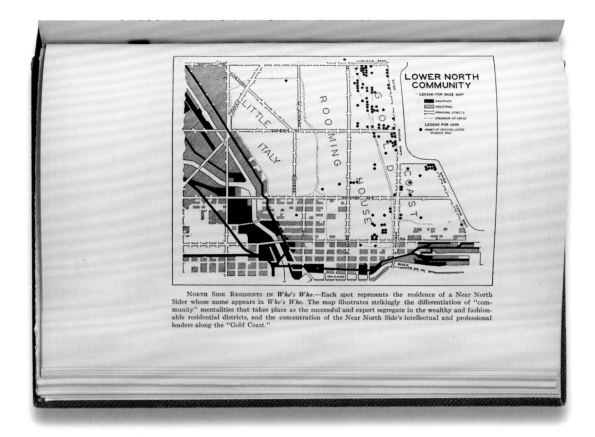

NORTH SIDE RESIDENTS IN *Who's Who.*—Each spot represents the residence of a Near North Sider whose name appears in *Who's Who.* The map illustrates strikingly the differentiation of "community" mentalities that takes place as the successful and expert segregate in the wealthy and fashionable residential districts, and the concentration of the Near North Side's intellectual and professional leaders along the "Gold Coast."

cago Press paperback series. But it remained in hardback as well, reaching its twelfth edition by 1969.

Scholarly success took longer. The book received only one or two periodical citations a year in the scholarly literature up through the 1970s, when sociologist Morris Janowitz's rehabilitation of the Chicago School of Sociology raised it to new visibility.[5] By 2008 *The Gold Coast* was up to ten to twelve citations a year. This new recognition reflected the book's status as an icon of the Chicago School, which, as the discipline has gradually internationalized, has become yet again the symbol for a sociology of substance and narrative, as opposed to one of surveys and quantitative analysis. Zorbaugh's compelling writing and rich data, and his analysis founded on the Chicago School themes of urban social psychology, community ecology, and social organization and disorganization, have made the book the exemplary monograph of the world's most famous sociological tradition.

Analyzing where educationally and economically privileged Chicagoans lived, alongside some of the city's most disadvantaged, this is one of the most influential titles of the Sociology Series published by the University of Chicago Press (see also nos. 39, 48, and 58). The series reflects the seminal role the university played in establishing a Chicago School of Sociology, which understood human behavior in terms of social and physical environments.

51

My Thirty Years' War: An Autobiography

MARGARET ANDERSON ∗ NEW YORK:
COVICI, FRIEDE PUBLISHERS, 1930

Liesl Olson

Margaret Anderson (1886–1973) titled the first of three volumes of her auto-biography *My Thirty Years' War*.[1] Anderson's account of her life—from leaving small-town Indiana for Chicago to the years when she edited the *Little Review*, a radical periodical she founded in Chicago in 1914, resembles a conversation with someone so self-possessed that her life seems more like a stage than a battle.

The book includes photos of Anderson and many of her literary and artistic peers—from Chicago (e.g., Carl Sandburg and Ben Hecht) to the European and expatriate American avant-garde (e.g., Constantin Brancusi and Ezra Pound). The book features a handsome modernist design, and typography by the fine-press printer S. A. Jacobs.

Anderson believed that an artist's personality—more than ideas or movements—is the impetus behind the most exciting writing, probably because she herself was mesmerizing. Statuesque, blonde, and blue-eyed, she was by all accounts beautiful. But her real charm was in making artists and writers feel her admiration. For example, the writer, dancer, and artist Mark Turbyfill, while still in high school, took some poems to Anderson. She turned him down but encouraged him to keep trying; three weeks later he returned with more poems, and she published one of them.[2]

For Anderson, art was naturally antipathetic to mainstream culture and the marketplace. In the first issue of the *Little Review*, she announced that the magazine was not connected with "any organization, society, company, cult or movement" but rather was "the personal enterprise of the editor."[3] She advocated a culture of youth and rebellion, and the *Little Review* became a forum for heated discussions between herself and artist Jane Heap, who in 1916 became her romantic partner and professional collaborator. "The quality of the L.R.," wrote Anderson, "its personality, the thing that set it apart from other magazines of its type was its reflection of these intense conflicts between its editors."[4]

The *Little Review* was not meant for the general public, but Anderson was herself an expert publicist. In 1914, trying to keep the *Little Review* afloat financially, she camped out on the Lake Michigan shore for six months to save rent—a stunt that brought much attention to the magazine. Writers Hecht and Maxwell Bodenheim walked miles to reach her and then pinned poems to her tent. She published the September 1916 issue with mostly blank pages, a dramatic protest of a lack of acceptable submissions and an advertisement for more.

But the greatest publicity came in 1920, when Anderson and Heap were charged with obscenity for serializing James Joyce's *Ulysses*. Their lawyer, the art collector John Quinn, told the women to remain "meek and silent" during the jam-packed trial in New York. Anderson thought it a bad strategy, "but, having promised, I sat still." The *Little Review* lost; Anderson and Heap were fined $100.[5]

In many ways *My Thirty Years' War* is a book about trials, experiments, and departures. On leaving Chicago for New York in 1917 with Heap, Anderson blithely concluded, "Chicago had had all it wanted from us, we had had all that it could give."[6] But Anderson sensed she had let go of something important in Chicago. She never adapted to the way people talked in New York, which to her felt less passionate, less animated. Paris as well "seemed so toned down." As she put it, "You feel too dazzling for the situation."[7] Refined and grown-up: this was not Chicago. Her first city was many things, but it was never old. Newness was Chicago's natural mode.

FACING Inspired by the 1913 exhibition at the Art Institute of Chicago of avant-garde art known as the Armory Show (see no. 35), Margaret Anderson founded the *Little Review*, a cutting-edge journal that championed radical change in the arts by publishing experimental writing and embracing cutting-edge art. She related the story of her tumultuous years publishing the journal in this, the first installment of her three-volume autobiography.

52

Chicago Gang Wars in Pictures: X Marks the Spot

[HAL ANDREWS] ✳ [ILLINOIS]: SPOT
PUBLISHING COMPANY, 1930[1]

William Mullen

More than big shoulders, Frank Lloyd Wright, or two great world's fairs, the standard reputation by which Chicago continues to be known around the globe is as the rollicking, booze-soaked Roaring Twenties city, its streets splattered with tommy-gun bullets and the blood of gangster wars. Fairly or not, the tawdry era of Al Capone and battling criminal gangs is the city's permanent legacy. Capone and a huge cast of sociopathic, homicidal tough guys such as "Machine Gun" Jack McGurn, "Little Hymie" Weiss, George "Bugs" Moran, and Samuel "Nails" Morton fought over huge fortunes made from selling bootleg Prohibition liquor. Though antiheroes, they figure as prominently in American folklore as Davy Crockett and Johnny Appleseed.

No published account better captures the gritty truth of that era than a rare little photographic book published in 1930, *Chicago Gang Wars in Pictures: X Marks the Spot*. Just sixty-four glossy pages in magazine format, it was the work of an enterprising journeyman Chicago reporter, Hal Andrews (1896–1961). Andrews covered crime for wire services and dailies during Chicago's most colorful, boisterous newspapering days, the "Front Page" era of Ben Hecht and Charles MacArthur fame that coincided with and chronicled the Prohibition wars.

While not much noted, Andrews, in full command of the gangster argot and Front Page journalistic idiom, infused his book with the rich flavor of the times. *X Marks the Spot* is a fast-paced tour of gang hideouts, crime scenes, and speakeasies, known as "thirst clinics" and "whoopee joints," the roughest ones patronized by "bootleggers, thugs and plug uglies."[2]

But the heart of the book is the stark black-and-white photographs—grisly assassination scenes showing the bloody, twisted corpses of gangsters—that Andrews bought from Chicago dailies. Squeamish newspaper editors until then had declined to publish pictures of bodies of slain thugs, instead running photos of empty crime scenes, an X marking the spot where the bodies had lain: thus the book's title. Andrews theorized that if people saw the gory reality of the violence, they would raise a hue and cry, "obliterating gangsters from the Chicago scene."[3]

Prohibition was in full flower when the book came out, and Andrews tabulated how the booze trade fed the rise of rampant crime. Enacted in 1919, Prohibition, he wrote, "made a swell law to break, the very best one on the book."[4] An estimated six to seven thousand speakeasies in the city and suburbs generated enormous profits for racketeers supplying alcohol and protection. Chief among them was Al Capone, heading the biggest gang, pulling in $70 million a year by 1926 from booze and beer operations. But disputes between rival gangs soon had them bombing one another's hideouts and speakeasies, hijacking delivery trucks, and shooting one another down, often publicly,

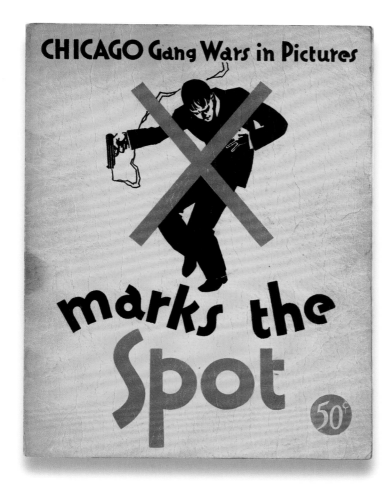

CHICAGO Gang Wars in Pictures

X marks the Spot

50¢

Hal Andrews, author of this survey of Chicago's most infamous criminals, is said to have first published *Chicago Gang Wars in Pictures* anonymously because he was afraid of reprisals from the underworld figures it exposed. Not for the faint of heart, this publication features bloody images of those violent decades that gave Chicago its reputation as the nation's crime capital.

even in the best neighborhoods. One rush-hour assassination occurred on a crowded sidewalk at Madison and Dearborn Streets. Two others, two years apart, took place directly in front of Holy Name Cathedral, center of the archdiocese, bullets pocking the church's stone.

"It begins with the murder of 'Diamond Jim' Colosimo at the dawn of prohibition," declared Andrews, "and it continues on up through the years, death by death, until the killers of Gangland finally graduated from murder to massacre on St. Valentine's Day, 1929."[5] Newspapers in Chicago and across the world ran photos of the massacre—seven bodies against a brick wall in a Chicago garage, slain by the Capone gang—conferring dubious fame on the city. It also scared Hal Andrews enough that he published *X Marks the Spot* anonymously, not taking credit for it until 1933.

53

Four American Books Campaign

Two Years before the Mast: A
Personal Narrative

RICHARD HENRY DANA JR. ✳
ILLUSTRATED BY EDW[ARD]. A. WILSON

Moby Dick, Or the Whale

HERMAN MELVILLE ✳ ILLUSTRATED BY
ROCKWELL KENT

Tales

EDGAR ALLAN POE ✳ ILLUSTRATED BY
W[ILLIAM]. A. DWIGGINS

Walden: Or Life in the Woods

HENRY DAVID THOREAU ✳ ILLUSTRATED
BY RUDOLPH RUZICKA

CHICAGO: THE LAKESIDE PRESS, 1930

Kim Coventry

While by the mid-1920s the design and production values of advertising materials, magazines, brochures, and other print products had become increasingly refined, books, especially in the literary genre, were neither well produced nor effectively marketed.[1] In 1926 the Chicago printing firm R.R. Donnelley & Sons seized the opportunity to fill this gap by positioning itself in this market, seeking as well to "add something to the philosophy of bookmaking" in America.[2]

Four American Books, as the bold and ambitious initiative came to be known, was the brainchild of Clarence Guy Littell (1882–1958), R.R. Donnelley's vice president and treasurer, and William A. Kittredge (1891–1945), head of the company's design and typography department.[3] The latter, a tastemaker and master typographer, had been hired in 1922 to make elegant graphic design synonymous with the company's identity and to imbue its advertising and its clients' products with a fresh aesthetic, one that married the book arts and industry.[4] A 1926 Donnelley advertising booklet stated, "Bookmaking at The Lakeside Press has become the fine thing it is because of the nice adjustment that has been struck between the craftsman and the machine."[5]

It had long been a Donnelley policy not to pursue publishing—its Lakeside Classics series (no. 24), launched two decades earlier, is not sold commercially—in order to avoid competing with clients. However, at the center of this advertising campaign was a publishing venture, which Kittredge predicted would create illustrated books that would set the standard for decades to come. The strategy, like that of the Classics series, was to demonstrate the company's ability to manufacture quality books on the same commercial equipment as long-run publications such as *Time* magazine, *Encyclopaedia Britannica*, mail-order catalogues for Sears, Roebuck (no. 8), and telephone directories (no. 9)—markets that Donnelley dominated.

A prepublication brochure for Four American Books claims that for each volume "the type will be set by machine, the paper made by machine, and the book printed in the regular book pressroom in the ordinary way on cylinder presses."[6] In addition, the volumes would involve an all-American cast of authors, illustrators, typographers, and manufacturing materials to full advantage.[7] Four artist-illustrators were asked to pick a title from a list of books that had never before been illustrated. W. A. Dwiggins (1880–1956) decided on Edgar Allan Poe's *Tales*; Rockwell Kent (1882–1971) selected Herman Melville's *Moby-Dick*;[8] Rudolph Ruzicka (1883–1978) opted for Henry David Thoreau's *Walden*; and Edward A. Wilson (1886–1970) chose Richard Henry Dana Jr.'s *Two Years before the Mast*.

The project was plagued by delays and the designers' demands. Dwiggins found the task daunting: "I knew that it was foolish to try to ornament Poe.

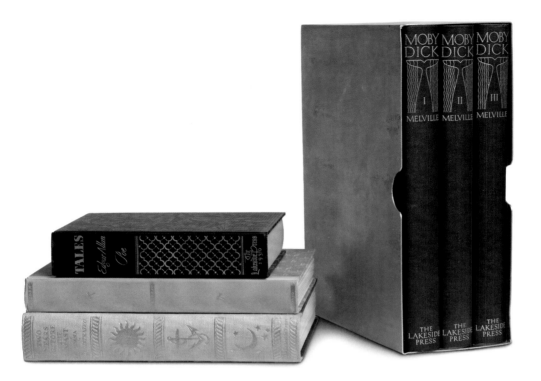

Nobody could hope to make pictures rich enough in weave to stand up beside the intricate embroidery of the text."[9] Kent designed a three-volume set in an aluminum slipcase, and some three hundred drawings, many full-page.[10] Wilson specified binding cloth from department stores (Lord & Taylor and Marshall Field's) rather than book manufacturing suppliers. Ruzicka determined it was necessary to decamp from Chicago for Concord, Massachusetts, to be near Walden Pond while completing his illustrations, which he did at Donnelley's expense.

Each title was printed in a limited edition of one thousand copies. *Moby Dick* sold out completely, and the other volumes, which did not do as well, were repackaged as Three American Books.[11] The campaign vastly expanded R.R. Donnelley's client base among book publishers and influenced the production and marketing of books. For the next several decades, Donnelley, and by extension Chicago, commanded a considerable position in the manufacture of mass-market books. The most lasting contribution of the undertaking, though, was Kent's *Moby Dick*. Still regarded as the definitive illustrated edition of this American classic, it positioned Chicago as a major center in the history of American book illustration, design, and production.

The Four American Books campaign was devised by Chicago's leading printing company, R.R. Donnelley, to expand its bookmaking business by proving that beautifully illustrated and produced books could be manufactured on commercial presses. Of the four novels selected, the most luxurious and ultimately the most collectible was Rockwell Kent's three-volume set of *Moby Dick* (see pp. 12–13).

54

Studs Lonigan: A Trilogy

JAMES T. FARRELL ∗ VOLUME 1, *YOUNG LONIGAN* ∗ VOLUME 2, *THE YOUNG MANHOOD OF STUDS LONIGAN* ∗ VOLUME 3, *JUDGMENT DAY* ∗ NEW YORK: THE VANGUARD PRESS, 1932 (VOL. 1), 1934 (VOL. 2), 1935 (VOL. 3)

Bruce Hatton Boyer

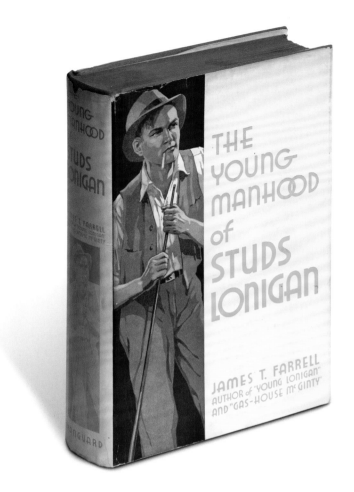

Ernest Hemingway famously wrote that "all modern American literature comes from one book by Mark Twain called *Huckleberry Finn.* . . . There has been nothing as good since."[1] He passed right over *Studs Lonigan.*

The epic trilogy by James T. Farrell (1904–79), published serially in the 1930s,[2] is surely our modern *Huckleberry Finn.* Both are picaresque journeys, Twain's a literal one down the Mississippi, Farrell's a constricted odyssey through Chicago's Irish South Side. Both are moral tales relayed with humor and irony: Twain's has the Duke and the Dauphin; Farrell's has the fatuous Father Gilhooley, Studs's bigoted father, his piously Catholic mother, and his hooligan street buddies.

What Hemingway most admired in *Huckleberry Finn* is also what makes *Studs Lonigan* so distinctive—its language. Twain was proud of his mastery of Mississippi River dialects, and Farrell was no less a master of the street jargon of 1920s and 1930s Chicago:

[Studs] took a close-up squint at his mug and decided that it, after all, was a pretty good mug, even if he almost had a sheeny's nose. He twisted his lip in sneers, screwed up his puss and imagined himself telling some big guy where to get off. He said, half aloud, see, bo, I don't take nobody's sass. And get this, bo, the bigger they are, de harder dey fall. See, bo![3]

It is little wonder that *Studs Lonigan*, with its slang and its depiction of blatant racism, anti-Semitism, and seamy sexual mores, was condemned when it first appeared, just as *Huckleberry Finn* has been disparaged. Unvarnished truth has a way of offending people.

Yet there is also a large difference between the two books. Twain made readers care about his hero because of—not in spite of—his rough-hewn virtues. Not so Farrell. Studs Lonigan can throw a verbal jab or a left hook with equal deftness but is never especially likable. Farrell lets readers know early on that Studs's grandiosity will doom him. We watch with equal measures of enjoyment and dread as the triumphant street fighter in *Young Lonigan* gives way to the lost man in *The Young Manhood of Studs Lonigan* until finally becoming the bitter alcoholic of *Judgment Day*:

Some day, some day, goddamn it, if he wouldn't make the f——n world take back everything it was doing to him. Some day he would make the world, and plenty of damn bastards in it, too, eat what he was eating, and in bigger doses. Some day, he, Studs Lonigan, was going to bust loose like hell on wheels, and when he did, look out, you goddamn world.[4]

Unlike Twain's hero, Farrell's struggles like a pinned insect against societal forces and constraints much stronger than he.

Studs Lonigan is impossible to imagine set anywhere else but Chicago. Farrell captured Carl Sandburg's "city of the big shoulders" (see no. 37) down to every gritty detail—the bars, pool halls, and coffee shops; the grim grayness of the South Side; the oppression of religious beliefs; the street corners, fights, and drunken brawls; the gangs and early deaths; the brothels and venereal disease: the dismal reality of the Great Depression. Chicago was Farrell's palette, and he painted life in the city with vivid strokes. Without James T. Farrell, American letters might not have produced Raymond Chandler, James M. Cain, Nelson Algren, Saul Bellow, and Philip Roth. And without *Studs Lonigan*, Chicago would not have had its most famous chronicler, a young University of Chicago Law School graduate-turned-actor who adopted the nickname by which he is known worldwide—Studs Terkel.

FACING Written in the depths of the Great Depression, this powerful tale, in three volumes, portrays the descent of an "average" Irish Catholic boy from South Side Chicago into an alcoholic adulthood, a descent that author James T. Farrell felt was inevitable given the destructive social forces of the spiritually empty society in which Studs Lonigan lived.

55

Esquire: The Magazine for Men

CHICAGO, 1933–50; NEW YORK,
1950–PRESENT

Teri J. Edelstein

On October 17, 1933, a large advertisement appeared on page 4 of the *Chicago Daily Tribune.* Its headline trumpets, "OUT TODAY and Gentlemen it leaves the Ladies flat!" An accompanying drawing depicts a disdainful beauty holding a lorgnette next to a man immersed in the first issue of a new quarterly magazine, *Esquire: The Magazine for Men.* An extensive text declares the publication's intended audience to be "a genuine adult male" who prefers "old wine and new stories," has a "healthy masculine taste for good clothes and strong language," likes "the inside on sports written by the men who have busted the records and not by some 'ghost writer,'" and would "rather read a brief saga by Ernest Hemingway than a sugar-coated tale of love in the suburbs." The possessors of such attributes are urged to procure a copy of this new magazine at men's shops, department stores, or newsstands before it sells out. Indeed, the entire first issue, of one hundred thousand copies—an astounding print run in its day—was quickly purchased.

The creators of this publishing phenomenon were the brothers David A. (1892–1952) and Alfred Smart (1895–1951), Arnold Gingrich (1903–76), and William H. Weintraub (1897?–1971).[1] Their new venture constituted an ambitious undertaking during the Depression.[2]

The same *Tribune* ad ran in the *New York Times* and the *Los Angeles Times*, revealing the founders' large national ambitions for the magazine. And those aspirations were immediately fulfilled. By December new ads announced that *Esquire* would now appear monthly.[3] The template for this success appears in the inaugural issue, a canny combination of serious and humorous writing on sports, politics, fashion, and travel. All is leavened with a healthy dose of sexual innuendo, especially in cartoons, sometimes featuring young women whose attributes are barely hidden.[4] The purported "lewd and lascivious" content led to a lawsuit in 1943, when the postmaster general asserted that the magazine had abused its favorable postal rate.[5] The case went to the Supreme Court, which found in 1946 that the First Amendment protected *Esquire*.[6] The magazine's contents created a precedent for another Chicago publishing phenomenon, *Playboy* (no. 77), created by Hugh Hefner, who had once worked for *Esquire*. But *Esquire* was a magazine one could legitimately say one read for the articles.

The first issue established the pattern of contributions by famous authors. In 1933 Gingrich met Ernest Hemingway, with whom he had corresponded as a collector of his works. Gingrich asked him to write for the forthcoming magazine, promising to double the fee he received from any other publication. Hemingway not only agreed but also aided the editor in soliciting other writers.[7] Hemingway, John Dos Passos, and Ring Lardner Jr. were featured in the first issue, along with, among others, Bobby Jones on golf and Gene Tunney on boxing. In the first decades of the magazine, the roster of distinguished authors also boasted Theodore Dreiser, F. Scott Fitzgerald, Graham Greene, Dashiell Hammett, Sinclair Lewis, Vladimir Nabokov (as Sirin), Luigi Pirandello, J. D. Salinger, Leon Trotsky, and Thomas Wolfe.[8]

From the first, *Esquire* included contributions by writers and artists from Chicago, but the magazine never fully venerated the city. For example, the Century of Progress exhibition, the greatest event in Chicago in 1933, features in the magazine only in the caption to a photograph, *The Cellophane Gown*, by Chicagoan Gilbert Seehausen. The text satirizes the visitors to the fair: "Bible-belt citizens coming to gasp—and gape . . . and returning, after a wondering examination of the multitudinous exhibits of science and the arts, with only this one memory sharp and clear: nudity and high buildings."[9] *Esquire*'s offices moved to New York in 1950; the magazine continues to publish to this day.

FACING Founded in Chicago in 1933, *Esquire* was published in the city for nearly twenty years before moving to New York. The contents of the suave men's magazine constituted a who's who of accomplished writers, photographers, and cartoonists. The January 1934 issue—the first to feature on the cover the magazine's personification, Esky—includes an essay by Ernest Hemingway, fiction by André Maurois, humor by Irving S. Cobb, and photographs by Margaret Bourke-White.

56

A Century of Progress International Exposition Chicago 1933–1934

[CHARLES D.] KAUFMANN & [HERMAN] FABRY; ARTHUR HERTZBERG & CRAFTSMEN ∗ [CHICAGO], 1933 OR 1934

Edward C. Hirschland

Chicago has a long history of holding its big celebrations in the wrong year. The World's Columbian Exposition, commemorating the four hundredth anniversary of the discovery of America in 1492 by Columbus, opened in 1893—off by a year. Millennium Park was built in honor of the start of the third millennium, which began in 2000.[1] It opened in 2004—off by four years.

What about A Century of Progress, which opened in 1933? Along with the rest of the world, Chicago was deep in the Great Depression. It was an opportune time to have a party to brighten the mood. And what better way than to stage a second world's fair, forty years after one of the great successes of the previous century, the World's Columbian Exposition (also known as the White City)?

The fair was to be the celebration of the hundredth anniversary—of what? Chicago was chartered as a city in 1837, so a centenary party would obviously have had to wait until 1937. However, Chicago was chartered as a town several times, once in 1833, which was the rationalization for the celebration. But in all honesty, it was a bit of a stretch.[2]

The theme of the fair was science and industrial development. In contrast to the White City, the 1933 fair was in magnificent color. Instead of the classical emphasis of the previous fair, this one featured the new style of architecture, art deco. Entertainment included the spectacular Skyride, which transported visitors 216 feet above the ground from the mainland to Northerly Island, the fair's site—landfill just off the shore of Lake Michigan between 12th Street (now Roosevelt Road) and 39th Street (Pershing Road). Another entertainment option was Sally Rand and her wildly popular fan dance. Eateries abounded. The fair was an enormous success, attracting about forty million visitors in the two seasons it was open. Thousands of books, maps, brochures, films, tourist guides, and the like were published both to promote and to describe the event. None, however, can match the beauty of the volume that is the subject of this entry, ironically a black-and-white presentation of a Technicolor fair.

A Century of Progress International Exposition Chicago 1933–1934 was the work of the company owned by Charles D. Kaufmann (1888–1948) and Herman Fabry (ca. 1880–1955), the fair's official photographers. Kaufmann was born to Jewish parents in Bohemia (now the Czech Republic), emigrated to the United States as a preteen, and took a job in 1901 as an errand boy for George R. Lawrence, a Chicago pioneer in aerial photography. In 1908 Kaufmann bought Lawrence's business and two years later was joined by Fabry, who had come to America from Germany as an infant.

Kaufmann and Fabry's book is unusual in that the fifty-one unnumbered pages are large silver gelatin photographs on heavy matte paper;[3] they are not printed reproductions of photographs. Each photo is identified by a caption handwritten in pencil.[4] The images tend to be more of architectural than of human interest. The binding is blue hard-grain morocco in a blue slipcase. The volume was bound in the Chicago shop of Arthur Hertzberg & Craftsmen, whose stamp appears on the inside front cover.[5]

Surprisingly little has been written about Kaufmann & Fabry—either the business or the men themselves. They claimed to have the most thoroughly equipped photographic plant in America.[6] We are lucky in the next century to have this splendid sample of their artistry and a magnificent souvenir of the Century of Progress.

Chicago's second world's fair, the 1933–34 Century of Progress, attracted an astonishing forty million visitors, despite the fact that people's discretionary income was so restricted during the Great Depression. Of the thousands of printed books and souvenirs produced around the fair, Kaufmann & Fabry's album of photographs is by far the most beautiful. Here we see the cutting-edge Nash Building and next to it the striking art-deco Transportation Building.

57

Down Beat

CHICAGO, 1934–PRESENT

Steve Tomashefsky

Jazz was not born in Chicago, but after 1918, when cornetist "King" Joe Oliver arrived from New Orleans, Chicago quickly became a major center of jazz creativity. Though many jazz artists achieved greatness in Chicago, the groundbreaking "Hot Five" and "Hot Seven" recordings by Louis Armstrong, who came in 1922, staked out the city's enduring claim as a key incubator of jazz talent.[1]

Chicago's central role in jazz history was bolstered in 1934, when Albert Lipschultz (1896–1979), an insurance salesman who cultivated a clientele among musicians, founded *Down Beat* magazine to expand his market. Lipschultz did not remain involved for long; within a year he sold the publication, after the formidable head of Chicago Musicians Union Local 10, James C. Petrillo, fearing competition for influence among union members, suggested he stick with insurance.

Down Beat's editor, Glenn Burrs (1897–1972), purchased the magazine for $1,500. Burrs hired a staff of writers whose work is still regarded as the foundation of American jazz journalism, including George Avakian, Stanley Dance, Dave Dexter, Leonard Feather, John Hammond, Helen Oakley, and many others.

There were jazz publications in Europe and some jazz journalism in mainstream American media, but *Down Beat* was the first periodical in the United States devoted to the topic. Early mastheads promised "Music News from Coast to Coast," covering "Ballroom, Cafe, Radio, Studio, Symphony, Theatre." *Down Beat*'s early pages were salted with showbiz slang and gossip. Most of the advertising came from musical instrument manufacturers, suggesting that the core readership comprised musicians and students. Photos of leggy "girl" singers featured frequently.

Unlike the union, *Down Beat* was never exclusionary.[2] From the start, it covered important African American innovators. To be sure, its 1939 readers' poll for members of an all-star band identified each winner as "(W)" or "(N)" to make sure readers did not miss that valuable information.[3] Chicago native and Hull-House alumnus Benny Goodman (W) was *Down Beat*'s first jazz superstar, but several *Down Beat* writers, most notably John Hammond (Goodman's brother-in-law), devoted many pages to African American artists.

In 1950 the magazine changed hands again. Burrs was deeply in debt to his printer, John Maher, who took ownership in lieu of payment. Maher (1899–1968) introduced many changes, including a substantial focus on jazz education and expanded attention to record reviews.

Probably *Down Beat*'s most important role in Chicago was its early coverage of the Association for the Advancement of Creative Musicians (AACM), a Chicago group that coalesced around pianist Muhal Richard Abrams in

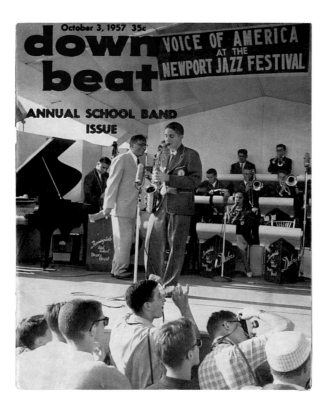

For over eighty years *Down Beat* has covered the world of jazz, highlighting this music scene in Chicago as well as nationally and beyond. The magazine has featured everything from outstanding high-school bands, as the cover of the October 3, 1957, issue demonstrates, to the Newport Jazz Festival. It remains to this day one of Chicago's most important periodicals.

the early 1960s. *Down Beat* never shied away from reporting what was new and controversial, including bebop in the 1940s and Ornette Coleman's near-atonal sounds in the late 1950s. But AACM members took that musical "freedom principle" (as *Down Beat* critic John Litweiler called it) to another level, while mixing in elements of African and Eastern music.[4] *Down Beat* gave AACM members national exposure when they were almost unknown outside Chicago.[5]

Since Maher's death, ownership of the magazine has continued in the family, though it is rumored that Hugh Hefner tried to buy it.[6] *Down Beat* remains based in metropolitan Chicago (in suburban Elmhurst) and is among the area's most important national periodicals.[7] Though many consider New York the center of jazz culture, *Down Beat*'s presence has helped to keep a spotlight on its hometown. As longtime *Down Beat* writer Howard Mandel wrote, "Jazz in the Windy City is carried out the Chicago Way: veterans pave the way for innovators; experimentalists and mainstreamers form supportive communities, and everyone values practicality, originality and integrity."[8] *Down Beat* has been a local institution every step of the Chicago way. Few music publications have gauged their readership so well and retained it for so long.

58

The Tenements of Chicago, 1908–1935

EDITH ABBOTT ∗ CHICAGO: THE
UNIVERSITY OF CHICAGO PRESS, 1936

Henry C. Binford

In Chicago's long history of activism aimed at improving the housing of poor citizens, *The Tenements of Chicago, 1908–1935* represents both a culmination and a bridge to new strategies. On the one hand, it is a monument to the extraordinary group of researchers and reformers gathered at Hull-House and the University of Chicago at the turn of the twentieth century. On the other, it is a product of the Great Depression and a justification for the new housing strategies introduced at the federal level in the 1930s. The book, which was reviewed in publications across the nation, was a clear indication of the leading roles Chicago academics and reformers would play in shaping the New Deal's policies.

Edith Abbott (1876–1957), who earned a PhD from the university in 1905, lived at Hull-House from 1908 until 1920. She and her equally talented sister, Grace, enjoyed the tutelage of Jane Addams, Julia Lathrop, and other, older settlement residents. The sisters worked together frequently. Edith's adult life was also almost inseparable from that of her mentor, colleague, collaborator, and life companion Sophonisba Breckinridge. When the three of them taught at the university's School of Social Service Administration, their students referred to them as "A2B."

Edith Abbott's book on tenements emerged from long-term projects of housing investigation and reform that became part of the agenda of Hull-House soon after it was founded. In 1892 Florence Kelley did door-to-door canvassing nearby, producing statistics used in the federal report *Slums of Great Cities* (1894) and in *Hull-House Maps and Papers* (1895). Robert Hunter, also working from Hull-House, wrote *Tenement Conditions in Chicago* (1901). In 1908 Abbott and Breckinridge renewed the research. With their students, they prowled Chicago's working-class neighborhoods and generated a stream of master's theses and articles about housing.

When the Depression hit and national discussion turned to housing issues, Abbott, Breckinridge, and their former students updated their older material. *The Tenements of Chicago* is thus in part a synopsis of progressive-housing research and reform. Half of the book's sixteen chapters are either authored or coauthored by members of the Abbott–Breckinridge team from twenty years earlier. However, the last few chapters, devoted explicitly to Depression challenges, showcase New Deal ideas and policies that went considerably beyond Progressive Era initiatives. Insisting that private housing could not meet the needs of the deprived, the book became a clarion call for an expanded federal program of slum clearance, coupled with new buildings to house those displaced. Some of the ideas championed in it would be embodied in the United States Housing Act of 1937. In addition to chapters reflecting the work that Edith Abbott and her students had done for decades on housing, *Tenements* deals with the problems of mothers, children, low-wage workers, immigrants, and African Americans. The book is held together by her strong voice, demonstrating her astonishing ability to move smoothly back and forth between cold data and fiery advocacy.

During the 1930s Abbott suffered the loss of several women who had nurtured her career: Julia Lathrop and Florence Kelley died in 1932; Jane Addams in 1935; and her sister, Grace, in 1939. She took some comfort from the construction in Chicago of two early examples of federally subsidized low-income housing and the naming of them for Lathrop and Addams. But she knew these were tiny actions when matched against need. Unlike many commentators on poor housing in the 1930s and long after, she recognized that any successful effort to get rid of tenements or slums required attention to inadequate wages and housing supply—a program of subsidy and social reform "on a really vast scale," not just deploying the bulldozers.[1] She also recognized that racial discrimination, which New Deal programs would reinforce, was in itself a barrier to housing progress.

FACING This study, one of the titles in the University of Chicago's Sociology Series (see also nos. 39, 48, and 50), surveys the terrible housing conditions in which Chicago's poorest citizens lived, highlighting the inadequacy of the city's attempts to improve conditions and the limitations of even the most enlightened private initiatives.

59

The Higher Learning in America

ROBERT MAYNARD HUTCHINS * NEW
HAVEN: YALE UNIVERSITY PRESS;
LONDON: HUMPHREY MILFORD, OXFORD
UNIVERSITY PRESS, 1936

John W. Boyer

FACING Robert Maynard Hutchins, seen here in an undated photograph, led the University of Chicago for two decades. In this book he outlined his belief that the purpose of a university education is to absorb civilizations' greatest achievements rather than prepare for a career. While responses to his ideas were mixed, his influence on the university's curriculum and on the national dialogue about the purposes of higher education was profound.

The Higher Learning in America, given as the Storrs Lectures at Yale University in 1935, was the most important attempt by Robert Maynard Hutchins (1899–1977) to diagnose and provide a cure for what he elsewhere called the "information disease" afflicting higher education in the United States.[1] In this accessible booklet of one hundred pages, Hutchins advanced the claim that universities alone have the ability in our society to pursue truth for its own sake. Yet in addition, we also—mistakenly—ask universities to train students for productive work beyond the academy. Hutchins believed that such vocationalism drives out the pursuit of truth, substituting the gathering of useful information for genuine inquiry. With vocationalism removed, universities could devote themselves to the cultivation of intellectual virtues through study of humankind's greatest achievements. Hutchins seemed fixed upon the university's responsibility to protect a discursive tradition of what his colleague Joseph J. Schwab later called "ultimate goals," a culture of permanent moral values.[2]

The Higher Learning in America was published at a key point in Hutchins's tenure as president of the University of Chicago, which stretched from 1929 to 1945, after which he served as chancellor until 1951. Witty, handsome, and charismatic, Hutchins had come to Chicago at age thirty from Yale as a rising star in higher education, though he lacked clear curricular ideas. Under the influence of his friend Mortimer Adler, he soon began to articulate the kind of educational vision suitable for the president of a major research university. By the later 1930s, Hutchins articulated a systematic approach to education, for which he owed a great debt to Adler and to their dialogue with a resistant faculty. A skillful writer and compelling orator, Hutchins summoned that vision in *The Higher Learning* to convey what he saw as the dangerous curricular incoherence of the modern university.

The curricular implications of the book were profound. Hutchins gave great weight to classical, humanistic, and philosophical study and was suspicious of specialized research as a useful component of undergraduate education. If mass education was to do more than train technical and professional elites for their careers, it would need a cultural and intellectual mission to replace the nineteenth-century classical curriculum, which had been thoroughly undermined by growing enrollments, the development of modern science, and the professionalization of scholarship. In practice this led to the establishment of the Great Books courses at the University of Chicago (no. 73), which Hutchins cotaught with Adler, and to the introduction and expansion of the general undergraduate curriculum in 1930s and 1940s, which would evolve into the college's distinctive Core. Both stimulated intense debate on campus. While Hutchins did win converts, there were many opponents on the university's faculty.[3]

The struggles between Hutchins and his enemies emblematized a collision of two curricular movements in liberal education. Hutchins's opponents sought to use leading works of the modern social and natural sciences, grounded in a strong historical perspective, to define a world of general knowledge that would prove useful for modern citizenship. In contrast, Hutchins sought to recover from the best classic works a more coherent but introspective vision of learning, stressing the skills of the individual student. Both constituted improvements over the curricular chaos of the 1910s and 1920s, and both resonated powerfully in the American academy.

In laying out Hutchins's vision of higher education, *The Higher Learning* broadcast the dynamism of the University of Chicago to a popular audience, amplifying its national influence. It also turned Hutchins into a national celebrity—a rarity among college presidents.

60

A History of Chicago

BESSIE LOUISE PIERCE ∗ VOLUME 1,
THE BEGINNING OF A CITY, 1673–1848
∗ VOLUME 2, *FROM TOWN TO CITY,
1848–1871* ∗ VOLUME 3, *THE RISE OF A
MODERN CITY, 1871–1893* ∗ NEW YORK:
ALFRED A. KNOPF, 1937 (VOL. 1); 1940
(VOL. 2); 1957 (VOL. 3)

Perry R. Duis

Bessie Louise Pierce (1886–1974) arrived in Chicago from Iowa in the fall of 1929. The first PhD student of Arthur Schlesinger Sr., a professor of American social and urban history at the University of Iowa, she had joined that school's faculty and had written three influential volumes on the role of noneducational lobbying groups in shaping schools in the United States. However, her master's-degree work at the University of Chicago attracted the attention of that institution's social science faculty, who decided that they needed someone trained in history to help them better understand Chicago. Pierce insisted on assembling her own research staff—easily done in the sinking economy of the Depression—and commenced work on a multivolume History of Chicago Project.

Chicago history books at that time were generally of two types: "mug" books, compilations of biographical sketches preceded by historical narratives designed to please civic boosters; and accounts of "comically criminal Chicago," a world of colorful scoundrels who have become a part of the city's international image (see no. 52). Pierce instead aimed to examine the city's past using objective scholarship without sensationalism, in effect paving the way for modern urban history. This social science approach alone made *A History of Chicago* a pioneering work. A few historians, most notably Milo Quaife, had begun to apply the tools of modern research to the early Illinois history. But no one had ever tried to tackle a place as large and complex as nineteenth-century Chicago.

The project first produced *As Others See Chicago* (1933), a scholarly collection of travelers' accounts.[1] Pierce drew back from examining earliest Chicago, deferring to Quaife's *Chicago and the Old Northwest, 1673–1835* (1913), which functioned as a prequel to her work. Instead, her first volume examines the land speculations of the 1830s and ends with the arrival of railroads in 1848. The second volume concludes with the Great Fire of 1871, and the third moves the narrative to the World's Columbian Exposition of 1893. The fourth, never completed, was to cover developments from 1893 to 1915, including Chicago's emergence as the nation's Second City and the attempts to reform the tempestuous metropolis. Pierce also contemplated a fifth, which would take the story up to the Depression.

Pierce's assistants pored through manuscripts and tens of thousands of newspaper articles. From their reports on the various subjects, Pierce would draft chapters. The influence of Schlesinger was clear in the inclusion of such social and cultural topics as everyday life and the role of women and immigrants. But the Depression doubtless contributed to the excessive treatment of economic topics, which became an increasingly dominant part of each subsequent volume. Page after page of detail about industries and trade displace the descriptions of domestic life, and especially the evolving ethnic neighborhoods, which are virtually ignored.

While the popular press expressed well-deserved awe at the detail and complexity of each volume, by the time the third appeared, in 1957, academic reviewers gently castigated Pierce for the complete lack of ideas. The new field of urban history, in its infancy in the late 1950s, was in search of cohesive, city-oriented interpretations of American history instead of the narratives Pierce offered. Her project—once considered groundbreaking for its scholarship and coverage of social history—had gone on so long without change that it was now criticized for being outmoded in approach.

Pierce struggled without success to complete the fourth volume, her advancing age, loss of staff, and the difficulties of obtaining grant support taking their toll.[2] She closed down the project and moved back to Iowa City, where she died. Her three-volume work—the first scholarly history of a major American city—remains her monument.[3]

Bessie Louise Pierce's ambitious three-volume history (a planned fourth volume was not realized) was groundbreaking not only for its scope and degree of detail but also for its objective, sociological approach to the development of the nation's second-largest city.

61

Illinois: A Descriptive and Historical Guide

American Guide Series

COMPILED AND WRITTEN BY THE
FEDERAL WRITERS' PROJECT OF THE
WORK PROJECTS ADMINISTRATION FOR
THE STATE OF ILLINOIS ∗ CHICAGO: A. C.
MCCLURG & CO., 1939

John Blew

The Federal Writers' Project (FWP) was created in August 1935 as a small part of the Works Progress Administration (WPA), the most ambitious of the New Deal government programs aimed at alleviating mass unemployment resulting from the Great Depression. A separate unit in each of the then forty-eight states (and one for New York City) reported to a central staff in Washington, DC. During its eight-year existence (1935–43), the FWP employed thousands of out-of-work writers, researchers, photographers, cartographers, clerks, and typists who collectively engaged in a bewildering variety of projects. The centerpiece, however, was the compilation and publication of a comprehensive historical and descriptive guide to each of the states (plus Alaska, Puerto Rico, and the District of Columbia), the aptly named American Guide Series.[1]

Each guide followed the same tripartite organization: a series of introductory essays on various historical, physical, economic, and cultural aspects of the state (fourteen in the Illinois *Guide*); detailed guides to those cities and towns in the state deemed most important (seventeen in the Illinois *Guide*); and individual road tours (twenty-seven in the Illinois *Guide*), designating the mileage from point to point and describing the highlights of each town, no matter how small or remote, and every natural or historical point of interest along the route. The FWP followed a policy of anonymity, so with few exceptions it is not possible to attribute to any particular author any part of the guides. Nevertheless, the Illinois unit employed some of the country's finest writers. Among them were Nelson Algren, Saul Bellow, Jack Conroy, Sam Ross, and Studs Terkel. A particularly strong cadre of African American members of the Illinois unit included Arna Bontemps, Katherine Dunham (before she became an accomplished dancer), Willard Motley, Margaret Walker, Frank Yerby, and, notably, Richard Wright. All of those writers lived in Chicago at some point.[2]

A freestanding guide to Chicago was started by the Illinois Project but was never completed. However, Chicago dominates the Illinois *Guide*. At 116 pages, its section is by far the most comprehensive in the volume. (The next-largest such city guide, to Rockford, contains just 10 pages.) The Chicago section is divided into nine geographic parts, each accompanied by a map (Loop and Vicinity, Grant Park, Near North Side, Lincoln Park, North and Northwest Side, West Side, Jackson Park, University of Chicago, and South Side).

The guide to Chicago focuses on important and obscure institutions, buildings, monuments, and other points of interest. Descriptions are often detailed but never boring. They are as interesting for the places now gone or repurposed as for what remains today. Who knew, for example, that the training ship used by the Illinois naval reserve at the time was the remodeled excursion steamer *Eastland*, on which occurred Chicago's most appalling disaster when the ship capsized in July 1915 in the Chicago River, drowning more than eight hundred persons?

There had been many previous guides to Chicago, but they were typically confined to its central area, tended to be superficial or of the booster variety, and were often issued in support of important events such as its two world's fairs (1893 and 1933–34). The Illinois *Guide*, like the others in the American Guide Series, contains no ephemeral "where to eat, where to stay" or similar recommendations. It was intended to be of enduring value. Its numerous reprints and revised editions are evidence of its success in that regard. The noted radio personality and writer Studs Terkel is quoted on the back of the 1983 reprint: "Don't hit the streets of Chicago—or anywhere else in Illinois—without this book."[3] While much has changed in the city since 1939, this Chicago guide remains relevant and useful to resident and tourist alike.

FACING Chicago-based writers Nelson Algren, Saul Bellow, and Richard Wright were among the many working on the Illinois volume of the American Guide Series, funded by the Federal Writers' Project during the Great Depression. The large section devoted to Chicago—116 pages—offers a thorough survey of places and structures. Even though many no longer exist, the book remains an informative read. Seen here is an advertisement for the *Guide*.

62

Native Son

RICHARD WRIGHT, AUTHOR OF *UNCLE TOM'S CHILDREN* ✳ NEW YORK AND LONDON: HARPER & BROTHERS PUBLISHERS, 1940

Davarian L. Baldwin

"Brrrrrriiiiiiiiiiiiiiiiiiinng." An abrasive alarm clock awakens the Thomas family to their "dark and silent" piece of inhumanity. The family is cramped into a small corner of Chicago's overcrowded South Side black community. Confined to a one-room kitchenette apartment, the two sons search for a place to avert their eyes as mother and sister quickly dress. Then a foot-long rat fills up any space that may be left for modesty, and the family jumps into action. The older son, Bigger, stands toe to toe with the rat, both baring their teeth as the only logical response to being cornered with nowhere to hide. Driven by fear, the rat emits a "long thin song of defiance" before Bigger kills it with a skillet. The boys regard the carcass of their formidable adversary with "awed admiration."[1] Trapped and terrified and therefore dangerous and defiant, Bigger is that rat. And so opens Richard Wright's *Native Son.* In this masterwork, Wright offered a protest novel wrapped in psychological thriller, and it became an instant best seller.[2]

The alarm clock also awakened America to the "accumulated injustice of the past" and its "lasting penalties."[3] With his unrelenting and pleading rage, Bigger Thomas challenged all acceptable representations of blackness. For Wright, Bigger was the literal native son of a "dislocated society; he is a dispossessed and disinherited man."[4] Wright, according to Lawrence Jackson, dared to "take the story of a black twenty-year-old reform school thug from Chicago's South Side, have him murder two women, and give him the standing of a tragic hero."[5] But as Wright rose to international prominence and cultivated his own "exile" status, it was easy to lose sight of how much *Native Son* is profoundly rooted in Chicago's Bronzeville community.[6]

The Mississippi-born Wright (1908–60) moved to Chicago in 1927, staying for ten years before decamping to New York. He saw Chicago as a "city of extremes" on a "new and terrifying plane of consciousness."[7] On the one hand, he encountered fresh possibilities within the black South Side Writers Group and the Communist Party's John Reed Club. On the other, he was ensnared by the looming specter of life in kitchenettes, which he called "our prison, our death sentence without a trial."[8]

When Bigger finally gets a break from his family's claustrophobic lodgings, he is further taunted by the city's "sense of possible achievement" as he gazes longingly at an airplane overhead.[9] His feeling of confinement is clearest when he works for a wealthy white family. He soon realizes that while the Daltons live only a few streets over, their "high, black, iron picket fence" confirms that they exist a world away.[10] Bigger's discomfort and racial shame in this new world condition him to lower his eyes, stoop his shoulders, tiptoe around, and answer "yessum" and "yessuh" in hushed tones.[11] His accidental murder of Mary Dalton infuses him with a sense of freedom and "terrified pride" because he has done the unexpected.[12]

Bigger's murderous turn was not to be celebrated, but for Wright his brutal rampage was a revolt against submission and "American oppression."[13] The author offered no easy resolutions. But in the world that produced Bigger, Wright perceived a "prophecy of our future."[14] To be sure, the tangled mix of the character's fear and defiance against a continual "dream deferred" can be found in both today's youth violence and their uprisings against police brutality.[15] We cannot forget that Bigger's ferocious rebuke erupted in "the urban environment of Chicago," where a "sense of possible achievement" became nothing more than a "taunting" mockery in the face of greater systems of submission and containment.[16] With such an insult, Bigger surmised, "They wouldn't let me live and I killed . . . what I killed for I am!"[17] What will we say to the Biggers of today?

FACING Trapped within a frame of beige, the narrow image of *Native Son*'s main character, Bigger Thomas, standing in a ghetto alley, expresses the socioeconomic and racial constraints that led inexorably to his tragic fate. This powerful dust-jacket design was the work of illustrator Richard Floethe (1901–88).

63

Forty-Four Cities in the City of Chicago

CHICAGO: THE CHICAGO PLAN
COMMISSION, 1942

Michael P. Conzen

Daniel Burnham's celebrated 1909 *Plan of Chicago* (no. 29) may have been the city's first comprehensive urban-planning document, but its panoptic scale left much of the city's internal sociogeographical character largely undefined. Even the formulation of the 1923 land-use zoning regulations, with their detailed block-level maps, treated the city as an essentially single spatial entity. The reorganization of the Chicago Plan Commission in 1939, the creation of a professional research unit, and the intensive planning process that led to the zoning revisions of 1942 finally brought official recognition that Chicago was a city of distinctive neighborhoods, not just a casual amalgam of political wards. Since the 1920s, University of Chicago sociologists had conceptually identified and defined "community areas" based on groupings of contiguous census tracts with similar social aspects, bounded by topographical margins such as rivers and railroads. But it took the commission's book, *Forty-Four Cities in the City of Chicago*, to give full voice and civic authority to the notion that Chicago's population resided in and contributed to the ever-changing character of many highly particular districts whose specific circumstances—indeed, their holistic geographical character—demanded nuanced responses from urban planners.

To counter any perception that the new planning involved a one-size-fits-all approach, the commission's research staff issued this earnest, descriptive summary of the history, character, and current condition of Chicago's chief districts, which it likens to forty-four "cities" within the city. Drawing on the vast cache of information provided by the 1939–41 Chicago Land Use Survey, the book provided for the first time a set of comprehensive, professionally researched, and officially sanctioned essays on the evolution, spatial structure, and planning challenges of these districts.

Forty-Four Cities is a conceptual product of Homer Hoyt (1895–1984), the commission's director of research. An influential land economist and real estate expert, Hoyt had forged a career at the Federal Housing Administration before joining the Chicago commission. His approach in this book was to combine the city's seventy-five already recognized, but in many ways statistically arbitrary, "community areas" into a more coherent group of larger districts for descriptive purposes. Hoyt authored sixteen of the resulting forty-four pithy essays, most of which run two to three pages in length, some with occasional photographs, while the remainder were written by other members of his interdisciplinary research team. Real estate economists Albert E. Dickens (1904–83) and Helen C. Monchow (1898–1950) contributed seven apiece, geographer Harold M. Mayer (1916–94) five essays, and other staffers the rest.

The essays represent "thick" description of their districts, infusing statistics of population and housing conditions with broader discussions—most

FORTY-FOUR CITIES
In the CITY of CHICAGO

THE CHICAGO PLAN COMMISSION, 20 N. Wacker Drive, Chicago, Ill. . . . April, 1942

of them singularly perceptive—of land-use characteristics and cultural features. Many districts in 1942 were largely residential, others heavily industrial, with commercial corridors the sinews binding them together. Underlying all essays is a concern for condition and imagined stability, with an eye to the incidence of "substandard" housing that should be addressed through planning action. The close ties of the Land Use Survey and the plan commission to the real estate industry explain the inclination to blame poor housing conditions on abstract overcrowding and generic economic conditions rather than slumlordism, redlining, and other failings of city governance and the social polity, particularly in neighborhoods undergoing racial change. "Creeping blight" was the watchword, hinting at possibilities for physical renewal—music to the ears of developers, notwithstanding the historical record of never-sufficient affordable housing on a citywide scale. Nevertheless, the essays succeed in revealing the immense physical and social diversity of Chicago's neighborhoods at the end of the Great Depression, suggesting the geographical subtleties in the city's fabric that future planners should act upon and not dismiss. As such, the volume takes its place as a foundational contribution to understanding Chicago.

The product of a newly reformed Chicago Plan Commission, *Forty-Four Cities in the City of Chicago* underscores the multiplicity of cultures that constitute the Midwest's largest metropolis. The authors urged planners to respect the diverse nature of Chicago's communities as they considered the future. While populations have changed and shifted since this book appeared over seventy-five years ago, the city remains one of many neighborhoods.

64

A Street in Bronzeville

GWENDOLYN BROOKS ∗ NEW YORK
AND LONDON: HARPER & BROTHERS
PUBLISHERS, 1945

Sara Paretsky

A Street in Bronzeville, Gwendolyn Brooks's first collection of poetry, appeared when she was twenty-eight, but the woman who went on to become one of North America's most important poets was already writing with assurance and authority. The poems, some poignant, some amusing, others harsh, depict experiences that any reader can share, but there is an edge to them as well, born of the segregated Chicago that Brooks inhabited.

Brooks (1917–2000) spent her entire life in Bronzeville, the heart of Chicago's black South Side.[1] Stretching from roughly Twenty-Second to Sixty-Seventh Street, between Cottage Grove and State Street, it was a deliberately contrived black ghetto, the result of the restrictive housing covenants created by the Chicago Association of Realtors.[2] CAR waited for population density on a given block to reach five people per room on average before opening up an adjoining block for black occupancy. Schools were so overcrowded that the city ran two half-day shifts rather than building new schools or integrating white schools.[3] Bronzeville had six times the mortality rate from tuberculosis in white neighborhoods and double the infant mortality rate.[4]

The streets Brooks walked and the people she knew were thus trying to keep their dignity or to find pleasure in life in the middle of highly stressful circumstances. This history gives an edge to poems such as the sonnet "kitchenette building":

> We are things of dry hours and the involuntary plan,
> Grayed in, and gray, "Dream" makes a giddy sound, not strong
> Like "rent," "feeding a wife," "satisfying a man."
>
> But could a dream send up through onion fumes
> Its white and violet, fight with fried potatoes
> And yesterday's garbage ripening in the hall,
> Flutter, or sing an aria down these rooms
>
> Even if we were willing to let it in,
> Had time to warm it, keep it very clean,
> Anticipate a message, let it begin?
>
> We wonder. But not well! not for a minute!
> Since Number Five is out of the bathroom now,
> We think of lukewarm water, hope to get in it.

Brooks had been writing poetry since childhood. Her mother, Keziah, took her writing seriously, saying she would become a "lady Paul Laurence Dunbar."[5] Keziah Brooks released her young daughter from most household

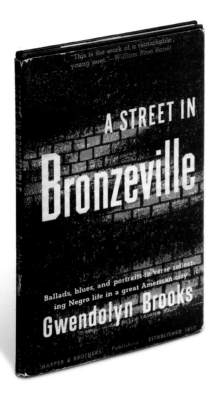

chores so that she could focus on her writing. Brooks was essentially self-taught. Her juvenilia include ardent imitations of Wordsworthian effusions on nature, but she rapidly moved to a more authentic voice after seeking advice from writers James Weldon Johnson and Langston Hughes, whose work she had long admired. Johnson advised her to study modernist poets such as T. S. Eliot.[6]

Brooks was part of a vital artistic scene in Chicago that was as dynamic as the Harlem Renaissance. However, writers such as Brooks did not portray the idealized relations between men and women that appear in such Harlem poets' work as Countee Cullen's. As Gary Smith pointed out, *Bronzeville* includes "the biting ironies of intraracial discrimination, . . . the devaluation of love [that society imposes on Black heterosexual relations] and . . . the suffering of poor Black women."[7]

Mainstream reviews from the *New York Times* to the *New Yorker* and the *Chicago Tribune* were enthusiastic about *A Street in Bronzeville;* Paul Engle wrote in the *Tribune* that Brooks had a "deep and imaginative talent, without relying on the facts of color to draw sympathy and interest."[8] While this is a startling statement, since the "facts of color" permeate the whole collection, Engle was right about Brooks's deep talent. The poems are complex and amazing and continue to jolt readers more than seventy years after their publication.

The strength, pain, love, alienation, humor, and resilience of the denizens of Bronzeville—a center of African American life where Gwendolyn Brooks, seen here in a 1950 photograph, grew up—are powerfully expressed in this poetic walk through the vital, if blighted, neighborhood on Chicago's South Side.

65

Black Metropolis: A Study of Negro Life in a Northern City

ST. CLAIR DRAKE AND HORACE R. CAYTON ✳
INTRODUCTION BY RICHARD WRIGHT ✳ NEW
YORK: HARCOURT, BRACE AND COMPANY,
1945

William Julius Wilson

Since the early twentieth century, Chicago has been a laboratory for the scientific investigation of the historical, social, and economic forces that shape urban neighborhoods. Social scientists associated with the University of Chicago—referred to as the Chicago School of Urban Sociology—conducted much of that research. By the mid-twentieth century, they had popularized the view that immigrant slums and the social problems that characterized them were temporary conditions in a cycle of inevitable progress. According to that view, the same process—initial conflict, followed by accommodation, and ultimately by assimilation—would also be the experience of the latest group of migrants: African Americans.

A fundamental revision of the Chicago framework appeared in 1945 with the publication of *Black Metropolis: A Study of Negro Life in a Northern City* by St. Clair Drake (1911–90) and Horace Cayton (1903–70). Drake and Cayton were among the small but growing number of African Americans drawn to sociology in the 1930s and 1940s. Drake would spend over two decades teaching at Roosevelt University and later at Stanford. Cayton's professional activities included teaching at Fisk University, researching, and journalism.

In *Black Metropolis*, Drake and Cayton first examined African American progress in employment, housing, and social integration, using census, survey, and archival data. Focused on Bronzeville—which includes the three Chicago communities of Douglas, Washington Park, and Grand Boulevard, where African Americans were concentrated—Drake and Cayton's analysis clearly revealed the existence of a color line that effectively blocked occupational, residential, and social mobility. In other words, the authors recognized that the unfolding racial patterns in Chicago could best be understood not as the manifestation of an organic and inevitable progression toward assimilation but as the result of racial decisions and practices embodied in social, political, and economic arrangements.

Drake and Cayton's classic study of Bronzeville provided the backdrop for subsequent examinations of Chicago's inner-city neighborhoods, studies that revealed a profound shift in the social organization of those neighborhoods after 1970.[1] In the last quarter of the twentieth century, the links between community institutions—including churches, schools, political organizations, businesses, and civic clubs—became far weaker and less secure. And illicit activities, such as drug trafficking, crime, prostitution, and the formation of gangs, accompanied the decreasing density and stability of formal organizations.

Two factors explained the weakening of social organization in Bronzeville neighborhoods and other Chicago inner-city areas after 1970. The first was changes in the broader society, including the nationwide decline in the fortunes of low-skilled workers and the growing suburbanization of jobs, which aggravated employment conditions in inner-city ghettos such as Bronzeville. The second was changes in the class, racial, and demographic composition of Bronzeville and other like areas, which experienced a higher concentration of poor and jobless individuals following the steady migration of more advantaged families to other neighborhoods in the city and to the surrounding suburbs. The declining presence of working- and middle-class African Americans deprived communities such as Bronzeville of key resources, including residents with incomes sufficient to sustain neighborhood services.

Thus one of the many values of *Black Metropolis* is that it provides a historical base for understanding the dynamic changes that have occurred in Chicago's inner-city neighborhoods. Current urban scholars rely on Drake and Cayton's comprehensive, empirically based descriptions of life in these residential areas prior to 1945 to highlight the profound transformations that have taken place in them since then. This is a major reason why *Black Metropolis*, which remains in print with a 2015 edition,[2] continues to be a widely cited and important study of urban neighborhoods.

This pathbreaking study of black life in America as lived on Chicago's South Side from the nineteenth into the mid-twentieth century is perhaps the best example of the way the city has served as "a laboratory," as William Julius Wilson calls it, for understanding the forces that have shaped change in America's inner cities. Shown here are two charts from the book related to work.

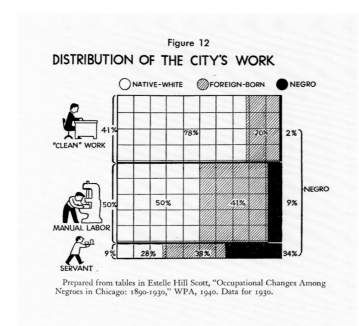

Figure 12

DISTRIBUTION OF THE CITY'S WORK

Prepared from tables in Estelle Hill Scott, "Occupational Changes Among Negroes in Chicago: 1890–1930," WPA, 1940. Data for 1930.

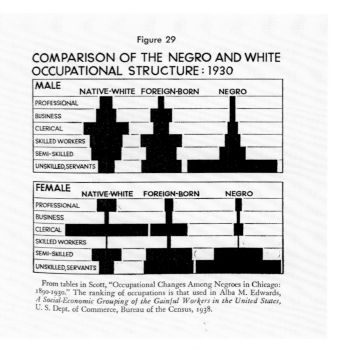

Figure 29

COMPARISON OF THE NEGRO AND WHITE OCCUPATIONAL STRUCTURE: 1930

From tables in Scott, "Occupational Changes Among Negroes in Chicago: 1890–1930." The ranking of occupations is that used in Alba M. Edwards, *A Social-Economic Grouping of the Gainful Workers in the United States*, U. S. Dept. of Commerce, Bureau of the Census, 1938.

66

Ebony

CHICAGO: JOHNSON PUBLISHING
COMPANY, 1945–2015; EBONY MEDIA
CORPORATION, 2016–PRESENT

Robert H. Jordan Jr.

Ebony magazine was created in Chicago and went on to become one of the nation's most important twentieth-century literary publications. It was responsible for elevating the battered spirits of an entire race that had been egregiously maligned for centuries. I know this to be true, because *Ebony* has been a part of my life for as long as I can remember.

I was born in Atlanta, two years before the first issue of *Ebony* hit the newsstands, on November 1, 1945. My mother bought that first issue and every single monthly issue thereafter for the rest of her life. The reason *Ebony* was so important to her and thousands of other African Americans is that it depicted them in true-to-life fashion for the *first* time in what became a mainstream national publication. It was groundbreaking.

Like many Negroes in the United States, my parents were disgusted with the manner in which black people had been shown in the media: From Aunt Jemima on pancake boxes to the children's book *Little Black Sambo*, portrayals of African Americans and Africans were often grotesque and demeaning.[1] In books, magazines, and most newspapers, Negroes were humiliatingly illustrated as pickaninnies with bulging eyes, unkempt hair, big red lips, and wide mouths into which they stuffed huge slices of watermelon. *Ebony*, by contrast, showed just how damaging, abusive, and mean-spirited such stereotypes were.

Ebony's publisher, John H. Johnson (1918–2005), was a visionary who realized that the time had come to offer African Americans a periodical that contained real, positive stories about them, told in an uplifting manner. Born in Arkansas, he moved with his family to Chicago in 1933. He started his first magazine, *Negro Digest*, in 1942. During one of many conversations I had with Johnson, he told me he originally envisioned *Ebony* as a photo magazine with news about black America. He planned to pattern this new monthly after *Life* magazine but explicitly designed it for African American readers. Johnson used black models in his advertisements. He told me he struggled, in the early days, to find major national sponsors.

Ebony was an immediate success. The entire run of the first issue—twenty-five thousand—sold out. Johnson clearly reached a nationwide audience that was starving for such a publication. The magazine initially highlighted African American entertainers and sports figures but gradually shifted its editorial focus to include black achievement of all sorts. Johnson improved the reporting and focused on issues such as African American militancy, black-on-black crimes, civil rights legislation, demonstrations, and freedom rides, with special emphasis on stories examining segregation and discrimination. He published a special edition of the magazine after the death of Dr. Martin Luther King Jr. By 2000 *Ebony*'s circulation had reached about 2.3 million; as of this writing, *Ebony* reaches 11 million readers. Now all issues are online.[2]

By the time my mother died, in 1991, she had amassed over five hundred issues of *Ebony*. She cherished her complete set, knowing that it chronicled the "black experience" in the United States like no other periodical in the history of the country.[3] She often told me that one day her prized collection would come to me to pass down to my progeny. She wanted them to see, through the pages of *Ebony*, the progress our people have made and to witness how difficult and tortuous the journey has been to get to where we are today, and where we hope to be in the future.

FACING The cover of the first issue of the Chicago-based *Ebony* conveys hope that race relations in the United States will improve in the next generation, although the single African American boy in the cover photograph, encircled by a crowd of boisterous Caucasian youths, seems overwhelmed and uncomfortable. For a later cover, see page 4.

67

Vision in Motion

L[ÁSZLÓ]. MOHOLY-NAGY ∗ CHICAGO:
PAUL THEOBALD, 1947

Lynn Martin Windsor

Man standing on four eggs—Print of Kandinsky's right hand—Space modulator—Fernand Léger drawing—Tactile chart—Chair made of one piece of bent plywood—Structure chart of Finnegans Wake—The packaged house—Photograph of fragrance of a coffee bean—Penguin pool in the London Zoo—Structural papercuts—Drawing made with a pinpoint flashlight—Guillaume Apollinaire ideogram

The above is a small sample of the 439 illustrations in *Vision in Motion*. The text is a manifesto by László Moholy-Nagy (1895–1946), the visionary Hungarian-born artist, experimenter, and Bauhaus teacher. He stated the foundation of his educational philosophy in his foreword:

This book takes as its basic premise the unity of the arts with life . . . though the inevitable logic of new technologies is willingly accepted on pragmatic intellectual terms, it is stubbornly opposed in the emotional sphere. . . . The remedy is to add to our intellectual literacy an emotional literacy, an education of the senses, the ability to articulate feeling through the means of expression.[1]

Moholy designed his book so that the illustrations and text are tightly integrated, which was unusual in 1947, the year in which it was published.

Moholy had been director of the advanced foundation course at the Bauhaus in Weimar, and later in Dessau. After he left the Bauhaus in 1928, he was a successful freelance designer in Berlin, Amsterdam, and London. But when the Association of Arts and Industries invited him in 1937 to become director of a new design school in Chicago, he accepted; the education of designers was of great importance to him. Writing to his wife, Sibyl, in August 1937 from Chicago, Moholy said, "There's something incomplete about this city and its people that fascinates me; it seems to urge one on to completion. Everything seems still possible. . . . Yes, I want to stay."[2]

Moholy's school, the New Bauhaus (later named the Institute of Design), opened in the autumn of 1937. It was modeled on the original Bauhaus to a great extent; it offered a year-long foundation course, supplemented by academic lectures and followed by more specialized workshops. The foundation course was an exploration of tools, machines, and materials in which students experimented with space, light, color, surface, and form. It was intended to be an "education of the senses." Moholy's utopian goal was to create a new unity of art, science, and technology for a better world. *Vision in Motion* mirrors the school and its philosophy; many of the illustrations are the work of its students and faculty, and many are by Moholy.

The combination of Moholy's pedagogy, an outstanding faculty, an international roll of lecturers, and the achievements of the students attracted

worldwide attention to the school and to Chicago. *Vision in Motion* added more acclaim: with forty thousand copies selling over a period of twenty-plus years,[3] it became a standard work in the literature of art education. Long out of print in English, *Vision in Motion* was republished in 2014 as Bauhaus Edition 39 in a German translation commissioned by the Bauhaus Dessau Foundation.[4] Now it has joined the famous series of Bauhaus books that Moholy codirected in the 1920s.

In 1990 the critic Richard Kostelanetz made clear the importance of this adventurous and prescient book:

Moholy's greatest single creation, representing the sum of his imagination and intelligence, is his book, *Vision in Motion*, written in America, in Chicago, a book that, appearing posthumously, concludes his life as only a book can do. Not only is it the single most illuminating survey I know of avant-garde modernism in the arts, it is also an "artist's book" of the very highest order, demonstrating that few artists ever wrote as well or as truly about their own esthetic aspirations.

In addition to his art, László Moholy-Nagy's greatest legacy was bringing the Bauhaus—the most influential art school of the twentieth century—from Germany to Chicago. He and his New Bauhaus faculty introduced students to a philosophy of art education—delineated in his book *Vision in Motion*—based on eliminating hierarchies between fine art and design and on creating a material world that reflects the unity of all the arts.

68

Chicago Railroad Fair Official Guide Book and Program for the Pageant 'Wheels a-Rolling'

[CHICAGO: CHICAGO RAILROAD FAIR], 1948

Will Hansen

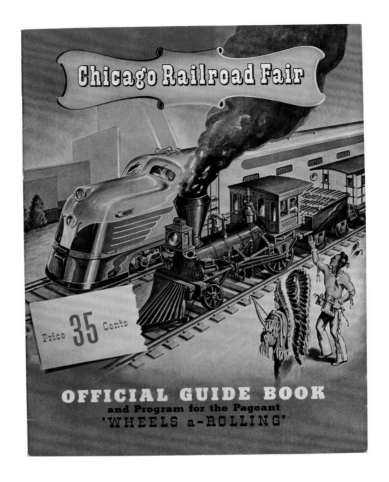

Transportation has always been central to Chicago's prosperity and, indeed, its reason for being. The city's status as the nation's transportation hub has also made it a magnet for spectacular, large-scale entertainments such as the World's Columbian and Century of Progress Expositions of 1893 and 1933–34, respectively. Those strands of Chicago's identity came together for the 1948 Chicago Railroad Fair.

The brainchild of the Chicago and North Western Railway,[1] the fair was funded and organized by nearly forty railroads and equipment manufacturers, led by Chicago's Museum of Science and Industry. The *Guide Book* explains that the fair commemorated the first successful trip west from Chicago on rails, by the *Pioneer* steam locomotive in October 1848; more broadly the railroads intended the fair as a "demonstration of their vital part in the daily life of America" over a century of explosive physical, technological, and economic growth.[2] The *Guide Book*'s text and illustrations were a collaborative effort between the fair's Publicity Department, led by Frederick J. Ashley, and staff in similar departments of the sponsoring companies.[3]

The *Guide Book* features a centerfold map of the fairgrounds, sprawling across fifty acres in Burnham Park. The map's key lists some of the exhibits sponsored by individual railroads and described in greater detail in the *Guide Book*. These included a "street scene . . . from the old French Quarter in New Orleans"; "a functioning replica of Old Faithful geyser" and "live bears"; a "45-foot tower of chromed rails"; a "nine-foot robot to answer questions"; and the "Deadwood Central" narrow-gauge railroad used to transport fairgoers across the grounds. Most infamously, a southwestern "Indian Village of 125 tribesmen and women . . . who live in . . . buildings typical of the tribes' natural habitats . . . staging legendary dances, singing age-old Indian songs in strange Indian tongues" exoticized and dehumanized Native Americans.[4]

Central to the fairgrounds—and the fair itself—were the five-thousand-seat grandstand and "ultra-modern, 450-foot pageant stage" for *Wheels a-Rolling*, a musical written by Edward Hungerford. Six of the *Guide Book*'s sixteen pages are devoted to synopses and illustrations of the play's fourteen scenes, which dramatized developments in American transportation from Father Jacques Marquette and Louis Jolliet's 1673 exploration of the Upper Mississippi region to the contemporary era of "Modern Transportation" and featured rolling stock such as the stainless-steel *Zephyr* train. The *Guide Book* also lists the hundreds of cast members and crew who put on the pageant, including four mechanics.

The Railroad Fair opened in July 1948 and was such a success that it returned for a second season in 1949.[5] The *Guide Book* too exceeded expectations: Chicago's Neely Printing Company produced an initial run of one hundred thousand copies, and inquiries were made before the fair's opening about doing a second printing of twenty-five or fifty thousand, and again shortly after the opening for another of one hundred thousand.[6] More than two hundred thousand copies were likely sold in 1948 for thirty-five cents each.

In many ways the Railroad Fair was self-consciously elegiac, forming the finale to an era: as the *Guide Book* writers exclaimed, "Nowhere, nowhere today is there a frontier! Modern transport has met the supreme challenge of the horizon! And so, an epic of progress . . . comes to a close."[7] While the fair has not lived on in the cultural memory of Chicago and the nation to the same degree as the 1893 and 1933–34 expositions, its blend of American triumphalism, frontier nostalgia, and corporate advertising surely had a lasting impact on the hundreds of thousands of attendees and positioned it as representative of its era and its host city.

Chicago has long been the United States' most important railroad center, serving as a hub for cross-country travelers and a major industrial capital and goods distributor. Moreover, freight and passenger cars, as well as engines, were manufactured in the city. Ironically, several fairs, beginning with this one in 1948, celebrated railroad history and innovation at the moment when airplane travel was becoming ascendant (see no. 69).

69

Master Plan of Chicago Orchard (Douglas) Airport: Prepared for City of Chicago

RALPH H. BURKE, AIRPORT CONSULTANT
∗ [CHICAGO], 1948

Charles Waldheim

FACING Ralph Burke's 1948 *Master Plan* for O'Hare Airport imagined the development of a modern airfield on the site of the World War II–era Douglas Aircraft plant northwest of Chicago. The postwar development of O'Hare at this location effectively erased what had been the sleepy farming village of Orchard Place, Illinois. William K. Kaiser made this presentation drawing in 1952 to show Burke's plan as seen from above. The gouache, watercolor, and crayon illustration is in the Art Institute of Chicago.

We modestly hope and confidently expect to construct an airport in Chicago finer, larger, safer and more convenient than any other in the World.[1]

Ralph H. Burke's plan for Orchard Airport is among the most significant documents in Chicago's history. In spite of its significance, the publication resides in near absolute obscurity. Perhaps a dozen copies of this modest pamphlet remain in public collections. Burke's plan was never published in any true sense of the word. It was simply a technical report from a consulting engineer to a mayor that was copied to perhaps a few hundred readers in positions of political, administrative, or professional significance to the subject matter at hand. It was never understood as a public document in the modern sense. Moreover, Burke's plan was not really a single publication at all but rather a series of short technical reports issued by Burke's consulting firm to Mayor Martin Kennelly between January 1948 and October 1954.

Yet beyond the significance of Burke's pamphlets for the development of Chicago, the original 1948 proposal is among the most important documents in the history of airport planning worldwide. More than any other document of its kind, Burke's plan anticipated the definitive typology of the modern jet-age airport. In so doing, the pamphlet shaped the airport on Chicago's Northwest Side that would come to be known as O'Hare. It also influenced the planning and design of airports around the world.

In the second half of the twentieth century, Chicago's O'Hare International Airport was the biggest and busiest facility of its kind anywhere. Characterized by a seamless integration of transportation infrastructure and architectural expression, it quickly became an international model for jet-age airport design. The largest public works project in Chicago's history, O'Hare exemplifies the relationships between public works patronage, machine politics, and the emergence of modern architecture in the public realm. As a work of modern architecture, the airport achieved a rare combination of popular and professional acclaim. Consulting engineer Ralph Burke and a team of Chicago architects led by C. F. Murphy Associates developed innovative design strategies at O'Hare, such as the movable jet bridge, the two-tiered entryway drive, the linear terminal building with finger piers, and the centralized parking garage. Those innovations were first synthesized and implemented at O'Hare and differed markedly from designs developed for comparable jet-age airports nationally and internationally.

Ralph Haney Burke (1884–1956) was a Republican Methodist who made his career as a public servant appointed to positions of public responsibility by Democratic Catholic mayors of Chicago. Born in Illinois and trained as an engineer at MIT, Burke began his career in Chicago public works when Rob-

O'HARE MASTER PLAN-1952
RALPH BURKE ASSOCIATES

ert R. McCormick hired him to work at the Chicago Sanitary District. From 1934 to 1946, Burke served as chief engineer for the Chicago Park District. In those roles as a civil servant, he was often tasked with developing public works infrastructure for a modern Chicago. Burke's plan for O'Hare would be among his greatest professional accomplishments in a consequential career of service to the citizens of the city.

In spite of Burke's prescience and his optimistic assertion that his plan was "ready for action" as early as January 1948, his proposal for O'Hare's development languished for many years.[2] It was only with the election of Mayor Richard J. Daley in April 1955, and Burke's death in August 1956, that the construction of O'Hare moved forward expeditiously. That had less to do with the considerable merits of Burke's plan than with Daley's success in negotiating with the airlines to fund the project. Unfortunately, it meant that Burke did not live to see the international impact of his innovative work of civic imagination.

70

History of the Development of Building Construction in Chicago

FRANK A. RANDALL, FRANK A.
RANDALL AND SONS, STRUCTURAL
ENGINEERS, SPECIAL LECTURER IN CIVIL
ENGINEERING, UNIVERSITY OF ILLINOIS
✳ URBANA: THE UNIVERSITY OF ILLINOIS
PRESS, 1949

Daniel Bluestone

Frank A. Randall's 1949 *History of the Development of Building Construction in Chicago* is an encyclopedic reference work focused on the architectural design, the structural techniques, and the palette of materials for buildings constructed in Chicago's Loop and adjacent downtown areas. The book constituted an important point of departure for popular and scholarly accounts of Chicago's commercial architecture, which had helped establish the city's international reputation as a center of architectural and engineering innovation. The first thirty-four pages provide a synopsis of the "evolution" of Chicago building, including wood-frame balloon construction, steel-skeleton construction, elevator technology, foundation techniques, and biographical notes on twelve leading architects of late-nineteenth and early-twentieth-century Chicago. Those include Daniel H. Burnham, William Holabird, William Le Baron Jenney, Martin Roche, John Wellborn Root, Louis Sullivan, and John M. Van Osdel. The book's main section lists individual buildings, organized by name and placed in chronological order of construction from 1830 to 1948. Eighty-two pages of separate indexes refer readers to building entries using name, location, architect, and engineer, or general information.

The entries range from a few lines to a paragraph to a full-page. Frank Alfred Randall (1883–1950), an engineer and instructor of civil engineering at the University of Illinois, and his collaborators combed through architecture, engineering, and real estate journals, and searched archive collections and secondary literature to assemble building narratives. The building accounts are keyed to fifty-eight bibliographic sources, including journals and primary and secondary sources, where additional information and images can be found. At times Randall's reliance upon those disparate sources produced inaccuracies. The Masonic Temple Building, for example, is variously listed as twenty and twenty-one stories and as standing 254 feet and 302 feet high.[1] Randall usefully explored the complex, layered history of urban sites, chronicling the succession of buildings on individual lots; he vividly captured the churning redevelopment of Chicago's urban landscape and the architectural, technological, economic, and cultural patterns of building construction, use, obsolescence, and demolition.

A sixty-four-page section of Randall's book reproduces material from an 1898 Rand, McNally guide to Chicago (no. 14). It includes twenty-two bird's-eye views of the downtown keyed to paragraphs on major buildings. Those historic images give considerable vibrancy to Randall's graphic presentation and easily eclipse in interest the book's forty other illustrations, which generally focus on individual buildings. The contrasts between Randall's book and the original Rand, McNally guide are striking. Randall focused narrowly on engineering structure, architectural form, and the central business district.

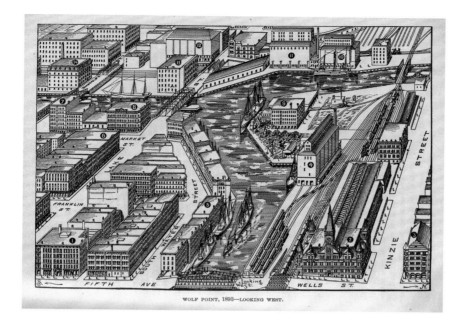

WOLF POINT, 1893—LOOKING WEST.

Chicago's reputation as a center of architectural and engineering innovation has been established by serious publications about the city's built environment, including this touchstone compendium about the history and construction of the city's downtown buildings. The volume borrowed some illustrations—such as this view of the Chicago River at Wolf Point—from a much earlier book, the 1893 *Rand, McNally & Co. Bird's-Eye Views and Guide to Chicago* (no. 14).

The parts of the Rand, McNally guide that Randall did not reproduce feature restaurants, streets, residences, the Lincoln Park Zoo, bicycling, short biographies of leading merchants and political leaders, "beautiful lights at night," "various nationalities," and far-flung neighborhoods such as the "Chinese Quarter" and the "Italian Quarter." Rand, McNally captured the cosmopolitan variety of the city as it surfaced in buildings and landscapes. This difference is apparent even when Randall focused on individual buildings. His entry on Burnham and Root's 1891 Monadnock Building notes the spread footings, Z-bar columns, small piers, load-bearing walls, and hardpan caissons. The Rand, McNally account profiles the Monadnock as a hive of business, with 1,600 offices and 7,500 inhabitants, prominent corporate tenants and the assortment of "attorneys, agents, capitalists, and commission merchants."[2]

Historian Carl W. Condit, whose subsequent work followed Randall's interest in the "structural art" and technological aspects of Chicago building, admired Randall's book. He felt that with Randall, Chicago was "well on the way to being adequately treated by the historians of architecture."[3] However, while Condit subsequently focused primarily upon the icons of structural expressionism within the so-called Chicago School, Randall's efforts to treat the downtown comprehensively opened people's eyes to the much more eclectic stylistic expressions of Chicago architectural production.

71

Chicago: City on the Make

NELSON ALGREN ✳ GARDEN CITY, NEW
YORK: DOUBLEDAY & COMPANY, INC.,
1951

Alex Kotlowitz

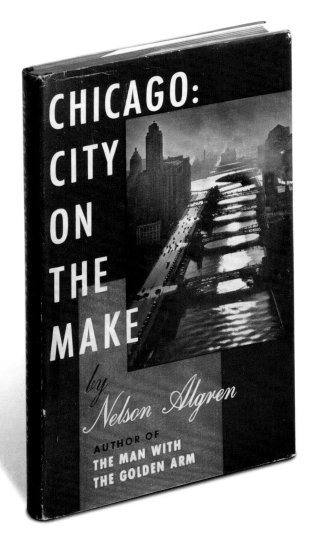

When I moved to Chicago in late 1983, I found an apartment on Evergreen
Street in Wicker Park, at the time a hardscrabble, working-class neighborhood. I soon learned that my street's name had recently been a source of
controversy. An author named Nelson Algren had lived down the street, and
shortly after his death a couple of years earlier, his friends convinced the city
to rechristen it Algren Avenue. Residents protested, and so the city reversed
course: it became Evergreen again. It was, I would learn, a fitting afterword
to Algren's unrequited love for the city.

I had never heard of Algren, and so I went to a used bookstore and found a slim volume, *Chicago: City on the Make*. On a blustery, cold winter night, I sat by the gas heater in my kitchen, riveted and warmed by this angry, blustery, yet tender prose poem. Algren wrote like John Coltrane playing sax, with a kind of disciplined improvisation, riffing on a city that, with all its contradictions, clearly gave him life. I was hooked. On Algren. On Chicago.

With the publication in 1950 of *The Man with the Golden Arm*—the first novel to win the National Book Award—Algren (1909–81) became a sought-after writer. On assignment for *Holiday Magazine*, he wrote this elegiac letter to Chicago, a city that he both loved and hated, and a city that both loved and hated him back. When it was published as a book in 1951, local critics panned it, and so it disappeared until the French philosopher Jean-Paul Sartre (whose wife, Simone de Beauvoir, was Algren's lover for a time) translated it into French.

Algren once took Beauvoir to a down-and-out tavern on what was then a down-and-out Madison Street. Dancing among drunks and prostitutes, she remarked, "It's beautiful." Algren laughed. "With us," he said, "ugliness and beauty, the grotesque and the tragic and good and evil—each has its place. Americans don't like to think these extremes mingle."[1] But Algren did, and that's the power of *City on the Make*: it holds the celebratory and the tragic side by side. Consider what may be the most oft-quoted passage: "Yet once you've come to be part of this particular patch, you'll never love another. Like loving a woman with a broken nose, you may well find lovelier lovelies. But never a lovely so real."[2]

In *City on the Make* and subsequent novels, Algren wrote about drug dealers and addicts, fighters and floozies. He gave voice to the inarticulate. In his ode to Chicago, he admired its beauty and boldness, along with its cruelty and hustling nature: "You'll know it's the place built out of Man's ceaseless failure to overcome himself. Out of Man's endless war against himself we build our success as well as our failures. Making it the city of all cities most like Man himself—loneliest creation of all this very old poor earth."[3]

Algren was speaking of Chicago, but he was also describing himself. He ultimately left the city for the East Coast. Though Chicago never named a street after him, it did build a memorial at the corner of Division Street and Milwaukee Avenue. It is an unremarkable fountain set in a small triangular park, a place inhabited by day laborers and drifters, though the area is becoming shinier and wealthier. Algren would have had something to say, no doubt, about the changing nature of his former neighborhood, but his sentiments are forever engraved on that fountain, even if they are hard to make out. The line is from *City on the Make*: "For the masses who do the city's labor also keep the city's heart."[4]

FACING Nelson Algren lived in Chicago on and off for much of his life, setting many of his stories and his most famous novel, *The Man with the Golden Arm* (1949), in the city. He dedicated his critical but also loving essay about Chicago, *City on the Make*, to another Chicago writer, Carl Sandburg, whose *Chicago Poems* (no. 37) he admired.

72

860–880 Lake Shore Drive, Ludwig Mies van der Rohe Architect, Associate Architects Pace Associates, Holsman, Holsman, Klekamp & Taylor

[CHICAGO]: 860 LAKE SHORE DRIVE TRUST, CA. 1951

John Ronan

How strange they must have looked when completed in 1951: elegant and mysterious, identical twin towers standing in dialogue at the city's edge, their radically reduced palette of steel, aluminum, and glass more like the cars rushing past on Lake Shore Drive below than the stone buildings nearby. Described in the sales brochure as "a spectacular upsweep of glass and steel,"[1] their facades seem to alternate between transparency and opacity, one face opening up while the other closes down. Each reveals, in a radical breach of protocol, the structural steel frame concealed behind the neighboring stone and brick edifices. The apartment interiors were similarly radical: windows of "thick plate glass . . . housed in specially designed aluminum frames"[2] are bisected by the horizon line of Lake Michigan, offering an ever-changing minimalist artwork, one's very own Mark Rothko.

The buildings' architect, Ludwig Mies van der Rohe (1886–1969), the German-born son of a stonemason, had made his name in Europe for his abandonment first of historical styles, then of ornament altogether, in such notable structures as the Barcelona Pavilion (1929). Mies was the director of the renowned Bauhaus when it was effectively shut down by the Nazis in 1933. With opportunities in his homeland dwindling, he fled in 1938 to the United States, where he was invited to run the school of architecture at the Armour Institute (later the Illinois Institute of Technology) in Chicago. Mies's stripped-down aesthetic found a welcome home in the city, the no-nonsense capital of the Midwest.

Commissioned by real estate mogul Herbert Greenwald, the developer-friendly (read: economical) design for 860–880 Lake Shore Drive is the result not of a burst of inspiration but rather of decades of research and experimentation into materials and construction. Here the architect realized his true expression of the steel-and-glass building, with all ornament stripped away until only essential elements remain. As the sales brochure for the buildings states, "The design is so simple, so clean, so uncluttered by meaningless detail."[3] Germans had a word for this—*Sachlichkeit*—a certain matter-of-fact quality that implies objectivity. Mies called it something else: "skin and bones architecture."

For Mies design was the result of a rational and empirical process, involving the important question of "how," not "what":

I tried . . . to develop a clear structure. We are just confronted with the material. How to use it in the right way is what you have to find out. It has nothing to do with the shape. What I do—what you call my kind of architecture—we should just call it a structural approach. We don't think about the form when we start. We think about the right way to use the materials. Then we accept the result.[4]

The two elegant glass-and-steel apartment buildings by Ludwig Mies van der Rohe that rose on Lake Shore Drive in 1949–51—shown here still under construction—reveal the formal purity and attention to detail that are hallmarks of the Chicago-based architect's style. They would spawn countless imitations throughout the world.

This represented not merely a stylistic alternative but a radical new approach to building design that even *sounded* different, for Mies spoke not in the flowery artistic terms of his some of his contemporaries but with the mathematical objectivity of a scientist. For him buildings are less artistic creations than objective "solutions" to the "problem" of building, his conclusions carrying with them the authority of an essential rightness with which any rational architect would concur. And so many did. Mies's steel-and-glass solution would be imitated ad infinitum across the American landscape (including by Mies himself), though it would never be improved upon. In retrospect the uneven quality of 860–880's descendants serves to foreground the deceptive simplicity of Mies's design and expose its *real* truth: 860–880 Lake Shore Drive is not an objective "solution" to a building "problem" but a rather subjective and enigmatic work of art.

73

Great Books of the Western World

ROBERT MAYNARD HUTCHINS, EDITOR ✳ MORTIMER J. ADLER, ASSOCIATE EDITOR ✳ ENCYCLOPAEDIA BRITANNICA, INC., IN COLLABORATION WITH THE UNIVERSITY OF CHICAGO ✳ [CHICAGO]: WILLIAM BENTON, 1952

Tim Lacy

Chicagoans did not, technically, invent the Great Books idea. But once the idea arrived in the city, it was transformed by its advocates into a movement so large and compelling that it could not be ignored by readers, authors, and publishers. The Great Books' links to Chicago became concrete and spectacular over three particular decades, owing to three individuals linked to three Chicago-based institutions. Through those thinkers—Mortimer J. Adler, Robert Maynard Hutchins, and William Benton—educators came to identify the city as the beating heart for Great Books circulation. This helped foster the city's reputation as an intellectual center for high culture. In the nation's cultural imagination, Chicago was the Great Books Capital of the United States.

The Great Books idea arrived in Chicago in 1930 with Mortimer Adler (1902–2001). An intellectual dynamo from Columbia University, Adler was invited by Robert Hutchins (1899–1977), the youthful and charismatic new president of the University of Chicago, to join the faculty. That occurred, in part, because of Adler's enthusiasm for Great Books. Hutchins saw Great Books as a vehicle to reinforce the power of the liberal arts and humanities, as well as to foster a literate and civically responsible populace. The pair taught an undergraduate course that required students to read one "great book" per week for two years. Through the 1930s, Adler and Hutchins turned the course into an academic destination and enhanced the university's already stellar reputation.[1]

By the 1940s, their work caused the Great Books idea to be seen as a Chicago-based national phenomenon. Adler's 1940 best seller, *How to Read a Book: The Art of Getting a Liberal Education*, presented Great Books as a logical challenge and endpoint for the techniques the book articulated.[2]

Adler and Hutchins taught a Great Books course in the early 1940s to executives and businessmen that was nicknamed "the Fat Man's Class." It won over a former advertising executive and future senator, William Benton (1900–1973), who had purchased the Encyclopaedia Britannica Corporation with the University of Chicago. He decided that Britannica would publish a set of the Great Books, with Hutchins as editor-in-chief and Adler as associate editor. In 1947 Hutchins and Adler also helped established the Great Books Foundation in Chicago to further their goals.[3]

With Benton and Britannica's backing, Hutchins and Adler labored through the end of World War II and the early Cold War years to produce the fifty-four-volume set in 1952.[4] The set includes examples of drama, economics, ethics, fiction, history, natural science, mathematics, natural science, philosophy, poetry, politics, and religion. The origins of the volumes' seventy-five authors and 443 works range, in time and place, from ancient Greece

Introductory Volumes:

1. A Liberal Education
2. The Great Ideas I
3. The Great Ideas II

4. HOMER
5. AESCHYLUS
   SOPHOCLES
   EURIPIDES
   ARISTOPHANES
6. HERODOTUS
   THUCYDIDES
7. PLATO
8. ARISTOTLE I
9. ARISTOTLE II
10. HIPPOCRATES
    GALEN
11. EUCLID
    ARCHIMEDES
    APOLLONIUS
    NICOMACHUS

12. LUCRETIUS
    EPICTETUS
    MARCUS AURELIUS
13. VIRGIL
14. PLUTARCH
15. TACITUS
16. PTOLEMY
    COPERNICUS
    KEPLER
17. PLOTINUS
18. AUGUSTINE
19. THOMAS AQUINAS I
20. THOMAS AQUINAS II
21. DANTE
22. CHAUCER
23. MACHIAVELLI
    HOBBES
24. RABELAIS
25. MONTAIGNE
26. SHAKESPEARE I
27. SHAKESPEARE II

28. GILBERT
    GALILEO
    HARVEY
29. CERVANTES
30. FRANCIS BACON
31. DESCARTES
    SPINOZA
32. MILTON
33. PASCAL
34. NEWTON
    HUYGENS
35. LOCKE
    BERKELEY
    HUME
36. SWIFT
    STERNE
37. FIELDING
38. MONTESQUIEU
    ROUSSEAU
39. ADAM SMITH
40. GIBBON I

41. GIBBON II
42. KANT
43. AMERICAN STATE
    PAPERS
    THE FEDERALIST
    J. S. MILL
44. BOSWELL
45. LAVOISIER
    FOURIER
    FARADAY
46. HEGEL
47. GOETHE
48. MELVILLE
49. DARWIN
50. MARX
    ENGELS
51. TOLSTOY
52. DOSTOEVSKY
53. WILLIAM JAMES
54. FREUD

and Rome to late-nineteenth-century America. The set also included an "idea index" (called the *Syntopicon*) of 102 essays on the so-called Great Ideas.[5]

Although initial sales were slow, by the late 1950s and early 1960s around fifty thousand sets sold annually.[6] However, as the enforced cultural consensus of the 1950s and 1960s gave way to acknowledgments of diversity in gender, race, ethnicity, and sexuality during the 1970s, the Great Books idea, criticized for its lack of inclusivity, temporarily faded into the background. By the end of that decade, both Benton and Hutchins had died. Adler, however, pushed and revived awareness of the Great Books in the 1980s, leading an initiative to reform the nation's K–12 institutions.[7]

Adler's popularity as an educator resulted in a Britannica plan to produce a second edition of Great Books of the Western World; the new, sixty-volume set was released in 1990, garnering both fanfare and controversy. Adler died in 2001, but Britannica continued to publish the set for another fifteen years. While the Great Books Foundation still exists, the larger cosmopolitan dynamics that fed midcentury Great Books efforts lives on in other, less ambitious educational endeavors.

The Great Books Series was the brainchild of University of Chicago president John Maynard Hutchins; William Benton, publisher of *Encyclopaedia Britannica* from 1943 to 1973; and philosopher Mortimer Adler. Seen here are the endpapers that appear in each volume.

74

Chicago: The Second City

A[BBOTT]. J[OSEPH]. LIEBLING ✳ DRAWINGS BY [SAUL] STEINBERG ✳ NEW YORK: ALFRED A. KNOPF, 1952

Thomas Dyja

Even if they've never read *Chicago: The Second City*—and at this point, who has?—Chicagoans know the phrase "Second City"; they have it tattooed on their heart so they can feel a little jolt of psychic pain whenever the city is jostled. And if few Chicagoans can claim to have read this collection of three *New Yorker* pieces by the magazine's staff writer A. J. Liebling (1904–63), published in January 1952, I think the total number of non-Chicagoans who have read it would fit inside an elevator at the Hancock Building. It likely would have been forgotten entirely, lost somewhere among Liebling's brilliant books about France, food, and boxing, if Chicago had not made such a fuss about it. Why did we care? Why do we still?

Bad trips—the missed connections and inedible food, the curious characters noted in detail, then barely escaped—make for the best travel writing. But they say as much about the writer as they do about the place, and *Chicago: The Second City* is really nothing more than an entertaining travel book. A dyed-in-the-wool New Yorker, Liebling hated the clothes women in Chicago wore and how the water tasted; he found his neighbors alternately too friendly and not friendly enough. He could not stand the Cubs or the White Sox and was mystified by the attractions of Lake Michigan. He was, in short, not a Chicago guy, and all the better—more lake water for us. His own blind spots are apparent: He wrote not a word about jazz or blues or gospel, or Saul Alinsky's work, or Ludwig Mies van der Rohe's new campus at the Illinois Institute of Technology, all of which would change the world in the years to come. But hey, to each his own.

What really hurt was that Liebling got so much right. The city in 1952 was at its postwar peak—some 3.5 million residents, shiny new buildings popping up in the Loop, factories thrumming. Then as now, Chicago kept the front room spotless and made sure to show everyone who visited the many wonders—the Art Institute and the Shedd Aquarium; the biggest, longest, tallest, and first of just about everything. To which Liebling had simply shrugged and made a beeline to the medicine cabinet to find out what we were *really* made of. Then, in *The New Yorker*—the magazine that *was* the eastern establishment, every perfect, self-satisfied paragraph dripping with supremacy—he announced that Chicagoans did not make their beds or wash their dishes, and there was evidence of mice in the corners: the city's politics were entirely corrupt; the lakefront facade hid miles of ghettos; racism was open and everywhere. He sneered at what he saw as the off-the-rack intellectualism of Robert M. Hutchins and Mortimer J. Adler's Great Books (no. 73) and the wealthy, parasitical suburbs.

Chicago's citizenry could have gotten out its collective broom and cleaned up. But Liebling was a terrible bringer of some messages Chicago needed to hear, and so instead of asking hard questions about machine politics or why the city's public housing had turned into a shameful circus, Chicagoans sulked with the stinging realization that despite their dreams, their city was never going to overtake New York. Then they brushed aside reform, voted Democratic, and made "The Second City" Chicago's version of *The Scarlet Letter*. Now it is the city's brand. And we still have not done nearly enough sweeping...

To say that *New Yorker* writer A. J. Liebling did not like Chicago is an understatement. His putdown of the city, especially its claims to be first and best at everything, made many Chicagoans angry, although at least one of Chicago's most celebrated institutions, the Second City comedy troupe (see no. 98), coopted the title of Liebling's book and considers it a badge of honor. *Chicago: The Second City* features witty line drawings by another New Yorker, Saul Steinberg (1914–99).

75

Give the Lady What She Wants! The Story of Marshall Field & Company

LLOYD WENDT AND HERMAN KOGAN ✱
CHICAGO: RAND, MCNALLY & COMPANY,
1952

Leslie Goddard

Marshall Field & Company, the grande dame of Chicago's department stores, celebrated its one-hundredth birthday in 1952. For many of Field's devoted fans, the highlight of the year was the publication of a store history, *Give the Lady What She Wants!*, by veteran Chicago newsmen Herman Kogan (1914–89) and Lloyd Wendt (1908–2007). Store officials gave away hundreds of copies, including special volumes for employees with ten years or more of service.[1]

The book attracted national notice. *Kirkus Reviews* called it "a friendly chronicle" that was "not without national business interest."[2] William Miller of the *New York Times* found it dull but gave the authors "an E for effort."[3] Readers, however, were enthralled. By June fifteen thousand copies had been sold, making it the highest-selling nonfiction title in Chicago at the time. Within a year the book was in its fifth printing. It remained steadily popular, appearing in paperback versions in 1966 and again in 1997. Today copies can be found online for as little as $4.

Kogan and Wendt used research, photographs, and illustrations from company archives to tell the story of the store's first century, tracing its beginnings to a dry-goods store, opened on Lake Street by Potter Palmer in 1852, which Marshall Field and Levi Leiter purchased in 1867. When Leiter retired in 1881, the store became Marshall Field & Company.[4]

Anecdotes from the book, usually unattributed, immediately became commonplace in articles about Field's. Some of them are legendary, such as when Field (1834–1906) ordered a manager arguing with a shopper to "give the lady what she wants," or when a customer received a full refund in 1946 for high-button shoes purchased in 1908.[5] For Wendt and Kogan, Field officials, in their efforts to stock the best and most exclusive products and create the most regal and welcoming store, personified the forces that propelled Chicago from a frontier community into a global metropolis between 1852 and 1952.

Much of the book's success was due to the authors' research. Using company archives, they drew on advertisements, official publications, store reports, and unpublished letters. They interviewed officials and employees and dug through various library archives. This resulted in a narrative that effectively weaves the history of the store and of its colorful leaders with those of the city. The rise of State Street (the location of the store for most of its history), the Great Fire of 1871 (which destroyed the store), changes in the status of women, economic depressions, the 1893 World's Columbian Exposition, and numerous other events all figure prominently.

The book's greatest strength, however, is its writing, which is lively and vibrant. The narrative includes a cinematic description of Palmer walking down Lake Street in 1852.[6] Mud oozes from wooden sidewalks, carpenters labor loudly, and farm carts trudge past. The street teems with wagon drivers, peddlers, and, everywhere, women shoppers.

Give the Lady includes neither footnotes nor a bibliography, and thus verifying its details is challenging. Did 1860s customers really carry home purchases in (then-rare) paper bags, for example? However, the book's intended readers were not academics but rather the many shoppers, employees, and officials who shared a heartfelt, often passionate devotion to Field's. For them Wendt and Kogan provided a compelling framework for understanding how the company became so prominent: impeccable customer service, high-quality merchandise, and the attitude that the customer is always right. *Give the Lady What She Wants!* was part of the process by which Field's created and strengthened its identity as Chicago's most prestigious and beloved department store.

For shoppers who remember Marshall Field & Company before its purchase by Macy's in 2006, this book remains a valuable—and delightful—history.

FACING Renowned for its elegant interiors, high-quality merchandise, up-to-the-minute fashions, and attentive service, Marshall Field & Company ranked as one of the nation's largest retail enterprises in the 1950s. The store's motto, "Give the lady what she wants," is an apt title for this engaging history of Chicago's preeminent department store.

76

The Adventures of Augie March: A Novel

SAUL BELLOW * NEW YORK: THE VIKING
PRESS, 1953

David Auburn

"Chicago" appears twice in the opening sentence of *The Adventures of Augie March*, repeated like an incantation: "I am an American, Chicago born—Chicago, that somber city." And though the novel moves beyond the city's borders—across the Midwest, down into Mexico, finally into Europe—it is sprawling, chaotic Chicago that gives the book its soul and, for large sections, its structure. Saul Bellow (1915–2005) seems to have designed the book to take us into as many parts of the city as possible and to let us meet everyone who lives there.

Though it is jammed with incident, the book is plotless. Augie is a poor Jewish boy growing up on Chicago's West Side in a strange, broken family (a vanished father, a nearly blind mother, and two brothers: one feeble-minded, one half-crazed with ambition). With nothing but an attitude toward life ("I . . . go at things as I have taught myself, free-style"),[1] he launches himself out into the city and a series of "adventures." He works in coal yards and pool halls and as the protégé of a Shakespeare-quoting autodidact slumlord. He organizes hotel workers in the Loop; he steals books to sell to students in Hyde Park. He is "adopted" by Evanston swells and rides the lake boats to Michigan as the corner man for a hopeless prizefighter. He meets gangsters, radicals, intellectuals, whores, heiresses, Poles, Italians, African Americans, Mexicans. The book sprawls like the city. It goes where it wants to go.

This quintessential Chicago novel was born in Paris. Bellow told Philip Roth how it happened: stuck on a novel, "deep in the dumps," he found himself watching the curbside flow of water released every morning for the Paris street cleaners. "I remember saying to myself, 'Well, why not take a short break and have at least as much freedom of movement as this running water.'" He remembered a childhood friend "whose surname was August—a handsome, freewheeling kid," and decided to tell his story, or his imagined story. "I was suddenly enriched with words and phrases. . . . It rushed out of me. I was turned on like a hydrant in summer."[2]

Bellow was not a native Chicagoan, or even American-born. His Canadian family moved to the Humboldt Park neighborhood from Montreal when he was a child, having been smuggled over the border by bootleggers. He arrived in Chicago on the Fourth of July 1924. He was nine years old.

The book he would write years later captures the exhilaration of that nine-year-old, overwhelmed and enthralled by his first glimpse of the gigantic new place that would become his home. The city, much more than its rather passive protagonist, is the engine of the book's discoveries. Chicago is so vivid in *Augie March* partly because Augie himself is not. An older Augie narrates the novel in rich, cascading, allusion-packed language, language that does not yet belong to the boy and young man he is recalling. Still in formation—in the process of becoming the person who can talk about his world that way—he is reactive: an observer, a describer.

But he described Chicago as well as anyone ever has.

Here is Augie, gazing from a skyscraper window at "the gray snarled city with the hard black straps of rails, enormous industry cooking and its vapor shuddering to the air, the climb and fall of its stages in construction or demolition like mesas, and on these the different powers and sub-powers crouched and watched like sphinxes."[3]

Augie March, a first-generation American, grows up in an immigrant-filled Chicago neighborhood much like the Humboldt Park in which the young Saul Bellow lived. Augie hopes to achieve the American dream without having to work too hard or commit himself to anything too much. His antic life is punctuated with more misses than hits, and the rough-and-tumble Chicago he inhabits, leaves, and returns to at once encourages his schemes and foils them.

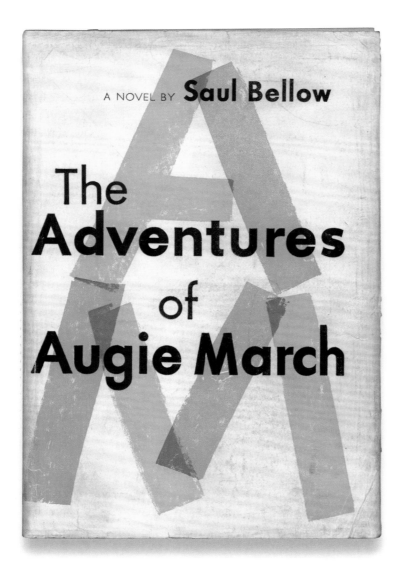

A NOVEL BY **Saul Bellow**

The **Adventures** of Augie March

Playboy

CHICAGO: HMH PUBLISHING COMPANY,
1953–PRESENT

Timothy J. Gilfoyle

Playboy magazine's inaugural issue appeared in December 1953 with Marilyn Monroe on the cover. During the ensuing half-century *Playboy* was an iconic publication in the pantheon of American magazines. The Chicago-based monthly has published works by many of the twentieth century's leading writers: Margaret Atwood, Arthur C. Clarke, Allen Ginsberg, LeRoi Jones, Gabriel García Márquez, Marshall McLuhan, Arthur Miller, Isaac Bashevis Singer, John Updike, Garry Wills, and others.[1] An extensive interview with a well-known public figure has been a common *Playboy* feature, including ones with President Jimmy Carter, Miles Davis, Martin Luther King Jr., John Lennon, and Vladimir Nabokov. Art by the likes of Art Spiegelman, Alberto Vargas, and Weegee has illustrated the pages. The magazine, however, has been best known for the provocative photo spreads of young women in various states of undress. *Playboy* came to symbolize sexual revolution, generated feminist outrage, and evoked new urban lifestyles.

The overt purpose of founding editor Hugh Hefner (1926–2017) was to feature "the girl next door" and promote "the Playboy lifestyle" for male readers. *Playboy* challenged the postwar domestic norms of early marriage, sexual fidelity, large families, and traditional concepts of masculinity.

Hefner, in both the magazine and life, glorified everything about bachelorhood: the city over the suburb, the apartment over the single-family home, urban adventure over suburban security, and heterosexual promiscuity over heterosexual monogamy. The *Playboy* ideal valorized unrestrained male heterosexuality, equating it with economic success and upward mobility. Hefner and his editors envisioned themselves as purveyors of sophisticated taste and expensive consumer behavior.[2]

Observers initially classified Hefner and *Playboy* as embodiments of a postwar sexual revolution. More accurately *Playboy* represented male rebellion. Hefner's resistance to Cold War cultural conservatism more often allied him with Beat writers Ginsberg and Jack Kerouac and rock-and-roll stars such as Elvis Presley. While *Playboy* never fully endorsed the alternative sexualities, aggressive anticapitalism, and recreational drug use that pervaded much of Beat and rock-and-roll culture, the latter's rejection of the white-collar "organization man," the female-controlled family, and the suburban ethos, however, revealed how much they shared.[3]

Playboy influenced the generations that came of age after World War II. By the 1970s, 20 percent of American men reportedly read it. Circulation peaked at 7.2 million in 1972. The magazine's success enabled Hefner to open Playboy Clubs in more than forty-five American and foreign cities, launch a television program, and purchase a property on Chicago's Gold Coast, which he named the Playboy Mansion.[4] The magazine served as a launching pad for numerous entertainers, including former Playmates Bettie Page and Anna Nicole Smith. Other celebrities appeared in the buff in *Playboy* to promote their careers: Drew Barrymore, Cindy Crawford, Bo Derek, Jayne Mansfield, and Sharon Stone. Pamela Anderson posed for fourteen different issues.[5]

Playboy also shaped other media. *Cosmopolitan* magazine aped *Playboy* in 1972 with a centerfold of the semiclad actor Burt Reynolds. In 1973 a counterpart for female audiences, *Playgirl* magazine, appeared. Hardcore pornographic competitors challenged *Playboy*, most notably Bob Guccione's *Penthouse* (1965) and Larry Flynt's *Hustler* (1974). The later magazines *FHM* (1985), *Maxim* (1995), and *Stuff* (1996) claimed to represent the new male lifestyle. These later competitors, along with internet-based publications and pornography, broke *Playboy*'s cultural dominance. In 2011 the magazine's circulation had dropped to 1.5 million, and by 2015, it was only eight hundred thousand.[6] The decline in circulation, however, did not hinder *Playboy*'s visibility. The *Playboy* logo—a rabbit head wearing a tuxedo bow tie—remains among the most recognized global brands into the twenty-first century. In 2016 the magazine decided to remove all nudity from the print edition. The experiment was short lived. In 2017 nudity returned.[7]

FACING In addition to the Playmate of the Month and a three-page spread of photographs of an unnamed nude female model, the April 1954 issue of *Playboy*'s contents included an installment of Ray Bradbury's science-fiction novel *Fahrenheit 451*; an article about jazz greats Benny Goodman, Count Basie, Gene Krupa, and others; and an essay by Benjamin Franklin, "Advice on the Choice of a Mistress."

78

Atoms in the Family: My Life with Enrico Fermi

LAURA FERMI * CHICAGO: THE
UNIVERSITY OF CHICAGO PRESS, 1954

Daniel Meyer

On a chilly evening in early December 1942, Italian physicist Enrico Fermi (1901–54) and his wife, Laura Capon Fermi (1907–77), stood inside the entrance of their Chicago home welcoming scientific colleagues to a dinner party. As the entering guests "shook the snow from their shoulders," recalled Laura Fermi in her memoir, *Atoms in the Family*, each scientist congratulated her beaming husband. Laura was puzzled, and it would be years before she learned that only hours earlier, working beneath the stands of the University of Chicago's Stagg Field, Fermi and his colleagues on the top-secret Manhattan Project had created the world's first controlled, self-sustaining nuclear chain reaction.[1]

Despite Fermi's leadership in the nation's rapidly developing nuclear program, he and his wife were recent immigrants. Both born in Rome, they had met at the University of Rome, where Enrico taught physics and Laura, the daughter of an upper-middle-class Jewish family, studied science. After their marriage in 1928, Enrico's scientific eminence grew, as did Benito Mussolini's regime and the imposition of anti-Semitic laws. Seizing the opportunity to leave Fascist Italy for Stockholm to accept the Nobel Prize in Physics in 1938, Enrico sailed with his family to a new life in the United States.[2] After conducting innovative research at Columbia University, Fermi and his colleagues were relocated to Chicago by Manhattan Project officials in 1942. He continued his investigations at other Manhattan Project labs, including Los Alamos, where he served on J. Robert Oppenheimer's team for the final stage of work leading to the Trinity test in New Mexico, the first detonation of a nuclear weapon. At the end of the war, Fermi joined the faculty of the University of Chicago's newly created Research Institutes.

By that time the Fermis and many of their immigrant colleagues had become American citizens, but the foreign origin of numerous key Manhattan Project scientists was the focus of ongoing postwar political suspicion. Seeking to broaden public understanding of nuclear scientists and their work, the University of Chicago Press asked Laura to write a biography of her life with Enrico.[3] She accepted with apprehension, since her command of English was awkward. "The actual writing was painful," she recalled. "I sat at the largest desk in our home with the dictionary on one side and Fowler's *Dictionary of [Modern] English Usage* on the other."[4] Over the next three years, drawing on memories, interviews, and official reports, she was able to complete *Atoms in the Family*. The book's dust jacket graphically depicts the narrative challenge faced by the first-time author: a Victorian stove and housewife's broom pose uneasily with stylized lab beakers and atoms.[5]

By the summer of 1954, the University of Chicago Press was in the midst of prepublication publicity for the book, with lengthy excerpts appearing in the

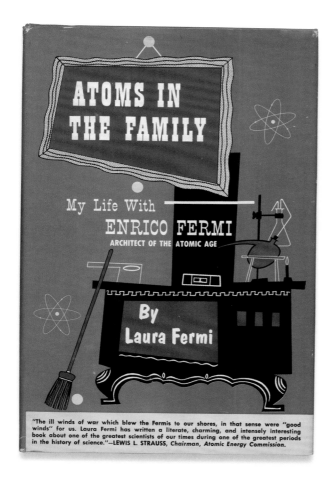

"The ill winds of war which blew the Fermis to our shores, in that sense were "good winds" for us. Laura Fermi has written a literate, charming, and intensely interesting book about one of the greatest scientists of our times during one of the greatest periods in the history of science."—LEWIS L. STRAUSS, Chairman, Atomic Energy Commission.

New Yorker and *Mademoiselle*. As the October publication date approached, however, Enrico's health gave way, and exploratory surgery disclosed cancer at an advanced stage. After several weeks of decline, he died on November 28, 1954.[6] Publicity tours and interviews planned for Laura had to be canceled, but the newly published book was still widely distributed: by mid-1955 nearly seventeen thousand copies had been sold. Reviewers were generally positive, although some thought the portrait of Enrico too personal; one noted that the mixture of charming family anecdotes and scientific detail left the reader "to wonder a little why he was so great."[7]

The strong sales of *Atoms in the Family* nonetheless helped to transform Laura Fermi into a successful author and reform advocate. She also represented her late husband at ceremonies marking anniversaries of the Manhattan Project, continuing her effort to humanize its work and put an individual face on the scientists whose lives it had transformed.[8]

In 1942 physicist Enrico Fermi and colleagues at the University of Chicago achieved the first self-sustaining nuclear chain reaction, which led to the creation of nuclear weapons and a campaign by scientists to control their use. The university's press asked Fermi's wife, Laura, to write about the life of the couple—seen here in 1954—to broaden appreciation for the work of nuclear scientists and reassure a nervous public about the potential peaceful applications of nuclear power.

79

Compulsion

MEYER LEVIN ∗ NEW YORK: SIMON & SCHUSTER, 1956

Nina Barrett

When Meyer Levin (1905–81) published *Compulsion* in 1956, more than three decades had passed since the historical event he was tackling: the infamous 1924 murder of fourteen-year-old Bobby Franks by Nathan Leopold Jr. and Richard Loeb. By then Loeb himself had been murdered in prison, and Leopold's 1953 parole request had been denied, suggesting that he too would die in jail sometime before his sentence of "life plus 99 years" expired.

Levin had briefly covered "the crime of the century" (see no. 44) as a cub reporter for the *Chicago Daily News*. But despite the killers' articulate confessions, the invasive and overwhelming media coverage, and the parade of psychiatric experts invited to testify by defense lawyer Clarence Darrow, the question that continued to haunt Levin for the next thirty years was *why*?

Levin interviewed Leopold in prison, and the two discussed collaborating on a memoir, but Leopold decided against it, and Levin blazed his own literary path. *Compulsion* wove together fact and fiction in an innovative style and is now often cited as the first "nonfiction novel," a precursor to Truman Capote's *In Cold Blood* (1966). The thinly veiled protagonists Judd Steiner and Artie Straus speak lines of dialogue lifted straight from the confession transcripts. The soaring eloquence of the fictional attorney Jonathan Wilk is mostly Darrow quoted verbatim. Yet some characters are wholly fictional or composites engineered in the service of the plot to help dramatize Levin's elaborate Freudian interpretation of the forces at work in the killers' psyches.

The book was an instant commercial and critical success, selling out its first printing in two days. Darryl Zanuck bought the film rights.[1] Erle Stanley Gardner pronounced it "an important book written in a highly readable style."[2] Robert R. Kirsch announced jubilantly in the *Los Angeles Times* that he felt he had found one of those very rare books "which still will be read in 50 or 100 years." Even with the names of the murderers changed, he said, "the Straus-Steiner story, though fiction, is truer than the Loeb-Leopold story. This may seem a strange thing to say. Yet, Nathaniel Hawthorne sensed this quality of fiction when he spoke of it as being 'true to the truth of the human heart.'"[3]

Leopold, however, was not pleased. He stated that the book made him "physically sick" and would damage his chance for parole.[4] Levin expressed "shock" that Leopold reacted this way, since he deeply believed Leopold *should* be paroled—and in fact Levin, Gardner, and Carl Sandburg all lent their voices to the parole effort.

Nevertheless Leopold, once released and living in Puerto Rico, sued Levin, alleging that the author had "unjustly appropriated Leopold's name, likeness and personality for profit" and that he had "intermingled fiction and fact so that they were indistinguishable."[5] The case dragged on for more than a decade before the Illinois Supreme Court ruled in Levin's favor in 1970.

Ironies abound: The intermingling of fact and fiction had been *the whole point*—the achievement that earned the novel a distinctive place in the history of American letters. And there is no doubt that *Compulsion*'s success helped create a climate in which Leopold could finally win parole. It humanized him in a way that neither Darrow's hired psychiatrists nor Leopold himself managed to do. When his own memoir, *Life Plus 99 Years*, was published about a year and a half after *Compulsion*, critics universally complained that it offered no insight whatsoever into why he had committed the murder. For that, wrote Edward de Grazia in his *New York Times* review, "the most satisfactory explanation has been poetic rather than psychiatric, that offered in Meyer Levin's recent novel, 'Compulsion.'"[6]

FACING The runaway success of Meyer Levin's 1956 fictionalization of the slaying of a boy by Nathan Leopold Jr. and Richard Loeb (see no. 44), inspired the author to write a play (1957) that, in turn, was the basis of the 1959 movie *Compulsion*, starring Orson Welles, Dean Stockwell, and Bradford Dillman.

80

A Raisin in the Sun: A Drama in Three Acts

LORRAINE HANSBERRY ∗ NEW YORK:
RANDOM HOUSE, 1959

Regina Taylor

What happens to a dream deferred?

Does it dry up
like a raisin in the sun?
Or fester like a sore—
And then run?
Does it stink like rotten meat?
Or crust and sugar over—
like a syrupy sweet?

Maybe it just sags
Like a heavy load.

Or does it explode?

Langston Hughes, 1951[1]

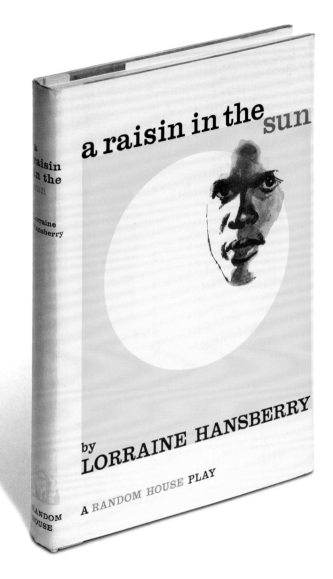

Lorraine Hansberry (1930–1965) exploded onto the American theater scene, shattering barriers when, in March 1959, her play *Raisin in the Sun* was produced at New York City's Ethel Barrymore Theatre. Its title inspired by a powerful 1951 poem by Langston Hughes (above), *Raisin* was the first play by an African American woman to appear on Broadway. That Hansberry wrote it and got it produced was a great act of revolt.

When *Raisin* won the 1959 New York Drama Critics Circle Award for best play, Hansberry became, at twenty-nine, the youngest playwright and only the fifth female to receive this prize.[2] For the first time, black bodies appeared on the Great White Way as authentic human beings rather than buffoons and stereotypes. The play is a rebellious document of Hansberry's times, prophetic in wrestling with the until-then rarely voiced themes—race, feminism, black aesthetics, and blacks' roots in Africa—before mainstream (white) audiences.[3]

Set in an overcrowded kitchenette tenement on Chicago's South Side, *Raisin* focuses on the Younger family grasping for the American Dream as they try to escape the city's restrictive housing covenants by being the first blacks to buy a house in a white neighborhood. The play ends on a note of hope and tension as the family steps into uncharted territory.

To write *Raisin*, Hansberry drew upon her own experiences growing up on Chicago's South Side. The fifth and youngest child of Nannie Perry Hansberry, a schoolteacher, and Carl Augustus Hansberry, a founder of the first African American bank in Chicago and a real estate broker, Hansberry grew up in advantageous circumstances. It was common for activists and artists such as Paul Robeson, W. E. B. Du Bois, and Hughes to visit the Hansberrys. She would ride with her father in a limousine on their monthly ritual of collecting rent. The working-class tenants would often invite them in for coffee. While conscious of her privileged status within her race, Hansberry understood that no matter one's economic status, skin color bound all blacks to a constrained existence.[4]

In 1938 the Hansberrys dared to test the margins of racism by crossing the lines of Chicago's Black Belt. They became the first black family to own a home on a street in a white residential section called Washington Park. The family was greeted by threats, violence, and even a lawsuit, which resulted in the Supreme Court of Illinois upholding a verdict to remove them from their home. Hansberry's father took the case to the US Supreme Court, which overturned the Illinois court's decision. *Hansberry v. Lee* was critical in ending restrictive housing codes in Chicago.[5]

Thus the history, memories, desires, and "dreams deferred" of Hansberry's life became the flesh and blood of her first play. She died of cancer only six years after *Raisin*'s New York premiere; she was thirty-four. Hansberry's all-too-brief life still has great resonance. Her dedication to art that "is ultimately social, that . . . agitates" has inspired many writers, including me.[6] Hansberry's reflections upon and questioning of the times in which she lived helped to define and redefine the margins of identity. Exploding boundaries and exposing her internal universes as she placed the social issues of the 1950s in Chicago under the spotlight, Lorraine Hansberry forever changed the American theatrical landscape.

FACING Lorraine Hansberry based her first play—about the struggles of an African American family seeking to leave Chicago's all-black South Side for the advantages of life in a Caucasian neighborhood—on the hostile treatment her own family received upon moving to a white area known as Washington Park.

81

Eight Men Out: The Black Sox and the 1919 World Series

ELIOT ASINOF * NEW YORK, CHICAGO, AND SAN FRANCISCO: HOLT, RINEHART AND WINSTON, 1963

Ira Berkow

In *Eight Men Out*, essentially a nonfiction novel published in 1963, Eliot Asinof (1919–2008) wrote that the "Black Sox scandal"—the tale of eight Chicago White Sox players who were involved and eventually banished from baseball for throwing the 1919 World Series—was "a betrayal of more than a set of ball games, even more than of the sport itself. It was a crushing blow at American pride."[1] Asinof recalled how the year before the United States had been victorious in World War I, "[s]aving Europe from the Hun" with "nobility and humanity."[2] Such glorious traits were reflective of baseball, which was perceived as pure Americana, our national pastime, and the ballplayers as quintessential icons.

Supposedly Major League Baseball followed the rules, and the best ball club, the one with consummate talent and team play, would legitimately emerge the winner in the World Series (which in 1919 was hardly "world," since it involved teams from a scattering of nine American cities, all east of the Mississippi River). For many, though, the Black Sox scandal shattered that image of purity, for the time being anyway. If you cannot believe that baseball is beyond corruption, what can you believe? Some called the shameful affair "the end of innocence," although there had been numerous "ends of innocence" in American history, just none quite to this degree in sports, even though it was no secret that in boxing, then perhaps the second most popular spectator sport in the United States, fights were fixed.

A graduate of Swarthmore College, Asinof played in the minor leagues before he became a writer of novels and nonfiction, primarily about baseball. His most successful publication was *Eight Men Out*, which became a movie (1988) for which he wrote the screenplay.

Eight Men Out takes the reader on a page-turning account of how gamblers, including the best known of them, Arnold Rothstein, managed to entice seven of the players to subtly fall down on the job, as it were, and thus lose to the decidedly underdog Cincinnati Reds five games to three. (An eighth man, third baseman Buck Weaver, sat in on the fixing plan but chose not to participate in it; yet the baseball commissioner, Judge Kenesaw Mountain Landis, threw him out anyway for not reporting the plan to the authorities.)

How did such great players of the time, such as outfielder "Shoeless" Joe Jackson, pitchers Ed Cicotte and "Lefty" Williams, and first baseman Chick Gandil, succumb to a conspiracy that, when discovered, shocked the nation? The intrigues, rationales, and greed (not just of the truly underpaid players but also of the skinflint team owner, Charles Comiskey) are portrayed with riveting drama and at times seeming insight. By "seeming," I mean that there is no way Asinof could have known the inner thoughts of characters such as Rothstein or Comiskey, since none of the protagonists ever spoke to

Asinof, who described his process as follows: "Little by little . . . the story gets pieced together[, though] most of the participants had died without talking, while those who survive continue to maintain silence."[3]

Indeed Asinof vividly captured the people, life, and times of the period. *Eight Men Out* illustrates why gambling remains today the greatest taboo in baseball. Just ask Pete Rose.

In 1919 members of the Chicago White Sox team, disgruntled over inadequate pay and poor treatment by the club's owner, Charles Comiskey, cooperated with a gambling syndicate to fix the World Series. The Black Sox scandal, as it is known, cast a shadow over the South Side team and baseball for many years. The decision to ban eight players from the game for life has never been rescinded.

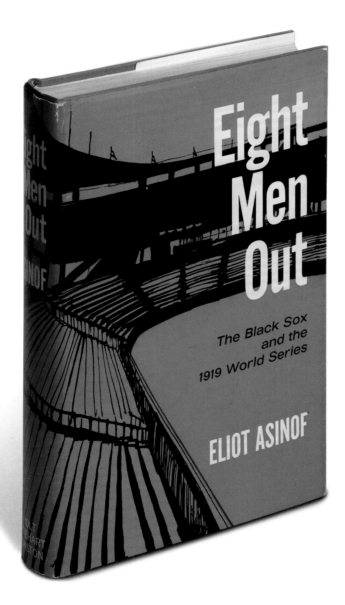

Eight Men Out

The Black Sox and the 1919 World Series

ELIOT ASINOF

82

The Chicago School of Architecture: A History of Commercial and Public Building in the Chicago Area, 1875–1925

CARL W. CONDIT ✳ CHICAGO AND
LONDON: THE UNIVERSITY OF CHICAGO
PRESS, 1964

Robert Bruegmann

Very few scholarly books catch fire with a large public. *The Chicago School of Architecture* by Carl W. Condit (1917–94) is one that did. Since it appeared in 1964, it has almost certainly been the most widely read and influential book on the history of Chicago architecture. One can hear echoes of it almost any day from the guides on the architectural boat tours plying the Chicago River or at hearings of the city's landmark commission.

Condit, who first trained as an engineer but then received a PhD in literature, taught for many years at Northwestern University.[1] *Chicago School* is by far his most influential book, but that influence is, at first glance, not easy to explain. It was not Condit's first attempt to trace the skyscraper's evolution. That was *Rise of the Skyscraper* (1952), which had little of the impact of his 1964 volume. Nor did Condit originate the term "Chicago School" or his basic plotline: that a small group of Chicago architects, including Louis Sullivan, John Root, and others, rejected nineteenth-century academic traditions and created a new and original architecture based on modern materials and needs. That argument had been proposed by European architects and historians before World War II.[2]

Most puzzling perhaps about *Chicago School*'s continuing influence is that subsequent scholarship, and even Condit's own later writings, have undermined many of the book's basic premises. For example, a central argument—that William Le Baron Jenney's Home Insurance Building (1885; demolished 1931) was the first fully skeletal building and thus the basis for Chicago's claim to being the skyscraper's birthplace—has been discredited. Scholars have also cast doubt on the "Chicago School" formulation itself.[3]

Of course, the fact that the skyscraper's actual evolution, like that of many important historical developments, is now acknowledged to have been a halting and often messy process suggests why Condit's book became so influential. Condit, a major authority on the history of engineering, must have known what he was sacrificing to make his book palatable for a general audience. And palatable it was. No longer were those familiar old buildings in the Loop dingy relics of a bygone era. They could now be seen as among the most important landmarks in the history of global culture.

To explain the full impact of this book, though, one must also take into account the context in which it was launched. Although for years Chicago had been one of the world's fastest-growing cities, with many Chicagoans hopeful that it would become the world's largest, by 1964 the region's growth was stalling while Los Angeles and other, newer cities surged. Suddenly Chicago was a mature, older metropolis.

What Chicago did not lose after World War II was intense local pride, unbounded ambition, and deep-seated anxiety about its place vis-à-vis New York. While it was increasingly difficult for Chicagoans to claim primacy in economic or cultural developments, Condit's claim that Chicago invented the skyscraper, and was therefore the birthplace of modern architecture, became the most resonant assertion anyone has made about the city's standing in the history of world culture. *The Chicago School of Architecture* was exactly the right story for its time and place, and Condit told it in a highly convincing way. It was so convincing and such a powerful argument that its influence has continued long after some of its central claims have been rebutted. Certainly no architectural history has contributed so much to redefining the image of a city for its own citizens and for the rest of the world.

FACING Historian Carl Condit's 1964 book was the first in-depth study of the city's influential architectural heritage, especially in the development of the skyscraper.

83

The Prairie School Review

EDITED BY WILBERT R. HASBROUCK
AND MARILYN WHITTLESEY HASBROUCK
* PARK FOREST AND PALOS PARK,
ILLINOIS: THE PRAIRIE SCHOOL PRESS,
1964–81

John Blew

The Prairie School Press was founded in 1961 by Wilbert R. ("Bill") Hasbrouck (1931–2018) and his wife, Marilyn Whittlesey Hasbrouck (born 1933), at their home in suburban Chicago. Bill was an architect employed by the Illinois Central Railroad; Marilyn, a former high-school algebra teacher, was raising their two children.[1] Both were passionate about the early-modern architecture of the so-called Chicago School (primarily commercial) and Prairie School (primarily residential) centered in Chicago and in the Midwest from the mid-1880s to about 1915 and led by Louis Sullivan and Frank Lloyd Wright.

While Sullivan and Wright have long been celebrated, at least fifty other architects—many outstanding, yet largely unknown—practiced during the same period; some had been employed by Sullivan or by Wright, but all were influenced by them. The Hasbroucks set out to publish a scholarly yet accessible journal that would feature the work of these less familiar Prairie School architects.

Thus was born the *Prairie School Review*. From 1964 through 1975, the Prairie School Press published forty-seven quarterly issues, including a double issue. A single issue followed in 1976 and a "final issue" in 1981.[2] Bill was editor and publisher and Marilyn assistant editor, though both stressed the joint nature of the enterprise. They composed each issue at their dining-room table, without benefit of staff or financial support. Annual subscriptions were $5 at the outset, gradually increasing to $10 near the end of the run. Since there were never more than two thousand paid subscribers, the Hasbroucks often subsidized the journal using other resources.[3]

Other than editorials and a few book reviews, the Hasbroucks did not write for the *Review*. It was the couple's policy from the beginning to give preference to the work of previously unpublished writers who were knowledgeable but, often like their subjects, relatively unknown or underrecognized. At first the couple had to seek out articles. They drew upon the research and writing of graduate students, serious amateurs, and a few young academics and other professionals. "These people became the real staff of the magazine since there never has been enough money to pay for articles," said the Hasbroucks.[4] Soon the word got out, and unsolicited manuscripts began to arrive. The *Review* provided an outlet for seminal scholarship on the Prairie School when other, more mainstream publications turned a blind eye to such work. Many of the young *Review* writers went on to distinguished professional careers.[5]

Among the architects whose work the *Review* published, some for the first time, are Parker Berry, Francis Barry Byrne, William Drummond, Harvey Ellis, Hugh Garden, Bruce Goff, Marion Mahoney Griffin, Walter Burley Griffin, George W. Maher, Purcell and Elmslie, E. E. Roberts, Henry Trost, and John Van Bergen.[6]

The
PRAIRIE
SCHOOL
Review

Volume VI, Number 2   Second Quarter, 1969

$1.50 a copy

While the *Review*'s subscriber base was small, its influence was outsized. The editorials were important and often prescient: They urged Chicago-based institutions to collect the papers and drawings of Prairie School architects; stressed the importance of preserving and restoring significant buildings in and around Chicago by these architects; and called for colleges and universities to teach the history of the Prairie and Chicago Schools and to train architectural preservationists.

During the twelve-plus years that the *Review* was published, scholarly and popular interest in Prairie School architecture took off, thanks in no small measure to the journal's influence. On the occasion of the Hasbroucks' 1992 gift of their *Prairie School Review* archive to the Ryerson and Burnham Libraries of the Art Institute of Chicago, Blair Kamin, the architecture critic of the *Chicago Tribune*, called the *Review* "an obscure, but important, magazine."[7]

In print from 1964 to 1981, the *Prairie School Review* spurred renewed interest in the turn-of-the-century work not only of the best-known Prairie School practitioners Louis Sullivan and Frank Lloyd Wright but also of many lesser-known designers, such as architect William Drummond (1876–1946), whose Recreation Building (1916–17) in Chicago's Shedd Park features on the cover of the review's volume 6, number 2 (1969).

84

Division Street: America

STUDS TERKEL * NEW YORK: PANTHEON
BOOKS (A DIVISION OF RANDOM HOUSE),
1967

Garry Wills

In classical antiquity, the poor were mute. Writing and reading, difficult and expensive exercises, were only for the privileged. Now we seem to be at an opposite extreme, when Twitter and other devices let anyone say anything anytime anywhere. Louis ("Studs") Terkel (1912–2008) found a way to avoid both extremes in his oral histories. He avoided interviews with the privileged, though he regularly had celebrities, authors, actors, and musicians on his radio talk show. For his books, he wanted to give voice to the voiceless:

There are deliberate omissions in this book, notably clergymen, college professors, journalists and writers of any kind. I felt that their articulateness and literacy offered them other forums. They had created their own books; my transcribing their attitudes would be nothing more than self-indulgence. It was the man of inchoate thought I was seeking rather than the consciously articulate.[1]

Terkel was encouraged to take this approach in 1967 by André Schiffrin, then the editor of Pantheon Books, who had just published Jan Myrdal's *Report from a Chinese Village*. The point of that book was to hear not what the Chinese government said was happening in the country but what the people themselves were experiencing. Schiffrin asked whether the same thing could be done, not in a small foreign village, but in a big city like Chicago. The aim was to hear from what are often called ordinary people, or common people. Terkel, however, did not believe there are any common people. Just people. He called those he spoke with not his subjects, or his informants, but his "companions."

Schiffrin and Terkel invented a new genre—neither the "man on the street" questionnaire nor answers to a pollster's list of questions. Terkel did not want to hear what people might say off the top of their heads but what they really felt in their hearts. To find this out, he had to spend time with his companions, let them get to know him, how he cared about them, how he listened. Then he could cull the most revealing comments from the conversations.

This approach was so successful that Terkel would repeat the operation in nine additional well-read volumes. He was fifty-four years old when *Division Street: America* came out in 1967. Neither he nor his publisher could have realized that he would live forty-two more years, working to the very end, able to do a whole series of such books. The later books modified the formula of *Division Street*. They were each devoted to a single theme: what did his companions think of working, or of World War II, of race, of music, of aging, of death? In that sense they were answering one leading question from the outset, though then they could range all over what the subject suggested to them.

While Terkel was a proud lefty himself, an important part of his liberalism was to hear everybody out with sympathy. He talked equably with Cold Warriors and pacifists, nuns and minor criminals, gay people and straight. Though these people differ widely and wildly, certain common traits emerge. Everyone wants to matter, to claim an individual dignity, whether that dignity is affirmed or denied by other people.

Terkel was able to spend so much time and energy in seeking out and listening closely to all kinds of people because that was his customary way of living. Being in his company made you want to change your own attitude toward other people and toward yourself. His books can have the same effect.

Studs Terkel, Chicago's legendary interviewer, wanted to call his first oral history "Halsted Street," after the second-longest street in Chicago, but decided on *Division Street* because it too runs through diverse neighborhoods and its name conveys layered meanings.

85

Miami and the Siege of Chicago: An Informal History of the Republican and Democratic Conventions of 1968

NORMAN MAILER ✳ NEW YORK AND
CLEVELAND: THE WORLD PUBLISHING
COMPANY, 1968

Frank Rich

Like the other explosive events of 1968, the tumult in Chicago that summer—a civil war within the Democratic National Convention, riots in the city beyond the arena's doors—required a new language to capture it. How could prose possibly match the instant eyewitness capabilities of television, the ubiquitous medium that was already pushing newspapers and magazines on their path to obsolescence?

Miami and the Siege of Chicago, a chronicle of both that year's Republican and Democratic conventions originally written by the novelist Norman Mailer (1923–2007) on assignment for *Harper's* magazine, was an effort to invent that new language. Mailer had long been captivated by the literary revolution known as New Journalism hatched in the 1960s by a pair of iconoclastic magazine editors, Harold Hayes of *Esquire* and Willie Morris of *Harper's*. Mailer's take on the 1960 Democratic convention for *Esquire* (no. 55), "Superman Comes to the Supermarket," was an early example of the genre. His book-length recounting of the 1967 antiwar march on the Pentagon, *The Armies of the Night* (subtitled *History as a Novel, the Novel as History*), was arguably his best-received literary venture since *The Naked and the Dead* (1948). *Miami and the Siege of Chicago* was its eagerly awaited sequel.

In lesser hands, New Journalism could be a recipe for self-indulgence, solipsism, and mischievous fictionalization, but that is not the case with Mailer's reportage from Miami and Chicago. His book holds up better than most political journalism written last week, let alone five decades ago—as history, as literature, and as a portrait of the United States both then and now. Mailer's Dickensian flourishes revivify the half-remembered figures of the time: Eugene McCarthy seemed less a presidential prospect than "the dean of the finest English department in the land," while Mayor Richard J. Daley looked at his worst "like a vastly robust peasant woman with a dirty gray silk wig" and at his best "respectable enough to be coach of the Chicago Bears."[1] Nor did Mailer forsake the wide-angle shot. He opened both chapters of his book with surveys of the conventions' respective settings. In Chicago, "the great American city," he apotheosized both the "clean tough keen-eyed ladies" of the Near North Side and "the fear and absolute anguish of beasts dying upside down" at the old slaughterhouses.[2] And beyond the urbanology, Mailer took the measure of the larger national dynamics at work, sketching in an emerging political landscape that persists in many ways to this day.

A classic New Deal liberal who thought Republicans "did not deserve the presidency, never," Mailer was nonetheless ambivalent about the armies of the Left he found in Chicago.[3] Contemplating the Yippies in Lincoln Park with their signs of "Vote Pig in '68" and situating himself in the scene in the third person, he wrote, "Were those unkempt children the sort of troops with

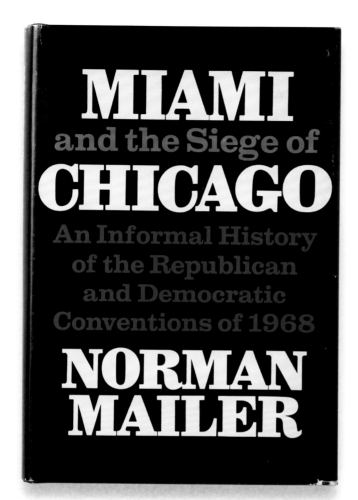

whom one wished to enter battle?" He fretted that Vietnam and Black Power were "pushing him to that point where he would have to throw his vote in with revolution," and asked, "What price was he really willing to pay?"[4]

This question is not resolved by the end of the book, which finds the author, manhandled but unbowed by Daley's rampaging cops, retreating to the revels at Hugh Hefner's Playboy Mansion. But if Mailer was not quite sure where he belonged in the maelstrom of 1968, he was certain about the trajectory that lay ahead for the country. "We will be fighting for forty years," he wrote.[5]

Even now that fight rages on. Many of its origins can be found in Mailer's one-of-a-kind account of a GOP in transition to the Reagan revolution in Miami, and of a divided Democratic party descending into chaos in Chicago.

Norman Mailer began the section of this book devoted to the 1968 Democratic Convention in Chicago with a description of the city's slaughterhouses. The brutality of that industry becomes a metaphor for the violence to which demonstrators were subjected in the streets. A number of them are seen here confronting the National Guard along Michigan Avenue at Grant Park.

86

Chicago on Foot: An Architectural Walking Tour

IRA J. BACH ✳ PHOTOGRAPHS BY
PHILIP A. TURNER ✳ CHICAGO: FOLLETT
PUBLICATIONS, 1969

Jay Pridmore

When Ira Bach's *Chicago on Foot* was first published, in 1969, crowd-pleasing books on architecture were a rarity. That was probably due to midcentury modernism, on the downward side of its long, unpopular run, and Ludwig Mies van der Rohe's terse aphorism "Build, don't talk."

It took a special author to understand that buildings can talk, we can hear what they have to say, and we can have conversations with them. Ira Bach (1906–85) was such a person, emerging from Chicago City Hall, of all places. As the city's director of planning, he oversaw most public building developments in Chicago from 1957, when he became Mayor Richard J. Daley's planning commissioner, to 1984, when he resigned as Mayor Harold Washington's assistant for development and planning.[1] Bach brought his skills as a city planner (he was trained at MIT) and a political appointee to many megaprojects, including Lake Meadows, Carl Sandburg Village, and O'Hare Airport. Bach filled other positions as well, including chairmanship of the city's Commission on Historical and Architectural Landmarks.

Bach's career reminds us that the best judge of architecture, more than a newspaper critic, more than early praise even, is longevity. A building's true worth can be assessed only after it has been around for a while. This lesson resonates in *Chicago on Foot*, which is an irony because it is by genre a guidebook, and by its nature a portrait of a moment.

Yet *Chicago on Foot* is an endlessly interesting snapshot. Bach wrote of the Rookery, then not many steps away from a heedless wrecker's ball, that the "glass-and-iron tracery [of its then-painted-over skylight] harmonizes with the extensive grillwork used below."[2] He praised the Daley Center, built in 1965, for its "appropriate setting," an instructive understatement to describe a work that was recently called "possibly the finest example of the International Style in America."[3] He lauded architect Walter Netsch's Circle Campus, now the University of Illinois–Chicago, for its network of elevated walkways, which later crumbled and were razed, reminding us again that time tells.

The thirty-six walking tours around the city in this book are as utilitarian, sometimes as terse, as a quintessential work of Chicago School architecture. Bear in mind, the high artistry of the Loop's early skyscrapers was recognized years after they were known for prosaic economy. Form always follows function. Likewise, Bach's literary merit is often visible beneath straightforward insight.

In its own time, this book's most important influence was to help revalue deteriorating neighborhoods with historic buildings, some restored, many not. Bach wrote of Old Town's townhouses, "You may think when you've seen one you've seen them all." But look deeper. "The rich texture of the fine brickwork and stone ornament make an architectural 'find' of many of the buildings."[4]

Chicago on Foot, which has been updated and republished many times since its original release (with Susan Wolfson as coauthor of later editions), highlights designs utterly buried in today's tours and architectural literature. It discusses the Civic Opera House with almost-fresh resentment of the man who built it: the indicted tycoon Samuel Insull. It cheers the over-the-top classicism of the 1896 Dewes mansion on Wrightwood, constructed for an otherwise forgotten beer mogul.

Of course, some of the buildings profiled in *Chicago on Foot* no longer exist, some lamented, some not. But that does not diminish Bach's book, which survives and ought to. Like a good building, it is a reveal of its specific time and place. Also like a good building, even an old one, it expresses universal values that are only magnified by time.

FACING The popularity among tourists and residents alike of this compact guide to Chicago and its neighborhoods by city planner Ira Bach has led to many printings and revised editions. This cover design for the second edition cleverly and succinctly projects the importance of walking through the city to learn about it.

87

Chicago, Chicago

PHOTOGRAPHS BY YASUHIRO ISHIMOTO
✳ FOREWORD BY HARRY CALLAHAN ✳
TEXT BY SHUZO TAKIGUCHI ✳ DESIGN BY
YUSAKU KOMEKURA ✳ [TOKYO]: BIJUTSU
SHUPPAN-SHA, 1969

Stephen Daiter

Designed and published in Japan, *Chicago, Chicago* is one of the most important photography books created about the city. In this beautifully printed volume, Yasuhiro Ishimoto (1921–2012) captured Chicago's public life of the 1950s and 60s in all its moods and complexity.[1]

Ishimoto's work was informed by a complicated dual perspective: Born in San Francisco, he was raised in Japan. He returned to the United States in 1939 to study, and during World War II was interned at Amache Camp in Colorado (1942–44), where he was introduced to photography. In 1946 he enrolled at Northwestern University to study architecture, but two years later he decided to focus on photography at Chicago's celebrated Institute of Design. Afterward he lived mainly in Japan, returning to Chicago regularly for more than fifty years, including a stay from 1958 to 1961 funded by the Minolta Corporation to photograph the city. This resulted in the publication *Chicago, Chicago.*

The book's seemingly straightforward photographs are filled with nuance and observations that only someone with Ishimoto's singular viewpoint could craft. Ishimoto's approach to photography is unique in its combination of Western modernism and Japanese formalism and attention to subtle beauty. His American influences included Harry Callahan and Aaron Siskind, his teachers at the Institute of Design (both made many iconic photographs of Chicago), as well as the architect Ludwig Mies van der Rohe.[2] On the other hand, Ishimoto was a devotee of the seventeenth-century Japanese poet Matsuo Bashō, a master of the short, austere poetic form known as haiku. This interest can be seen in the gentle, humanistic character and elegant structure of Ishimoto's photographs.

Chicago, Chicago has a distinct narrative flow created by a sensitive observer who was largely apolitical. It begins with photographs that allude to the end of an industrialized era: changing and decaying neighborhoods, urban renewal, and the tough and determined people who live there. These are followed by images of a city that is also rebuilding and vibrant. While some of them focus on the abstract and tactile properties of surfaces and building elements, people, whether solitary or in small groups (often children), predominate. We see them celebrating, waiting on street corners, sitting on stoops, looking out windows, congregating at beaches and parks. The book's last, enigmatic image, of newspaper pages blowing through Grant Park, seems to suggest the ever-changing, elusive meanings of modern life and the apparently random twists and turns that shape the future.

Since its publication, *Chicago, Chicago* has helped mold Japanese perceptions of Chicago.[3] It has also inspired Chicago's photography community.

This is because Ishimoto's images are both particular and universal: astute comments on physical, political, historical, and cultural relationships of Chicagoans, they constitute an homage to the city that is at once clear-eyed and affectionate.[4]

The photographer Yasuhiro Ishimoto had two homes: Tokyo and Chicago. This book was for many years regarded as his most personal statement. In the book's last photograph, he used contrasts of shadow and light to capture a sense of wind blowing newspaper pages randomly over an otherwise still park scene.

88

Chicago: Growth of a Metropolis

HAROLD M. MAYER AND RICHARD
C. WADE, WITH GLEN E. HOLT ✳
CARTOGRAPHY BY GERALD F. PYLE ✳
CHICAGO AND LONDON: THE UNIVERSITY
OF CHICAGO PRESS, 1969

Pauline Saliga

Chicago: Growth of a Metropolis is a pictorial history that examines the geographical features, historic events, and entrepreneurial citizens that shaped Chicago's development. First published in 1969, *Growth of a Metropolis* was written at a time when architectural historians were laying a foundation of scholarship on the history of Chicago architecture in books such as Sigfried Giedion's *Space, Time and Architecture: The Growth of a New Tradition* (1941), which places Chicago architecture within the development of international modernism, and the four volumes by Carl Condit that form the bedrock of Chicago's architectural history: *The Rise of the Skyscraper* (1952); *The Chicago School of Architecture: A History of Commercial and Public Building in the Chicago Area, 1875–1925* (1964; no. 82); *Chicago, 1910–29: Building, Planning and Urban Technology* (1973); and *Chicago, 1930–70: Building, Planning, and Urban Technology* (1974).

Mayer and Wade's book takes a different approach. It considers how Chicago's geographic features enabled it to prosper as a port and railroad capital, while its entrepreneurs and ordinary citizens spurred the city's early growth by rebuilding after the Great Fire of 1871 and by continuing to innovate through the 1893 and 1933–34 world's fairs and the 1909 *Plan of Chicago* (no. 29).

As a pictorial history, with more than one thousand historic photos and fifty maps, *Chicago: Growth of a Metropolis* is a uniquely useful introduction to the city's history for both researchers and casual readers. A major focus throughout is housing of all types, from architect-designed mansions to workers' cottages, bungalows, and two-flats. Rather than focus on prominent citizens as a standard study might, Mayer and Wade created more of a social history, exposing ordinary and sometimes gritty life in Chicago over time. They did this by publishing hundreds of street views interpreted in long captions that summarize complex social and economic histories with an amazing economy of language. A seventy-four-word photo caption for the 1850s Galvin residence in Bridgeport, for example,[1] sheds light on the local industries (lime), the area's predominant first-wave immigrant groups (Irish and German), and the catalytic role the Illinois and Michigan Canal played in the development of the South Side Bridgeport neighborhood. It also hints that the humble worker's cottage seems short because the street level was raised but the house was not.

This welcoming format allows one to skim Chicago history or delve into how people inhabited the city. The book includes everything from small-scale personal and recreational spaces—houses, beaches, parks, neighborhood shopping areas—to large-scale public and commercial spaces: skyscrapers, industrial corridors, airports, and expressways. The use of historic photos,

1. Clarendon Beach and Bath House, 1916
(Courtesy Chicago Historical Society.)

2. Northern End of Lincoln Park, from Irving Park Boulevard (Now Irving Park Road), 1936
Adjacent to the Edgewater and Uptown communities, a hook-shaped, man-made peninsula enclosed Montrose Harbor and beach. On this new land fill, running beside Waveland Golf Course, Lake Shore Drive was extended from Montrose to Foster avenues. The engineers who built this section of the drive were among the pioneers in their use of the grade separation cloverleafs. (Courtesy Chicago Historical Society.)

3. Junction of River Street (Wacker Drive) and Rush Street Bridge, Eastward, 1914 or Early 1915
Rush Street Bridge was one of the worst traffic bottlenecks in the city, with two different streets feeding into it. At the right is the Hoyt Building erected in 1872 on the site of Fort Dearborn. It stood until 1921 when it was torn down to make way for the London Guarantee Building (now the Stone Container Building). The wharves in the foreground were used by the Goodrich Line steamboats from Civil War times until the thirties. These vessels connected Chicago with ports on both the east and west shores of Lake Michigan. Across the bridge, on the extreme left is the steamer *Eastland* (not a Goodrich liner), which capsized at Clark Street in 1915 with loss of over 800 lives. (Courtesy Chicago Historical Society.)

4. South on Michigan Avenue from the Chicago River, Probably 1918
A narrow and congested Michigan Avenue in the foreground contrasts with the already widened Michigan Avenue in the distance. The three blocks of buildings on the east side of Michigan Avenue were soon demolished and a widened thoroughfare was completed from Grant Park to the river. (Courtesy Chicago Historical Society.)

5. Michigan Avenue (then called Pine Street), North from Ohio, 1918
This photograph was taken just before the widening of Michigan Avenue from the River northward to the Lake at Oak Street. (Photograph, Charles Barker. Courtesy Chicago Historical Society.)

ingly intolerable traffic jams. Among the worst bottlenecks was North Michigan Avenue. The portion in front of Grant Park had already been widened, but at Randolph Street what was known as "the Splendid Mile" suddenly narrowed to sixty-six feet. Walter Moody described it in 1919 as a strip which "presented the appearance of a poor, tenth rate city" where "many vacant buildings showed the grime of years upon their windows, the door-lintels were hung with cobwebs, and a general air of decadence prevailed." At the river, traffic moved across the Rush Street Bridge, which carried seventy-seven per cent of all the automobile and twenty-six per cent of all the commercial vehicles coming into the Loop from the North Side —a heavier burden than was borne by the famous and larger London Bridge in England.

As early as 1914 the people had voted a bond issue to begin widening the street and to building a new bridge. Opponents of the project declared it a boon only to "rich automobile owners" and "the swells," and took the issue to court. Before litigation had been finished, over 8,700 property settlements were made and years of construction were lost. But, in May, 1920, an immense public celebration greeted the widened street and the new double-leaf bascule span. The bridge, in Lloyd Lewis' words, "rose into the air like an alligator's jaws when ships whistled" and carried commercial vehicles in the lower level while accom-

included as a narrative tool, is one reason the book endures today. Equally important, scholars find *Growth of a Metropolis* as relevant now as it was when it first appeared. It has been cited in untold numbers of publications.[2]

Lead authors Harold M. Mayer (1916–94) and Richard C. Wade (1922–2008) documented the city from the perspective of a geographer and an urban planner, respectively. Mayer was a prolific scholar who wrote influential geographic histories, including *The Port of Chicago and the St. Lawrence Seaway* (1957) and *Readings in Urban Geography* (1959).[3] A pioneer in the interdisciplinary study of urban history, Wade used social science as a way to analyze the growth of cities in such books as *Slavery in the Cities: The South 1820–1860* (1964) and *A History of the United States* (1966). Assisting the lead authors was historian Glen E. Holt, who studied Chicago's neighborhoods.[4] Gerald F. Pyle, a medical geographer and epidemiologist, produced the volume's maps. Pyle's area of expertise was using maps to analyze the spread of disease over time and space.[5]

Over one thousand photographs, accompanied by informative captions, tell the story of Chicago's development, from historical events and influential personalities to the city's many neighborhoods. The wide-ranging subjects of this spread include a beach and bath house, an aerial shot of the north end of Lincoln Park, the wharves of the Chicago River, and the development of Michigan Avenue.

89

Rules for Radicals: A Pragmatic Primer for Realistic Radicals

SAUL D. ALINSKY ∗ NEW YORK: RANDOM HOUSE, 1971

Don Rose

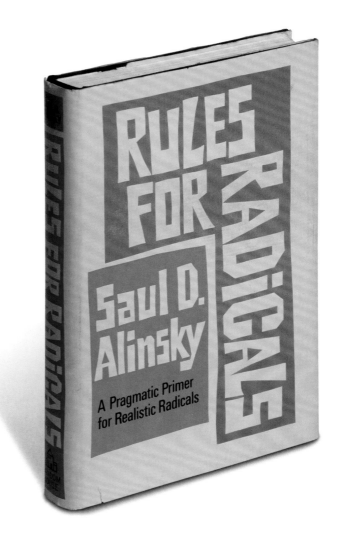

"What does a community organizer do?" Sarah Palin asked with a sneer at the 2008 Republican National Convention. Months later she found out, when a former community organizer from Chicago named Barack Obama and his cohorts organized enough communities politically to achieve an overwhelming electoral-vote victory for the United States presidency.

Between the settlement-house movement of Jane Addams, during violent episodes of social upheaval in the late nineteenth and early twentieth centuries, and the neighborhood empowerment thrust of Saul Alinsky (1909–72), ranging from early union drives to the civil rights movement, Chicago must be viewed as the original laboratory and proving ground of community organizing. Born in Chicago, Alinsky attended the University of Chicago, majoring in archeology. His first job was as a criminologist for the state of Illinois, followed by a stint as an organizer for the Congress of Industrial Organizations (CIO). By 1939 he was active as a community organizer.

Although the rhetoric and styles of Addams and Alinsky differed vastly, they shared a virtually identical aim: to empower the powerless. For Alinsky this involved entering a struggle between the "haves" and "have-nots." His most quotable quote, "The despair is there; now it's up to us to go in and rub raw the sores of discontent, galvanize [people] for radical social change,"[1] would have been too crude for Addams. For her, "a settlement constantly endeavors to make its neighborhood realize that it belongs to the city as a whole and can only improve as the city improves."[2]

But despite the difference in their times and style, Addams's goal was essentially what Alinsky and his Industrial Areas Foundation, established in 1940, achieved. From the white ethnic Back of the Yards Neighborhood Council to the African American Woodlawn Organization to the Latino United Neighborhood Organization, his groups integrated themselves into the Chicago power structure and got their pieces of the pie, as had the immigrant, largely Italian, neighborhoods Addams had helped organize politically. Alinsky's organizational tactics have become enshrined for succeeding generations, all across the nation and in social and political groups both left and right, thanks in large part to his final testament, *Rules for Radicals*.

While Alinsky's 1946 book *Reveille for Radicals* is more philosophically and ideologically grounded, in *Rules* he codified and simplified the techniques and procedures of organizing by offering thirteen tenets of "power tactics," supplemented by eleven dealing with the ethics of ends and means. Found in the book are such epigrammatic statements as "'The Prince' was written by Machiavelli for the Haves on how to hold power. 'Rules for Radicals' is written for the Have-Nots on how to take it away" and "If the ends don't justify the means, what does?" Each chapter offers lessons through mini-dialogues between the aspiring organizer and those he is organizing, bolstered by rhetorical verities of democracy. Though this *vade mecum* today sounds a bit old hat ("never go outside the experience of your people," "a good tactic is one your people enjoy," and so forth), it remains useful, as even some Tea Partiers attest, while at the same time others vilify Hillary Clinton as an "Alinskyite."[3] The organizer's confrontational strategies were at once praised and highly criticized.

Alinsky laid the groundwork for today's far more sophisticated organizers who have the tools of the internet, data, and social media to work with instead of shoe leather and the mimeograph machine, but he set the wheels in motion and inspired many successors, including Obama and Chicago's Midwest Academy, whose founder, Heather Booth, credits Alinsky's work and books as fundaments, much as Alinsky looked to those of Addams.

FACING The legacy of Jane Addams's Hull-House (no. 30) was updated by Chicago activist Saul Alinsky, who urged groups and neighborhoods to organize politically and penetrate existing power structures in order to achieve change. *Rules for Radicals* has influenced generations of community organizers nationwide.

90

Boss: Richard J. Daley of Chicago

MIKE ROYKO * NEW YORK: E. P. DUTTON & CO., INC., 1971

Paul M. Green

Simply stated, Mike Royko (1932–97) was one of Chicago's greatest newspaper columnists. The Pulitzer Prize–winning writer covered the city's government and politics in weekly and then daily columns that appeared for over forty years in three Chicago papers. His book *Boss: Richard J. Daley of Chicago* remains the most widely read and discussed biography of the city's most famous mayor, not because of any groundbreaking research or analysis but rather because of the author's journalistic talent, unique satiric wit, and feel for his city's citizens.[1]

Boss captures not only the personality and power of Richard J. Daley (1902–76) but also the political rhythms of Chicago. Published after the raucous 1968 Democratic National Convention in Chicago, it prompted stiff criticism from Daley loyalists, including the mayor's wife, who demanded that her local supermarket chain take the book off its shelves. That did not happen.

Many authors (including me) have tried to fully understand Daley as both an individual and a politician. Most skim through his first sixty years and zero in on the issues of Daley versus racial change and Daley versus anti–Vietnam War protesters. Royko avoided that trap, attempting to create a full picture of this man, who rose from the working-class neighborhood of Bridgeport, which bordered the stockyards, to become the most powerful mayor in Chicago's history.

Royko described Daley's long climb up the political ladder as one of "luck" and "pluck." His takeover of the Cook County Democratic Central Committee in 1953 was helped by the death of his chief rival. His mayoral victories in the 1955 primary and general elections were due in large part to his reenergizing the city's Democratic organization; the machine was firmly under his control.[2]

Boss lists a series of episodes when the mayor crushed any and all opposition, demanded total loyalty from elected and appointed officials, and ran the city with an iron hand. The book points out some of the dubious members of Daley's Democratic machine, focusing on those with open ties to organized crime. It also suggests how Daley's personal lifestyle—one of family, church, and neighborhood—kept him from being totally linked with those nefarious individuals.

In a book filled with insights and inside stories, perhaps Royko's best contribution was debunking the myth that Chicago was a "city of neighborhoods"; he saw it instead as a "city of ethnic states," with many residents suffering from ethnic and religious discrimination. Royko understood that this forced Chicago's huge and diverse European immigrant populations to isolate themselves—each in their own ethnic state—to create a sense of safety and belonging. That history makes neighborhood fights against desegregation

more understandable, if not acceptable, and provides true insight into Daley the man and politician. Royko dramatized Daley and the race issue by centering on Dr. Martin Luther King Jr.'s 1966 visit to Chicago, demonstrating the mayor's slickness in agreeing with his high-profile visitor's goals but, in the end, making no significant policy changes. Such tactics revealed Daley's "Bridgeport bias" on race, as well as the political reality he faced.

Describing Chicago's unpreparedness for the 1968 Democratic Convention, Royko mocked Daley's combative hostility toward "outside people" who came to *his* city to disrupt *his* convention with their antiwar protest.[3] Almost sadly, Royko related how the master politician became an amateurish bully in dealing with this critical moment in Chicago's history.

While acknowledging Daley's background and his vast governmental experience, Royko condemned his unwillingness to deal seriously with the issues of race and dissent and his use of his "machine" to intimidate and dominate those who challenged his authority, especially reformers. Nonetheless, *Boss* did little to hurt Daley politically. He was reelected in 1971 and 1975 by landslide margins.[4]

In the April 4, 1971, issue of the *New York Times*, Studs Terkel opined about *Boss*: "Fortunately, nothing can stop a book whose time has come. Mike Royko, Chicago's most incisive and impertinent journalist since Finley Peter Dunne [see no. 20], has produced such a work." Terkel praised this bare-all account of Richard J. Daley, the city's most famous, and infamous, mayor, as "an occasion for celebration."

91

Forever Open, Clear and Free: The Struggle for Chicago's Lakefront

LOIS WILLE ✳ CHICAGO: HENRY REGNERY COMPANY, 1972

Julia Bachrach

Chicago residents and visitors often agree that the twenty-six-mile stretch of lakefront parkland is one of the city's most valuable assets. Until the 1972 publication of Lois Wille's book *Forever Open, Clear and Free: The Struggle for Chicago's Lakefront,* however, the history of the movement to protect the lakefront's open character was not widely known. Reissued in 1991 and still in print, the volume has been engaging and informative to broad and diverse audiences for more than four decades. *Forever Open* has helped foster new battles for the protection of the city's lakefront and has inspired other authors to produce scholarship related to this rich and complex topic.

One of the nation's groundbreaking women newspaper reporters, Lois Wille (b. 1931) began her career at the *Chicago Daily News* in 1956. Though few women journalists were able to write about serious issues at that time, Wille won a 1963 Pulitzer Prize for public service for a series about the dearth of birth-control services in Illinois. She became associate editor at the *Chicago Sun-Times* and then editorial page editor for the *Chicago Tribune*, receiving a second Pulitzer Prize for editorial writing in 1989. Wille often covered stories about Chicago politics and problems. In a 1991 interview with the Washington Press Club Foundation, she explained that her work with Chicago Metropolitan Council, a nonprofit that advocated for good planning in housing and environmental issues, inspired her to write *Forever Open*.[1]

Written in a narrative style, *Forever Open* tells a long and complicated story in a compelling way. The book introduces the early explorers Father Jacques Marquette and Louis Jolliet, who suggested a canal to link Lake Michigan with the Mississippi River after Native Americans showed them how to travel this route by portaging canoes through areas too shallow for paddling. This leads to the visionary canal commissioners and the legal precedent they established in the 1830s by marking a land-sale map "forever Open, Clear, & free."[2] Businessman Aaron Montgomery Ward's two-decades-long battle to keep Grant Park from being cluttered with buildings is covered in a colorful, though slim, chapter. Daniel H. Burnham and his seminal 1909 *Plan of Chicago* (no. 29) are taken up in a discussion that includes the development of the south lakefront parks up to Chicago's 1933–34 World's Fair. The last three chapters, which can be considered the most important of the book, focus on lakefront issues from the post–World War II period to the early 1970s. This was the era in which Wille herself worked with the Metropolitan Planning Council, covering relevant stories as a newspaper reporter and editor.

The book relies on only limited primary sources and lacks citations throughout. Recent scholarship has revealed inaccuracies in some of the materials that Wille used. The final chapters are more accurate, since Wille was able to rely more on firsthand experience. Despite such weaknesses, there is no doubt that *Forever Open* is extremely valuable and influential. It helped pave the way for the adoption of Chicago's 1973 Lakefront Protection Ordinance. A 2016 lawsuit to prevent the construction of the Lucas Museum demonstrates that the need to safeguard the lakefront is as relevant today as when the book was first published nearly half a century ago.[3] *Forever Open, Clear and Free: The Struggle for Chicago's Lakefront* continues to foster civic pride in Chicago's legacy of green space and inspires new generations of activists who are committed to protecting this priceless asset.

This photograph of the Field Museum as it looked around 1921 reveals the degree to which the its surroundings have been transformed into what is today one of the great public spaces of any North American city. The long and arduous struggle to achieve this goal is relayed in *Forever Open, Clear and Free*.

92

Chicago
Breakdown

MIKE ROWE * LONDON: EDDISON PRESS,
LTD., 1973

Paul Garon

In *Chicago Breakdown*, Mike Rowe (b. 1938), a former editor of the pioneering English journal *Blues Unlimited*, provided a detailed history of blues in Chicago, tracing it through the multiple perspectives of blues artists, record-label entrepreneurs, nightclub proprietors, and disk jockeys. He elaborated upon those varied testimonies to form the main structure of the book: Chicago blues broken down into analyses of styles, regions, and eras.

Blues artists in Chicago included the likes of Big Bill Broonzy, Memphis Minnie, and Tampa Red, all big names in the 1930s and early 1940s. However, the sobriquet "Chicago blues" came into being to designate the new electric sounds pioneered by Elmore James, Howlin' Wolf, Jimmy Reed, Sunnyland Slim, Muddy Waters, and Sonny Boy Williamson II, to name a few, who spawned a new generation that included Buddy Guy, Magic Sam, Otis Rush, and other younger artists.

Blues singers have been recording in Chicago since the 1920s, but the sound we now recognize as the Chicago blues grew out of Waters's first recordings for Aristocrat in 1947 and the sounds shaped by Waters and Little Walter shortly after that.

Artists from the Mississippi Delta region migrated north to Chicago, bringing with them their musical traditions, and it was those traditions, reworked with the new sounds of the city, that became the Chicago blues. As more traditional singers like Memphis Minnie and Tampa Red saw their club dates disappearing in the face of the new electric sounds produced by a new generation of blues artists, the major labels that had recorded them, like RCA Victor and Columbia, lost interest and stopped recording them. It took independents like Chess and VeeJay to capture the new sounds; without those small labels, the Chicago blues might not have appeared as it did and when it did. The tradition of Chicago blues being recorded by local labels has not ended, with music still being recorded by local labels like Bob Koester's Delmark Records and Bruce Iglauer's Alligator Records.

The structure of *Chicago Breakdown* illuminates the development of Chicago blues in ways that are still relevant in assessing this musical tradition. While Waters, Wolf, and many of their colleagues hailed from the South Side, a new, younger crop of West Side singers began recording for labels such as Cobra, Artistic, and Chief. All of those players—who began their recording careers in 1956–58—derived their guitar styles from B. B. King, emphasizing single-note picking between lines, rather than building on country-blues traditions. King himself was inspired by the sophisticated styles of Lonnie Johnson and T-Bone Walker.

The audience for *Chicago Breakdown* was the thousands of new blues fans who participated in the folk-blues revival of the 1950s and 1960s; they were joined by others who came to postwar Chicago blues from the world of rock.

Thus as the great blues pioneers disappeared and the music became less relevant in African American culture, it grew more popular in white American culture than it had ever been before. Rowe's book kept the focus on the African American contribution to the history of Chicago, just as important as that of the city's black visual artists, writers, and poets, who have received more attention.

Chicago Breakdown is remarkable for its well-researched, comprehensive view. Perhaps equally remarkable is that this essential book on one of Chicago's artistic and cultural treasures was written by a Londoner. The book was first published in Britain by Eddison Press and, two years later, in the United States by Drake Publishers. DaCapo Press obtained the paperback rights in 1981, and the book became popular, ultimately undergoing a name change to *Chicago Blues*. So thorough is Rowe's work that it has never been replaced, and it is still in print from DaCapo.

FACING The evocative 1971 photograph of dancers at the Chicago blues club Theresa's that graces this dust jacket is by Valerie Wilmer (b. 1941), a celebrated photographer of European and American jazz and blues personalities and settings. Both Wilmer and Mike Rowe, the author of this important book, are English, signaling the impact Chicago's music has had worldwide.

93

Sexual Perversity in Chicago and The Duck Variations[1]

Two Plays by David Mamet

NEW YORK: GROVE PRESS, 1978

Chris Jones

"As a kid in high school, I hung around Second City quite a bit," David Mamet (b. 1947) wrote in 1991. "I was friendly with the owners and their families and was permitted to frequent the joint. Later I worked there as a busboy, and, occasionally, I played piano for the kids' shows on the weekend." The great comedy theater Second City was in Old Town; for Mamet it was the closest thing in Chicago to *la vie bohème*. As Mamet recounted in his reminiscence, its denizens hung out at the Hotel Lincoln and shot craps in the men's room. "When it came time for me to go out into the world, I applied to the hotel and was rented a room," Mamet wrote.

I lived at the Hotel Lincoln. I went downstairs several times a day to the restaurant and sat in the same booths that once sheltered [Jack] Burns and [Avery] Schreiber, Fred Willard and the great Severn Darden. . . . I received messages at the switchboard and had beautiful young women up to my room. . . . I also worked as a waiter at a club just up Clark Street and as a busboy in the final days of The London House. I wrote plays in my notebook, sitting in the Laff-In and on various benches in the park across the street.[2]

So the Hotel Lincoln was where Mamet first learned how to be Mamet. To a large extent, that colorful residence and Second City combined in Mamet's head to forge *Sexual Perversity in Chicago*, first produced at the city's Organic Theatre in 1974 under the direction of Stuart Gordon. One of the most famous plays ever written in Chicago,[3] it not only defined Mamet but also reflected a broad swath of the city's theater scene. Its staccato style and unflinching bluntness were widely perceived as an early example of the raw honesty that typified the early years of Chicago's Off-Loop theater movement.

Sexual Perversity started out as a series of Second City–style blackout sketches, which Gordon helped Mamet shape into a coherent play against a backdrop of the singles bars located on Division Street, south of the Lincoln Hotel. Like so much of the material associated with the famous comedy citadel, *Sexual Perversity* is an impressionistic look at failed relationships set in an archetypical Second City locale—the Chicago pickup bar. It follows the travails of two Jewish couples, both unable to keep their relationships together. The piece begins with guys bragging about their sexual exploits and concludes, after the relationships dissolve, with an expression of desperate loneliness. *Sexual Perversity* is full of profanity, putting in place the Mametian brand but also making it difficult for the writer to escape what he set in motion in Chicago.

Sexual Perversity is not a catalogue of erotic misbehavior. The titular perversity is, fundamentally, emotional. The play's characters talk, date, drink, and fight mostly as a way of avoiding any expression of true emotion. In the cynical tone and sad, downbeat ending of this great play, one can see Mamet's ability both to profit from the shallowness of life and, at the same time, to indict it. The 1986 movie version of *Sexual Perversity* (retitled *About Last Night* because the film's producers believed the original title would be too offensive) is set in Chicago, but its characters are younger and thus their mistakes more easily forgivable.[4] Hollywood producers like optimism (or at least the possibility thereof); Mamet's script is merely a reflection of life in Chicago, as he saw it from the Lincoln Hotel. He forgave nothing.

Slang and profanities punctuate the interchanges of four working-class Chicago twentysomethings struggling with intimate relationships in *Sexual Perversity in Chicago*. The powerful play established Chicago-born David Mamet as an important new voice in American realist theater when it was introduced off-Broadway in 1976.

94

The House on Mango Street

SANDRA CISNEROS * HOUSTON: ARTE
PÚBLICO PRESS, 1984

Carlos Tortolero

There it was: a line . . . a line of people . . . of all ages. For several hours it stretched from inside the National Museum of Mexican Art, Chicago, to outside the building for almost a block. What were these people waiting to see? The writer Sandra Cisneros. She had come to sign copies of her 1984 book *The House on Mango Street* in conjunction with a traveling exhibition organized by the museum. What was beautiful about the line was that hardly anyone was talking. People were patiently waiting their turn, reading *The House on Mango Street*. Those who did not have their nose in the book were discussing their favorite parts of it.

The House on Mango Street consists of vignettes of varying lengths (some no longer than a few lines) about a twelve-year-old Mexican girl named Esperanza (meaning Hope) Cordero, whose family has moved into a new home on Mango Street in a largely Latino neighborhood in Chicago, much like the one where Cisneros's large family settled. This coming-of-age story follows Esperanza as she experiences the realities of living amid immigrant families in the city. Told by her in first-person present tense, the vignettes reveal her sensitive observations about the world around her and her desire to one day leave the neighborhood in order to achieve more in life. She learns eventually that she can never leave Mango Street entirely. She says to herself and to her readers: "You will always be Esperanza. You will always be Mango Street. You can't erase what you know. You can't forget who you are."[1]

In writing this novel, Cisneros (b. 1954) did not break a glass ceiling: she took a sledgehammer and shattered it. While Mexico and Latin America boast a rich history of excellent contemporary writers—Isabel Allende, Julia Alvarez, Carlos Fuentes, Eduardo Galeano, Gabriel García Márquez, Octavio Paz, Elena Poniatowska, and Mario Vargas Llosa are only a few—they were ignored for the most part by the Eurocentric literary world. Whenever Mexican and Latino writers approached publishing houses in the United States, editors told them that their books had to have universal appeal. It was as if this extremely large cultural group of people with family names such as García, Hernández, Martínez, and Cordero (in Esperanza's case) had no stories to tell, no human experiences worth sharing. *The House on Mango Street* was in fact first published by Arte Público Press, Houston, which is dedicated to writing by Latinos living in the United States. The great success of Cisneros's book proved how ridiculous and, yes, racist the Eurocentric literary world could be (and still is). A best seller, reissued in many editions, forms, and languages, Esperanza's story has captured the interest of and brought hope to millions of readers everywhere.

In the years since the initial 1984 publication of the book, Esperanza's dreams, experiences, and desires have become as American as tacos, tamales, and enchiladas. It is important to note that of all of the fine titles included in the present volume, *The House on Mango Street* is one of the few to be required reading in schools throughout the nation.[2] Moreover, this book is significant for its setting: the Mexican and Latino neighborhoods of Chicago. *The House on Mango Street* put Chicago's Mexican community—currently about 1.5 million people—on the map. Yet there are still too few books focused on this cultural group. Cisneros's was the first, opening the door to many stories that must be told.

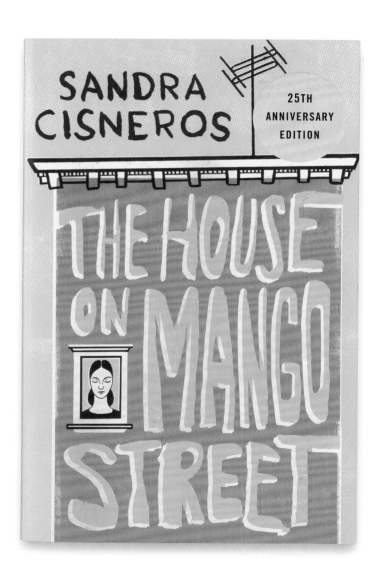

Chicago's Humboldt Park neighborhood, which has been settled over the decades by waves of European, Latino, and Mexican immigrants, provides the setting of at least two influential coming-of-age novels: Saul Bellow's *Adventures of Augie March* (no. 76) and Sandra Cisneros's *House on Mango Street*. Cisneros's affecting book has become a standard text for schoolchildren throughout the United States.

95

Nature's Metropolis: Chicago and the Great West

WILLIAM CRONON * NEW YORK AND LONDON: W. W. NORTON & COMPANY, 1991

Kathleen Neils Conzen

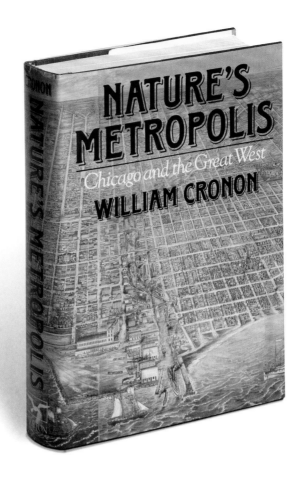

A quarter century after its first publication, this prize-winning environmental history by William Cronon (b. 1954) remains an indispensable key to understanding nineteenth-century Chicago and a provocative challenge for Chicagoans today.[1] The unexpected juxtaposition of metropolis and western nature in the book's title signals its framing concern to understand the "naturalness" of cities and their place within, rather than opposed to, the natural world. Nineteenth-century Chicago, this magisterial case study argues, derived its growth from converting the stored bounty of the countryside into market-defined commodities and in turn transmuted that natural environment into "second nature," the superimposed landscape of a new human order. *Nature's Metropolis* is thus at once a deeply researched and engrossing history of Chicago's economic origins, a creative geographical analysis of its role within the nation's emergent urban system, and an impassioned plea for an expanded environmental consciousness that includes the city and cultural landscapes within its purview.

For most readers today, the compelling core of the book still lies in the three fascinating chapters that trace the complex linkages created as Chicago used its favorable water and rail systems to mine the fields, forests, and grasslands of its vast hinterland, in the process reshaping countryside and city alike. Readers follow a sack of grain from fertile midwestern prairies through the ever greater abstractions of grain elevators, the Chicago Board of Trade, commodity futures, cornered markets, and demands for state regulation. They observe Chicago's reliable market similarly converting the region's quickly cut-over forests into lumber for the city itself and for buildings and fences that enabled the treeless prairies to become agriculturally productive. And unlike tourists who could only marvel at the city's "dis-assembly-line" stockyards, readers learn to link Chicago's meat backward to annihilated bison herds, Indian reservations, cowboys, cattle drives, and feedlots, and forward to ice harvests, refrigerated railcars, and the decline of the neighborhood butcher shop.

But Chicago's transformation of nature into commodities also created an equally significant new geography of capital. Bankruptcy records helped Cronon chart the flows of capital into and through Chicago, the contours of the far-flung wholesaling networks the city's merchants developed, and the truncated structure of the western urban system that emerged in this gateway city's lengthy shadow. Innovative entrepreneurialism thrived in the city's "busy hive" built upon nature's bounty, and soon armies of traveling salesmen and newfangled mail-order catalogues selling Chicago products and services accelerated the environmental transformation of its hinterland.

Cronon's elegant narration avoids becoming a jeremiad for a lost natural paradise while making clear the environmental consequences of choices made by nineteenth-century Chicago merchants and manufacturers and their customers and workers. While a final chapter uses the 1893 World's Columbian Exposition as a vehicle for attention to some ecological and social consequences within Chicago itself as well, those issues have now received fuller consideration from subsequent scholarship. However, numerous other Chicago commodity chains still await their historical interpreter, from coal and iron (among the most obvious) to cut flowers (among the more obscure), as does the linkage of human systems of passage to and through Chicago to the transformative movements of goods and capital that Cronon analyzed, and the continuation of his story into Chicago's present.

Nature's Metropolis concludes with an insistence on the inextricable unity of city and countryside. A generation of fruitful scholarship in environmental and urban history now reflects the influence of this book's example and exhortation. In our own age of globalization and global warming, its message retains all of its original urgency.

FACING This critical study interprets the evolution of Chicago in the last half of the nineteenth century into the nation's Gateway City as the result of a dialogue between nature—the vast resources of North America's West—and urban conglomerates and the financial means and interests of the East.

96

There Are No Children Here: The Story of Two Boys Growing Up in the Other America

ALEX KOTLOWITZ ✳ NEW YORK,
LONDON, TORONTO, SYDNEY, AUCKLAND:
NAN A. TALESE / DOUBLEDAY, 1991

D. Bradford Hunt

Heartbreakingly, the title of Alex Kotlowitz's book reporting on the lives of two young African American brothers on Chicago's Near West Side originated with their mother, who explained, "You know, there are no children here. They've seen too much to be children."[1] White Chicagoans writing about the black community usually produce complex sociologies rather than nuanced tragedies. Kotlowitz's intimate and gut-wrenching look at the childhoods of Lafayette and Pharoah is definitely the latter, breaking through rhetorical barriers and revealing the deeply human costs of the city's disdain toward its black poor.

Chicago is internationally known as a city harshly divided by race. Generalized racism, governmental housing policies, and deindustrialization have had disastrous consequences. *There Are No Children Here* takes place near the nadir of the city's black ghettos, with crime peaking statistically in 1991 and homicides in 1992. But the data cannot describe the personal devastation of being beaten, witnessing a murder, or losing a family member, all of which happen relentlessly in the world of Lafayette and Pharoah. Kotlowitz's on-the-ground storytelling uncovers the mental toll of violence and poverty, whipsawing the reader between sharp, tragic vignettes and fleeting glimpses of optimism. The cumulative emotion is entrapment without physical walls but with immense practical and always psychological ones. The boys' mother, LaJoe, despite her many strengths, cannot leave her environment, as she supports eight children using welfare benefits; public housing's rock-bottom rent is her only safety net, and a tattered one at that.

Like Upton Sinclair, who aimed at the nation's heart with *The Jungle* (no. 27) but, as he put it, hit its stomach, Kotlowitz (b. 1955) wanted to show the devastating human costs of urban poverty but instead provided momentum to public housing's demolition. The "Here" in the title became not the broader black ghetto but Chicago's monolithic projects. LaJoe's family lives in the Henry Horner Homes, opened in 1957 but utterly dysfunctional three decades later.[2] "Nothing here, the children would tell you, was as it should be," Kotlowitz related.[3] *There Are No Children Here* expanded the library of grim stories about public housing in disarray, contributing to a radical shift in policy by the mid-1990s.[4] Chicago's "Plan for Transformation" tore down projects like Horner, scattered families to private rental housing in other poor black neighborhoods, and rebuilt "mixed-income communities" with carefully selected tenants. Root causes of poverty remained unaddressed, and solutions centered on place rather than people.

Kotlowitz's empathetic and measured reporting of the world of Lafayette and Pharoah is ultimately a deep indictment of Chicago's urban social systems. Law enforcement, courts, welfare departments, and public housing—

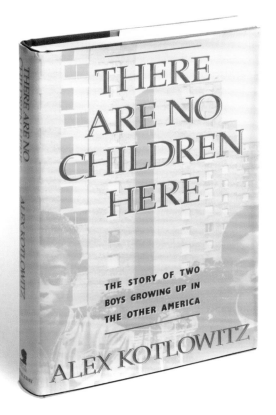

all have served the city badly, with the poor trapped in systemic failure. His description of clashes with that system are maddening; problems are readily apparent, solutions less so.

There Are No Children Here won several awards[5] and has been taught widely in high schools and colleges; 722,000 copies have been sold. In 1993 Oprah Winfrey starred as LaJoe in a made-for-TV movie version of the book. This surprising success allowed the self-effacing Kotlowitz to write further narratives of injustice on society's margins and to coproduce a documentary titled *The Interrupters* (2011) about community-based efforts to head off recriminating violence in Chicago's black communities. He never abandoned Lafayette and Pharoah; the three remain close, although both brothers have spent time in jail for drug offenses. A happy ending to Kotlowitz's story was not in the cards. While *There Are No Children Here* could not shake the city's political class out of its ambivalence toward the black poor, Kotlowitz's devotion to the family's story produced a book that resonates today as a reminder of the massive psychological toll that poverty and violence exact.

In 1985 photojournalist Stephen Shames (b. 1947) captured Lafayette Rivers, one of the two brothers at the heart of Alex Kotlowitz's searing narrative, at age ten in a hallway of the Henry Horner Homes. The image conveys the grim conditions in Chicago's high-rise public housing projects.

97

Jimmy Corrigan: The Smartest Kid on Earth

CHRIS WARE ✳ NEW YORK: PANTHEON
BOOKS, 2000

Hillary Chute

FACING On this page of *Jimmy Corrigan*, Jimmy's father (as a child) and grandfather visit the 1893 Chicago World's Columbian Exposition; they climb to an observation platform overlooking outsized classical-style sculptures. One depicts a mother proudly extending her baby toward the heavens. A few minutes later Jimmy's grandfather will walk away, disappearing from his son's life forever.

Chris Ware, arguably the most important cartoonist writing and drawing today, has a great line he told me about the United States: if New York is the brains of the country and Los Angeles is its asshole, then Chicago is its heart. Born in Omaha in 1967, Franklin Christenson "Chris" Ware moved to Chicago in 1991 to attend graduate school at the School of the Art Institute, and he never left.

Set mainly in Chicago, *Jimmy Corrigan: The Smartest Boy on Earth* began as a weekly comic strip in *Newcity* and was published as a 380-page book in 2000. It traces filial sadness across four generations of Corrigan men; eschewing chronology, it interweaves the nineteenth century with the 1980s. *Jimmy Corrigan* has two main plotlines—both featuring lonely characters named James, or "Jimmy," Corrigan—that eventually intersect. One is an eight-year-old boy living with a cold, unsympathetic single father on Chicago's South Side in the early 1890s. We encounter the other in late-twentieth-century Chicago, first as a child—a guileless Superman fan with a single mother—and then as an isolated thirty-six-year-old office employee. The two Jimmys are grandfather and grandson, each dramatically abandoned by his father.

The intensity of the response to the book—in both publishing and fine-arts contexts—demonstrates Ware's success in harnessing the unique properties of comics to mimic processes of remembering, dreaming, and imagining.[1] Different typefaces—from neat script within panels to stylized block letters framed as taglines in colorful blue and red boxes ("Later," "Anyway," "Suddenly")—give readers access to characters' interiority and a sense of the complete control of the storyteller as a visual artist orchestrating every detail. Each panel exists in meaningful relation to others on the page, not only building the story but also creating a stunning graphic whole. Ware uses color as patterning to great effect, helping readers to see the page as a complete composition, an aesthetic unit.

Throughout *Jimmy Corrigan*, Chicago is visualized in Ware's stylish, masterfully precise lines and swaths of subtle hues. The city comes to life through detailed topographies, with buildings both prosaic and grand: ordinary residences, businesses, schools, parks—and the magnificent display of Chicago's 1893 World's Columbian Exposition, which is a central plot point and presence in the book.

The defining—and most crushing—moment of *Jimmy Corrigan* is when Jimmy Corrigan is abandoned by his father atop the Manufactures and Liberal Arts Building at the 1893 Exposition. With decisive lines, Ware drew the outsized building in intricate architectural detail, inside and out. "I followed him like a loyal animal right up to the edge of the largest building in the world," tiny black cursive explains, floating in the sky above father and

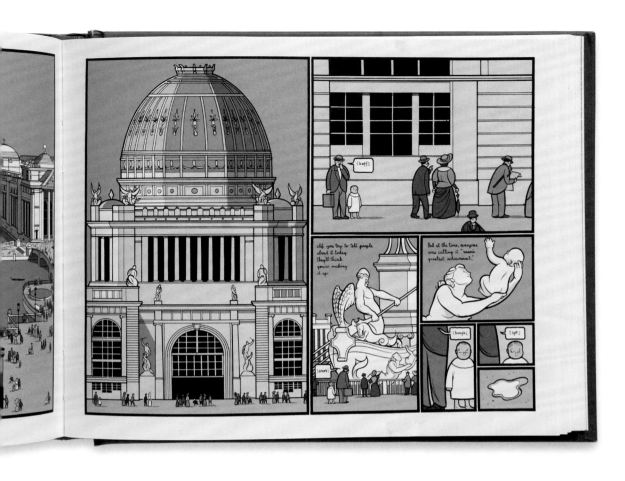

son, who stand looking out from the top of the building.[2] The weight and yet the ephemerality of this big fairground building capture the inexplicable, affective contradictions of family ties.[3]

Ware's work confronts the interrelation of past and present; it is about the arbitrary and difficult process of sifting through the past, and how memories intertwine and collide. We see this in his *Building Stories* (2012), also set in Chicago, whose stories readers must themselves "build" by piecing together fourteen different unordered print elements, contained in an 11 × 17 inch box. If in *Jimmy Corrigan* Chicago buildings are so lovingly rendered as to feel like characters, in *Building Stories* they actually speak, narrating their occupants' lives, tallying every orgasm, broken bone, birth, replaced radiator. In his meticulous attention to Chicago's spaces and spirit in the spatially site-specific medium of comics, whether in turn-of-the-century neighborhoods, fairgrounds, or contemporary skyscrapers, Ware's work presents a Chicago attuned to the past yet full of possibility.

98

Days and Nights at the Second City: A Memoir, with Notes on Staging Review Theatre

BERNARD SAHLINS ✳ CHICAGO: IVAN R. DEE, 2001

Kelly Leonard

The entire recent tradition of American theatrical satire can be summed up in three words: The Second City.   **Clive Barnes, 1969**[1]

It is no exaggeration to say that one of Chicago's chief exports in the last fifty-nine years has been improv-based sketch comedy and the impressive list of artists who have steeped themselves in that work. The proliferation of this indigenous art form and its purveyors span mediums and generations. Its origins can be traced to a small cabaret theater that opened its doors in Chicago in 1959: the Second City.

Bernard Sahlins (1922–2013) not only cofounded the Second City (with Paul Sills and Howard Alk) but was also the primary creative and business leader of that institution through its first twenty-five years. In 1953 he had become a producer at Playwrights Theatre Club in Chicago, where the likes of Ed Asner, Elaine May, Mike Nichols, and Sills honed skills that would bring them all fame.[2] Sahlins's book *Days and Nights at the Second City* is both a memoir and manual. It tells the story of one of the world's most influential theatrical institutions while providing the reader with brilliant and concise instruction on how to create and stage review theater.

Sahlins's memoir is rich and engaging, filled with the boldfaced names of comedians who were virtual unknowns when they came under his care: John Belushi, Robert Klein, Bill Murray, Gilda Radner, Harold Ramis, George Wendt, Fred Willard, and so many more. Beyond the incredible list of talents, the evolution of the Second City is a journey through the cultural zeitgeist of a city and a nation. The work on stage at the Second City spoke to changing values, political figures, the powerful, and the underrepresented. The culture of the theater has mirrored the city in which the company was created, taking its name from a column by A. J. Liebling in the *New Yorker* declaring Chicago to be a second-class metropolis (see no. 74).[3] By donning the insult, Sahlins and the Second City thumbed their noses at East Coast elitism while also suggesting that there may be something emboldening in embracing the insult itself. Quite simply, *Days and Nights at the Second City* tells us about our own civic history, but played back with a lot of laughter and spiked with wonderful irreverence.

The instructional aspect of the book, on the other hand, is a timeless and invaluable account of the conditions, methodologies, and outcomes that Sahlins and his cohorts honed over many years and that are commonly recognized as nothing less than the dominant source of modern American humor: wearing characters lightly, playing to the top of one's intelligence, and paying fierce attention to focus and being in the moment. Sahlins provided a step-

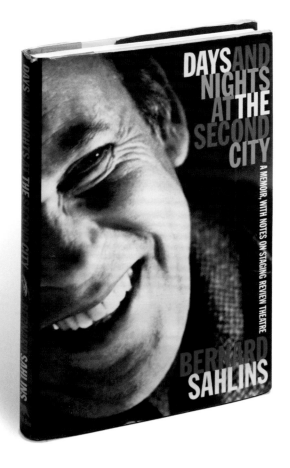

by-step summary of the defining characteristics of review comedy, creating a template for what is funny and what is true.

Later in his career, Sahlins and his wife, Jane Nicholl Sahlins, cofounded the International Theatre Festival in Chicago. For many years thereafter, Sahlins produced, directed, and taught in the city he loved.

If recent indicators are to be believed, the Second City will continue to provide the world with some of the best and brightest minds in American comedy. An understanding of the history of this august institution is both important and essential. That understanding would be wholly incomplete without Sahlins's *Days and Nights at the Second City*, which gives readers a front-row seat for wondrous acts of innovation. Better yet, the narrator was the troupe's chief architect, erstwhile champion, and legendary raconteur. His story will forever be a valuable resource for generations of performers and audiences invested in the art of laughter.

Chicago's improvisational theater group the Second City—its story told here by one of its cofounders—has spawned some of the nation's most creative comedians. A 1960 photograph shows one of the early ensembles taking a break on a sightseeing boat on the Chicago River. Left to right: Severn Darden, Eugene Troobnick, Howard Alk, Charles Lewson, William Matthieu, Alan Arkin, Paul Sills, Mina Kolb, Paul Sand, and unidentified.

99

The Great Chicago Fire and the Myth of Mrs. O'Leary's Cow

RICHARD F. BALES ✳ FOREWORD BY
THOMAS F. SCHWARTZ ✳ JEFFERSON,
NORTH CAROLINA, AND LONDON:
MCFARLAND & COMPANY, INC., 2002

Glenn Humphreys

FACING Richard Bales's investigation of Chicago's 1871 Fire led to the exoneration of Catherine O'Leary, whose barn was identified as the fire's origin. Bales countered the conventional story—depicted in this nineteenth-century colored lithograph on the book's cover—by demonstrating that a chief witness against O'Leary had lied: Daniel Sullivan testified that he had seen a fire in the barn from where he stood, but as the diagram shown here proves, the barn was not visible from that spot.

Mrs. O'Leary and her cow are innocent! In 1997 one of Chicago's legendary stories was officially rewritten when the City Council exonerated Catherine O'Leary, long blamed for the Great Chicago Fire of 1871. The council's action was the direct result of Richard Bales's analysis of archival sources from the 1870s. He published his preliminary findings in an article in the *Illinois Historical Journal* in 1997. Bales (b. 1951) expanded his work into a book published in 2002, *The Great Chicago Fire and the Myth of Mrs. O'Leary's Cow.*

Bales's dogged research involved locating nineteenth-century primary sources, a challenging task, as most city and county documents, such as real estate records, burned in the fire. Undaunted, Bales gained access to land records of the Chicago Title Insurance Company. He also spent two years painstakingly transcribing the handwritten, often difficult-to-decipher testimony given by Catherine O'Leary and dozens of others before the Board of Police and Fire Commissioners. He combined these archival sources with photographs and other records to log the locations of houses and barns on the street where the fire originated, as well as the width of the lots, street, and side alley. Then he and graphic designer Douglas Swanson created simple, clear, yet dramatic, scale drawings of the block to reveal new aspects of the fire.

The inferno that destroyed the core of Chicago raged over three days, from October 8 until October 10, 1871. It began on DeKoven Street, on Chicago's West Side. O'Leary and her family lived in a house on DeKoven Street with a barn at the back of the property where they kept cows. Few people dispute those points. How the fire began is another matter.

As early as October 9, while the fire was still burning, the *Chicago Evening Journal* blamed O'Leary: "The fire . . . being caused by a cow kicking over a lamp in a stable in which a woman was milking." The O'Leary story became one of Chicago's best-known tales, morphing from anti-immigrant and anti-Irish versions to being the subject of a Norman Rockwell painting.[1] But Bales's research convinced him that Catherine O'Leary did not cause the fire.

So who started it? Through a careful study of the records, Bales identified and investigated several suspects. Ultimately, he made a strong case that Daniel "Peg-Leg" Sullivan, a neighbor of the O'Learys, was the culprit. He reviewed Sullivan's testimony before the commissioners and plotted his movements on Swanson's scale drawings of the block to demonstrate discrepancies in the man's statements. For example, Sullivan swore that from his perch across DeKoven Street he saw the fire in the O'Leary barn. But Bales determined that this was impossible, given that, from there, the house owned by the Dalton family blocked the view of the O'Leary barn.

In his foreword, Illinois State Historian Thomas F. Schwartz described Bales's book as "an engaging and entertaining piece of detective work."[2] And

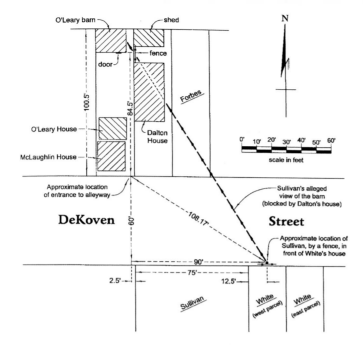

O'Leary Property and Surrounding Area

October 8, 1871

FIGURE 54—O'LEARY PROPERTY AND SURROUNDING AREA. This diagram of the O'Leary neighborhood is based primarily on Chicago Title Insurance Company records, inquiry testimony, and post-fire photographs. It shows the O'Leary, Dalton, and Forbes properties on the north side of DeKoven Street and the Sullivan and White parcels on the south side of the street. Note that the O'Leary barn, located at the rear of their property, is less than fifty feet away from their home, which is in back of the McLaughlin house. Other information contained in this drawing is discussed in the following chapter. (Diagram by Douglas A. Swanson)

that it is. We are taken on a journey to DeKoven Street in October 1871 and introduced to firemen, journalists, and residents of the neighborhood. Along the way we learn how the city worked, including how the fire boxes operated, or did not. To do this, Bales used seemingly mundane business and government archives in new ways to investigate one of Chicago's seminal events. He also commissioned artist Marshall Philyaw to create drawings of many of the characters in this story. While Bales's book led to Mrs. O'Leary's name being officially cleared of any responsibility, nearly 150 years after the fire, it remains difficult to determine with certainty who started the blaze. That is, unless new archival sources are discovered.

100

The Devil in the White City: Murder, Magic, and Madness at the Fair That Changed America

ERIK LARSON ✳ NEW YORK: CROWN PUBLISHERS, 2003

Victoria Lautman

FACING This book weaves together two loosely related narratives: the planning and execution of the World's Columbian Exposition, represented in C. D. Arnold's sweeping photograph of the Agriculture Building, and the tale of serial murderer H. H. Holmes, whose victims were young women staying at his residential hotel on Sixty-Third Street, seen here. Erik Larson's extensive primary research lends the story a sense of immediacy and authenticity, plunging readers fully into a defining moment in the city's history.

There are thousands of photographs documenting the 1893 World's Columbian Exposition in Chicago and the pearly neoclassical buildings that inspired the fair's nickname, the White City. An unparalleled Gilded Age spectacle, it became permanently embedded in the chronicles of Chicago history after hosting nearly twenty-six million visitors during its sixth-month run. It also burnished the fame of architect Daniel Burnham, who oversaw the fair's highly complex design and wrangled other creative minds into participating.

Such details about the Columbian Exposition are not particularly newsworthy to anyone knowledgable about the fair and Chicago's past. But in 2003, a book by Erik Larson (b. 1954), a writer of historical nonfiction, molded a massive amount of fair-related information into a riveting saga. *The Devil in the White City* is not a dense, formulaic history book but rather a vivid, novelistic page-turner. It captures the fair's incandescent birth, life, and aftermath with such deftly handled minutiae that readers feel intimately connected to the event and its originators. When first published, the book rocketed to the top of the best-seller lists, where the paperback edition, as of this writing, continues to remain. No wonder Leonardo DiCaprio snapped up film rights.[1]

Larson's approach to the subject is ingenious, interweaving two parallel storylines that gradually coalesce into a suspenseful epic of good versus evil, personified in the actions of a pair of real-life characters. Chapters alternate between these disparate protagonists, whose lives orbit around the momentous exposition: Burnham (1846–1912), a dazzling visionary whose public reputation was staked on the fair's success or failure; and H. H. Holmes (1861–96), a largely unknown but astonishingly malevolent figure who arouses breathless apprehension as the narrative progresses.

The real-life Holmes (born Herman Mudgett) is considered to have been America's first documented serial killer, committing gory murders in the shadow of Burnham's grandiose dream. He anticipated that the fair would lure young women to Chicago in search of jobs and lodging and erected the World's Fair Hotel at Sixty-Third and Wallace streets to accommodate them. Holmes's sinister edifice ensured the ultimate nightmare of checking in but not checking out.

Unlike other authors who have written about Burnham or Holmes, Larson connected the two men through the fair's exhilarating milieu. He also recognized several traits that they shared, including the ability to apply their acute intelligence and powers of persuasion to achieve their desires. Like Burnham, Holmes was egocentric and ambitious, able to maintain a sociable public persona while under astonishing duress. And as sole designer of the so-called Murder Hotel, he was a de facto architect.

The juxtaposition of a famous civic figure and a seductive psychopath

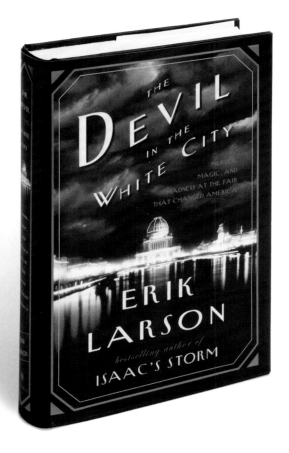

HOLMES' "CASTLE"   (63d St , Chicago, Ill)

makes for a more engrossing read than two separate biographies, and *The Devil in the White City* offers a refreshing alternative vision of that pivotal moment in Chicago's past. It is as though Larson single-handedly pushed a weighty freight train onto a different track, since the World's Columbian Exposition has always been associated with beauty, the glory of Chicago, and such newfangled inventions as Cracker Jacks, dishwashers, and the Ferris Wheel. Larson has added an additional, colorful way to enter that celebrated moment, even inspiring several *Devil in the White City* tours of the once-swanky nineteenth-century Englewood neighborhood, where the fair was constructed. Larson did not actually rewrite history, but his efforts have enlightened tens of thousands of readers about one of the most significant events in Chicago's past.

101

Brush Back

SARA PARETSKY ✳ NEW YORK: G. P.
PUTNAM'S SONS, 2015

Gini Hartzmark

At its heart Chicago is a city of neighborhoods, a checkerboard of small communities, each with its own distinct character and personality, its own set of rules. *Brush Back*, by Sara Paretsky (b. 1947), explores the deep and lasting impact of neighborhoods on the people who grew up in them and the relentless pull of place even on those, like her protagonist, V. I. Warshawski, who think that they have successfully escaped such bonds.

Warshawski, the lawyer turned hardboiled private investigator and protagonist of the seventeenth installment of Paretsky's popular and highly regarded mystery series, is a daughter of Chicago's Southeast Side. A strong female character who has paved the way for other tough female sleuths, Warshawski (Vic to her friends) made her first appearance in *Indemnity Only* in 1982. Vic believed that she had left behind the shuttered steel mills of the tough blue-collar environs of her youth when she went to the University of Chicago (Paretsky earned an MBA and PhD there) on scholarship and then moved on to law school and into more affluent and intellectually open parts of the city. But in nearly every book either she finds herself involved in some aspect of her earlier life or her earlier life finds her. In *Brush Back*, when an old high-school flame, Frank Guzzo, asks her to investigate a thirty-year-old murder, Vic is pulled back into old animosities and long-buried trouble.

It all starts when Guzzo shows up at her office to tell her that his mother, Stella, has just been released from jail after serving a sentence for beating his sister, Annie, to death, a crime for which she now insists she was framed. Vic starts asking questions, at first reluctantly, but finds herself drawn deeper into a mystery involving everything from corruption and crime to her own tangled past.

Set entirely in Chicago, *Brush Back* takes the reader to parts of the city that tourists seldom see: the inside of the Fourth District police station, the construction site of a downtown skyscraper, the edge of Calumet Harbor, where a body is found half-buried in a mountain of petroleum coke.

Described in rich detail, Chicago is woven into the narrative fabric of the book. As Vic battles traffic, rides the "L," and drops into her favorite bar, the city serves not merely as backdrop but rather as an important protagonist in the story. The Chicago we see through Paretsky's Vic is not just physical but metaphorical. Vic describes a retired judge, one of the witnesses she interviews during her investigation: "He threw his head back, laughing as if delighted that he had something I couldn't afford. It didn't surprise me: growing up behind the old stockyards, you competed for every beam of sunlight that filtered through the haze of blood and smoke."[1]

The touchstones of the plot are also pure Chicago. Political corruption, organized crime, and professional sports—in this case, baseball (Paretsky

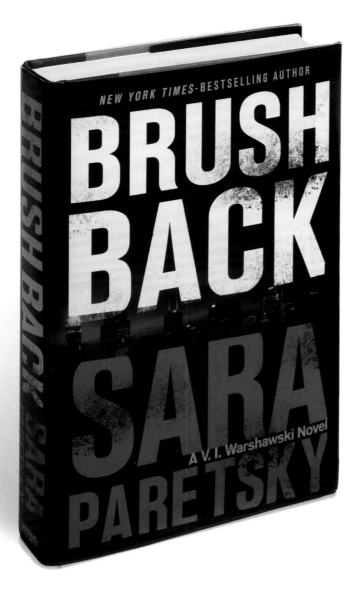

NEW YORK TIMES–BESTSELLING AUTHOR

BRUSH BACK

SARA PARETSKY

A V. I. Warshawski Novel

In *Brush Back*, Sara Paretsky's pathbreaking female investigator, V. I. Warshawski, is once again embroiled in the criminal life of Chicago's South Side. Paretsky's depictions of the ethnic neighborhoods and gritty industrial sectors in which her thrillers take place are as vivid as the dangerous exploits of her intrepid detective.

is a Cubs fan)—are all integral to the story. Guzzo had a tryout with the Cubs but wound up driving a truck. His son might have a shot at a scholarship if the patron saint of the neighborhood—an insurance agent with powerful connections—will put in a good word for him. Even the title of the book, *Brush Back,* is a baseball reference: the term refers to a fastball, high and inside, meant to intimidate the hitter, an apt metaphor for the ways in which the people from Vic's old neighborhood attempt to protect their secrets.

Notes

NOTE TO THE READER

For the most part, we used the first edition of
publications featured in the present volume.
In a few instances we photographed a different
edition when it offered particularly relevant
visual or textual information. All such instances
are noted.

PREFACE

1. Nicholas Basbanes, "Madness Redux," in *Patience &
Fortitude* (New York: HarperCollins, 2001), 142–43. Here Basbanes discussed the late Jay Fliegelman and his work to link
his collection of some five hundred association copies to "the
cultural history of America."

LISTING CHICAGO

1. Norman Mailer, *Miami and the Siege of Chicago: An
Informal History of the Republican and Democratic Conventions of 1968* ([New York]: New American Library, 1968), 89
(no. 85).

2. For the committee's members and activities, see the
preface and acknowledgments.

3. In the end, two committee members who had assumed
responsibility for two entries ended up writing three each,
when assigned contributors could not produce them.

4. Richard Junger, *Becoming the Second City: Chicago's
Mass News Media, 1833–1898* (Urbana: University of Illinois
Press, 2010), 192–93.

5. G. W. Steevens, *The Land of the Dollar* (Edinburgh:
Blackwood, 1897), 144.

6. Writing in the early twentieth century, the Hungarian
critic Lajos Hatvany likened his native Budapest to Chicago;
see Gwen Jones, *Chicago of the Balkans: Budapest in Hungarian Literature 1900–1939* (Oxford: Legenda, 2013), 1.

1

1. Juliette Kinzie was not included in the official roster
of the early Chicago Historical Society because she was a
woman. But evidence from letters she sent in 1858 and 1860
to her daughter in Savannah, Nellie Kinzie Gordon, shows
that she was very much an active participant and supporter.
She attended annual meetings and lectures that were held in
the homes of members. In January 1860 she hosted a meeting
of the Historical Society, according to a letter of January 22
from Kinzie to Gordon. Letters from Kinzie to Gordon dated
December 2, 1858, and June 13 and December 10, 1860, refer
to the former's attendance at society meetings. A letter of
September 22, 1858, from John Kinzie to Gordon mentions
his attendance at a meeting of the organization. See Juliette
Kinzie papers, microfilm, Chicago History Museum.

2. [Juliette A. Kinzie], *Narrative of the Massacre at Chi-

cago, *August 15, 1812, and of Some Preceding Events* (Chicago: Ellis & Fergus, 1844), frontis.

3. Milo M. Quaife, "Historical Introduction," in Juliette A. Kinzie, *Wau-Bun, the "Early Day" in the Northwest* (Chicago: Lakeside, 1932), lii; and Nina Baym, introduction to Kinzie, *Wau-Bun, the "Early Day" in the Northwest* (Urbana: University of Illinois Press, 1992), xv–xvi.

4. Quaife (note 3), p. liii.

5. For more on Kinzie, see Rima Lunin Schultz, "Juliette Kinzie," in *Women Building Chicago*, ed. Rima Lunin Schultz and Adele Hast (Bloomington: Indiana University Press, 2001), 472–76; and Constance R. Buckley, "Searching for Fort Dearborn: Perceptions, Commemoration, and Celebration of the Urban Collective Memory" (PhD diss., Loyola University Chicago, 2005), esp. 72–79. Kinzie's legacy has been enhanced by the achievements of her granddaughter and namesake Juliette Gordon Low, founder of the Girl Scouts; see Gladys Denny Shultz and Daisy Gordon Lawrence, *Lady from Savannah: The Life of Juliette Low* (Philadelphia: J. B. Lippincott, 1958, rev. ed. 1988).

2

1. Ellsworth had the unfortunate distinction of being the first Union officer to die in the Civil War. His regiment entered Alexandria, Virginia, after Confederate troops had vacated the city. Ellsworth took it upon himself to remove the secessionist flag from the rooftop of the Marshall House Inn. Descending the stairs after completing this task, he was shot in the chest by the inn's proprietor, who was in turn shot by Ellsworth's troops. Ellsworth died on May 24, 1861. Both casualties in this skirmish became martyrs for their respective causes. For more on Ellsworth, see Charles A. Ingraham, *Elmer E. Ellsworth and the Zouaves of '61* (Chicago: Chicago Historical Society and University of Chicago Press, 1925).

2. In his 1868 history of Chicago (no. 5), John S. Wright praised the firm for building a business that "is unsurpassed by any in the country, and may now claim to be the great central music publishing house of the country." Wright, *Chicago: Past, Present, Future* (Chicago: Sold by the Western News Co., and All Chicago Booksellers, 1868), 279 (no. 5). For more on Root & Cady, see I. D. Guyer, *History of Chicago: Commercial and Manufacturing Interests and Industry* (Chicago: Church, Goodman & Cushing, 1862), 179–80; and A. T. Andreas, *A His-*

tory *of Chicago*, vol. 2, *From 1857 until the Fire of 1871* (Chicago: A. T. Andreas, 1885), 593 (no.11). For more on the city's early sheet-music industry, see Dena Epstein, *Music Publishing in Chicago before 1871: The Firm of Root & Cady, 1858–1871* (Detroit: Information Coordinators, 1969), especially chapter 1, "Chicago Music Publishers Other Than Root & Cady."

3. Not long after Ellsworth's death, Vaas composed "Col. Ellsworth Requiem March," which Root & Cady published. The company splintered after the fire. Cady established C. M. Cady in New York City in 1875, and it remained in business until his death in 1889. See Dena J. Epstein (note 2), 29. Root's firm underwent several management changes and names from 1873 to at least 1891, at which point, according to George Frederick Root's autobiography, it was still in business. See Geo. F. Root, *The Story of a Musical Life: An Autobiography* (Cincinnati: John Church, 1891), 167.

3

1. Thirteen monthly parts were issued. They are housed in highly ornamented paper covers, and each contains four tinted lithographs (measuring 8½ × 12 inches) of buildings, street scenes, and important public works, accompanied by eight pages of descriptive text. While twenty-five such parts were planned, publication ceased in 1867, probably because the project was losing money.

2. See John W. Reps, *Views and Viewmakers of America* (Columbia: University of Missouri Press, 1984).

3. When the plate of the Water Tower was printed in 1867, the structure had not yet been built. Designed by W. W. Boyington, it was erected in 1869. The artist must have derived the image from architectural drawings.

Special thanks are due to Paul F. Gehl, custodian emeritus of the John M. Wing Foundation on the History of Printing at the Newberry Library, for his knowledge and assistance.

4

1. On the construction of the tunnel, see Carl Smith, *City Water, City Life: Water and the Infrastructure of Ideas in Urbanizing Philadelphia, Boston, and Chicago* (Chicago: University of Chicago Press, 2013), 38–52.

2. Robert Williams, ed., *The Chicago Diaries of John M. Wing 1865–1866* (Carbondale: Southern Illinois University Press and the Caxton Club, 2002).

3. Joel L. Samuels, "The John M. Wing Foundation on the History of Printing at the Newberry Library," *Library Quarterly* 58, no. 2 (April 1988): 164–89.

5

1. Wright's first-person account appears in Augustine W. Wright, *In Memoriam. John S. Wright, An Address Delivered before the Chicago Historical Society, Friday Evening, July 21, 1885* (Chicago: Fergus Printing, 1885), 26–27; and in many subsequent discussions of him. The only modern biography is Lloyd Lewis, *John S. Wright: Prophet of the Prairies* (Chicago: Prairie Farmer Publishing, 1941), but aspects of Wright's career are discussed in William Cronon, *Nature's Metropolis: Chicago and the Great West* (New York: W. W. Norton, 1991), 45, 47, 52, 82 (no. 95); and Carl Smith, *Urban Disorder and the Shape of Belief: The Great Chicago Fire, the Haymarket Bomb, and the Model Town of Pullman*, 2nd ed. (Chicago: University of Chicago Press, 2008), 46–47.

2. John S. Wright, *Wright's Proposition to a Chicago Railway Capitalist with Important Addendum* (Chicago: Beach and Barnard, 1871), 42.

3. John S. Wright and J. Holmes Agnew, *Citizenship Sovereignty* (Chicago: Published for American Citizens, the True Maintainers of State Sovereignty, 1864), iii. The prospectus for the 2,500-page work appears on the inside of the front paper wrapper.

4. John S. Wright, *Chicago: Past, Present, Future* (Chicago: Sold by the Western News Co., and All Chicago Booksellers, 1868), xxv.

5. Wright (note 4), 281 (parks), 100n ("I am poor").

6. John S. Wright, *Chicago: Past, Present, Future . . . Second Edition, for the Chicago Board of Trade* (Chicago: For Sale by All Chicago Booksellers, 1870), ix.

7. Wright removed the appendix (one copy survives at the Chicago History Museum and another in a private collection), but the contents page had already been printed, and the controversy still registers in the author's acknowledgments to the second edition. It is titled *Appendix. Obligations of Promise, Contract and Covenant, according to the Code of Honor. Privilege and Duty of the President and Directors of the Board of Trade of Chicago, to maintain their plighted faith in regard to the Book, 'Chicago: Past, Present, Future.'* Wright (note 6), vi.

8. See *Proceedings of the Common Council of the City of Chicago for the Municipal Year of 1869–70* (Chicago: Republican Company, 1870), 653, 668; *Proceedings of the Common Council of the City of Chicago for the Municipal Year 1870–71* (Chicago: J. S. Thomson, 1871), 21, 32, 45.

9. *Chicago Daily Tribune*, November 26, 1874.

10. *Chicago Daily Tribune*, September 30, 1874.

11. See Lewis (note 1).

6

1. William Bross to F. L. Olmsted, April 28, 1866, Frederick Law Olmsted Papers, Library of Congress, Washington, DC.

2. *The Papers of Frederick Law Olmsted*, suppl. series vol. 1, *Writings on Public Parks, Park Systems, and Parkways*, ed. Charles E. Beveridge and Carolyn F. Hoffman (Baltimore: Johns Hopkins University Press, 1997), 211, 213.

3. The sources used for this essay include Victoria Post Ranney, *Olmsted in Chicago* (Chicago: Open Lands Project, 1972); *Papers of Frederick Law Olmsted* (note 2), 206–38; and William H. Tishler, ed., *Midwestern Landscape Architecture* (Urbana-Champaign: University of Illinois Press, 2000), 41–56.

7

1. Roe published more than fifteen books, almost all of them novels, in the course of his relatively short life.

2. Roe's life and career are described in Glenn O. Carey, *Edward Payson Roe* (Boston: Twayne, 1985).

3. Edward Payson Roe, *Barriers Burned Away* (New York: Dodd & Mead, 1872), ix.

8

1. Ward developed his retail acumen working as a traveling salesman for a Michigan general store, an experience that shaped his perception of consumer tastes and needs and steeled his commitment to fair and honest business practices. He resettled in Chicago in 1865, working for a variety of dry-goods retailers and wholesalers, including Field, Palmer, Leiter & Co. He hatched his business plan to buy products cheaply, eliminate middlemen, and sell directly to consumers by mail based on his experiences with rural communities as a traveling salesman. The destruction of Ward's first inventory of goods in the Great Chicago Fire of 1871 forced him to delay the launch of his new venture until the following year.

2. The Homestead Act of 1862 and the expansion of the railroads into the western territories opened up this area for rapid settlement. Farmers organized the Patrons of Husbandry (commonly called the Grange) in 1867 to eliminate the middleman through cooperative ventures and thus reduce exorbitant prices they paid for inferior goods. In 1874 Montgomery Ward & Co. was designated as the official Grange Supply House, which earned the company the trust and business of the more than eight hundred thousand members of the Grange. See Daniel J. Boorstin, "A. Montgomery Ward's Mail-Order Business," *Chicago History* 2, no. 3 (Spring-Summer 1973): 142–46. See also Elizabeth Rae Rips, "An Introductory Study of the Role of the Mail Order Business in American History, 1872–1914" (M.A. thesis, University of Chicago, 1938), 15–17, 61–63; William Cronon, *Nature's Metropolis: Chicago and the Great West* (New York: W. W. Norton, 1991), 310–40 (no. 95); and Hal S. Barron, *Mixed Harvest: The Second Great Transformation in the Rural North* (Charlotte: University of North Carolina Press, 1997), 155–242.

3. Rips (note 2), 8–10.

4. Richard W. Sears (1863–1914) founded the R. W. Sears Watch Company in Minneapolis in 1886 as a mail-order watch business. Watchmaker Alvah C. Roebuck (1864–1948) joined the firm in 1887. Sears moved company operations to Chicago in 1887, eventually expanding its products to include diamonds and jewelry. It assumed the name Sears, Roebuck and Co. in 1893 and the following year issued its first mail-order catalogue, with a broad range of consumer products. Sears bought out Roebuck in 1895, and Julius Rosenwald (1862–1932), who supplied the company with men's clothing, bought into the firm. Rosenwald significantly expanded Sears's catalogue products and modernized its mail-order operations, He became president of the company in 1908. See Boris Emmet and John E. Jeuck, *Catalogues and Counters: A History of Sears, Roebuck and Company* (Chicago: University of Chicago Press, 1950), 23–136. See also the Sears Archives, http://www.searsarchives.com/history/ (accessed November 2, 2016).

5. For a more detailed description of the catalogues, see Rips (note 2), 15–22, 31–33.

6. Rips (note 2), 52–58.

7. Boorstin (note 2), 149.

8. The Montgomery Ward trade name was sold in the bankruptcy proceeding and is now owned by Colony Brands, a direct-marketing firm in Wisconsin.

9. Ancestry.com, the family-history online resource, offers digital copies of Sears catalogues from 1896 to 1993 to give people a snapshot of the kinds of clothes and other products their ancestors wore and used. See http://search.ancestry.com/search/db.aspx?dbid=1670 (accessed November 2, 2016).

9

1. See Mary T. Schmich, "'Ol' Yellows Are Mirrors of the Times," *Chicago Tribune*, May 26, 1986.

By 1844 there were several business directories in the United States. The first ones used maps to locate businesses. In 1878, two years after the invention of the telephone, New Haven, Connecticut, published a directory listing the numbers of the city's twenty-two telephones. Previous versions of the Chicago directory, before Donnelley took over, were published by Edwards & Co., Chicago.

2. David Anderson, "City's First Phone Book: Time Was . . . No Clear Tone Back in 1886," *Chicago Sun-Times*, January 12, 1976.

3. Bettye H. Pruitt, *Donnelley and the Yellow Pages: The Birth of an Advertising Medium* (Chicago: Reuben H. Donnelley, 1986), 10.

4. "The History of the Yellow Pages." http://inventors.about.com/od/xyzstartinventions/a/yellow_pages.htm (accessed November 14, 2015, but no longer active).

5. Pruitt (note 3), 17.

6. Pruitt (note 3), 14.

7. Pruitt (note 3), 7.

8. Pruitt (note 3), 14.

9. Chicago Vacuum Medical and Surgical Institute, "A Method of Cure without Medicine," advertisement in *The Lakeside Annual Directory of the City of Chicago*, May 1886.

10. Pruitt (note 3), 13.

11. Pruitt (note 3), 21.

12. Pruitt (note 3), 24.

13. *The Reuben H. Donnelley Corporation*, brochure (1948), Special Collections Research Center, University of Chicago Library.

1. A. T. Andreas, *History of Chicago: From the Earliest Period to the Present Time*, vol. 2, *From 1857 to the Fire of 1871* (Chicago: A. T. Andreas, 1885), 485 (no. 11).

2. *General Directory and Business Advertiser of the City of Chicago for the Year 1844: With a Historical Sketch and Statistics Extending from 1837 to 1844.*

3. A. T. Andreas, *History of Chicago: From the Earliest Period to the Present Time*, vol. 1, *Ending with the Year 1857* (Chicago: A. T. Andreas, 1885), 414 (no. 11).

4. Paul M. Angle, *The Chicago Historical Society, 1856–1956: An Unconventional Chronicle* (Chicago: Rand, McNally, 1956), 80–84. On July 14, 1874, a fire in the South Loop destroyed more than eight hundred buildings over a sixty-six-acre area. Among these was the Marine Bank Building, where, in J. Young Scammon's office, the collections of the Chicago Historical Society that had survived the 1871 fire were stored. All but a few items perished in the later fire.

5. Following is a complete list of publications in Fergus' Historical Series: No. 1, *The Annals of Chicago: A Lecture Delivered before the Chicago Lyceum, January 21, 1840*, by Joseph N. Balestier, 1876. No. 2, *Fergus' Directory of the City of Chicago, 1839*, compiled by Robert Fergus, 1876. No. 3, *The Last of the Illinois and a Sketch of the Pottawatomies, with Origin of the Prairies*, by John D. Caton, 1876. No. 4, *Early Movement in Illinois for the Legalization of Slavery: An Historical Sketch*, by Wm. H. Brown, 1876. No. 5, *Biographical Sketches of Some of the Early Settlers of the City of Chicago*, pt. 1, *S. Lisle Smith, George Davis, Dr. Philip Maxwell, John J. Brown, Richard L. Wilson, Col. Lewis C. Kerchival, Uriah P. Harris, Henry J. Clarke, Samuel J. Lowe*, 1876. No. 6, *Biographical Sketches of Some of the Early Settlers of the City of Chicago*, pt. 2, *William H. Brown, Benjamin W. Raymond, J. Young Scammon, Charles Walker, Thomas Church*, 1876. No. 7, *Early Chicago: A Lecture Delivered before the Sunday Lecture Society at McCormick Hall, on Sunday Afternoon, May 7th, 1876*, by John Wentworth, 1876. No. 8, *Early Chicago: A Lecture Delivered before the Sunday Lecture Society at McCormick Hall, on Sunday Afternoon, April 11, 1875, "With Supplemental Notes,"* by John Wentworth, 1876. No. 9, *The Present and Future Prospects of Chicago: An Address Delivered before the Chicago Lyceum, January 20, 1846*, by Henry Brown, with *Rise and Progress of Chicago*, by James A. Marshall, and *Chicago in 1836, "Strange Early Days,"* by Harriet Martineau, 1876. No. 10, *Addresses Delivered at the Annual Meeting of the Chicago Historical Society, November 19, 1868*, by J. Young Scammon and Isaac N. Arnold, *A Sketch of the Late Col. John H. Kinzie*, by Juliette A. Kinzie, *Sketches of Billy Caldwell and Shabonee*, by William Hickling and G. S. Hubbard, and *"The Winnebago Scare,"* by Hiram W. Beckwith, 1877 (copies of Fergus No. 10 are scarce; see *Chicago History* 2, no. 1 [Fall 1948]: 13: "But the collector who aims at a complete set—a laudable ambition—is warned that he will probably hunt far and long for Number Ten. . . . Number Ten is a real rarity"). No. 11, *Early Medical Chicago*, by James Nevins Hyde, 1879. No. 12, *Illinois in the Eighteenth Century—Kaskaskia and Its Parish Records: Old Fort Chartres; and Col. John Todd's Record-Book*, by Edward G. Mason, 1881. No. 13, *Recollections of Early Illinois and Her Noted Men*, by Joseph Gillespie, 1880. No. 14, *The Earliest Religious History of Chicago*, by Jeremiah Porter, *Early History of Illinois*, by William H. Brown, *Early Society in Southern Illinois*, by Robert W. Patterson, *Reminiscences of the Illinois-Bar Forty Years Ago: Lincoln and Douglas as Orators and Lawyers*, by Isaac N. Arnold, *The First Murder-Trial in Iroquois County for the First Murder in Cook County*, 1881. No. 15, *Abraham Lincoln*, by Isaac N. Arnold, *Stephen A. Douglas: An [sic] Eulogy*, by James W. Sheahan, 1881. No. 16, *Early Chicago—Fort Dearborn*, by John Wentworth, 1881. No. 17, *William B. Ogden and Early Days in Chicago*, by Isaac N. Arnold, 1882. No. 18, *Chicago River-and-Harbor Convention*, by William Mosley Hall, John Wentworth, Samuel Lisle Smith, Horace Greeley, and Thurlow Weed, together with *Statistics concerning Chicago*, by Jesse B. Thomas and James L. Barton, 1882. No. 19, *Early-Chicago Reminiscences*, by Charles Cleaver, 1882. No. 20, *A Winter in the West: Letters Descriptive of Chicago and Vicinity in 1833–4*, by Charles Fenno Hoffman, 1882. No. 21, *Biographical Sketch of John Dean Caton, Ex-Chief-Justice of Illinois*, by Robert Fergus, 1882. No. 22, *Recollections of the Early Chicago and the Illinois Bar*, by Isaac N. Arnold, *Recollections of the Bench and Bar of Central Illinois*, by James C. Conkling, *The Lawyer as a Pioneer*, by Thomas Hoyne, 1882. No. 23, *Early Illinois Railroads*, by William K. Ackerman, 1884. No. 24, *Congressional Reminiscences: Adams, Benton, Clay, Calhoun, and Webster*, by John Wentworth, 1882. No. 25, *Norris' Business Directory and Statistics of the City of Chicago for 1846*, by J. W. Norris, 1846, revised and corrected by Robert

Fergus, 1883. No. 26, *A Discourse on the Aborigines of the Ohio Valley*, by William Henry Harrison, *The Fort-Wayne Manuscript: An Old Writing (Lately Found) Containing Indian Speeches and a Treatise on the Western Indians*, by Hiram W. Beckwith, 1883. No. 27, *The Illinois and Indiana Indians*, by Hiram W. Beckwith, 1884. No. 28, *Directory of the City of Chicago Illinois, for 1843*, compiled by Robert Fergus, 1896. No. 29, *Biographical Sketch of Joseph Duncan, Fifth Governor of Illinois*, by Julia Duncan Kirby, 1888. No. 30, *Narrative of the Massacre at Chicago [Saturday], August 15, 1812, and of Some Preceding Events*, 2nd ed., by Juliette Augusta (Magill) Kinzie, 1914. No. 31, *Early Illinois*, pt. 1, *Pierre Menard, and Pierre-Menard Papers, Historical Sketch and Notes*, by Edward Gay Mason, *Noel Le Vasseur*, by Stephen R. Moore, *Lists of Early Illinois Citizens*, intro. by Edward Gay Mason, 1890. No. 32, *Early Illinois*, pt. 2, *John Rice Jones* and *Rice Jones*, by W. A. Burt Jones, 1889. No. 33, *Early Illinois*, pt. 3, *John Todd, John Todd's Record-Book and John-Todd Papers, Historical Sketch and Notes*, by Edward Gay Mason, 1890. No. 34, *Early Illinois*, pt. 4, *Philippe de Rocheblave and Rocheblave Papers, Historical Sketch and Notes*, by Edward Gay Mason, *Court of Enquiry at Fort Chartres*, by John Moses, 1890. No. 35, *Eleazer Williams Not the Dauphin of France*, by William Ward Wight, 1903.

11

1. A. T. Andreas, *History of Chicago from the Earliest Period to the Present Time*, vol. 2, *From 1857 until the Fire of 1871* (Chicago: A. T. Andreas Co., 1885), 3.

2. Andreas (note 1), 3.

3. "Literature . . . The History of Chicago," *Chicago Daily Tribune*, March 22, 1884, 9.

4. "Literature . . . The Second Volume of Andreas' History of Chicago," *Chicago Daily Tribune*, November 7, 1885, 9.

5. Andreas (note 1). For the biographical tally, see Paul M. Angle, "The Great Repository of Chicago History," *Chicago History* 8 (1969): 290.

6. Andreas lost his first fortune when he overextended into sumptuous illustrated state atlases of Minnesota and Iowa, but he gained another when he pared back to barebones midwestern county histories packed with paid-for biographies—"mug" books—that he then tested on a broader scale in histories of Milwaukee and northern Wisconsin. Failure again threatened in late 1884, in the midst of his Chicago venture, with the collapse of a touring theatrical company that he had backed. He subsequently amassed another fortune by producing giant panoramas of Civil War battles—and the Crucifixion—in partnership with various Civil War generals. But following an expensive trip to Europe, that fortune also disappeared in Columbian Exposition speculations, including the projected 6,124-room Andreas Hotel at Seventy-Third and Cregier. See Angle (note 5); and Michael P. Conzen, "Maps for the Masses: A. T. Andreas and the Midwestern County Atlas Map Trade," in *Chicago Mapmakers: Essays on the Rise of the City's Map Trade*, ed. Michael Conzen (Chicago: Chicago Historical Society for the Chicago Map Society, 1984), 47–63. See also "The 'Mountain Pink' Ruined Him," *New York Times*, October 7, 1884, 1; "Largest Hotel in the World," *Staunton* [Virginia] *Spectator*, November 9, 1892, 3; and "Alfred T. Andreas Dies," *Chicago Daily Tribune,* February 11, 1900, 4.

7. "Letter from Washington . . . Capt. A. T. Andreas," *Troy* [New York] *Weekly Times,* November 3, 1886, 1.

8. . *Chicago Daily Tribune*, October 9, 1884, 8; and Conzen (note 6), 60.

12

1. John P. Altgeld, *Reasons for Pardoning Fielden, Neebe and Schwab* ([Springfield, IL?,]: n.p. 1893), n.p.

2. Ibid.

3. Clarence Darrow, "Eulogy for John P. Altgeld," in Clarence Darrow, *The Story of My Life* (New York: Charles Scribner's Sons, 1932), 457.

13

1. Henry Blake Fuller, "My Early Books," typewritten manuscript, 1919. Henry Blake Fuller Papers, Box 11, Folder 361, p. 5, Newberry Library, Chicago. On the Fuller Papers at the Newberry, see finding aid at http://mms.newberry.org/xml/xml_files/fuller.xml (accessed August 16, 2016).

2. These include *The Chevalier of Pensieri-Vani* (1890) and *The Chatelaine of La Trinité* (1892).

3. "Advertised as just ready PW Sept. 16, 1893." Jacob Blanck, comp., *Bibliography of American Literature* (New Haven, CT: Yale University Press, 1959), 3, 257–58, no. 6465.

4. Henry Blake Fuller, *The Cliff-Dwellers: A Novel* (New York: Harper & Brothers, 1893), 1.

5. Fuller (note 4), 50.

6. Fuller lamented that his theme of marriage as an alliance of families was not "detected" by critics. See Fuller (note 1), 1.

7. Fuller (note 4), 235.

8. Quoted by Henry Regnery in *The Cliff Dwellers: The History of a Chicago Cultural Institution* (Evanston, IL: Chicago Historical Bookworks, 1990), 7.

9. Regnery (note 8), 8.

10. Ann Massa, "Henry Blake Fuller and the Cliff Dwellers: Appropriations and Misappropriations," *Journal of American Studies* 36, 1 (April 2002): 70.

11. Henry Blake Fuller, *The Cliff-Dwellers*, ed. Joseph A. Dimuro (Peterborough, ON: Broadview Editions, 2010), includes the text of the novel along with contemporary reviews, literary criticism, and cultural commentary.

14

1. James R. Grossman et al., *The Encyclopedia of Chicago* (Chicago: University of Chicago Press, 2004), 941.

2. The book is bound in gold-stamped red cloth and has maroon endpapers. The inside rear cover features a map pocket containing a large folded folio sheet with two maps on the recto and one on the verso. The book features a total of ninety-one line engravings.

3. *Rand, McNally & Co.'s Bird's-Eye Views and Guide to Chicago* (Chicago: Rand, McNally, 1893), 2.

15

1. For more information on the relationship between African Americans and Africans and the World's Columbian Exposition, see Christopher Robert Reed, *All the World Is Here! The Black Presence at White City* (Bloomington: Indiana University Press, 2000).

2. Ida B. Wells, Frederick Douglass, I. Garland Penn, and F. L. Barnett, *The Reason Why the Colored American Is Not in the World's Columbian Exposition: The Afro-American's Contribution to Columbian Literature* (Chicago: Ida B. Wells, 1893), 7.

3. In 1895 Wells married Ferdinand Barnett, an attorney with whom she had four children. Calling herself Ida B. Wells-Barnett, she was ahead of her time in choosing to keep her own last name as well as taking her husband's.

16

1. William H. Carwardine, *The Pullman Strike* (Chicago: Charles H. Kerr, 1894), 125.

2. Pullman Town, surrounding the Pullman Sleeping Car Company shops and containing some five hundred employee houses, opened as a planned industrial community in 1884, one that could sustain itself economically rather than rely on the owner's philanthropy. Quickly hailed for its integrated design and wholesome layout (by architect Solon S. Beman), it nevertheless attracted criticism even before the labor conflict of 1894 for its effectively top-down and arbitrary governance.

3. Carwardine (note 1), 14.

4. Carwardine (note 1), 29.

5. Heath W. Carter, *Union Made: Working People and the Rise of Social Christianity in Chicago* (New York: Oxford University Press, 2015), 134–36.

6. Carwardine (note 1), 111.

17

1. The book was also published in London later in 1894 by the *Review of Reviews*.

2. Catalyzed by Stead's book, city leaders founded the Civic Federation in 1893, with a mission to better the quality of life in Chicago by improving its political, economic, and moral climate. The organization now focuses on increasing the efficacy of Chicago-area governments.

3. William T. Stead, *If Christ Came to Chicago! A Plea for the Union of All Who Love in the Service of All Who Suffer* (Evanston, IL: Chicago Historical Bookworks, 1994), 421.

4. "The Church of God in Chicago has only one belief," he wrote, "and that is to do what Christ would have done if He were confronted with the problems with which they had to deal." Stead (note 3) 429.

5. W. Sydney Robinson, *Muckraker: The Scandalous Life and Times of W. T. Stead: Britain's First Investigative Journalist* (London: Robson Press, 2012), 250–51.

18

1. *The Chap-Book* is a perennial subject for literary historians. The standard references are Sidney Kramer, *History of Stone & Kimball and Herbert S. Stone & Co, with a Bibliography of Their Publications, 1894–1905* (Chicago: N. W. Forgue, 1940); and Wendy Clauson Schlereth, "*The Chap-Book*, a

Journal of American Intellectual Life in the 1890s" (PhD diss., University of Iowa, 1980).

2. Harriet Monroe, "Aere Perennius," *Poetry* 6, no. 4 (July 1915): 197.

19

1. The four essays were authored by well-known figures: Charles Mulford Robinson contributed "The Fair as a Spectacle"; William Anderson Coffin, "The Fair as a Work of Art"; Thomas Corwin Mendenhall, "Science and the Fair"; and Selim Hobart Peabody, "The Educational and Moral Value of the Exposition."

20

1. For further reading, see Elmer Ellis, ed., *Mr. Dooley at His Best* (New York: Charles Scribner's Sons, 1938); Elmer Ellis, *Mr. Dooley's America: A Life of Finley Peter Dunne* (New York: Alfred A. Knopf, 1941); Charles Fanning, *Finley Peter Dunne and Mr. Dooley: The Chicago Years* (Lexington: University Press of Kentucky, 1978); and Charles Fanning, ed., *Mr. Dooley and the Chicago Irish: The Autobiography of a Nineteenth-Century Ethnic Group* (Washington, DC: Catholic University of America Press, 1987).

2. Ellis (note 1), 120.

21

1. It followed the publication, in pamphlet form, of Dewey's shorter *My Pedagogic Creed* in 1897.

2. Quoted in William Harms and Ida DePencier, *Experiencing Education: 100 Years of Learning at the University of Chicago Laboratory Schools* (Chicago: University of Chicago Laboratory School, 1996), 2.

3. John Dewey, *The School and Society: Being Three Lectures* (Chicago: University of Chicago Press, 1899), 18, 28.

4. See for example Richard Hofstadter, *Anti-Intellectualism in American Life* (New York: Alfred A. Knopf, 1963). Hofstadter, the great American historian and the most astute of progressive education's critics, carefully excused Dewey for many of the movement's failings and characterized later progressive educators as having strayed from the "sound and important" ideas for reform that he had articulated in works such as *The School and Society* (360).

22

1. Theodore Dreiser, *Sister Carrie* (New York: Bantam Books, 1958), 48.

2. Dreiser (note 1), 65.

3. Dreiser (note 1), 93.

23

1. Frank Norris, *The Pit: A Story of Chicago*, ed. Joseph R. McElrath Jr. and Gwendolyn Jones (New York: Penguin Books, 1994), 57.

2. Norris (note 1), 39.

3. McElrath and Jones, introduction to Norris (note 1), vii.

4. See Warner Berthoff, *The Ferment of Realism: American Literature 1884–1919* (Cambridge: Cambridge University Press, 1981), 223–26; Carl S. Smith, *Chicago and the American Literary Imagination 1880–1920* (Chicago: University of Chicago Press, 1984), 60–70; and Howard Horwitz, *By the Law of Nature: Form and Value in Nineteenth-Century America* (New York: Oxford University Press, 1991), 146–67.

5. The subtitle *A Romance of Chicago* used in the *Saturday Evening Post* was changed to *A Story of Chicago* when the book was published in 1903.

24

1. Richard Robert Donnelley and Thomas Elliott Donnelley were members of the Caxton Club starting in 1895, the year of its founding. Many of their descendants, as well as Donnelley company executives, have been active Club members. The company provided pro bono design and printing to the Club for decades. See Kim Coventry, "Donnelley Family and Caxton Club: Five Generations of Involvement," *Caxtonian* 6, no. 4 (April 1998): 1–4.

2. The Lakeside Classics were distributed to customers and friends of the company. After it went public in 1957, shareholders were added to the list. Print-run figures are unknown for the first seven decades, except for 1935 when, according to the preface to that year's volume, fifteen hundred books were printed. By the 1970s, tens of thousands of copies of each title were being distributed. See Susan M. Levy, "The Lakeside Classics: A Christmas Gift That Keeps on Coming," *Caxtonian* 20, no. 12 (December 2012): 1–5. Collectors the world over strive to own the full series, for which there is a sustained market.

3. The Lakeside Press imprint was used in the early years of the company for publishing (as opposed to printing) ventures. The company ceased publishing in the 1930s except for the Lakeside Classics and the Four American Books (no. 53), an advertising initiative undertaken to attract literary publishers. For other materials printed by the company, see nos. 8–9, 18, 29, and 38. See also Kim Coventry, "R.R. Donnelley & Sons Company: Its Role in the Development of Commerce, Craft, and Culture in Chicago," *Caxtonian* 15, no. 1 (January 2007): 111.

4. Richard Robert Donnelley was born in Hamilton, Ontario, Canada, in 1836 and moved to Chicago in 1864 to join a printing partnership that was renamed Church, Goodman & Donnelley.

5. For a brief history of the company, see Kim Coventry, *Printing for the Modern Age: Commerce, Craft, and Culture in the RR Donnelley Archive* (Chicago: University of Chicago Library, 2006).

6. [Thomas Elliott Donnelley], introduction to *The Autobiography of Benjamin Franklin*, Lakeside Classics 1 (Chicago: Lakeside Press, 1903), vi.

7. A complete list of the titles can be found on WorldCat, the OCLC, and www.rrdonnelley.com/about/lakeside-classics/ (accessed August 6, 2017).

8. J. Christian Bay, "Scarce and Beautiful Imprints of Chicago," *Papers of the Bibliographical Society of America* 15, no. 2 (1921): 101.

9. A scan of the literature neither confirmed nor refuted this long-held claim. I am grateful to Alice Schreyer for her help with this research.

10. [Thomas Elliott Donnelley], "Publishers' Preface," in John Bidwell, *Bidwell's Echoes of the Past*; and Rev. John Steele, *In Camp and Cabin*, Lakeside Classics 26 (Chicago: Lakeside Press, 1928), viii.

25

1. For the fire's immediate impact, see John R. Freeman, *On the Safeguarding of Life in Theaters: A Study from the Standpoint of an Engineer* (New York: American Society of Mechanical Engineers, 1906), reprinted from the *Transactions* of the Society, vol. 27.

2. For more on Bishop Fallows and the slightly different *Chicago's Awful Theater Horror*, see the introduction by Perry R. Duis and Cathlyn Schalhorn to Nat Brandt, *Chicago Death Trap: The Iroquois Theatre Fire of 1903* (Carbondale: Southern Illinois University Press, 2003). For the lawsuits and investigations, see Brandt, 122–32.

3. Vincent Starrett, "Books Alive," *Chicago Sunday Tribune*, June 6, 1943, 12.

4. See Joanne L. Goodwin, *Gender and the Politics of Welfare Reform: Mothers' Pensions in Chicago, 1911–1929* (Chicago: University of Chicago Press, 1997).

5. *Chicago Daily Tribune*, August 15, 1939.

27

1. "'The Jungle' and the Way Out," *Westminster Review* 166, no. 4 (October 1906): 365.

2. Before it came out as a book, it was serialized, in 1905, in another socialist magazine, *One-Hoss Philosophy*, published in Girard, Kansas.

3. Christopher Wilson, "The Making of a Bestseller, 1906," *New York Times*, December 22, 1985; and Isaac F. Marcosson, *Adventures in Interviewing* (London: John Lane, 1919), 280–85.

4. Louise Carroll Wade, "The Problem of Classroom Use of Upton Sinclair's *The Jungle*," *American Studies* 32, no. 2 (Fall 1991): 79–101.

5. Cited in Wade (note 4), 79.

6. For a discussion of *The Jungle* and the reaction to it, see Dominic A. Pacyga, *Slaughterhouse: Chicago's Union Stock Yard and the World It Made* (Chicago: University of Chicago Press, 2015), 124–32. Jack London is quoted on page 129.

28

1. Thomas served as the orchestra's first musical director from its founding in 1891 until his death in early 1905. Upton persuaded Thomas to write an autobiography, to which the critic contributed a reminiscence. *Theodore Thomas: A Musical Autobiography*, ed. George P. Upton (Chicago: A. C. McClurg, 1905), was originally issued in two volumes: 1, *Life Work*, and 2, *Concert Programmes*. In 1964 the first volume was reissued under the same title, with a new introduction by Leon Stein (New York: Da Capo).

2. The most momentous event of Upton's college years was the night he heard Jenny Lind—the "Swedish nightingale"—

sing before a wild and adoring crowd. To his last days, he cited her consummate grace and radiant sound as his life's inspiration.

3. For a dramatic and more detailed account, see James W. Sheahan and George P. Upton, *The Great Conflagration* (Chicago: Union Publishing, 1871).

4. In 1887 Upton prepared for William Frederick Poole, first librarian of the Newberry Library, Chicago, a list of books, periodicals, scores, and other documents that came to form the nucleus of the library's stellar music collection. Upton subsequently donated numerous works from his own library and facilitated the Newberry's acquisition of the Theodore Thomas archive from the conductor's family.

29

1. They included Washington (DC), Cleveland, and San Francisco, and Manila and Baguio in the Philippines.

2. The majority of the original drawings are in the Art Institute of Chicago; others are held by the Chicago History Museum.

3. Effective publicity for the plan was also provided by the publication, in 1911 and subsequent years, of *Wacker's Manual of the Plan of Chicago* (no. 33).

4. See Carl Smith, *The Plan of Chicago: Daniel Burnham and the Remaking of the American City* (Chicago: University of Chicago Press, 2006).

30

1. These include child welfare legislation, housing and sanitation reform, vocational education, immigrant protection, labor mediation, women's suffrage, and civil rights advocacy.

2. The illustrations are those of the artist Norah Hamilton (1873–1945), a resident of Hull-House and sister of another resident, Dr. Alice Hamilton, who developed the field of occupational health. Norah eventually became director of Hull-House's children's art program.

3. Jane Addams, *Twenty Years at Hull-House with Autobiographical Notes* (New York: Macmillan, 1910), 42.

4. Addams (note 3), 292.

5. Addams (note 3), 396. Addams rejected Tolstoy's admonition to only live by one's own labor and to cast off property and wealth, and she consequently offered her American audience a way to translate ideals into action without extremism.

6. Addams wrote hundreds of articles and speeches. Only *Twenty Years* was published in more than one edition during her life; it is also the only work to be translated while she was alive. It went into German in 1913 and more recently into Spanish and Japanese. Addams coedited two books and coauthored a number of articles and studies. See Mary Lynn McCree Bryan, ed., *The Jane Addams Papers: A Comprehensive Guide* (Bloomington: Indiana University Press, 1996), 95–98.

7. The scholarship documenting this interpretation of Addams is voluminous. In recent decades her significance as a philosopher of democracy, a sociologist, and a public intellectual has been well established. See for example Mary Jo Deegan, *Jane Addams and the Men of the Chicago School, 1892–1918* (Piscataway, NJ: Transaction Books, 1988); Jean Bethke Elshtain, *Jane Addams and the Dream of American Democracy* (New York: Basic Books, 2002); and Marilyn Fischer, Carol Nackenoff, and Wendy Chmielewski, eds., *Jane Addams and the Practice of Democracy* (Urbana: University of Illinois Press, 2009).

31

1. See Anthony Alofsin, *Frank Lloyd Wright: The Lost Years, 1910–1922; A Study in Influence* (Chicago: University of Chicago Press, 1993), esp. chap. 2 and appendix B. Wright saw this as a business opportunity, offering copies to architects at $50 payable in increments over five years and urging friends to hawk these volumes for him. See Alofsin's introduction to the 1998 edition of his *Studies and Executed Buildings by Frank Lloyd Wright* (New York: Rizzoli), especially p. 8.

2. Joseph August Lux, *Joseph M. Olbrich, Eine Monographie*, 4 vols. (Berlin: Ernst Wasmuth, 1913–19); and Paul Wenzel and Maurice Krakow, *A Monograph of the Work of McKim, Mead & White, 1879–1915*, 4 vols. (New York: Architectural Book Publishing, 1914–15).

3. Paul Kruty, "Graphic Depictions: The Evolution of Marion Mahony's Architectural Renderings," in *Marion Mahony Reconsidered*, ed. David Van Zanten (Chicago: University of Chicago Press, 2011), 51–93.

4. Kruty (note 3), 67.

32

1. The sisters had run a lucrative bordello in Nebraska and used the profits to create their Chicago club. They employed

many strategies to keep the establishment from being closed by the authorities, including vetting their members carefully and charging enormous fees, brooking no misbehavior, and freely entertaining officials who might otherwise have given them trouble.

2. [Ada and Minna Everleigh,] *The Everleigh Club Illustrated* (Chicago, 1911), 1.

3. Illustrations in the booklet are as follows, preceded by page number: 2. Everleigh Club, 2131, 2133 Dearborn St.; 3. Silver Parlor; 4. Gold Parlor; 5. Green Parlor; 6. Copper Parlor; 7. Japanese Parlor; 8. Corner View of Ball Room; 9. View of Ball Room; 10. Club Room; 11. Japanese Throne Room; 12. Entrance to Hall of 2131; 13. Mosque Looking into Moorish Room; 14. East View of Moorish Music Room; 15. Oriental Music Room; 16. Rose Parlor, Louis Quatorze; 17. Green Parlor, Louis Quinze; 18. Oriental Anteroom; 19. Rose Parlor Looking into Green Parlor; 20. Entrance to Hall of 2133; 21. Stairway off of Ballroom; 22. Blue Parlor Suite; 23. Alcove of Blue Room; 24. Parlor of Rose Room; 25. Alcove of Rose Room; 26. Hallway off of Rose Room; 27. Breakfast Room in 2133; 28. Dining Room in 2131; 29. Red Parlor Bed Room; 30. Green Parlor Bed Room; 31. Private Car Buffet.

4. A second edition of the booklet (also scarce) was published in the mid-1960s by "Willie Everleigh," an obvious pseudonym. This version, apparently used by Karen Abbott for her book (referred to in the text two paragraphs below), contains several photos and illustrations not in the original.

5. Washburn's book was published in New York by Knickerbocker Publishing; Hibbler's was published by Volitant (place of publication unknown); and Abbott's in New York by Random House.

6. Norman Mark, *Mayors, Madams, and Madmen* (Chicago: Chicago Review Press, 1979), 29.

33

1. Walter D. Moody, *Teachers' Hand Book: Wacker's Manual of the Plan of Chicago, Municipal Economy* (Chicago, 1911), 4. Note that *Teachers'* appears in the cover title. Inside, the apostrophe is moved: *Teacher's* (11).

2. Several page numbers are repeated, so a student told to turn to a page later in the book could get lost. And the table of contents is wrong for the last seven chapters.

3. Two chapters were renumbered, and a new chapter called "Developing the Lake Front" was added.

4. A twenty-page progress report (called "Addenda") was included.

5. As in the previous edition, the last chapter is an update, but this time up to "1925, when this chapter was written" [*Wacker's Manual* (Chicago, 1924), 141]. This is just one more curiosity to add to the story, since the stated printing date is 1924.

34

1. *Poetry, A Magazine of Verse* 1, no. 2 (November 1912): 64.

2. All quotes in this paragraph are from Harriet Monroe, *A Poet's Life: Seventy Years in a Changing World* (New York: Macmillan, 1938).

3. Cited in *The Poems of T. S. Eliot*, vol. 1, *Collected and Uncollected Poems*, ed. Christopher Ricks and Jim McCue (London: Faber and Faber, 2015), 374.

4. *Poetry* was also first to recognize many poems that are now widely anthologized: "We Real Cool" by Gwendolyn Brooks, "Briggflatts" by Basil Bunting, "anyone lived in a pretty how town" by E. E. Cummings, "Chez Jane" by Frank O'Hara, "Fever 103" by Sylvia Plath, "Chicago" by Carl Sandburg, "Sunday Morning" by Wallace Stevens, and countless others.

5. Adam Kirsch, "*Poetry* Magazine's Rebirth," *The Sun*, December 20, 2005, http://www.nysun.com/arts/poetry-magazines-rebirth/24685/ (accessed September 6, 2016).

35

1. Two editions of the catalogue were printed. Other than including a lengthier introduction by F. J. Gregg, the second edition differs only slightly from the first. Only in Chicago was the exhibition staged at an art museum. After its showing at the Art Institute, the exhibition traveled to Boston, where it was displayed at the Copley Society of Art.

2. Edward E. Hale, "Vincent Van Gogh: Post-Impressionist," *Dial* 54 (June 1, 1913): 455.

3. *Nude Descending a Staircase (No. 2)* (1912) is in the Philadelphia Museum of Art.

4. These include Cor Ardens, the Salon des Refusés, Neo-Arlimusc, and most especially the Chicago No-Jury Society of Artists. See Paul S. Kruty, "Declarations of Independents:

Chicago's Alternative Art Groups of the 1920s," in *The Old Guard and the Avant-Garde*, ed. Sue Ann Prince (Chicago: University of Chicago Press, 1990), 77–93.

36

1. "The Top 100 Sports Books of All Time," *Sports Illustrated*, December 16, 2002.

2. Ring Lardner, *You Know Me Al: A Busher's Letters* (Charleston, S.C.: BookSurge LLC, 2004), 48.

3. Lardner (note 2), 113.

4. Lardner (note 2), 178.

5. Lardner (note 2), 179.

6. Cited in Colin Fleming, "The Greatest Baseball Novel Ever Written: Ring Lardner's *You Know Me Al*," *Atlantic*, August 28, 2013.

37

1. Carl Sandburg, "I Am the People, the Mob." All poems cited in this essay were published in *Chicago Poems* and can be found in Sandburg, *The Complete Poems of Carl Sandburg* (New York: Harcourt Brace and Company, 1970).

2. "Chicago" was first published in *Poetry* magazine (no. 34) in March 1914. It is included in *Chicago Poems*.

3. The 1940 prize was for the second volume of his biography of Lincoln; the 1951 award was for his *Collected Poems*.

4. See Archibald MacLeish, preface to Sandburg (note 1), xx.

5. William Pritchard, *Frost: A Literary Life Reconsidered* (Oxford: Oxford University Press, 1984), 118.

38

1. For discussions of the competition and publication, see Leslie Coburn, "Considering the People on the Back Streets: Urban Planning at the City Club of Chicago," in *Drawing the Future: Chicago Architecture on the International Stage, 1900–1925*, ed. David Van Zanten (Evanston, IL: Northwestern University Press, 2013), 84–106; and Neil Levine, "The Quadruple Block Plan Expanded into an Entire Neighborhood Scheme for the Chicago City Club Competition of 1912–13," in Levine, *The Urbanism of Frank Lloyd Wright* (Princeton, NJ: Princeton University Press, 2016), 77–115.

2. Minutes of the City Club of Chicago, City Planning Committee, April 11, 1913. At this meeting City Club members sought to draw up a general statement of the "good and bad features of the Burnham Plan for Chicago." This and subsequent references to City Club of Chicago minutes and manuscripts are drawn from the City Club of Chicago Collection, Chicago History Museum.

3. George E. Hooker, "Program of a Competition," in *City Residential Land Development: Studies in Planning*, ed. Alfred B. Yeomans (Chicago: University of Chicago Press, 1916), p. 1.

4. George E. Hooker, "A Plan for Chicago," *Survey*, September 4, 1909, 790.

5. Minutes of the City Club of Chicago, City Planning Committee, September 20, 1911.

6. Minutes of the City Club of Chicago, City Planning Committee, April 25, 1913.

7. Minutes of the City Club of Chicago, City Planning Committee, July 14, 1914.

8. Rudolph F. Schuchardt to Charles H. Wacker, July 28, 1914, in Minutes of the City Club of Chicago, City Planning Committee, July 1914.

9. Hooker (note 4), 778–90.

10. Hooker (note 4), 790.

11. Yeomans (note 3), 39.

12. Minutes of the City Club of Chicago, Committee on Housing Conditions, October 28, 1912: "Mr. Hooker briefly outlined the plan for the architects' prize exhibit to be held in connections with the Housing Committee's exhibit." See also Minutes of the City Club of Chicago, Committee on Housing Conditions, November 27, 1911. This plan for the display followed one initially offered by Hooker for a national exhibition on cities that would include three sections, one on historical developments of the city, a second devoted to cities of the present day, and a third for "speculative department, in which there should be plans as depicting an entirely idealistic physical organization of a considerable number of existing cities" aimed at envisioning future urban form. See Hooker to Jens Jensen, April 27, 1910, Minutes of the City Club of Chicago, City Planning Committee, May 11, 1910.

13. "Garden Cities in England," *City Club Bulletin* 4 (June 7, 1911): 133–40.

14. Minutes of the City Club of Chicago, Committee on Housing Conditions, April 16, 1912, July 1, 1912; and "Co-partnership Housing and Garden Cities," *City Club Bulletin* 5 (October 12, 1912): 281–89. See also "The Garden City Idea in City and Suburban Development," *City Club Bulletin* 7 (May 29, 1914): 182–87.

15. Frank Lloyd Wright, "A Home in a Prairie Town," *Ladies Home Journal* 18 (February 1901): 17.

16. Levine (note 1).

17. Minutes of the City Club of Chicago, City Planning Committee, March 22, 1912.

18. Donald Leslie Johnson, "Origin of the Neighbourhood Unit," *Planning Perspectives* 17 (2002): 227–45.

40

1. The apostrophe in "toddling" is placed differently in the title and in the lyrics.

2. He changed his name from Alfred Breitenbach.

3. Wikipedia lists seventy-five recordings of "Chicago" by individuals, groups, and orchestras; https://en.wikipedia.org/wiki/Chicago_(That_Toddlin%27_Town) (accessed September 8, 2016).

4. George F. Root wrote some of the best Civil War tunes, which his firm, Root & Cady, published (see no. 2). Fannie Bloomfield Zeisler, wife of the lawyer who defended the 1888 Haymarket Riot anarchists, was a legendary concert pianist. Her conservatories were led as well by another great pianist, Rudolf Ganz. Homer Rodeheaver promoted early twentieth-century white gospel music; Thomas A. Dorsey published and Mahalia Jackson later sang black gospel music. For white jazz, think Benny Goodman and the Austin High Gang. The African American musicians who performed, recorded, and published their ragtime, gospel, and jazz compositions in Chicago are legion. The uncompromising rigor of avant-garde composer Ralph Shapey was fostered at the University of Chicago. The Eighth Blackbird ensemble is a leading proponent of new music.

41

1. The title on the book's cover is *1001 Afternoons in Chicago* (p. xv), but the title page lists *A Thousand and One Afternoons in Chicago* (p. 97).

2. H. L. Mencken, "The Literary Capital of the United States," *The Nation* (London), April 17, 1920 (American suppl.). The following May 12, it was reprinted on the book page of the *Chicago Daily News*.

3. Henry Justin Smith recounted the origins of the column and Hecht's "idea that just under the edge of the news as commonly understood . . . lay life" on the second page of his preface to Ben Hecht, *A Thousand and One Afternoons in Chicago* (Chicago: Covici-McGee, 1922).

4. Hecht (note 3), 174.

5. Hecht (note 3), 160.

6. The Dutch-born Rosse was an architect and designer. During his time in Chicago (1918–23), he served as head of the Design Department at the School of the Art Institute and also created stage sets for the Chicago Grand Opera Company. He later designed sets for many New York theatrical productions and Hollywood films (including the 1931 *Frankenstein* featuring Boris Karloff).

7. For Hecht's reminiscence of Pascal Covici, Herman Rosse, and their first mutual publishing efforts, see Ben Hecht, "How We Raised a Small Flag Once," in *A Child of the Century* (New York: Simon and Schuster, 1954), 337–40.

8. The offending novel was *Fantazius Mallare: A Mysterious Oath* (Chicago: Covici-McGee, 1922). For a short while Hecht continued his 1001 column in the *Chicago Literary Times*, a biweekly paper he copublished with poet Maxwell Bodenheim. Years later he wrote a column titled "1001 Afternoons in New York" for Ralph Ingersoll's magazine *PM*. Those columns, largely expressing anger at the failure of the United States to respond to growing anti-Semitism abroad, were also collected into a book of the same title published by Viking Press in 1941 (with illustrations by George Grosz, whom Hecht had befriended during his time in Germany after World War I).

9. The award was for *Underworld*, a silent film about Chicago gangsters directed by Josef von Sternberg that was released in 1927. Other films Hecht wrote (in some cases he was not credited) include *Scarface* (1932), *Wuthering Heights* (1935), *Gunga Din* (1939), *Spellbound* (1945), *Notorious* (1946), and *Ride the Pink Horse* (1947).

10. *1001 Afternoons in Chicago* was reprinted by the University of Chicago Press in 1992 and again in 2009 (with a new introduction by William Savage). In 2014 a radio play featuring stories from the book, with music by Seth Boustead and Amos Gillespie, was presented in Chicago by ACM (Access Contem-

porary Music) and Strawdog Theatre Company. A recording of the play is available on CD-ROM.

42

1. The book comprises 103 pages of text and 281 black-and-white plates. The Tribune Company planned to send copies to the competition's participants and then sell the rest at bookstores for $5 (about $70 in 2016).

2. These designs were never considered for awards. The *Tribune* did not include them in its follow-up articles, and American architecture journals did not discuss them (at least not in the 1920s).

3. Stanley Tigerman, *Tribune Tower Competition Late Entries*, 2 vols. (New York: Rizzoli, 1980).

4. About this and other aspects of the competition, see Katherine Solomonson, *The Chicago Tribune Tower Competition: Skyscraper Design and Cultural Change in the 1920s* (New York: Cambridge University Press, 2001).

5. Eliel Saarinen's well-integrated handling of a stepped-back top would inspire myriad emulators. One of them was Raymond Hood, who collaborated on the design of the competition's winning entry. A year later he and his partner, André Fouilhoux, drew inspiration from Saarinen's entry for the American Radiator Building (New York, 1923–24; currently the Bryant Park Hotel). Hood would go on to design other noteworthy skyscrapers in New York, including the New York Daily News Building (1929) and the RCA Building at Rockefeller Center (1933). Hood's career would also inform a character in Ayn Rand's novel *The Fountainhead* (1943): Peter Keating, a deeply ambitious architect who, in contrast to Rand's hero, Howard Roark (based on Frank Lloyd Wright), follows fashion in his designs. On Hood and *The Fountainhead*, see Merrill Schleier, *Skyscraper Cinema: Architecture and Gender in American Film* (Minneapolis: University of Minnesota Press, 2009), 310n11; and Frank Heynick, "Peter Keating Designed Rockefeller Center?" *Atlasphere*, September 7, 2009, http://www.theatlasphere.com/columns/090907-heynick-rockefeller.php (accessed August 9, 2016).

43

1. Quoted in Carlo Rotella, "The Genre Artist," *New York Times Magazine*, July 19, 2009, 24. This article provides information on Jack Vance and writers who influenced him and were influenced by him (20–25).

2. On early twentieth-century Chicago as a center of magic, esoteric hucksterism, and weird publishing, see Owen Davies, *Grimoires: A History of Magic Books* (Oxford: Oxford University Press, 2009), 210–18.

3. The magazine was first headquartered in Indianapolis; it moved to Chicago in 1926. Edwin Baird was the first editor, succeeded by Wright in 1924.

4. H. P. Lovecraft, "The White Ship," *Weird Tales* 9, no. 3 (March 1927).

5. Robert E. Howard, "A Witch Shall Be Born," *Weird Tales* 24, no. 6 (December 1934).

6. C. L. Moore, "Shambleau," *Weird Tales* 22, no. 5 (November 1933).

7. Steven Heller, "The Revenge of Margaret Brundage, 'Queen of the Pulps,'" *Atlantic*, January 31, 2013, https://www.theatlantic.com/entertainment/archive/2013/01/the-revenge-of-margaret-brundage-the-queen-of-the-pulps/272715/ (accessed September 8, 2017).

44

1. Although Clarence Darrow was never a member of the Caxton Club, the printer of *The Plea of Clarence Darrow*, Ralph Fletcher Seymour, was a member from 1902 until his death in 1966. Noted for its arts and crafts style, his Alderbrink Press produced a number of notable books, including two by Frank Lloyd Wright (*The Japanese Print* [1914] and *Experimenting with Human Lives* [1923]) and Henry Blake Fuller's *Bertram Cope's Year* (1919), which has been called the first American homosexual novel.

2. *The Plea of Clarence Darrow, August 22nd, 23rd & 25th, MCMXXIII, in Defense of Richard Loeb and Nathan Leopold Jr. on Trial for Murder: Authorized and Revised Edition, Together with a Brief Summary of the Facts* (Chicago: Ralph Fletcher Seymour, [1924]), 8.

3. Julian Mack, "The Juvenile Court," *Harvard Law Review* 23 (1909): 120. See also David S. Tanenhaus, "Justice for the Child: The Beginning of the Juvenile Court in Chicago," *Chicago History* (Winter 1998–89): 4, 19 ("The [juvenile] court, much like an esteemed cultural institution, would be displayed as a symbol of civilization and a badge of civic pride for Chicagoans for years to come").

4. Clarence Darrow, *The Story of My Life* (Boston: Da Capo, 1996), 236–37.

5. *The Plea of Clarence Darrow* (note 2), 112.

6. *The Plea of Clarence Darrow* (note 2), 7.

7. *The Plea of Clarence Darrow* (note 2), 27.

8. *The Plea of Clarence Darrow* (note 2), 35.

9. *The Plea of Clarence Darrow* (note 2), 72.

10. *The Plea of Clarence Darrow* (note 2), 55 and 30, respectively.

45

1. Louis H. Sullivan, *The Autobiography of an Idea* (New York: American Institute of Architects Press, 1924). See also Robert C. Twombly, *Louis Sullivan: His Life and Work* (New York: Viking, 1986); and John Vinci, Ward Miller, Richard Nickel, and Aaron Siskind, *The Complete Architecture of Adler & Sullivan* (Chicago: University of Chicago Press, 2010).

2. Frank Lloyd Wright, *An Autobiography* (New York: Duell, Sloan and Pearce, 1943), 267.

3. Arthur Wesley Dow, *Composition: A Series of Exercises in Art Structure for the Use of Students and Teachers* (New York: Baker and Taylor, 1900); Denman Ross, *A Theory of Pure Design* (Boston: Houghton Mifflin, 1907); and Ernest Batchelder, *Design in Theory and Practice* (New York: Macmillan, 1910).

4. See Jonathan Massey, *Crystal and Arabesque: Claude Bragdon, Ornament, and Modern Architecture* (Pittsburgh: University of Pittsburgh Press, 2009).

47

1. For more information on Stagg and the history of football at the University of Chicago, see Robin Lester, *Stagg's University: The Rise, Decline, and Fall of Big-Time Football at Chicago* (Urbana: University of Illinois Press, 1995, 1999); John W. Boyer, *The University of Chicago: A History* (Chicago: University of Chicago Press, 2015); and John Kryk, *Stagg vs. Yost* (Lanham, MD: Rowman & Littlefield, 2015).

2. One Hearst columnist termed Stagg an "Unreconstructed Amateur" just after the coach's one hundredth birthday. See Bob Considine, *The Unreconstructed Amateur: A Pictorial Biography of Amos Alonzo Stagg* (Whitefish, MT: Literary Licensing, 1962). In fact Stagg was a "constructed amateur." His own behavior along those lines began when he finagled a higher salary from Harper by threatening to sign elsewhere after he had already agreed to terms. See Lester (note 1), 16.

3. Barry Bearak, "Where Football and Higher Education Mix," *New York Times*, September 16, 2011.

48

1. See Robert E. Park and Ernest W. Burgess, *The City* (Chicago: University of Chicago Press, 1925).

2. Park and Burgess (note 1), 40.

3. Frederic Thrasher, *The Gang: A Study of 1,313 Gangs in Chicago* (Chicago: University of Chicago Press, 1927), 22.

49

1. [Richard Cahan], *Celebrating 1855–2005: 150* ([Chicago]: Baird & Warner, 2005).

2. Foreword to *A Portfolio of Fine Apartment Homes* (Chicago: Baird & Warner, 1928).

3. For a fuller geographic and chronological discussion of such buildings in Chicago, see Neil Harris, *Chicago Apartments: A Century of Lakefront Luxury* (New York: Acanthus, 2004).

4. The author of this publication was possibly identified in an article in the *Chicago Daily Tribune*. "De Luxe Flats to be pictured in a New Booklet" describes a forthcoming work authored by "Howard Kenworthy Hall, formerly of Mark Levy and Brother and for some time with Baird & Warner." *Chicago Daily Tribune*, January 29, 1928, B4. The article mentions that the forthcoming booklet will include "120 buildings within the city limits." Apparently Hall died sometime in the 1920s—the obituary of his son, in the *Panama City News Herald*, October 24, 2014, states that he was born in 1922 and "orphaned at an early age." Hall's death might explain the changed nature of the publication from a booklet to a book that features fewer buildings—eighty-three—located in a geographic reach extended beyond the city limits.

5. Harris (note 3), 18.

6. *Portfolio of Fine Apartment Homes* (note 2), 21 (6–12 East Scott Street), p. 65 (227–237 East Delaware).

7. *Portfolio of Fine Apartment Homes* (note 2), 22 (1550 North State Parkway).

50

1. The convention in *Chicago by the Book* is to cite each entry as it appears on the title page of the first edition. In this case, a strange one, the title page of the first printing (April 1929) reads, seemingly in error, *Gold Coast and Slum: A Sociological Study of Chicago's Near North Side*, while the front cover and spine read *The Gold Coast and Slum*. The title page of the second printing two months later (June 1929) was corrected, with the two definite articles added: *The Gold Coast and the Slum*.

2. Harvey Warren Zorbaugh, *The Gold Coast and the Slum: A Sociological Study of Chicago's Near North Side* (Chicago: University of Chicago Press, 1929), 8–9, 69–86.

3. The first use of this term referred specifically to New York's high society. It is found in an unbylined interview with Ward McAllister (social aide-de-camp of Mrs. Jacob Astor), "Secrets of Ball-Giving," *New York Daily Tribune*, March 25, 1888, 11. McAllister said, "Why, there are only about four hundred people in fashionable New-York Society. If you go outside that number you strike people who are either not at ease in a ball-room or else make other people not at ease."

4. University of Chicago Press Records, Joseph Regenstein Library, University of Chicago, Box 506, Folder 14.

5. Janowitz started the Heritage of Sociology series at the University of Chicago Press, which reissued many of the Chicago classics (and eventually much more; forty volumes ultimately appeared). See Robert E. Park, Ernest W. Burgess, and Roderick D. McKenzie, *The City* (Chicago: University of Chicago Press, 1967), vii–x.

51

1. Anderson dedicated the autobiography to the opera star and actress Georgette Leblanc, with whom she was in love at the time. The second volume is *The Fiery Fountains* and the third *The Strange Necessity*.

2. Turbyfill recounted his meeting with Margaret Anderson in his unpublished autobiography, Mark Turbyfill Papers, Series 1, Box 1, Folders 1–2, Newberry Library, Chicago.

3. Margaret Anderson, "Announcement," *Little Review* 1, no. 1 (March 1914): 2.

4. Margaret Anderson, *My Thirty Years' War* (New York: Covici, Friede, 1930): 231.

5. *The Little Review* published about half the novel in installments over a two-year period. The fine was paid by an unknown "lady from Chicago." For Anderson's discussion of the trial, see Anderson (note 4), 219–22.

6. Anderson (note 4), 136.

7. Anderson (note 4), 150.

52

1. The Spot Publishing Company was most likely not an established publishing firm but a name simply made up for the occasion of a short print run in 1930 of *Chicago Gang Wars* by a job printer. While some bibliographic sources list Rockford, Illinois, as the location of the printer, there is no clear documentation for that city or any other.

2. Hal Andrews, *Chicago Gang Wars in Pictures: X Marks the Spot* ([Illinois]: Spot Publishing, 1930), 5.

3. Andrews (note 2), 1.

4. Andrews (note 2), 5.

5. Andrews (note 2), 1.

53

1. Claire Badaracco, *American Culture and the Marketplace: R.R. Donnelley's Four American Books Campaign, 1926–1930* (Washington, DC: Library of Congress, 1992), 1. I relied heavily on this excellent history of the Four American Books campaign.

2. William A. Kittredge to W. A. Dwiggins, January 4, 1927. William A. Kittredge Papers, Series 1, Box 1, Folder 31, Newberry Library, Chicago.

3. Kittredge was only thirty-one years old when he joined Donnelley. Despite his youth, he was an experienced designer, having worked for Riverside Press (Cambridge, MA), Oxford Print (Boston), Oswald Press (New York), and Franklin Printing Company (Philadelphia). In an article written four years after Kittredge's death, Rudolph Ruzicka stated, "Kittredge accepts the materials as well as the life of his time and in this sense his work is modern; the conscientious regard he has for the purpose of the work in hand and a certain natural reserve save him from the modish." *News-Letter of American Institute of Graphic Arts* (1939). Of the books produced under Kittredge's supervision while at Donnelley, forty-three were selected for inclusion in the American Institute of Graphic Arts' "Fifty Books of the Year" competition. See *William A.*

Kittredge: His Work at the Lakeside Press, a memorial booklet designed by Rudolph Ruzicka and published by the company in 1945.

4. Even before he moved to Chicago, Kittredge designed a book for the Caxton Club: Pierre François Xavier de Charlevoix, *Journal of a Voyage to North America*, with a historical introduction, notes, and index by Louise Phelps Kellogg (1923).

5. *Fine Book Making at the Lakeside Press Chicago*, vol. 2, no. 3 (Chicago: R.R. Donnelley & Sons, 1926), 3.

6. Four American Books prepublication prospectus, 1930. The Lakeside Press imprint was used for publishing (as opposed to printing) during the first sixty years of the company's existence, most famously for the Lakeside Classics (no. 24).

7. In the end, the stock and font for *Moby Dick* were English in origin rather than American.

8. The hyphen in the title used by Melville does not appear in the title of this edition.

9. Dwiggins's illustrator's note for his Lakeside edition of Poe's *Tales*. William A. Kittredge Papers, Series 1, Box 1, Folder 37, Newberry Library, Chicago.

10. All of Kent's correspondence with Kittredge is in the William A. Kittredge Papers at the Newberry Library, Chicago. On November 11, 1926, he wrote to Kittredge, "Moby Dick is a most solemn, mystic work, with the story and the setting serving merely as the medium for Melville's profound and poetic philosophy. . . . I would like to determine the typography of the book before I commit myself to the style of drawing; for even more important than the color of the cuts is the scale of the line. The color, so far as I can see, is determined; night, the midnight darkness enveloping Human existence, the darkness of the human soul, the abyss,—such is the mood of Moby Dick."

11. A one-volume trade edition of *Moby Dick* was published in late 1930 by Random House. Fifty thousand of the 69,167 copies were distributed by the Book-of-the-Month Club. Since then many trade editions have used Kent's illustrations. Both *Moby Dick* and *Walden* were recognized for superior design by the Fifty Books of the Year competition in 1931.

54

1. Ernest Hemingway, *Green Hills of Africa* (orig. 1935; New York: Charles Scribner's Sons, 2003), 22.

2. Random House / Modern Library published the three parts in one volume in 1938 (see note 3).

3. James T. Farrell, *Studs Lonigan: A Trilogy* (New York: Random House / Modern Library, 1938), 68.

4. Farrell (note 3), 381–82.

55

1. The Smarts specialized in publications aimed at retailers of men's clothing. An earlier publication, *Apparel Arts*, which they had asked the twenty-eight-year-old Gingrich to edit, had enjoyed a huge success. Interestingly, Gingrich credited Marshall Field's publication *Fashions of the Hour* as an inspiration. Arnold Gingrich, *Nothing but People: The Early Days at Esquire—A Personal History, 1928–1952* (New York: Crown, 1971), 27.

2. According to Gingrich, the very day that *Esquire* salesmen began to solicit advertisements, President Franklin D. Roosevelt closed the banks. Gingrich (note 1), 84.

3. The success of *Esquire* solidified the Smarts' publishing empire, which went on to include the short-lived magazines *Coronet*, *Ken*, and *Verve* (the American successor to the French periodical *Minotaure*). See Hugh Merrill, "Other Parts of the Empire," in *Esky: The Early Years at Esquire* (New Brunswick, NJ: Rutgers University Press, 1995), chap. 5. The Smarts also founded Coronet Films, which, after World War II, successfully created and distributed educational films to schools (Merrill, 104).

4. The first issue featured cartoons by Chicago artists George Petty and E. Simms Campbell, who were prominent contributors for many years. According to Gingrich (note 1), 96–97, Campbell was the only contributor included in every issue from the inaugural one until his death in 1971. An alumnus of the University of Chicago and graduate of the School of the Art Institute of Chicago, he was one of the first celebrated and syndicated black cartoonists. Beginning in 1940, New York artist Alberto Vargas was featured. Petty and Vargas girls became emblematic of *Esquire*.

5. See "Mail Rights Denied to *Esquire*; Magazine to Fight Order in Court," *New York Times*, December 31, 1943, 1.

6. Merrill (note 3), 103–23.

7. Gingrich (note 1), 84–90.

8. See Don Erickson, ed., *Esquire: The Magazine for Men: 40th Anniversary Celebration* ([New York]: Esquire, 1973).

Fitzgerald's "The Crack-Up" premiered in the February 1936 issue. The following August, the magazine introduced Hemingway's "Snows of Kilimanjaro."

9. *Esquire: The Magazine for Men* 1, no. 1 (October 1933): 45. Other writers featured in the magazine when it was published in Chicago include Clarence Darrow, James T. Farrell, H. L. Mencken, John O'Hara, William Saroyan, Georges Simenon, and Joseph Wechsberg.

56

1. Technically, the millennium started on January 1, 2001, but most celebrations worldwide took place in 2000.

2. Arguably, Chicago was officially founded in 1830, when the plat of the town of Chicago was filed in Peoria County. See Edmund J. James, *The Charters of the City of Chicago*, pt. 1, *The Early Charters 1833–1837* (Chicago, 1898), p. 18. The town was chartered in 1833 and again in 1835. It became a city on March 4, 1837, the date on Chicago's seal.

3. Each image measures 8 × 11 inches, plus margins, in either landscape or portrait orientation.

4. The fifty-one photos are as follows (numbers added by author): 1. Circle at Twelfth Street Entrance; 2. Grand Fountain; 3. Grand Fountain from Planetarium Bridge; 4. Avenue of Flags; 5. Looking North from West Skyride Tower; 6. Lagoon Theatre; 7. Hall of Science—North Facade; 8. Hall of Science—Court; 9. Hall of Science—Great Hall; 10. Administration Building—Trustees Room; 11. Administration Building—East Facade; 12. Looking South East from West Skyride Tower; 13. Looking East from West Skyride Tower; 14. Golden Temple of Jehol; 15. General Exhibits Group Looking South; 16. Good Housekeeping Pavilion and Tower of Hall of Religion; 17. Swiss Village; 18. Looking South from West Skyride Tower; 19. Byrd's South Pole Ship *City of New York*; 20. Aerial View—23rd Street Area; 21. Swift's Orchestra Hall; 22. Aerial View—Looking North; 23. Village Area—Looking North; 24. Mexican Village; 25. Belgian Village; 26. Italian Village; 27. Colonial Village; 28. Village Plaza—Looking South; 29. English Village; 30. Fort Dearborn; 31. Black Forest Village; 32. Black Forest Village; 33. Transportation Building; 34. Transportation Building; 35. Chrysler Motors Building; 36. Aerial View at 31st Street; 37. Indian Village and General Motors Building; 38. Wings of a Century; 39. Aerial View—Looking North [photo by Chicago Aerial Survey Company,

not Kaufmann & Fabry]; 40. Food and Agricultural Building; 41. U.S. Government Building and States Group; 42. U.S. Government Building; 43. Fireworks; 44. Electrical Building; 45. Electrical Building; 46. Electrical Building—Circular Court; 47. Horticultural Gardens; 48. Streets of Shanghai; 49. Dutch Village; 50. Balbo Aeroplane Squadron July 15, 1933; 51. Planetarium and Terrazzo Reflecting Pool.

5. Each volume, an unknown number of which were printed, was presented, presumably gratis, to a recipient whose name was printed on the cover and hand-lettered on the title page. An uncommon limited edition of the book was produced in red hard-grain morocco with a red slipcase. This special numbered edition has nine extra photographs and was signed by Rufus C. Dawes, president of the fair, and Lenox R. Lohr, general manager. The extra photos show the exhibits or pavilions of Sears, Roebuck & Co., Eastman Kodak Company, International Business Machines Corporation, American Can Company, Studebaker Exhibit, Nash Motors Company, Standard Oil Company, International Harvester Company, and General Electric Company. Though this red version had a stated limitation of 257 copies, it is almost certain that far fewer were actually produced; only three had been located as of October 2016.

6. Advertisement for Kaufmann & Fabry, 425 S. Wabash Avenue, in *Polk's Chicago (Illinois) City Directory 1928–1929*, vol. 72 (Chicago, 1928), 289.

57

1. Armstrong moved to Chicago at Oliver's invitation. The Hot Five and Hot Seven records, made for the Okeh label between 1925 and 1928, comprised seventy-nine individual songs and a revolving group of musicians under Armstrong's leadership.

2. Petrillo's Local 10 was restricted to white musicians until the 1960s.

3. *Down Beat* 6, no. 1 (January 1939): 1.

4. John Litweiler, *The Freedom Principle: Jazz after 1958* (New York: William Morrow, 1984). Early AACM members included Lester Bowie, Malachi Favors, Joseph Jarman, Roscoe Mitchell, and Don Moye (who performed together as the Art Ensemble of Chicago), along with Fred Anderson, Anthony Braxton, Jodie Christian, Kelan Phil Cohran, Kahil El'Zabar, Chico Freeman, Steve McCall, Kalaparusha Maurice

McIntyre, Leo Smith, Henry Threadgill, and many others—a tremendous gathering of musical talent.

5. My old boss Bob Koester of Chicago's Delmark Records released their first albums; he often said he did not really appreciate the music (Louis Armstrong was more his style), but John Litweiler (see note 4) and others he respected convinced him it was important.

6. *Playboy* (no. 77) has covered jazz extensively, but its taste is somewhat more mainstream than *Down Beat*'s.

7. *Down Beat*'s last headquarters in Chicago was an old building at 222 West Adams Street, which was later demolished and replaced by a Skidmore Owings & Merrill office tower where, coincidentally, I now work.

8. Howard Mandel, "Toddlin Town," *Down Beat* 83, no. 3 (March 2016): 56.

58

1. Edith Abbott, *The Tenements of Chicago, 1908–1935* (Chicago: University of Chicago Press, 1936), 495.

59

1. On "information disease," see *Report of the President, 1930–1934*, February 1, 1935, 21–22. Special Collections Research Center, University of Chicago Library.

2. Joseph J. Schwab, interview with George W. Dell, April 12, 1976, Robert M. Hutchins and Associates Oral History Interviews, Box 2, Folder 9, Special Collections Research Center, University of Chicago Library.

3. Adler (1902–2001) was a well-known philosopher and public author. Hutchins and he first met in 1927 at Columbia University, where Adler was a doctoral student. Hutchins angered the philosophy faculty at Chicago by attempting to appoint Adler to that department; he eventually found a position for Adler in the Law School, where he taught until 1952.

60

1. Bessie Louise Pierce, comp. and ed., *As Others See Chicago: Impressions of Visitors, 1673–1933* (Chicago: University of Chicago Press, 1933). Publication of this title coincided with the 1933–34 Century of Progress exposition in Chicago. It was reprinted in 2004 by the University of Chicago Press, with a new foreword by me.

2. Sales of the second volume had almost killed the third. Because the run of the latter was small, it is hard to find a copy in its original blue binding. Alfred A. Knopf gave hundreds of signatures of the first two volumes, which his firm had published, to the Chicago Historical Society, which bound them in black.

3. The University of Chicago Press reissued all three volumes in paperback in 2007.

61

1. For readers wishing to learn more about the FWP, see the classic work on the subject, Jerre Mangione, *The Dream and the Deal: The Federal Writers Project 1935–1943* (Boston: Little, Brown, 1972). Mangione was a senior member of the project's central staff in Washington, DC.

2. The approximately three hundred employees of the Illinois unit, one hundred in the central office in Chicago and the rest distributed in field offices and elsewhere in the state, were ably led by John T. Frederick (1893–1975), the director for most of its existence. Regarded as one of the best of the state directors, Frederick had been plucked for the job from the English Department at Northwestern University. He had an eye for writing talent and was an outstanding recruiter. It is generally believed that during the one year Richard Wright spent with the Illinois unit before transferring to the one in New York City, he carried out the research that formed the basis for his groundbreaking novel *Native Son* (no. 62).

3. The Illinois *Guide* was first published in an edition of five thousand on August 7, 1939. Copies sold for $3 each. Within the first year four thousand copies were sold, and by October 1942 so were all remaining copies. A slightly revised edition was published in 1947, followed by a more ambitious revision in 1974. And yet, as if to attest to the enduring value of the original 1939 edition, two verbatim reprints have been issued, one in 1973 and a second in 1983. The 1983 facsimile printing was published by the University of Chicago Press in a handsome and portable paperback format. It includes a scholarly fifty-one-page introduction by Neil Harris and Michael Conzen, then professors of history and geography, respectively, at the University of Chicago.

62

1. Richard Wright, *Native Son: With an Introduction "How*

'Bigger' Was Born" by the Author*, abridged ed., original 1940 text (New York: Perennial, 1966), 7–8.

2. Adopted by the Book-of-the-Month Club, *Native Son* sold well over two hundred thousand copies in a matter of weeks.

3. Wright (note 1).

4. Wright (note 1), xiii, xx.

5. Lawrence P. Jackson, *The Indignant Generation: A Narrative History of African American Writers and Critics, 1934–1960* (Princeton, NJ: Princeton University Press, 2011), 114.

6. Liesl Olson, *Chicago Renaissance: The Midwest and Modernism* (New Haven, CT: Yale University Press, 2017), 8. See also Robert Bone, "Richard Wright and the Chicago Renaissance," *Callaloo* 28 (Summer 1986): 446–68; Robert Bone and Richard A. Courage, *The Muse in Bronzeville: African American Creative Expression in Chicago, 1932–1950* (New Brunswick, NJ: Rutgers University Press, 2011); and Elizabeth Schroeder Schlabach, *Along the Streets of Bronzeville: Black Chicago's Literary Landscape* (Urbana: University of Illinois Press, 2013).

7. Wright (note 1), xv, xxvi. Also see Richard Wright, *12 Million Black Voices: A Folk History of the Negro in the United States* (New York: Viking, 1941); and *12 Million*'s 3rd ed. (New York: Thunder's Mouth, 1992).

8. Wright, *12 Million Black Voices*, 3rd ed. (note 7), 31.

9. Wright (note 1), xv.

10. Wright (note 1), xi, 24, 45.

11. Wright (note 1), 46, 50, 67.

12. Wright (note 1), 101.

13. Wright (note 1), xxi.

14. Wright (note 1), xx.

15. Langston Hughes, *Montage of a Dream Deferred* (New York: Holt, 1951). For another, later exploration of the theme, see Lorraine Hansberry, *A Raisin in the Sun* (New York: Vintage, 2004) (no. 80).

16. Wright (note 1), xv.

17. Wright (note 1), 391–92. *Native Son* was turned into a play of the same title by Paul Green and Richard Wright, produced by Orson Welles and John Houseman, in the year following publication of the novel (New York: Harper & Brothers, 1941). In 1951 Wright played Bigger Thomas in a film version made in Argentina. It was not well received. Another film version appeared in 1986.

64

1. Brooks was born in Topeka, Kansas, but her family migrated to Chicago when she was six weeks old.

2. The term *black ghetto* was first appropriated for urban black quarters by St. Clair Drake and Horace Cayton in *Black Metropolis,* their seminal study of race in Chicago (New York: Harcourt Brace, 1945) (no. 65).

3. By 1940 Chicago had more racially restrictive covenants than any other American city, according to Beryl Satter, *Family Properties: Race, Real Estate and the Exploitation of Black Urban America* (New York: Metropolitan Books, 2009), 40.

4. Drake and Cayton (note 2), 204–5.

5. The son of slaves, the poet Paul Laurence Dunbar (1872–1906) also began to write stories and verse while still a child.

6. The longest poem in *Bronzeville*, "The Sundays of Satin-Leg Smith," pays ironic homage to Eliot's "Love Song of J. Alfred Prufrock," as Brooks wrote of "men estranged / From music and from wonder and from joy / But far familiar with the guiding awe / Of foodlessness."

7. Gary Smith, "Gwendolyn Brooks's *A Street in Bronzeville*, the Harlem Renaissance and the Mythologies of Black Women, the Love Poems in Bronzeville," in *MELUS* 10, 3 (1983): 37. For example, the brilliant, caustic "Ballad of Pearl May Lee" turns the love ballad on its head: "Then off they took you, off to the jail / A hundred hooting after. / And you should have heard me at my house, / I cut my lungs with my laughter. . . . / The sheriff, he peeped in through the bars, / And (the red old thing) he told you, / 'You son of a bitch, you're going to hell!' / 'Cause you wanted white arms to enfold you."

8. Quoted in *Gwendolyn Brooks: Reliant Contemplation*, ed. Stephen Caldwell Wright (Ann Arbor: University of Michigan Press, 2001), 3.

65

1. See for example William Julius Wilson, *When Work Disappears: The World of the New Urban Poor* (New York: Alfred A. Knopf, 1996); Mary Pattillo, *Black on the Block: The Politics of Race and Class in the City* (Chicago: University of Chicago Press, 2007); Robert J. Sampson, *Great American City: Chicago and the Enduring Neighborhood Effect* (Chicago: University of Chicago Press, 2012); and William Julius Wilson, *The Truly Disadvantaged: The Inner City, the Underclass, and Public Policy* (Chicago: University of Chicago Press, 1987, 2nd ed. 2012).

2. St. Clair Drake and Horace R. Cayton, *Black Metropolis: A Study of Negro Life in a Northern City*, with a new foreword by Mary Pattillo (Chicago: University of Chicago Press, 2015).

66

1. First published in England in 1899, Helen Bannerman's *Story of Little Black Sambo* enjoyed widespread popularity until critics from the 1930s on decried its stereotyping of "black" peoples.

2. *Ebony* has partnered with Google to offer its entire archive for free browsing online: "Each issue appears just as it did at its original time of publication, complete with period advertisements"; http://www.ebony.com/archives#ixzz3nHb-TuRLS (accessed November 2, 2016). *Jet*, a weekly news digest that Johnson started in 1951, is today an online publication.

3. During an interview on October 22, 1992, Johnson told me that, beside my mother's, he knew of only two other complete editions of *Ebony*: his and that of the Carnegie Library in New York, which is now part of the Schomburg Center for Research in Black Culture, a research center of the New York Public Library.

67

1. László Moholy-Nagy, foreword to *Vision in Motion* (Chicago: Paul Theobald, 1947), n.p.

2. László Moholy-Nagy to Sibyl Moholy-Nagy, August 8, 1937, in Sibyl Moholy-Nagy, *Moholy-Nagy: Experiment in Totality* (Cambridge, MA: MIT Press, 1969), 145. The New Bauhaus opened in autumn 1937 and closed in spring 1938. In 1939 Moholy began his own nonaffiliated school, the School of Design. In 1944 the name was changed to Institute of Design, and in 1949 the Institute of Design merged with the Illinois Institute of Technology.

3. Richard Kostelanetz, "Moholy-Nagy: The Risk and Necessity of Artistic Adventurism," *Salmagundi* 10–11 (Fall 1969–Winter 1970): 283–84.

4. László Moholy-Nagy, *Sehen in Bewegung*, Bauhaus Edition 39 (Leipzig: Spector Books, 2014).

68

1. Chicago Railroad Fair records, Box 29, Folder 848, Special Collections and University Archives, University of Illinois at Chicago.

2. *Chicago Railroad Fair Official Guide Book and Program for the Pageant 'Wheels a-Rolling'* [Chicago: Chicago Railroad Fair, 1948], 1.

3. Chicago Railroad Fair records (note 1), Box 8, Folder 239; and Box 29, Folders 840–48.

4. *Chicago Railroad Fair Official Guide Book* (note 2), 8–9.

5. A fair was also held in the same location in 1950, branded as The Chicago Fair of 1950. While it featured many transportation-themed attractions and a pageant called *Frontiers of Freedom*, it was unaffiliated with the Railroad Fair.

6. Chicago Railroad Fair Records (note 1), Box 6, Folder 182; and Box 13, Folder 4.

7. *Chicago Railroad Fair Official Guide Book* (note 2), 7.

69

1. Ralph H. Burke, consulting engineer, "Remarks Given before Chicago Plan Commission," January 10, 1948, 5. Municipal Reference Library, Harold Washington Library, Chicago.

2. Ralph H. Burke, cover letter to Hon. Martin H. Kennelly, Mayor, City of Chicago, accompanying publication of *Master Plan of Chicago Orchard Airport* (January 1948), 2. Municipal Reference Library, Harold Washington Library, Chicago.

70

1. Frank A. Randall, *History of the Development of Building Construction in Chicago* (Urbana: University of Illinois Press, 1949), 5, 128. A second edition, revised and expanded by John Randall, the author's son, was published by the same press in 1999.

2. Rand, McNally & Company, *Rand, McNally & Co.'s Bird's-Eye Views and Guide to Chicago* (Chicago: Rand, McNally, 1893), 24. Randall used an 1898 version of this guide, misidentifying it as a "unique guide" despite the fact that it was published in 1893 for use by visitors to the World's Columbian Exposition.

3. Carl W. Condit, review of *History of the Development of Building Construction in Chicago* by Frank A. Randall, *Isis* 43 (December 1952): 383.

71

1. Simone de Beauvoir, cited in Nelson Algren, *Nonconformity: Writing on Writing* (New York: Seven Stories, 1998), 53.

2. Nelson Algren, *Chicago: City on the Make* (New York: Doubleday, 1951), 23.

3. Algren (note 2), 73.

4. Algren (note 2), 68.

72

1. *860–880 Lake Shore Drive* ([Chicago]: 860 Lake Shore Drive Trust, [ca. 1951]), n.p.

2. *860–880 Lake Shore Drive* (note 1).

3. *860–880 Lake Shore Drive* (note 1).

4. Cited in Moises Puente, *Conversations with Mies van der Rohe* (Princeton, NJ: Princeton Architectural Press, 2008), 58.

73

1. It was an iteration of what was called General Honors, a course made famous at Columbia University by Adler's intellectual mentor, John Erskine.

2. Although the ambitious Adler confessed that he wrote the book to make money, its contents and educational ideas grew out of genuine experiences and important issues. Defining three levels of reading, he sought, out of concern for the fate of democracy in a world at war, to motivate citizens toward a higher level of political discourse.

3. Adler and Hutchins served on the Great Books Foundation's first board of trustees, and Chicago business leaders Lynn Williams and Walter Paepcke were named first president and vice president, respectively. The foundation has aspired to be a national and international institution that supports adult education programs. It trains leaders for local reading groups focused on Great Books, basic ideas, and common problems around those ideas. The larger goals are to further good citizenship and democracy. The foundation explicitly avoids the formalities of offering credits or degrees.

4. The following selection criteria for the set were devised by a Britannica-based advisory board: The book or work should (1) be important by itself without reference to any other and seminal and radical in treatment of basic ideas and problems; (2) belong to the Western tradition in that it is intelligible in relation to other great books; (3) be immediately (if superficially) understandable for the ordinary reader; (4) possess many levels of intelligibility for diverse grades of readers; and (5) be indefinitely rereadable. To make the set an instrument of liberal education, it was decided that certain ideas be used to test each title for inclusion.

5. The construction of the *Syntopicon* involved a team of indexers that worked from 1943 to 1945, initially, to catalogue just the Greek classics in relation to a list of 1,003 terms. Eventually that work expanded to each of the set's 443 works in relation to 102 fundamental, or "Great," ideas that helped make the set an instrument of liberal education. Managed by Adler, that team included, at one point, forty indexers and seventy-five clerks working on a part-time or hourly basis. William Gorman and Milton Mayer were Adler's top assistants. The indexing project, about which *Life* and *Look* magazines ran picture stories in 1948, was completed in 1949. The 102 Great Ideas begin with Angel and end with World, and include Beauty, Duty, Family, Honor, Labor, Man, Oligarchy, Progress, Science, Theology, and other themes. A complete list can be found in Tim Lacy, *The Dream of a Democratic Culture: Mortimer J. Adler and the Great Books Idea* (New York: Palgrave Macmillan, 2013), 232–35.

6. Early on Benton complained about cost overruns related to editorial work (expenses ranging from one to two million dollars). By early 1956, a backlog of three thousand sets remained after terrible sales in the previous four years (1,863 sets in 1952 and 138 in 1953). The publication was almost written off, but Kenneth Harden, hired in 1956, revamped sales tactics and techniques such that 5,256 sets were sold by the end of the same year. Sales rose to 26,607 in 1959, more than 40,000 in 1960, and 51,083 in 1962. See Lacy (note 5), 75–78.

7. In 1982 Adler published *The Paideia Proposal: An Educational Manifesto*, in which he did not explicitly promote Great Books as a solution to the American education system's ills but rather embraced utilizing them for larger understanding and the enhancement of critical thinking through regular seminars focused on primary texts.

75

1. These employees received "presentation copies," each with a preprinted inscription from Hughston McBain, then chairman of the board.

2. Vivien Kellems, "Give the Lady What She Wants," *Kirkus Reviews*, May 5, 1952, www.kirkusreviews.com/book-reviews/vivien-kellems-2/give-the-lady-what-she-wants/ (accessed May 30, 2015).

3. William Johnson Miller, "Came Early, Left Late: *Give the Lady What She Wants! The Story of Marshall Field & Co.*, by

Lloyd Wendt and Herman Kogan," *New York Times*, July 20, 1952, BR11.

4. In the 1860s Marshall Field's moved to State Street, where it overcame economic downturns, several fires, and fierce competition to become Chicago's most prestigious department store. Field's prided itself on the store's Tiffany-mosaic vaulted ceiling, matching eight-ton bronze clocks, and spectacular window displays. Its first suburban branch opened in 1928 in Lake Forest. At the time of *Give the Lady*'s publication, construction was under way for its first shopping-mall stores, opened in Park Forest Plaza in Park Forest in 1955 and at Old Orchard in Skokie in 1956.

5. Lloyd Wendt and Herman Kogan, *Give the Lady What She Wants! The Story of Marshall Field & Company* (Chicago: Rand, McNally, 1952), 223 and 376, respectively. Other stories are lively and amusing, like the one about a shoplifter who stole only from Field's. Asked why, she retorted, "I'm no jitney thief. . . . I work your store because you got all the best stuff in the city!" (231).

76

1. Saul Bellow, *The Adventures of Augie March: A Novel* (New York: Alfred A. Knopf, 1995), 5.

2. Quoted in Zachary Leader, *The Life of Saul Bellow: To Fame and Fortune, 1915–1964* (New York: Alfred A. Knopf, 2015), 370–71.

3. Bellow (note 1), 489.

77

1. Other writers included Ray Bradbury, Truman Capote, Arthur C. Clarke, James T. Farrell, Jack Kerouac, Henry Miller, Norman Podhoretz, William Styron, and Kurt Vonnegut.

2. See John C. Burnham, *Bad Habits: Drinking, Smoking, Taking Drugs, Gambling, Sexual Misbehavior, and Swearing in American History* (New York: New York University Press, 1993), 194–96; Elizabeth Fraterrigo, "The Answer to Suburbia: Playboy's Urban Lifestyle," *Journal of Urban History* 34 (July 2008): 747–74; Elizabeth Fraterrigo, *Playboy and the Making of the Good Life in Modern America* (Oxford/New York: Oxford University Press, 2009); and Carrie Pitzulo, *Bachelors and Bunnies: The Sexual Politics of Playboy* (Chicago: University of Chicago Press, 2011).

3. See Barbara Ehrenreich, *The Hearts of Men: American Dreams and the Flight from Commitment* (New York: Anchor, 1983); and Lillian B. Rubin, *Erotic Wars: What Happened to the Sexual Revolution?* (New York: Farrar, Straus and Giroux, 1990).

4. Burnham (note 2), 193. An international list of clubs appears in "Playboy Clubs"; https://en.wikipedia.org/wiki/Playboy_Club (accessed February 23, 2017).

5. Ravi Somaiya, "Nudes Are Old News at Playboy," *New York Times*, October 12, 2015, http://www.nytimes.com/2015/10/13/business/media/nudes-are-old-news-at-playboy.html?smprod=nytcore-iphone&smid=nytcore-iphone-share&_r=0 (accessed July 30, 2016); and "Playboy in Popular Culture," *New York Times*, October 13, 2015, http://www.nytimes.com/interactive/2015/10/13/business/playboylisty.html (accessed July 30, 2016).

6. Somaiya (note 5); "Playboy in Popular Culture" (circulation figure); "*Penthouse* (magazine)," Wikipedia, https://en.wikipedia.org/wiki/Penthouse_(magazine) (accessed July 30, 2016); and "*Hustler*," Wikipedia, https://en.wikipedia.org/wiki/Hustler (accessed July 30, 2016).

7. Mike Snider, "'Playboy' Brings Nudity Back to Magazine," *USA Today*, February 13, 2017, http://www.usatoday.com/story/money/business/2017/02/13/playboy-brings-nudity-back-magazine/97868038/ (accessed February 18, 2017).

78

1. Laura Fermi, *Atoms in the Family: My Life with Enrico Fermi* (Chicago: University of Chicago Press, 1954), 177. From 1943 to 1945, the Manhattan Project's operations expanded to laboratories and production facilities across the United States. Research at the University of Chicago was designated with the code name Metallurgical Laboratory, or Met Lab.

2. Fermi (note 1), 125–41.

3. University of Chicago Press Records, Box 176, Folder 2, Special Collections Research Center, University of Chicago Library.

4. Laura Fermi Papers, Box 1, Folder 5, Special Collections Research Center, University of Chicago Library.

5. University of Chicago Press Records (note 3), Box 176, Folders 1–2. The title of the book was an obvious play on *The Addams Family*, the popular series of cartoons by Charles Addams published in the *New Yorker*.

6. University of Chicago Press Records (note 3), Box 176, Folders 2–3.

7. Sales data can be found in the University of Chicago Press Records (note 3), Box 175, Folder 5. This review—Earl Ubell, "A Housewife on the Atom," *The Nation*, November 27, 1954, 467—is located, along with others, in Box 176, Folders 4–5; and in the Laura Fermi Papers (note 4), Box 1, Folder 7.

8. Laura's subsequent books include *Mussolini* (1961) and *Illustrious Immigrants* (1968). She campaigned against urban air pollution and handgun violence in Chicago. For other writings and more on her public activities, see the Laura Fermi Papers; Cleaner Air Committee of Hyde Park–Kenwood Records; and Civic Disarmament Committee for Handgun Control Records; Special Collections Research Center, University of Chicago Library.

79

1. The book has enjoyed a significant afterlife. Levin wrote a play version of it (1957), which was adapted for the movie starring Orson Welles, Dean Stockwell, and Bradford Dillman (1959). *Compulsion* first appeared in paperback in 1957, has been reissued several times and remains in print.

2. Erle Stanley Gardner, "Killers for Kicks," *New York Times*, October 28, 1956.

3. Robert R. Kirsch, "The Book Report," *Los Angeles Times*, November 21, 1956.

4. Nathan Leopold Jr., "Leopold Is Pained by Levin's 'Novel,'" *New York Herald Tribune*, November 29, 1957.

5. "Leopold Is Suing over 'Compulsion,'" *New York Times*, October 3, 1959.

6. Edward de Grazia, "Aftermath of a 'Thrill,'" *New York Times*, March 23, 1958.

80

1. Langston Hughes, "Harlem," from *The Collected Poems of Langston Hughes,* ed. Arnold Rampersad and David Roessel (New York: Alfred A. Knopf, 1994), 426. Copyright © 1994 by the Estate of Langston Hughes, reprinted with the permission of Harold Ober Associates Incorporated. Writing about African American activism, Hansberry mentioned Hughes's poem: "Some Negroes my own age and younger say that we must now lie down in the streets, tie up traffic, do whatever we can—take to the hills with guns if necessary—and fight back."

Fatuous people remark these days on our 'bitterness.' Why of course we are bitter. The entire situation suggests that the nation be reminded of the too little noted final lines of Langston Hughes' mighty poem." Lorraine Hansberry, *To Be Young, Gifted, and Black: Lorraine Hansberry in Her Own Words*, adapted by Howard Nemiroff, original drawings and art by Lorraine Hansberry, intro. by James Baldwin (Englewood Cliffs, NJ: Prentice-Hall, [1969]), 51.

2. It took about a year for producers Philip Rose and David Cogan to raise enough money from 150 investors to finance the play. They had trouble finding a Broadway theater to stage it until tryouts in New Haven, Philadelphia, and Chicago received enthusiastic reviews. Directed by Lloyd Richards (making him the first African American to direct a play on Broadway), the original cast included Ruby Dee, Lonne Elder III, Lou Gossett, Claudia McNeil, Sidney Poitier, Diana Sands, and Glynn Turman, among others. Ossie Davis later replaced Poitier. The play was nominated for four Tony awards. The film version (1961) included several cast members of the original Broadway production.

3. As James Baldwin declared in his introduction to Hansberry's posthumously published memoir *To Be Young, Gifted, and Black*, "Never before in the entire history of the American theater had so much of the truth of black people's lives been seen on the stage." In Hansberry (note 1), xii.

4. Hansberry recalled going to kindergarten "in white fur in the middle of the depression and the kids beat me up. I think it was at that moment I became a rebel." Hansberry (note 1), 64.

5. As Hansberry described the situation, "Howling mobs surrounded our house. One of their missiles almost took the life of [this] eight-year-old [Hansberry]. . . . My memories . . . included being spat at, cursed and pummeled in the daily trek to and from school. And I also remember my desperate and courageous mother, patrolling our house all night with a loaded German Luger, doggedly guarding her four children, while my father fought the respectable part of the battle in the Washington court." Hansberry (note 1), 51.

On the state and federal cases, see *Lee v. Hansberry*, 372 Ill. 369, 24 N.E. 2d 37 (Ill. 1939), and *Hansberry v. Lee*, 311 U.S. 32 (1940). Hansberry believed that her father never recovered from his struggles against racial segregation. He died from a cerebral hemorrhage in 1946, at age fifty, while visiting

Mexico, where he planned to move his family. Hansberry (note 1), 51.

6. Hansberry went on to say, in a talk presented to the American Society of African Culture on March 1, 1959, "The question is not whether one will make a social statement in one's work—but only what the statement will say, for if it says anything at all, it will be social." Lorraine Hansberry, "The Negro Writer and His Roots: Toward a New Romanticism," *Black Scholar* 12, no. 1 (March-April 1981): 5.

81

1. Eliot Asinof, *Eight Men Out: The Black Sox and the 1919 World Series* (New York: Henry Holt, 1987), 197.

2. Asinof (note 1).

3. Asinof (note 1), viii.

82

1. Born in Cincinnati, Condit received a degree in engineering from Purdue University, followed by an MA and a PhD in English literature from the University of Cincinnati, where he wrote a dissertation on Geoffrey Chaucer. His growing interest in the history of urban architecture drew him to Chicago. He began teaching in the English Department at Northwestern University in 1945, but he moved into architecture, art history, and urban planning. Among his many achievements during his thirty-year career at the university was establishing a history of science program.

2. For example, Sigfried Giedion put it in succinct form in his 1941 opus *Space, Time and Architecture*: *The Growth of a New Tradition.*

3. A number of authors have demonstrated that not only was the Home Insurance not a completely skeletal structure, but New York City could boast taller buildings in the previous decade and the development of skeletal construction was the result of important contributions by many individuals in several European and American cities. For a summary of arguments about the "Chicago School," see Robert Bruegmann, "The Myth of the Chicago School," in *Chicago Architecture: Histories, Revisions, Alternatives*, ed. Katerina Ruedi Ray and Charles Waldheim (Chicago: University of Chicago Press, 2005).

83

1. From 1968 through 1975, Bill Hasbrouck was executive director of the Chicago Chapter of the American Institute of Architects, and in 1976 he opened his own architectural office, specializing in restoration of landmark buildings. In 1974 Marilyn Hasbrouck opened the Prairie Avenue Bookshop, which served architecture and design professionals and architecture enthusiasts in Chicago and elsewhere for over thirty years before closing in 2009.

2. Each issue of the *Review* is 8½ × 11 inches, averages about thirty pages in length, and is printed in black and white on heavy cream-colored stock. The journal adhered to a consistent format: a full-page photograph on the cover, followed by an editorial, a lead article usually showcasing the work of a particular architect or firm (always accompanied by photographs and drawings, a list of its extant buildings, and a bibliography) or a particular building or group of related buildings, one or more book reviews, and occasional letters to the editors.

3. Demand for a number of issues of the *Review* led the Hasbroucks to reprint them. Thousands of copies of the issue devoted to the California architects Greene & Greene have been reprinted and sold at the architects' Gamble House in Pasadena; nearly as many reprints of the issue on the Mason City, Iowa, community known as Rock Crest / Rock Glen community—which features buildings by Wright, Drummond, Walter Burley Griffin, and others—have been sold there. But those are the exceptions. Complete runs of the first printing of the *Review* are rare and collectible.

4. "From the Editors," *Prairie School Review* 10, no. 4 (1973): 4.

5. Authors of major articles in the *Review* include architectural historians H. Allen Brooks, Sally Chappell, Carl W. Condit, Leonard Eaton, David Gebhard, Donald Hoffman, Paul Sprague, and David Van Zanten. Another contributor, Roger Kennedy, was a prolific author, museum administrator, and director of the National Park Service. Occasionally, renowned scholars such as Henry Russell Hitchcock wrote for the journal as well.

6. In addition to studies on specific architects and buildings, the journal featured several articles on sculptors and painters, such as Richard Bock and Alphonso Iannelli, whose work was incorporated into buildings by Wright and other

Prairie School architects. One issue focused on Prairie School furniture, and another was devoted to the work of the Prairie School landscape architect Ossian Simonds. Two issues took on the vexing problem of defining the "Chicago School of Architecture."

7. Blair Kamin, "A New Legacy: Prairie School Archive Given to Art Institute," *Chicago Tribune*, September 10, 1992, C12.

84

1. Studs Terkel, *Division Street: America* (New York: Pantheon Books, 1967), xix.

85

1. Norman Mailer, *Miami and the Siege of Chicago: An Informal History of the Republican and Democratic Conventions of 1968*, intro. by Frank Rich (New York: New York Review of Books, 2008), 99 ("the dean of"), 114 ("a vastly robust" and "respectable enough").

2. Mailer (note 1), 85 ("great American" city), 86 ("clean tough"), 88 "fear and . . . anguish"). In his opening paragraph (85), Mailer memorably said of Chicago, "Perhaps it is the last of the great American cities."

3. Mailer (note 1), 63.

4. Mailer (note 1), 88 ("unkempt children"), 187 ("pushing him"), 188 ("What price").

5. Mailer (note 1), 223.

86

1. See Stanley Ziemba and Thom Shanker, "Ira Bach to Leave City Post: Planner to Remain on Landmarks Commission," *Chicago Tribune*, November 9, 1984, B1.

2. Ira J. Bach, *Chicago on Foot: An Architectural Walking Tour*, photographs by Philip A. Turner (Chicago: Follett, 1969), 44.

3. Gerard Wolfe, *Chicago: In and around the Loop, Walking Tours of Architecture and History* (New York: McGraw-Hill, 2004), 65.

4. Bach (note 2), 193.

87

1. The large square quarto book, bound in cloth, has a photo-illustrated slipcase with an obi (sash).

2. Ishimoto's architectural studies also shaped his aesthetic approach to photography. The curator Colin Westerbeck, visiting the artist in Japan in the late 1990s, related that the artist showed him a circa 1951 sales brochure for Ludwig Mies van der Rohe's twin residential towers at 860–880 Lake Shore Drive, Chicago (no. 72), which he had taken with him to Japan in 1953. He enthusiastically pointed out the similarities between Mies's buildings and the imperial villa at Katsura, which he photographed extensively. Westerbeck, "The Ten Foot Square Hut," in Colin Westerbeck, *Yasuhiro Ishimoto: A Tale of Two Cities*, with contributions by Arato Isozaki and Fuminori Yokoe (Chicago: Art Institute of Chicago, 1999), 35.

3. Ishimoto's Chicago photographs deeply impacted his subsequent images in Japan. As the art historian and curator Yasufumi Nakamori observed, exhibitions and publications of Ishimoto's work in Japan "brought the New Bauhaus and the American street esthetic to postwar Japanese art." Nakamori, in conversation with Stephen Daiter, spring 2016. This statement by Nakamori appears in an article in *ArtDaily*, May 9, 2009, when the Museum of Fine Arts, Houston, acquired three hundred photographs by Ishimoto. Ishimoto's importance was acknowledged in 1983, when the Japanese government awarded him the distinguished Medal of Honor with Purple Ribbon, and again in 1996, when he was named a Person of Cultural Merit.

4. In 1983 the artist published another book, also called *Chicago, Chicago* (Tokyo: Japan Publications), which features different photographs.

88

1. Harold M. Mayer and Richard C. Wade, with Glen E. Holt, *Chicago: Growth of a Metropolis*, cartography by Gerald F. Pyle (Chicago: University of Chicago Press, 1969), p. 155.

2. They range from the 1973 article by A. J. Krim, "Photographic Imagery of the American City, 1840–1860," *Professional Geographer* 25, no. 2 (May 1973), to the 2015 book by John F. McDonald, *Chicago: An Economic History* (New York: Routledge, Taylor and Francis Group).

3. In recognition of Mayer's influence on the field of geography, the American Geographical Society commissioned a book on his life's work, *Harold M. Mayer, Fifty Years of Professional Geography*, ed. Lutz Holzner and Jeane M. Knapp (Milwaukee: American Geographical Society Collection of the Golda Meir Library, University of Wisconsin–Milwaukee, 1990).

4. See Glen E. Holt and Dominic A. Pacyga, *Chicago: A Historical Guide to the Neighborhoods; The Loop and South Side* (Chicago: Chicago Historical Society, 1979).

5. Among Pyle's many publications are *The Spatial Dynamics of Crime*, with Edward W. Hanten et al. (Chicago: University of Chicago, Department of Geography, 1974); and *Applied Medical Geography* (Washington, DC: V. H. Winston & Sons, 1979).

89

1. See Jim Britell, "WWAD: 'What Would Alinsky Do?,'" *Playboy*, March 1972; http://www.freerepublic.com/focus/f-chat/2367150/posts (accessed October 30, 2016). The interview was conducted a few weeks before Alinsky died.

2. Cited in Maurice Hamington, "Community Organizing: Addams and Alinsky," http://www.philosophy.uncc.edu/mleldrid/SAAP/MSU/P04R.html (accessed November 1, 2016).

3. Clinton (then Rodham) wrote her senior thesis at Wellesley College on Alinsky's work, with Alinsky's cooperation.

90

1. *Boss* spent twenty-six weeks on the best-seller list of the *New York Times*. Royko's columns were syndicated in over six hundred newspapers.

2. That rival, Alderman Clarence Wagner, died in an automobile accident. In 1955 Daley knocked off incumbent Democratic mayor Martin Kennelly in the primary and then defeated the reform-minded alderman Robert Merriam in the general election. However, Royko allowed that in his 1955 double triumph Daley had the full support of such liberal reform stalwarts as US senator Paul Douglas, former Illinois governor Adlai Stevenson, and several prominent members of the Hyde Park–based Independent Voters of Illinois. It must be remembered that for most of his political life Daley considered himself a liberal.

3. Mike Royko, *Boss: Richard J. Daley of Chicago* (New York: E. P. Dutton, 1971), 177.

4. In 1980, less than four years after Daley's death. Royko helped elect the mayor's eldest son, Richard, as Cook County state's attorney. Late in that campaign Royko wrote a series of brutal columns castigating Daley's opponent (incumbent Bernard Carey) for mishandling the case of serial killer John Wayne Gacy. Young Daley, with Royko's help, won this office by a narrow margin and eventually became mayor of Chicago. He topped his father's record as the city's longest serving mayor (1989–2011).

91

1. Interviews with Lois Wille for the Washington Press Club Foundation, as part of its Oral History Project, Women in Journalism, recorded by Diane K. Gentry, 1991, http://beta.wpcf.org/oralhistory/will.html (accessed March 18, 2016).

2. Lois Wille, *Forever Open, Clear and Free: The Struggle for Chicago's Lakefront* (Chicago: Henry Regnery, 1972), 23. The title of the first edition has no comma after "Clear"; a comma was added in the second edition, published by the University of Chicago Press in 1991. A special edition, numbered, signed, and bound in marbled boards, enclosed in a custom slipcase, and limited to 250 copies, was produced for the hundredth anniversary of Montgomery Ward & Co. in 1972.

3. Blair Kamin, "Hobson's Argument on Lucas Museum Rings False," *Chicago Tribune*, May 5, 2016.

93

1. In *The Duck Variations* (1972), two elderly men meet, perhaps randomly, sitting on a bench. They talk about the ducks swimming in a lake before them. Their conversation leads, inevitably, to their view of themselves and the world. See note 3.

2. David Mamet, "Reminiscing without Reservations: Salad Days at the Lincoln Hotel," *Chicago Tribune Magazine*, December 8, 1991. All of those comedians were associated with Second City.

3. The play opened off-off-Broadway in New York in 1976. It was paired in another New York production with Mamet's *Duck Variations* (see note 1) in 1976. Both won the 1976 Obie Award as Best New American Play.

4. Mamet did not approve of *About Last Night*. A second film version, also called *About Last Night*, appeared in 2014. It features an African American cast.

94

1. Sandra Cisneros, *The House on Mango Street* (New York: Vintage Books, 1984), 105.

2. Another text that is often assigned as required reading is Lorraine Hansberry's *Raisin in the Sun* (no. 80).

95

1. Cronon is a professor of history, geography, and environmental studies at the University of Wisconsin–Madison, where he has taught since 1992. *Nature's Metropolis* was awarded the Bancroft Prize for History in 1992 and was nominated as well for a Pulitzer Prize.

96

1. Alex Kotlowitz, *There Are No Children Here: The Story of Two Boys Growing Up in the Other America* (New York: Nan A. Talese / Doubleday, 1991), x.

2. In my book *Blueprint for Disaster: The Unraveling of Chicago Public Housing* (Chicago: University of Chicago Press, 2009), I inverted Kotlowitz's title to argue that "there are too many children here," documenting the extraordinary density of youth created by public housing planners. This youth density made it difficult for parents, managers, and the police to establish social order. Place large numbers of youth in elevator buildings in sprawling projects, and gangs will multiply; mix in poverty, systemic racism, drug addiction, and gross mismanagement, and a failed community is all but certain.

3. Kotlowitz (note 1), 8.

4. Other works about Chicago public housing also added momentum to radical policy change in the 1990s: Nicholas Lemann, *The Promised Land: The Great Black Migration and How It Changed America* (New York: Alfred A. Knopf, 1991); and LeAlan Jones and Lloyd Newman, with David Isay, *Our America: Life and Death on the South Side of Chicago* (New York: Scribners, 1997).

5. These include the Helen Bernstein Award for Excellence in Journalism, Christopher Award, and Carl Sandburg Award.

97

1. *Jimmy Corrigan* won Britain's prestigious Guardian First Book Award, as well as an American Book Award. Pages from the book were exhibited in the 2002 Whitney Biennial.

2. Chris Ware, *Jimmy Corrigan: The Smartest Kid on Earth* (New York: Pantheon, 2000), n.p.

3. Despite their monumental character, the buildings were all temporary. The Manufactures and Liberal Arts Building at the time was the largest building ever constructed.

98

1. Clive Barnes, "Stage: 'The Second City,' Revue in New Version at East Side Playhouse," *New York Times*, October 15, 1969.

2. In 1955 Sills had cofounded, in Chicago's Hyde Park neighborhood, the Second City's predecessor, Compass Players, with which Asner, May, and Nichols, along with Alan Alda, Shelley Berman, Linda Lavin, Jerry Stiller, and many more were associated. Sills left the Second City in 1965 to pursue other ventures. Alk, who was also active in Compass Players, left the Second City in the early 1960s.

3. A. J. Liebling, "Second City," *New Yorker*, January 12, 1952, 29–37.

99

1. Norman Rockwell (American, 1894–1978), *Mrs. Catherine O'Leary Milking Daisy*, 1930/40, oil on canvas, 37 × 34 in. Chicago History Museum, gift of the Office of the Mayor of Chicago, 1949.28.

2. Thomas F. Schwartz, foreword to Richard F. Bales, *The Great Chicago Fire and the Myth of Mrs. O'Leary's Cow* (Jefferson, NC: McFarland, 2002), 2.

100

1. *The Devil in the White City* was nominated for a number of literary prizes, winning several, including an Edgar Award (best fact crime). DiCaprio bought the rights for the movie in 2010.

101

1. Sara Paretsky, *Brush Back* (New York: G. P. Putnam's Sons, 2015), 141–42.

Contributors' Biographies

Andrew Abbott (no. 50) is Gustavus F. and Ann M. Swift Distinguished Service Professor, Department of Sociology and the College, at the University of Chicago. Known for his ecological theories of occupations, Abbott also pioneered algorithmic analysis of social sequence data. He has written on the foundations of social science methodology and on the evolution of the social sciences and the academic system.

A Chicago native, **David Auburn** (no. 76) is a playwright, director, and screenwriter. His plays include *Proof* (2000; it won a Pulitzer Prize and a Tony Award), *The Columnist* (2012), and *Lost Lake* (2014). His stage adaptation of Saul Bellow's *Adventures of Augie March* will premiere in 2019. His film work includes *The Girl in the Park* (2007), which he wrote and directed, and the forthcoming *Georgetown*.

Julia Bachrach (nos. 26, 91) is a historian and preservation planner. Previously she served as the Chicago Park District's historian and preservationist. She has written extensively on Chicago's parks and public spaces. Her books include *The City in a Garden: A History of Chicago's Parks* (2001) and *Inspired by Nature: The Garfield Park Conservatory and Chicago's West Side* (2008). She contributed to such publications as *Midwestern Landscape Architecture* (2000), the *Oxford Companion to the Garden* (2006, 2008), and *Art Deco Chicago* (2018).

Davarian L. Baldwin (no. 62) is Paul E. Raether Distinguished Professor of American Studies at Trinity College, Hartford. His books include *Chicago's New Negroes: Modernity, the Great Migration, and Black Urban Life* (2007); and *Escape from New York: The New Negro Renaissance beyond Harlem* (co-edited with Minkah Makalani; 2013). Baldwin is currently writing *Land of Darkness: Chicago and the Making of Race in Modern America* and *In the Shadow of the Ivory Tower: How Higher Education Is Transforming Urban America*.

Nina Barrett (no. 79) has authored several books, including *The Leopold and Loeb Files: An Intimate Look at One of America's Most Infamous Crimes* (at press), in addition to literary essays and reviews for the *New York Times Magazine*, *The Nation*, and other publications. A trained chef, she has won two James Beard Awards for her food reporting on the Chicago public radio station WBEZ. She owns Bookends & Beginnings, an independent bookstore in Evanston.

A Pulitzer Prize winner and former sports columnist for the *New York Times*, Chicago-born and -raised **Ira Berkow** (no. 81) is the author of *Maxwell Street: Survival in a Bazaar* (1977) and *The DuSable Panthers: The Greatest, Blackest, Saddest Team from the Meanest Street in Chicago* (1978).

Henry C. Binford (no. 58) is a social historian focused on the United States in the nineteenth century. A professor at Northwestern University, he is particularly interested in urbanization and city growth.

John Blew (nos. 61, 83) is a Chicago-based lawyer, now retired, and bibliophile who has formed important collections of Chicagoana, architecture, and Federal Writers' Project materials, among others. He is a member of the Caxton Club's Publications Committee.

Daniel Bluestone (nos. 38, 70), professor of the history of art and architecture at Boston University, has worked on Chicago preservation and community revitalization. His prizewinning books are *Constructing Chicago* (1991) and *Buildings, Landscapes, and Memory: Case Studies in Historic Preservation* (2011). Important essays on Chicago include "Chicago's Mecca Flat Blues" (1998); "Louis H. Sullivan's Chicago: From 'Shirt-Front' to Alley, to 'All-Around Structures'" (2013); and "Framing Landscape while Building Density: Chicago Courtyard Apartments, 1891–1929" (2017).

Bruce Hatton Boyer (no. 54) is the author of one novel and many books and articles on Chicago history, including *A Natural History of the Field Museum* (1993) and *The Great Chicago Trivia and Fact Book* (1997). He teaches writing at Roosevelt University. He served as president of the Caxton Club from 2013 to 2015.

John W. Boyer (no. 59) is Dean of the College and Martin A. Ryerson Distinguished Service Professor of History at the University of Chicago. A specialist in the history of the Habsburg Empire

and of Central Europe, Boyer has written three books on the history of Vienna. He has also authored a major scholarly history of University of Chicago (2015). His current project is a book on Austria from 1867 to 1893.

Robert Bruegmann (no. 82) is a historian and critic of architecture, landscape, preservation, urban development, and the built environment. A Distinguished Professor Emeritus of Art History, Architecture and Urban Planning at the University of Illinois at Chicago, he has authored or edited numerous publications, including books on Chicago architects Holabird & Roche (1997) and Harry Weese (2010). He edited and contributed to *Art Deco Chicago* (2018).

David Buisseret (no. 3) taught at the University of the West Indies (Jamaica campus; 1964–80) and then served as director of the Hermon Dunlap Smith Center for the History of Cartography at the Newberry Library (1980–96). Subsequently he held the inaugural Jenkins and Virginia Garrett Chair in the History of Cartography at the University of Texas–Arlington. He has published widely on seventeenth-century France, the early modern Caribbean, and the history of cartography and exploration.

Hillary Chute (no. 97), professor of English and art and design at Northeastern University, has taught at the University of Chicago and Harvard University. She is the author of *Graphic Women: Life Narrative and Contemporary Comics* (2010), *Outside the Box:*

Interviews with Contemporary Cartoonists (2014); *Disaster Drawn: Visual Witness, Comics, and Documentary Form* (2016); and *Why Comics? From Underground to Everywhere* (2017).

Kathleen Neils Conzen (nos. 11, 95) is Thomas E. Donnelley Professor Emeritus, Department of History and the College at the University of Chicago. Her teaching and publications have focused on nineteenth-century American social history, with particular emphasis on immigration, ethnicity, religion, western settlement, and urban development. For a change of pace, she is working with Michael P. Conzen on a book about the role of German immigrants in the early California wine industry.

Michael P. Conzen (no. 63) is professor of geography at the University of Chicago. His research interests include urban historical geography, international urban morphology, and American landscape studies. Among his publications are *Mapping Manifest Destiny: Chicago and the American West* (with Diane Dillon; 2007), *The Making of the American Landscape* (2010), and *Shapers of Urban Form: Explorations in Morphological Agency* (with Peter Larkham; 2014).

Kim Coventry (nos. 24, 53) is executive director of the Richard H. Driehaus Foundation. Among her publications are *Classic Country Estates of Lake Forest: Architecture and Landscape Design 1856–1940* (coauthor; 2003), *Printing for the Modern Age: Commerce, Craft, and Culture in the RR Donnelley Archive* (2006), and *The History of Crab Tree Farm* (2012). Cochair of the

Caxton Club's Publications Committee, she originated the concept that evolved into *Chicago by the Book*.

The Chicago-based gallery of **Stephen Daiter** (no. 87) specializes in fine art and documentary photography, including a focus on photographers connected with the Chicago Bauhaus and Institute of Design.

Perry R. Duis (no. 60) is professor emeritus of history at the University of Illinois-Chicago. Specializing in urban social history, he has written extensively about Chicago, including *The Saloon: Public Drinking in Chicago and Boston* (1983) and *Challenging Chicago: Coping with Everyday Life, 1837–1920* (1998).

Thomas Dyja (no. 74) is the author of the award-winning *The Third Coast: When Chicago Built the American Dream* (2013). A native of Chicago, he has written several novels and a biography of the civil rights leader Walter White (2008).

Teri J. Edelstein (nos. 49, 55) served as director of the Mount Holyoke College Art Museum and the University of Chicago's Smart Museum, and as deputy director of the Art Institute of Chicago. She has focused her research on the intersection of high art and popular culture. Most recently she edited and coauthored *Art for All: British Posters for Transport* (2015) and contributed an essay to *Art Deco Chicago* (2018).

Charles Fanning (no. 20) is professor emeritus of English and history at Southern Illinois University. His publications include *Finley Peter Dunne and Mr. Dooley: The Chicago Years* (1978), *The Irish Voice in America: 250 Years of Irish-American Fiction* (1990, 2000), and *Mapping Norwood: An Irish-American Memoir* (2010). Currently he is completing a novel set in Chicago in the 1880s.

Leon Fink (no. 16) is Distinguished Professor Emeritus of History at the University of Illinois–Chicago. He focuses on labor unions in the United States, immigration, and the nature of work. He edits *Labor: Studies in Working-Class History of the Americas*, the nation's premier journal of labor history. His dozen books include *The Long Gilded Age* (2016) and *Labor Justice across the Americas* (2018).

Rick Fizdale (no. 9), retired chairman, chief executive officer, and chief creative officer at the advertising firm Leo Burnett, is the author of *999: A History of Chicago in Ten Stories* (2014), which uses the building in which he lives as a backdrop to describe the battle for control of the lakefront between 1871 and 1910.

Paul Garon (no. 92) is an author, writer, and editor noted for his meditations on surrealist works, as well as a scholar on blues as a musical and cultural movement. In 1970 he cofounded *Living Blues* magazine. Garon and his wife, Beth, operate Beasley Books, a used and antiquarian book business in Chicago.

Paul F. Gehl (no. 18) is curator emeritus at the Newberry Library. A historian of printing and education, he is the Caxton Club's archivist and historian.

Timothy J. Gilfoyle (no. 77) is a professor of history at Loyola University Chicago. His writing and teaching concentrate on the history of American cities. His books include *City of Eros: New York City, Prostitution, and the Commercialization of Sex, 1790–1920* (1992); *A Pickpocket's Tale: The Underworld of Nineteenth-Century New York* (2006); *Millennium Park: Creating a Chicago Landmark* (2006); and *The Urban Underworld in Late Nineteenth-Century New York: The Autobiography of George Appo* (2013).

Leslie Goddard (no. 75) is an award-winning actress and scholar who for over a decade has been portraying famous women and presenting history lectures. A former museum director, she is the author of two books on Chicago history—*Remembering Marshall Field's* (2011) and *Chicago's Sweet Candy History* (2012)—and currently works as a historical interpreter, author, and public speaker.

Elliott J. Gorn (no. 22) holds the Joseph A. Gagliano Chair in History at Loyola University Chicago, where he teaches courses in nineteenth- and twentieth-century American history. His publications include *Mother Jones: The Most Dangerous Woman in America* (2001) and *Dillinger's Wild Ride: The Year that Made America's Public Enemy Number One* (2009). His book on Emmett Till is currently at press.

Hanna Holborn Gray (no. 46) is president emeritus and professor emeritus of early modern European history at the University of Chicago. Her memoir, *An Academic Life*, was published in 2018.

Adam Green (no. 39), associate professor of American history at the University of Chicago, focuses on twentieth-century American and African American history, as well as on cultural studies and social movements. His publications include *Selling the Race: Culture and Community in Black Chicago, 1940–1955* (2006); and *Time Longer than Rope: Studies in African American Activism, 1850–1950* (coedited; 2003). His current book project concerns the history of the black struggle for happiness.

The late **Paul M. Green** (no. 90) was an educator, author, researcher, and media pundit whose passion was political analysis. He taught for nearly three decades at Governors State University, followed by Roosevelt University, where he directed the Institute for Politics. He also enjoyed a public life as a speaker, television commentator, and newspaper contributor. His books include *The Mayors: The Chicago Political Tradition* (1987, 2013) and *World War II Chicago* (2003).

Ron Grossman (no. 12) is a reporter for the *Chicago Tribune* who covers the city's ethnic neighborhoods, among other subjects. Before turning to journalism, Grossman was a professor of history at Lake Forest College, Michigan State University, and the University of Nebraska. He is the author of *Guide to Chicago Neighborhoods* (1981).

Will Hansen (no. 68) has a dual role at the Newberry Library. As director of reader services, he manages reading-room and reference-desk operations and the collections housed in the library's book-stack building. As curator of Americana, he collects current monographs, antiquarian books, and manuscript Americana. Previously, Hansen worked as assistant curator of collections at the Rubenstein Rare Book & Manuscript Library, Duke University. He is a Caxtonian.

Neil Harris (introduction; nos. 7, 19, 25) is Preston and Sterling Morton Professor Emeritus of History at the University of Chicago, where he has taught since 1969. Focusing on the evolution of American cultural life and its supporting institutions, his many publications include *Chicago Apartments: A Century of Lakefront Luxury* (2004) and *The Chicagoan: A Lost Magazine of the Jazz Age* (2008). He is a member of the Caxton Club's Publications Committee.

Gini Hartzmark (no. 101) writes mysteries set in Chicago that center on the investigations of socialite and attorney Kate Millholland. They include *Principal Defense* (1992), *Final Option* (1994), *Fatal Reaction* (1998), and *Dead Certain* (2000).

Cultural historian **Celia Hilliard** (nos. 28, 41) has written and spoken extensively about Chicago's diverse arts and social institutions. Her publications include *The Woman's Athletic Club of Chicago 1898–1998* (1999) and two issues of the Art Institute of Chicago's *Museum Studies*, one on the Antiquarian Society, the museum's oldest support group (2002), and the other on the Art Institute's early president and benefactor Charles L. Hutchinson (2010). She is a member of the Caxton Club's Publications Committee.

Alison Hinderliter (no. 2), manuscripts and archives librarian at the Newberry Library, has been an archivist since 1991. Her areas of expertise include literature, journalism, performing arts, corporate records, family histories, and photograph history. She has published many articles and finding aids about the Newberry's modern manuscript collections. She is also an amateur pianist, and her lifelong goal is to learn and perform all thirty-two Beethoven piano sonatas.

Edward C. Hirschland's (nos. 32, 33, 56) collection of Chicago-related books, maps, ephemera, music, photographs, manuscripts, and artifacts is one of the most important in private hands. A management consultant, Ed lectures and publishes on Chicago history and has served on the boards of the Adler Planetarium, American Statistical Association (Chicago), Field Museum, Illinois Institute of Technology's College of Architecture, Society of Architectural Historians, and Caxton Club. He is a member of the Caxton's Publications Committee.

Librarian and archivist **Glenn Humphreys** (no. 99) is in charge of special collections at the Chicago Public Library's Harold Washington Library Center. He holds an MA and certificate in bibliography from the Library School at the University of California, Berkeley, where he focused on rare books and archives. He is a Caxtonian.

D. Bradford Hunt (no. 96) is vice president for research and academic programs at the Newberry Library, where he has worked since 2015. Previously he was a dean and professor of social science and history at Roosevelt University, Chicago. His research focuses on the history of public housing and city planning in Chicago; among his publications is the prize-winning *Blueprint for Disaster: The Unraveling of Chicago Public Housing* (2009). He is a Caxtonian.

Gary T. Johnson (no. 44) has been president of the Chicago History Museum since 2005. A lawyer for over three decades, he studied history while a Rhodes Scholar at Oxford University. For ten years, he served as president of Museums in the Park, an association of eleven Chicago institutions.

Chris Jones (no. 93) is the chief theater critic for the *Chicago Tribune* and its Sunday cultural columnist. He also directs the National Critics Institute at the Eugene O'Neill Center in Waterford, Connecticut. He was awarded the George G. Nathan Award for dramatic criticism in 2015. Jones holds a PhD from Ohio State University; his book *Bigger, Brighter, Louder: 150 Years of Chicago Theater* appeared in 2013.

A longtime television news journalist and anchor mainly at WGN-TV, Chicago, **Robert H. Jordan Jr.** (no. 66) is also a producer, writer, and playwright. Jordan, who earned a PhD in education, was the first journalist-in-residence at the University of Chicago. He retired from broadcasting in 2015 to devote more time to his company, Video Family Biographies, which makes legacy videos for families across the country to help them protect and preserve their history.

Ann Durkin Keating (no. 1) is Dr. C. Frederick Toenniges Professor of History at North Central College, Naperville, Illinois. She is coeditor of *The Encyclopedia of Chicago* (2004) and author of *Chicagoland: City and Suburbs in the Railroad Age* (2005); *Chicago Neighborhoods and Suburbs: A Historical Guide* (2008); and *Rising Up from Indian Country: The Battle of Fort Dearborn and the Birth of Chicago* (2012).

Alex Kotlowitz (no. 71) is the award-winning author of the national best seller *There Are No Children Here* (1991; no. 96), *The Other Side of the River* (1998), and *Never a City So Real* (2004). A former staff writer at the *Wall Street Journal,* he has contributed to the *New York Times Magazine,* the *New Yorker*, and *This American Life*. He was a producer of the 2011 film *The Interrupters*. He is a writer-in-residence at Northwestern University.

D. W. Krummel (no. 40) taught in the Graduate School of Library and Information Science at the University of Illinois–Urbana-Champaign from 1970 to 2014. His writing on music bibliography includes the Grove/Norton handbook *Music Printing and Publishing* (1990), *The Literature of Music Bibliography* (1992), and the *Bibliographical Handbook of American Music* (1987), among other titles. He is a Caxtonian.

Paul Kruty (no. 35), professor emeritus at the University of Illinois, has written extensively on American art and architectural history, particularly the work of Frank Lloyd Wright, Walter Burley Griffin, and Marion Mahony. His publications range from studies on art patron Arthur Jerome Eddy to Chicago's radical art groups of the 1920s. His books include *Frank Lloyd Wright and Midway Gardens* (1997), *Marion Mahony and Millikin Place* (2007), and *On His Own: Walter Burley Griffin's First Two Houses* (2017).

A scholar specializing in American intellectual and cultural history, as well as the history of education, **Tim Lacy** (no. 73) has taught at several Chicago-area colleges and universities. He is author of *The Dream of a Democratic Culture: Mortimer J. Adler and the Great Books Idea* (2013). He is currently working on projects about "great books cosmopolitanism" and anti-intellectualism.

Victoria Lautman (no. 100) is a writer and lecturer specializing in arts and culture. After receiving an MA in art history, she worked at the Smithsonian's Hirshhorn Museum before embarking on a career in journalism. She has hosted long-running radio programs in Chicago, reported on the arts for television, and contributed to many international publications. Her book *The Vanishing Stepwells of India* was published in 2017.

Kelly Leonard (no. 98) is the executive director of insights and applied improvisation at the Second City, where he has worked for nearly three decades in various artistic and leadership positions. He was a major force behind the renaissance and expansion of the famed comedy troupe. His book *Yes, And* appeared in 2015. He coleads the Second Science Project, a collaboration with the Center for Decision Research at the University of Chicago.

A social historian, **Robin Lester** (no. 47) is the author of *Stagg's University: The Rise, Decline, and Fall of Big-Time Football at Chicago* (1995). He has published op-eds in the *New York Times* and the *Chicago Tribune* and has written a novel, *Princes of New York* (2013), based on his experiences as a school headmaster in New York, San Francisco, Chicago, and Minneapolis.

Russell Lewis (nos. 8, 10) is executive vice president and chief historian at the Chicago History Museum, where he has worked in various capacities since 1982. His areas of expertise include the Great Chicago Fire, early Chicago history and settlements, segregation, Camp Douglas and the Civil War, Chicago's world fairs, and nineteenth- and

early-twentieth-century merchandising history. He is author of *Historic Photos of Chicago* (2006) and *Historic Photos of the Chicago's World's Fair* (2010).

Martin E. Marty (no. 17) is Fairfax M. Cone Distinguished Service Professor Emeritus of the History of Modern Christianity at the University of Chicago, where he taught from 1963 to 1998. One of his many books, *Righteous Empire: The Protestant Experience in America* (1970), won a National Book Award. The Martin Marty Center is the University of Chicago Divinity School's institute for interdisciplinary research in religious studies.

Daniel Meyer (no. 78) is director of special collections and university archivist at the University of Chicago Library. He is coauthor of *Classic Country Estates of Lake Forest* (2003) and has curated exhibitions and digital collections, including *The University and the City* (1992); *American Environmental Photographs* (1999); *The First American West* (2002); *Our Lincoln* (2009); *Firmness, Commodity and Delight* (2011); and *Fermi, CP-1, and the Atomic Scientists' Movement* (2017).

William Mullen (no. 52) wrote for the *Chicago Tribune* for forty-five years, covering local police, politics, and cultural affairs. His work on vote fraud in Chicago and city abuses of federal housing policy resulted in Pulitzer Prizes for the newspaper. Overseas he covered war and foreign news, including three years as *Tribune* London

bureau chief. He and *Tribune* photographer Ovie Carter won a Pulitzer for international reporting.

Lester Munson (no. 36) was a reporter and writer at ESPN and *Sports Illustrated* who specialized in legal affairs and investigations. For twenty-eight years he wrote about money, celebrity, violence, sex, drugs, race, gender, greed, court decisions, and falls from grace in the sports industry. He currently works as a freelance writer and commentator on sports and politics from his home in Chicago.

Kenneth Nebenzahl (no. 14) founded Kenneth Nebenzahl, a rare-books firm, in 1957. He has lectured and written extensively on early mapping, exploration, and American history. In 1967 he started an annual lecture series named for his deceased son, Kenneth Jr., on the history of cartography. He is a trustee emeritus of the University of Chicago and a past president of the Caxton Club.

Liesl Olson (no. 51) is author of *Modernism and the Ordinary* (2009) and *Chicago Renaissance: Literature and Art in the Midwest Metropolis* (2017). She is director of Chicago studies at the Newberry Library.

Dominic A. Pacyga (no. 27) was a professor of history in the Department of Humanities, History, and Social Sciences at Columbia College Chicago, where he taught for thirty-seven years before retiring in 2017. He has authored or coauthored six books concerning Chicago's history, includ-

"North End of the Transportation Building, December 31, 1891" (top), and "Interior of the Woman's Building, December 30, 1891," photographs by C. D. Arnold (1844–1927) in Rossiter Johnson, ed., *A History of the World's Columbian Exposition*, 1897–98 (no. 19).

ing *Slaughterhouse: Chicago's Union Stock Yard and the World It Made* (2015). He lectures widely on a variety of topics, including urban development, labor history, immigration, and racial and ethnic relations.

Andrew V. Papachristos (no. 48) is a professor in the Department of Sociology at Northwestern University. His research focuses on social networks, neighborhoods, street gangs, and interpersonal violence.

Sara Paretsky (no. 64) is an award-winning crime writer based in Chicago. To date she has written twenty novels and two volumes of short stories. The central character in all but two of her novels, V. I. Warshawski—an intrepid female private investigator working in Chicago—has transformed the role and image of women in crime fiction (see no. 101).

Since 2010 **Toni Preckwinkle** (no. 15) has been president of the Cook County Board, where she has championed criminal justice reform and the expansion of health care. Previously she served four terms in the Chicago City Council, representing the city's Fourth Ward. She is known for her advocacy of affordable housing, sponsorship of living-wage ordinances, and strong stance against police brutality and excessive force. She earned BA and MA degrees from the University of Chicago.

Jay Pridmore (no. 86) has worked as a journalist in Chicago and has written extensively about architecture. Among his many books are *Marshall Field's: A Building Book* (2002), *Chicago Architecture and Design* (2005), *Building Ideas: An Architectural Tour of the University of Chicago* (2013), and *I. W. Colburn: Emotion in Modern Architecture* (2015).

Victoria Post Ranney (no. 6) is a scholar of the work of the landscape architect Frederick Law Olmsted. She wrote *Olmsted in Chicago* (1972) and edited *The Papers of Frederick Law Olmsted*, volume 5, *The California Frontier* (1990). She cofounded Chicago's Friends of the Parks in 1975 and, with her husband, George Ranney, developed Prairie Crossing in Grayslake, Illinois, a community of four hundred homes built around open land in a manner that conserves the environment.

Frank Rich (no. 85) is a writer-at-large for *New York* magazine and an executive producer of the HBO series *Veep* and *Succession*. He was previously an op-ed columnist and chief theater critic for the *New York Times*. His books include *Ghost Light: A Memoir* (2000) and *The Greatest Story Ever Sold: The Decline and Fall of Truth in Bush's America* (2006).

John Ronan (no. 72) is founding principal of the eponymous Chicago-based architecture firm, which has produced numerous award-winning designs, including the Poetry Foundation in Chicago (2011). The firm's work has been widely exhibited and published. Ronan is currently the John and Jeanne Rowe Endowed Chair Professor of Architec-

ture at the Illinois Institute of Technology College of Architecture.

Don Rose (no. 89), a political activist and consultant, heads Don Rose Communications and the Urban Political Group. He writes a weekly online column for the *Chicago Daily Observer* (CDOBS.com). He has been an on-air commentator for WLS-TV and hosted a weekly community-affairs talk show for twenty-two years on WPNT-FM and its predecessor stations. Rose has published widely on political and cultural affairs.

Bonnie Rosenberg (photo editor), is an expert in intellectual property currently serving as manager of rights and images at the Museum of Contemporary Art, Chicago. She worked previously as executive assistant to architectural historian Victoria Newhouse at Condé Nast Publications and was editorial assistant at the *Art Newspaper* in New York. She holds a BA in art history and English from Saint Louis University and an MA in journalism from Syracuse University.

Susan F. Rossen (editor) directed the Publications Department at the Art Institute of Chicago for twenty-eight years, shepherding over two hundred publications into print. Previously she was an educator, curator, and publisher at the Detroit Institute of Arts. Currently a freelance editor, she is cochair of the Caxton Club's Publications Committee.

Carlo Rotella (no. 43) is director of American studies at Boston College. His books include *October Cities* (1998), *Good with Their Hands* (2002), *Cut Time* (2003), and *Playing in Time* (2012). A Guggenheim fellow, he received the Whiting Writers Award and the L. L. Winship / PEN New England Award. He writes for the *New York Times Magazine* and has been a regular op-ed columnist for the *Boston Globe*. His work has also appeared in the *New Yorker*, *Harper's*, and *The Best American Essays*.

Since 1995 **Pauline Saliga** (no. 88) has been the executive director of the Society of Architectural Historians, which promotes the study, interpretation, and preservation of the built environment worldwide. Before that she worked as a curator at the Museum of Contemporary Art, Chicago, and then at the Art Institute of Chicago, where she organized exhibitions about architecture and their accompanying catalogues, including *Fragments of Chicago's Past* (1990) and *The Architecture of Bruce Goff 1904–1982* (1995).

Alice Schreyer (no. 13) is the Roger and Julie Baskes Vice President for Collections and Library Services at the Newberry Library. Previously she was associate university librarian for area studies and special collections and curator of rare books at the University of Chicago. A leader in the field of special collection librarianship, she is a past chair of the board of directors of the Rare Book School at the University of Virginia. She is a Caxtonian.

A historian of social movements with particular emphasis on women's history, **Rima Lunin Schultz** (no. 30) coedited *Women Building Chicago 1790–1990: A Biographical Dictionary* (2001). She wrote the introduction and edited the 1895 classic *Hull-House Maps and Papers* (2007). Her article "Jane Addams, Apotheosis of Social Christianity" was published in *Church History* (2015). She is coauthor of *Eleanor Smith's Hull-House Songs: The Music of Protest and Hope in Jane Addams's Chicago* (2018).

Don Share (no. 34) edits *Poetry* magazine and is the author, editor, or translator of twelve books. His work at *Poetry* has earned three National Magazine Awards from the American Society of Magazine Editors and a VIDA Award for his "contributions to American literature and literary community."

Eric Slauter (no. 5) is associate professor of English and director of the Karla Scherer Center for the Study of American Culture at the University of Chicago. He focuses chiefly on transformations in political thought and behavior in eighteenth-century America. His book *The State as a Work of Art: The Cultural Origins of the Constitution* appeared in 2009.

Carl Smith (nos. 4, 29) is Emeritus Franklyn Bliss Snyder Professor of English and American Studies and professor of history at Northwestern University. His books include *Chicago and the American Literary Imagination, 1880–1920* (1984); and the award-winning *Urban Disorder and the Shape of Belief: The Great Chicago Fire, the Haymarket Bomb, and the Model Town of Pullman* (1994) and *The Plan of Chicago: Daniel Burnham and the Remaking of the American City* (2009).

Katherine Solomonson (no. 42) teaches architectural and urban history at the University of Minnesota. She focuses on the complex roles that built environments—and the processes involved in shaping them—play in the production of values, identities, and social relations. She authored *The Chicago Tribune Tower Competition: Skyscraper Design and Cultural Change in the 1920s* (2001), coedited *Making Suburbia: New Histories of Everyday America* (2015), and is completing *Cass Gilbert's Architecture in the Great Northwest: Constructing a National Landscape*.

Timothy Spears (no. 23) is professor of American studies and vice president for academic development at Middlebury College, where he has taught since 1990. He is the author of *Chicago Dreaming: Midwesterners and the City, 1871 to 1919* (2005).

Actress and playwright **Regina Taylor** (no. 80) has received a Golden Globe Award and an NAACP Image Award for her role in the TV series *I'll Fly Away*. Her plays include *Oo-Bla-Dee*, which won a best new play award from the American Critics Association in 2000. Her prize-winning 2002 musical *Crowns* has been performed extensively throughout the nation. She is the writer-in-residence at Signature

Theater, New York, and Distinguished Artistic Associate at the Goodman Theatre, Chicago.

Steve Tomashefsky (no. 57) is a Chicago-based lawyer and book collector. Before starting his legal career, he spent ten years working at Delmark Records, a jazz and blues label based in Chicago. Specializing in construction law and intellectual property, he has represented major record labels and recording artists. A Caxton Club member, he has contributed to the Club's monthly *Caxtonian* and *Other People's Books* (2011).

Carlos Tortolero (no. 94) is founder and president of the National Museum of Mexican Art, Chicago (NMMA), which opened in 1987. It has become a national model for its exhibitions, performances, arts education programs, advocacy of cultural equity issues, and demonstration of how museums need to change. In 1997 NMMA became the first Latino museum to be accredited. Tortolero has served on the boards of the University of Illinois and American Alliance of Museums, among others.

David Van Zanten (nos. 31, 45), Mary Jane Crowe Professor Emeritus in Art and Art History at Northwestern University, teaches modern architecture and urbanism. His publications include *Designing Paris: The Architecture of Duban, Labrouste, Duc, and Vaudoyer* (1987); *Building Paris: Architectural Institutions and the Transformation of the French Capital, 1830–1870* (1994); *Sullivan's City: The Meaning of Ornament for Louis Sullivan* (2000); and *Drawing the Future: Chicago Architecture on the International Stage, 1900–1925* (2013).

Michael P. Wakeford (no. 21) is a historian and associate professor in the Division of Liberal Arts at the University of North Carolina School of the Arts. He teaches courses in US cultural and intellectual history, with particular interest in the histories of the arts in American life, education, and the urban landscape. He earned his PhD at the University of Chicago.

An architect and urbanist, **Charles Waldheim** (no. 69) is John E. Irving Professor at Harvard University's Graduate School of Design, where he directs the school's Office for Urbanization. He examines the relations between landscape, ecology, and contemporary urbanism. Among his numerous publications is *Airport Landscape: Urban Ecologies in the Aerial Age* (coedited with Sonja Dümpelmann; 2016).

Rosanna Warren (no. 37) is Hanna Holborn Gray Distinguished Service Professor in the Committee on Social Thought at the University of Chicago. A translator and editor, she has also published six poetry collections, including *Departure* (2003) and *Ghost in a Red Hat* (2011). A book of criticism, *Fables of the Self: Studies in Lyric Poetry*, appeared in 2008.

Emeritus professor of history at Northwestern University, **Garry Wills** (no. 84) is an author, journalist, and historian specializing in American history, politics, and religion. His *Lincoln at Gettysburg* (1982) won a National Book Critics Award and a Pulitzer Prize. The most recent of his nearly forty books is *What the Qur'an Meant: And Why It Matters* (2017). Since 1973 he has been a frequent contributor to the *New York Review of Books*.

The sociologist **William Julius Wilson** (no. 65) is Lewis and Linda L. Geyser University Professor, Harvard University. Before his Harvard appointment, he spent twenty-four years at the University of Chicago. His many books include the award-winning *The Declining Significance of Race* (1978, 1980, 2012), *The Truly Disadvantaged* (1987, 2012), and *When Work Disappears* (1996). He is a recipient of the 1998 National Medal of Science, the highest scientific honor bestowed in the United States.

The Chicago-based graphic designer **Lynn Martin Windsor** (no. 67) was a student at László Moholy-Nagy's Institute of Design, Chicago. She has designed major projects for the University of Chicago and books for the Art Institute of Chicago, among many other institutions. Currently she is involved in efforts to preserve the legacy of Moholy-Nagy's schools. She is a Caxtonian.

This book was generously supported by the following donors:

John Blew
John P. Chalmers
Donald E. Chatham
Kim Coventry
G. Kevin Davis
James R. Donnelley
Shawn M. Donnelley and Christopher M. Kelly
The Richard H. Driehaus Foundation
Doug Fitzgerald
Joan M. Friedman
Susan R. Hanes
Lee Harrer
Neil Harris and Teri J. Edelstein
Celia Hilliard
Leslie S. Hindman
Edward C. Hirschland
Wendy Cowles Husser
Norman O. Jung
Alvin R. Kantor
Ronald G. Klein
William Locke
Eileen Madden
David S. Mann
Robert and Margaret McCamant
David C. Meyer
Deborah Mitts-Smith
Anthony J. Mourek
Nebenzahl-Spitz Foundation
John K. Notz Jr.
Richard W. Renner
Susan F. Rossen
Anne Royston
Alice Schreyer
Ronald K. Smeltzer
Terra Foundation for American Art
Thomas E. Swanstrom
Steve Tomashefsky
Donna M. Tuke
Jerome C. Yanoff

FACING
The entry of German-born architect Walter Gropius (1883–1969) to the Tribune Tower *International Competition*, 1923 (no. 42).

Plate Number 197

Photo/Image Credits

ity for Males, Sodality for Young Ladies, and St. Ann's
for Married Ladies ; there is also an acolytical and
ociety of young men.

everend A. Damen is the Hercules who has in a few
ought all this work. To his energy, his ability, his
his perseverance, and his great practical intelligence is
only the erection of this magnificent edifice, but the
piritual success which has crowned the labors of the
With him, and all actively engaged in the arduous
the parish, are Reverend Father De Blieck, Reverend
erkorn, Reverend Andrew O'Neill, Reverend Michael
Reverend C. F. Smarius, Reverend Florentine Boudreaux
erend James Van Goch. Four of these gentlemen are
ly engaged in giving missions throughout the United

ason work of the church was done by Reid and Sher-
the carpenter's work by M. Donahue. The description
building is not given herein as fully as it would have
cause on the first of May the towers and whole front are
ken down, and the church extended thirty feet, and some
terations will be made at the same time. It will then,
w proportions, be a really splendid structure.

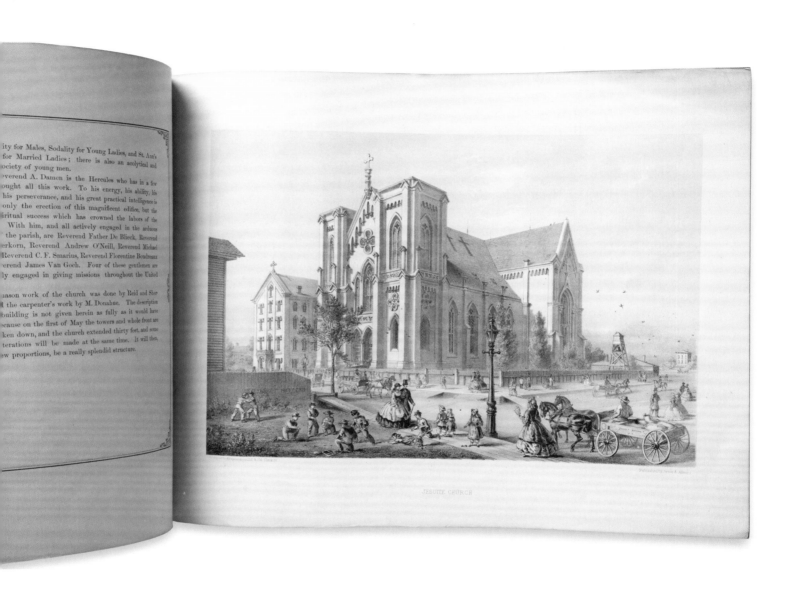

JESUITE CHURCH

Holy Name Church (1860) survived the Chicago Fire of 1871
and is featured in *Chicago Illustrated 1830–1866* (no. 3).

Index

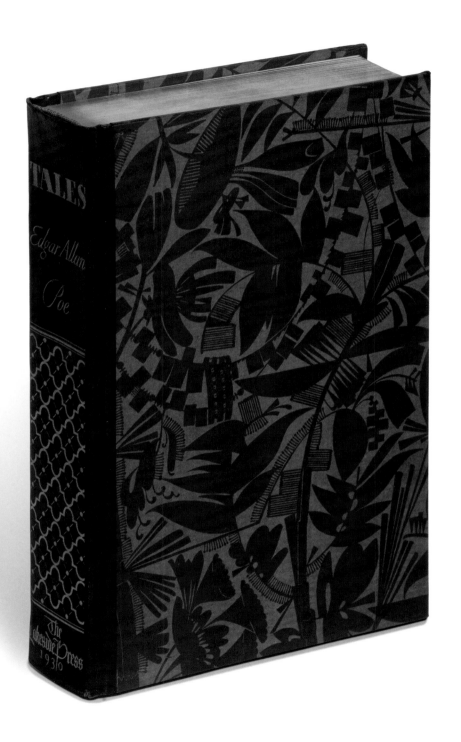

Edgar Allan Poe, *Tales*, one of the titles in Lakeside Press's Four American Books Campaign, 1930 (no. 53).

The Caxton Club

The Caxton Club was founded in 1895 by fifteen Chicago bibliophiles who desired to support the publication of fine books in the spirit of the prevailing arts and crafts movement. They named the new organization the Caxton Club in honor of the first English printer, William Caxton (ca. 1422–ca. 1491).

The Club's founders were businessmen, lawyers, publishers, a librarian, and a bookseller. They intended the high-quality books—in both content and design—primarily for their own personal libraries. The founders had three other goals: to establish clubrooms where they could escape from the day-to-day exigencies of family and the business world; to hold exhibitions for the edification of members, family, friends, and the general public; and to form a library of reference material about books.

In the Caxton Club's early years, excellent progress was made in meeting all the objectives. From 1899 to 1918, the Club maintained rooms in the Fine Arts Building on Michigan Avenue, in the heart of Chicago's growing cultural community. An occasional luncheon was held in conjunction with lectures that accompanied the opening of exhibitions. In later years, financial difficulties forced the Club to forgo the rooms, regular exhibitions, and the library.

After World War I, the Club focused on providing a monthly dinner for its members with distinguished speakers addressing topics related to literature and the book arts. In 1936, after experimenting with a variety of locations, the organization began a long association with the Mid-Day Club in the First National Bank Building (rebuilt in 1969 on roughly the same site and now called Chase Tower), where its meetings took place through 2007. Currently Club social events occur mostly at the Union League Club. Dinner meetings are held on the third Wednesday and luncheon meetings on the second Friday of each month. The programs reflect the Club's purpose "to promote the arts pertaining to books and to foster their appreciation."

The Club forged an important long-term relationship with R.R. Donnelley & Sons through several company executives who were Club members. For more than a century, Donnelley provided pro bono graphic design and printing to the Club. A sustained relationship with the Newberry Library has enabled the Club to house its offices there, giving rise to shared initiatives, including programming.

In recent years the Caxton Club has extended its reach by collaborating with universities and colleges, museums, libraries, and other bibliophilic organizations, both regional and national; organizing exhibitions; and making grants to young book artists and librarians. It has continued to publish books: over one hundred publications bear the Club device. The list features numerous titles on midwestern Americana; Chicago history, journalism, and literature; the book arts (especially in Chicago and the Midwest); and other topics.

The Caxton Club's membership currently represents a diverse group of authors, binders, collectors, conservators, dealers, designers, editors, librarians, publishers, and scholars. Through this fellowship, the Caxton Club provides a forum to learn about the history, production, and preservation of books; to heighten appreciation of outstanding content, design, and production; and to share in the joys of book collecting.

FACING Louis Sullivan, *A System of Architectural Ornament*, 1924, plate 20 (no. 45).

FINIS

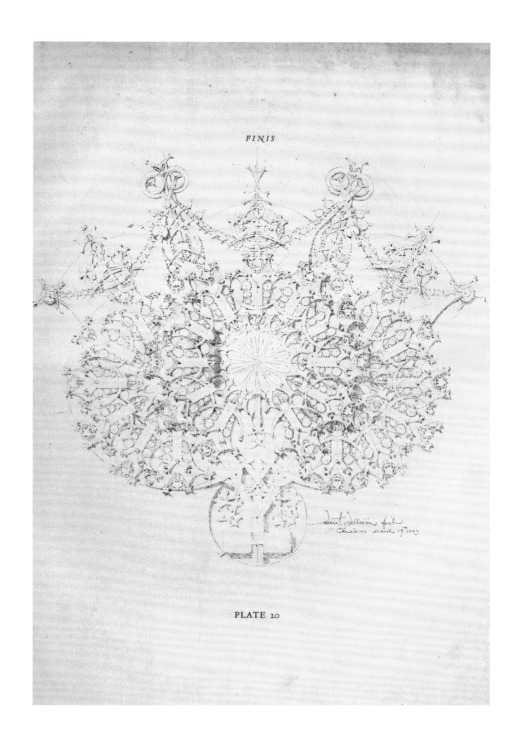

PLATE 20